THE BIG BOOK OF

RUNES AND RUNE MAGIC

How to Interpret Runes, Rune Lore,
and the Art of Runecasting

EDRED THORSSON

WEISER
BOOKS

This edition first published in 2018
by Weiser Books, an imprint of
Red Wheel/Weiser, LLC
With offices at:
65 Parker Street, Suite 7
Newburyport, MA 01950
www.redwheelweiser.com

ISBN: 978-1-57863-652-5

Library of Congress Control Number: 2018954581

Cover and text design by Kathryn Sky-Peck

Printed in the United States of America
IBI
10 9 8 7 6 5 4 3 2 1

CONTENTS

PART THREE: READING THE RUNES

PART FOUR: RUNE MAGIC

ABBREVIATIONS

All translations from Old Norse, Old English, and other old languages found in this book are those of the author. An attempt has been made to strike a balance between poetic and literal translations, but often favor is given to the literal for the sake of correct understanding. In such cases notes may be added.

B.C.E.	Before Common Era (= B.C.)
C.E.	Common Era (= A.D.)
Gmc.	Germanic
Go.	Gothic
MS(S)	Manuscript(s)
OE	Old English
OHG	Old High German
ON	Old Norse
pl.	plural
sg.	singular

ACKNOWLEDGMENTS

Thanks go to Paul Newell, Mitchell Edwin Wade, David Bragwin James, Robert Zoller, James Chisholm, Alice Rhoades, Anthony Looker, Ian Read, Ingrid Fischer, Adolf and Sigrun Schleipfer, Michael Moynihan, Ralph Tegtmeier, and Michael A. Aquino.

PREFACE

This book represents some of the very best and most popular of my early work as a researcher and operative rune magician. The work represents a distillation of the most essential knowledge one can have on the lore of the runes. If your interests are broad and run the gamut from historical information to the actual practical application of runic knowledge in working the magic of these symbols, then this is the book that will serve as a reliable resource.

When dealing with runes, or really any comprehensive, culturally authentic form of magic, there are essentially four levels of information and activity that students must be aware of and engage in. These are: (1) basic historical knowledge; (2) inner, or esoteric, knowledge; (3) knowledge of how to read the symbols; and (4) how to use the information in an active, practical way. One must know, understand, read, and write within the system in question. Historical knowledge is internalized and reflected upon to develop theoretic frameworks, then the world is read or understood according to these ideas before the stage of active creativity in that system is attempted. This book takes the student through all of these phases in the most basic and fundamental way. For this reason, its contents are divided into four parts: Historical Lore, Hidden Lore, Reading the Runes, and Rune Magic.

In many regards this text consists of a republication of earlier works, but I have taken the opportunity to update and expand ideas originally offered to make them more in keeping with my current understanding. I found very little to "change," but there are some new ideas and resources that are beneficial to learn.

The greatest challenge in creating this new work was in keeping the tone and spirit of the original texts. The original works, written in the late 1970s and early 1980s, had a certain energy reflective of my stage of development at that time. That energy has been appreciated by my most loyal students over the years, so I have tried to keep it in the contents of this book. One of the interesting things about having a writing career that has spanned over forty years is the ability to see the different tones and energies present in earlier works that have yet to be refined and distilled as they would be in later works, but that very energy is similar to a sort of white lightning, which would be a shame to lose.

Edred Thorsson
Woodharrow
March 20, 2018

INTRODUCTION

Long have we dwelt outside the gates of the gard of our indwelling gods. We were not expelled from their knowledge by some irreversible transgression—but rather have only turned our backs on their troth. We can again turn to face their radiant power—but only by knowing the roadways of that journey. Those gangways are the runes—the mysteries of our path—and the keys to their own hidden dimensions.

This book is made up of four parts: the historical and hidden lore of the runes, knowledge of how to read them, and knowledge of how to rist them upon the fabric of the world. Taken as a whole, this volume is a complete course in undertaking the acquisition of active knowledge of the runes and their uses. This process begins with learning the historical and objective lore surrounding the runes from antiquity. The first part of this book makes up a sort of brief introduction to runology. Once the basic knowledge has been learned, the student, or runer, moves on to deeper esoteric contemplation of the symbolic, cosmological, and psychological world of the ancestors. This takes the runer to a new level of consciousness about the symbolic world surrounding us, its origin and purpose. The next level involves what has been called reading the runes: this includes forms of what is called divination, but also requires the runer to interact with the symbols of the runes and his or her own life events in an active way. Before the child speaks, it understands. Before it writes, it must learn to read. The passive skills are relatively easier to use than the active ones. These passive skills also incur less in the way of possible negative repercussions, or "unintended consequences." It has been known for magic to work too well and too quickly— before the magician has had time to develop the life skills necessary to deal with that success. So, learning to read the runes aright is a major step in balanced development. Once the reading exercises are mastered, the runer moves on to active writing, or risting, into the very fabric of the universe. With the foundations already built, success is better assured.

In an elder age it seems we made a mistake. We rejected—slowly and incompletely to be sure, but nevertheless, we as a people rejected—the wisdom of our own gods. No wondrous "cure" will reverse this rejection overnight; no "grace" is forthcoming from Odin! Only our own hard effort will bring each of us back to the long-lost lore. To this difficult yet noble task, all of the efforts of this book are dedicated.

Although we lost much through our mistakes in ancient times, we have continued to lose more in recent years by some misguided efforts of limited vision at the "revival" of the old ways of the North. Again and again, would-be revivalists have rejected the timelessly eternal and positive vision of the Master of Ecstasy in favor of historical, limited schemes of negative ideologies. It is not who or what we stand against which defines us, but who and what we stand for. One of our most important works is to help shape a philosophical foundation for the growth of this positive vision of timeless relevance, that we may win by example and conquer the world from within our Selves. Personal transformation must come before world transformation.

In the twentieth and twenty-first centuries the runes have often been seen to serve what appear to be political ends. This spans the gamut from the Nazis, to the use of the "peace sign" in the 1960s to more recent use by right-leaning groups. The runes are first and foremost sacred symbols of an archaic culture with eternal values and meaning. It is this eternal meaning which operative runlogists of today seek to activate in their lives. As such we oppose holding these ancient symbols hostage to unprincipled present-day squabbles involving politics and virtue-signaling. The runes are powerful and must be used for the purposes they came into this world to serve.

The runes, and the ideology they encompass, serve a wide variety of ends, through both "direct," or magical, means and more intellectual pathways. In the magical realms, runework is used for personal transformation, building wider consciousness, psychic development, healing, investigation of Wyrd, and shaping the environment according to the inner will.

While in the intellectual realms, the topic of the first few chapters of this book, runelore and rune wisdom can serve as a mental framework for the development of a new philosophy based on a timeless pattern and expressed through a potent meta-language. Many "traditions" have tried and failed to construct such a successful meta-language, with a precise and meaningfully beautiful grammar—for example, Christianity and Islam and their cultural variants. But these may be called failures because of the inherent weakness in their inorganic systems. If you work through the runic system and make it a part of your life, you will have given yourself a gift no one else could have bestowed: knowledge of *thine own self*—unique yet part of a whole. The runes will serve as a language with which you may "converse" with aspects of yourself and at the same time *communicate* this knowledge to others, which is a hard yet necessary test for any true understanding. This understanding can then be taken to a new level and activated in accordance with your will to effect changes in the world.

We must not only understand the runes as the ancients understood them—that is only the beginning—but we must come to a *new knowledge* of them. As they have transformed us, so must our comprehension of them be transformed. They were, are, and shall ever be eternally changing and eternally demanding of change. Therefore, those who wish only to reinforce their personal prejudices and who have little interest in, or indeed fear of, the transmuting powers housed in the runes should be warned now. The runes describe a road of metamorphosis, not a tower of justification.

Like all things *worth* knowing, these mysteries are stubborn secrets (and mischievousness is not beyond them). Often, they will wrap themselves in a riddle, but they will always tell more by their riddle than if they had spoken with a clear tongue. There is little grace in their characters, and their Master has even less. But this is as it *must* be. Anyone who says differently must indeed be a priest of the lie—for he would tell you that the only gain is by the gift, whereas we Odians know well that true wisdom must be won by the human will. This will and its attendant human consciousness is the only true Gift—it is the sword cast before infant humanity in the cradle. It is by this sword alone that our ways in the world shall be won.

This book is designed to facilitate an effective use of the shaping and imaginative intellect in conjunction with the most recent and best scholarship in the fields of runic studies and in the history of the old Germanic religion. It contains a detailed historical account of the development of ancient runic traditions and the ways in which runestaves were used in the elder age. These historical data are combined with esoteric investigations into the nature of the runes themselves—the ways in which they relate to one another—and into the realms of esoteric teachings of cosmogony, cosmology, numerology, psychology (soul-lore), and theology. This lore is then made active, both as a skill in reading the mysteries which surround us, and as a skill for writing our own wills in the world in which we live. It is hoped that the deeper runelore held in the pages of this work will open the way to a broader understanding of the runes and help to awaken that great god that lies sleeping within. Now its voice may be but a whisper, but with will and craft we shall awaken it, so that its voice becomes a roar—and we will know it more truly than ever before.

Part One

HISTORICAL LORE

Chapter 1

ELDER RUNES

(TO 800 C.E.)

T his chapter is intended to provide the runer with a basic outline of runic history and development from the oldest times to around 800 C.E. (or the beginning of the Viking Age) and includes a section on the Old English and Frisian traditions that continue beyond that time frame. It is necessary for anyone entering upon the esoteric study of the runes to have a fundamental notion of the historical context of the tradition. The discussion here will provide the foundation for this task; independent readings and studies must build the larger edifice. The majority of the information contained in this first part of the book has been gleaned from scholarly works on runology (see Bibliography). The exoteric facts and interpretations contained in these pages will serve the runer well as an introduction to the wondrous world of rune wisdom developed in later parts of the book.

The Word Rune

The most common definition for the word *rune* is "one of the letters of an alphabet used by ancient Germanic peoples." This definition is the result of a long historical development, the entirety of which we must come to know before we can see how incomplete such a definition is. Actually, these "letters" are much more than signs used to represent the sounds of a language. They are in fact actual *mysteries*, the actual "secrets of the universe," as one who studies them long and hard enough will learn.

Rune as a word is only found in the Germanic and Celtic languages. Its etymology is somewhat uncertain. There are, however, two possible etymologies: (1) from Proto-Indo-European *reu-* (to roar and to whisper), which would connect it with the vocal performance of magical incantations, and (2) from Proto-Indo-European *gwor-w-on-*, which would connect it to the Greek and Old Indic gods *Ouranos* and *Varuna*, respectively, giving the meaning of "magical binding." This is also an attribute of Odin. The word may have had the essential meaning of "mystery" from the beginning.

In any case, a Germanic and Celtic root *runo-* can be established, from which it developed in the various Germanic dialects. That the word is very archaic in its technical sense is clear from its universal attribution with a rich meaning. The root is found in every major Germanic dialect (see table 1.1). What is made clear from the evidence of this table is that "rune" is an ancient, indigenous term and that the oldest meaning was in the realm of the abstract concept (mystery), *not* as a concrete sign (letter). The definition "letter" is strictly secondary, and the primary meaning must be "mystery."

This root is also found in the Celtic languages, where we find Old Irish *rūn* (mystery or secret) and Middle Welsh *rhin* (mystery). Some people have argued that the root was borrowed from Celtic into Germanic; however, more have argued the reverse because the Germanic usages are more vigorous, widespread, and richer in meaning. Another possibility is that it is a root shared by the two Indo-European dialects and that there is no real question of borrowing in the strict sense. Perhaps the term also was borrowed into Finnish from Germanic in the form *runo* (a song, a canto of the *Kalevala*), but the Finnish word may actually come from another Germanic word meaning "row" or "series."

Table 1.1. Germanic rune definition.

Dialect	Word	Meaning
Old Norse	*rūn*	secret, secret lore, wisdom; magical signs; written characters
Gothic	*rūna*	secret, mysterium
Old English	*rūn*	mystery, secret council
Old Saxon	*Rūna*	mystery, secret
Old High German	*rūna*	mystery, secret

Although the word is clearly of common Germanic stock, the actual word in modern English is not a direct descendant from the Old English *rūn* but was borrowed from late scholarly (seventeenth-century) Latin—*runa* (adjective, *runicus*)—which in turn was borrowed from the Scandinavian languages.

The Odian definition of rune is complex and is based on the oldest underlying meaning of the word—a mystery, archetypal secret lore. These are the impersonal patterns that underlie the substance/nonsubstance of the multiverse and that constitute its being/nonbeing. Each of these runes also may be analyzed on at least three levels:

- Form (ideograph and phonetic value)

- Idea (symbolic content)

- Number (dynamic nature, revealing relationships to the other runes)

With the runes, as with their Teacher, Odin, all things may be identified—and may be negated. Therefore, any definition that makes use of "profane" language must remain inadequate and incomplete.

Throughout this book, when the word *rune* is used, it should be considered in this complex light; whereas the terms *runestave*, or simple *stave*, will be used in discussions of them as physical letters or signs.

Early Runic History

The systematic use of runestaves dates from at least 50 C.E. (the approximate date of the Meldorf brooch) to the present. However, the underlying traditional and hidden framework on which the system was constructed cannot be discussed in purely historical terms—it is ahistorical.

Essentially, the history of the runic system spans four epochs: (1) the elder period, from the first century C.E. to about 800 C.E.; (2) the younger period, which takes us to about 1100 (these two periods are expressions of unified runic traditions bound in a coherent symbology); (3) the middle period, which is long and disparate and which witnessed the decay of the external tradition and its submersion into the unconscious; and finally, (4) the periods of rebirth. Although the use of runes continued in an unbroken (but badly damaged) tradition in remote areas of Scandinavia, most of the deep-level runework took place in revivalist schools after about 1600.

It may be argued that a historical study is actually unnecessary or even detrimental for those who wish to plumb the depths of that timeless, ahistorical, archetypal reality of the runes themselves. But such an argument would have its drawbacks. Accurate historical knowledge is necessary because conscious tools are needed for the rebirth of the runes from the unconscious realms; the modern runic investigator must know the origins of the various structures that come into contact with the conscious mind. Only in this context can the rebirth occur in a fertile field of growth. For this to take place, the runer must have a firm grasp on the history of the runic tradition. For without the roots the branches will wither and die. In addition, the analytical observation and rational interpretation of objective data (in this case the historical runic tradition) is fundamental to the development of the whole runemaster and vitki. If a system is not rooted in an objective tradition, many erroneous elements can more easily find their way into the thinking process of the practitioner. Clarity and precision are valuable tools for inner development.

Runic Origins

As the runes (mysteries) are ahistorical, they must also be without ultimate origin—they are timeless. When we speak of runic origins, we are more narrowly concerned with the origins of the traditions of the futhark stave system. The questions of archetypal runic origins will be taken up later on. The runes may indeed be said to have passed through many doors on the way to our perceptions of them and to have undergone many "points of origin" in the worlds.

There are several theories on the historical origins of the futhark system and its use as a mode of writing for the Germanic dialects. These are essentially four in number: the Latin theory, the Greek theory, the North-Italic (or Etruscan) theory, and the indigenous theory. Various scholars over the years have subscribed to one or the other of these theories; more recently a reasonable synthesis has been approached, but it is still an area of academic controversy.

The Latin or Roman theory was first stated scientifically by L. F. A. Wimmer in 1874. Those who adhere to this hypothesis generally believe that as the Germanic peoples came into closer contact with Roman culture (beginning as early as the second century B.C.E. with the invasion of the Cimbri and Teutones from Jutland), along the Danube (at Carnuntum) and the Rhine (at Cologne, Trier, etc.), the Roman alphabet was adapted and put to use by the Germans. Trade routes would have been the means by which the system quickly spread from the southern region to Scandinavia and from there to the east. This latter step is necessary because the oldest evidence for the futhark is not found near the Roman limes and spheres of influence but rather in the distant northern and eastern reaches of Germania. The idea of trade routes poses no real problem to this theory because such routes were well established from even more remote times. The Mycenaean tombs in present-day Greece (ca. 1400–1150 B.C.E.) contain amber from the Baltic and from Jutland, for example. More recently, Erik Moltke has theorized that the futhark originated in the Danish region and was based on the Roman alphabet.

This theory still holds a number of adherents, and some aspects of it, which we will discuss later, show signs of future importance. In any case, the influence of the cultural elements brought to the borderlands of the Germanic peoples by the Romans cannot be discounted in any question of influence during the period between approximately 200 B.C.E. and 400 C.E.

It must be kept in mind when discussing these theories that we are restricted to questions of the origin of the idea of writing with a phonetic system (alphabet) among the Germanic peoples in connection with the runic tradition, and not with the genesis of the underlying system or tradition itself.

The Greek theory, first put forward by Sophus Bugge in 1899, looks more to the east for the origins of this writing system. In this hypothesis it is thought that the Goths adapted a version of the Greek cursive script during a period of contact with Hellenic culture along the Black Sea, from where it was transmitted back to the Scandinavian homeland of the Goths. There is, however, a major problem with this theory because the period of Gothic Greek contact in question could not have started before about 200 C.E., and the oldest runic inscriptions date from well before that time. For this reason most scholars have long since abandoned this hypothesis. The only way to save it is to prove a much earlier, as yet undocumented connection between the two cultures in question. More research needs to be done in this area. Also, it is probable that Hellenistic ideas, even if they played no role in runic origins, may have had a significant part in the formation of some elements of the traditional system.

The North-Italic or Etruscan theory was first proposed by C. J. S. Marstrander in 1928 and was subsequently modified and furthered by Wolfgang Krause, among others, in 1937. Historically, this hypothesis supposes that Germanic peoples living in the Alps adopted the North-Italic script at a relatively early date—perhaps as early as 300 B.C.E.—when the Cimbri came into contact with it and passed it on to the powerful Suevi (or Suebi), from whom it quickly spread up the Rhine and along the coast of the North Sea to Jutland and beyond. There can be no historical objections to the plausibility of this scenario, except for the fact that the initial contact came some three to four hundred years before we have any record of actual runic inscriptions.

As a matter of fact, there is an example of Germanic language written in the North-Italic alphabet—the famous helmet of Negau (from ca. 300 B.C.E.). The inscription may be read from right to left in figure 1.1.

The inscription may be read in words *Harigasti teiwai* . . . and translated "to the god Harigast (Odin)," or "Harigastiz [and] Teiwaz!" In any case the root meanings of the first two words of the inscription are clear.

Figure 1.1. Inscription on the helm of Negau.

Hari-gastiz (the guest of the army) and Teiwaz (the god Tyr). In later times, it would be normal to expect Odin to be identified by a nickname of this type, and we may well have an early example of it here. Also, this would be an early proof of the ancient pairing of the two Germanic sovereign deities (see chapter 13).

As can be seen from the Negau inscription, the scripts in question bear many close formal correspondences to the runestaves; however, some phonetic values would have to have been transferred. No one Etruscan alphabet forms a clear model for the entire futhark. An unfortunate footnote to runic history has recently been added by a certain occult writer who in two books has represented a version of the Etruscan script as "the runic alphabet." This has perhaps led to some confusion among those attempting to unravel runic mysteries.

The idea that the runes are a purely indigenous Germanic script originated in the late nineteenth century and gained great popularity in National Socialist Germany. This theory states that the runes are a primordial Germanic invention and that they are even the basis for the Phoenician and Greek alphabets. This hypothesis cannot be substantiated because the oldest runic inscriptions date from the first century C.E. and the oldest Phoenician ones date from the thirteenth and twelfth centuries B.C.E. When this theory was first expounded by R. M. Meyer in 1896, the runes were seen as an originally ideographic (the misnomer used was "hieroglyphic") system of writing that then developed into an alphabetic system acrophonetically (i.e., based on the first sound of the names attached to the ideograph). One aspect of this is probably correct: the Germanic peoples seem to have had an ideographic system, but it does not appear to have been used as a writing system, and it is here that the indigenous theory goes astray. It is possible that the ideographic system influenced the choice of runestave shapes and sound values.

From the available physical evidence it is most reasonable to conclude that the runestave system is the result of a complex development in which both indigenous ideographs and symbol systems and the alphabetic writing systems of the Mediterranean played significant roles. The ideographs were probably the forerunners of the runestaves (hence the unique rune names), and the prototype of the *runic system* (order, number, etc.) is probably also to be found in some native magical symbology.

One piece of possible evidence we have for the existence of a pre-runic symbol system is the report of Tacitus in chapter 10 of his *Germania* (ca. 98 C.E.), where he mentions certain *notae* (signs) carved on strips of wood in the divinatory rites of the Germans. Although the recent discovery of the Meldorf brooch has pushed back the date of the oldest runic inscription to a time before Tacitus wrote the *Germania*, these still could have been some symbol system other than the futhark proper. In any case, it is fairly certain that the idea of using such things as a writing system, as well as the influence governing the choice of certain signs to represent specific sounds, was an influence from the southern cultures.

In the end it is most likely that the runes originated in the Latin script. The amount of economic and cultural exchange between Rome and Germania was far more vigorous than is often assumed. What is most interesting about the whole process is that the Germanic people did not just accept the Latin script as a practical way of writing (as other peoples did), but rather they entirely reformed it in a variety of ways to make it part of their own unique and particular worldview. It is this incontestable fact that most obviously leads reasonable people to conclude that there is something *mysterious* about the runes. They encode esoteric cultural secrets.

This summarizes the story with regard to the *exoteric* sciences. But what more can be said about the esoteric aspects of runic origins? The runes themselves, as has been said, are without beginning or end; they are eternal patterns in the substance of the multiverse and are omnipresent in all of the worlds. But we can speak of the origin of the runes in human consciousness (and as a matter of fact this is the only point at which we can begin to speak about the "origins" of anything).

For this we turn to the *Elder* or *Poetic Edda* and to the holy rune song of the "Hávamál," stanzas 138 to 165, the so-called "Rúnatals tháttr Ódhins" (see also chapter 8). There, Odin recounts that he hung for nine nights on the World Tree, Yggdrasill, in a form of self-sacrifice. This constitutes the runic initiation of the god Odin: he approaches and sinks into the realm of death in which he receives the secrets, the mysteries of the multiverse—the runes themselves—in a flash of inspiration. He is then able to return from that realm, and now it is his function to teach the runes to certain of his followers in order to bring wider consciousness, wisdom, magic, poetry, and inspiration to the world of Midhgardhr—and to all of the worlds. This is the central work of Odin, the Master of Inspiration.

The etymology of the name Odin gives us the key to this "spiritual" meaning. Odin is derived from Proto-Germanic *Wōdh-an-az*. *Wōdh-* is inspired numinous activity or enthusiasm: the *-an-* infix indicates the one who is master or ruler of something. The *-az* is simply a grammatical ending. The name is also something interpreted as a pure deification of the spiritual principle of *wōdh*. See chapter 13 for more details of Odinic theology.

The figure of Odin, like those of the runestaves, stands at the inner door of our conscious/unconscious borderland. Odin is the communicator to the conscious of the contents of the unconscious and supra-conscious, and he/it fills the "space" of all of these faculties. We, as humans, are conscious beings but have a deep need for communication and illumination from the hidden sides of the worlds and ourselves. Odin is the archetype of this deepest aspect of humanity, that which bridges the worlds together in a webwork of mysteries—the runes.

Therefore, in an esoteric sense the runes originate in human consciousness through the archetype of the all-encompassing (whole) god hidden deeply in all his folk. For us the runes are born simultaneously with consciousness. But it must be remembered that the runes themselves are beyond his (and therefore our) total command. Odin can be destroyed, but because of his *conscious* assumption of the basic pattern of the runic mysteries (in the Yggdrasill initiation) the "destruction" becomes the road to transformation and rebirth.

Age of the Elder Futhark

As mentioned before, the oldest runic inscription yet found is that of the Meldorf brooch (from the west coast of Jutland), which dates from the middle of the first century C.E. From this point on, the runes form a continuous tradition that is to last more than a thousand years, with one major formal transformation coming at approximately midpoint in the history of the great tradition. This is the development of the Younger Futhark from the Elder, beginning as early as the seventh century. But the elder system held on in some conservative enclaves, and its echoes continued to be heard until around 800 C.E, and in hidden traditions beyond that time.

The elder system consists of twenty-four staves arranged in a very specific order (see Table 1 in Appendix I). The only major variations in this order apparently were also a part of the system itself. The thirteenth and fourteenth staves: ᛇ : and : ᛈ : sometimes alternated position; as did the twenty-third and twenty-fourth staves : ᛞ : and : ᛟ :. It should be noted that both of these alternations come at the exact *middle* and *end* of the row.

By the year 250 C.E., inscriptions are already found over all of the European territories occupied by the Germanic peoples. This indicates that the spread was systematic throughout hundreds of sociopolitical groups (clans, kindreds, tribes, etc.) and that it probably took place along preexisting networks of cultic traditions. Only about three hundred inscriptions in the Elder Futhark survive. (To this about 250 bracteates with runic stamps can also be added.) This surely represents only a tiny fraction of the total number of inscriptions executed during this ancient period. The vast majority done in perishable materials, such as wood and bone—the most popular materials for the runemaster's craft—have long since decayed. Most of the oldest inscriptions are in metal, and some are quite elaborate and developed. Those on gold objects were mostly melted down in the following centuries.

In the earliest times runestaves were generally carved on mobile objects. For this reason the distribution of the locations where inscriptions have been found tells us little about where they actually were carved. A good illustration of this problem is provided by the bog finds (mostly from around 200 C.E.) on the eastern shore of Jutland and from the Danish archipelago. The objects on which the runes were scratched were sacrificed by the local populace after they had defeated invaders from farther east. It was the invaders who had carved these runes somewhere in present-day Sweden, not the inhabitants of the land where the objects were found. As the situation stands, it seems that before about 200 C.E. the runes were known only in the regions of the modern areas of Denmark, Schleswig-Holstein, southern Sweden (perhaps also on the islands of Öland and Gotland), and southeastern Norway. As the North Germanic and East Germanic peoples spread eastward and southward, they took the runes with them, so that scattered inscriptions have been found in present-day Poland, Russia, Romania, Hungary, and Yugoslavia. The runic tradition remained continuous in Scandinavia until the end of the Middle Ages. One of the most remarkable Scandinavian traditions was that of the bracteates, thin disks of gold stamped with symbolic pictographs and used as amulets, carved between 450 and 550 C.E. in Denmark and southern Sweden (see figure 1.6 on page 15). Two other distinct yet organically related traditions are represented by the Anglo-Frisian runes (used in England and Frisia from ca. 450 to 1100 C.E.) and the South Germanic runes (virtually identical to the North Germanic futhark) used in central and southern Germany (some finds in modern Switzerland and Austria) from approximately 550 to 750 C.E.

Futhark Inscriptions

We have seven examples of inscriptions that represent the futhark row, completely or in fragments, from the elder period. They appear in chronological order in figure 1.2. on page 12.

The Kylver stone (which was part of the *inside* of a grave chamber), combined with later evidence from manuscript runes, shows that the original order of the final two staves was D-O and that the Grumpan and Vadstena bracteates were very commonly fashioned with runes as part of their designs. The Kylver stone has, however, reversed the thirteenth and fourteenth staves to read P-EI instead of the usual EI-P order. The Beuchte brooch contains only the first five runes scratched into its reverse side in the futhark order, followed by two ideographic runes—: ᛉ : *elhaz* and : ᛃ : *jera*—for protection and good fortune. On the column of Breza (part of a ruined Byzantine church and probably carved by a Goth) we find a futhark fragment broken off after the L-stave and with the B-stave left out. The Charnay brooch also presents a fragment, but it seems intentional for magical purposes. The brooch of Aquincum bears the first aett, or section of runes, for the futhark complete. (For discussions of the various aspects of the aett system, see chapters 7 and 9.)

Survey of the Elder Continental and Scandinavian Inscriptions

The most convenient way to approach exoteric runic history is based on the study of the various types of materials or objects on which staves are carved seen through a chronological perspective. Generally, there are two types of objects: (1) loose, portable ones (jewelry, weapons, etc.), which may have been carved in one place and found hundreds or thousands of miles away; and (2) fixed, immobile objects (stones), which cannot be moved at all, or at least not very far.

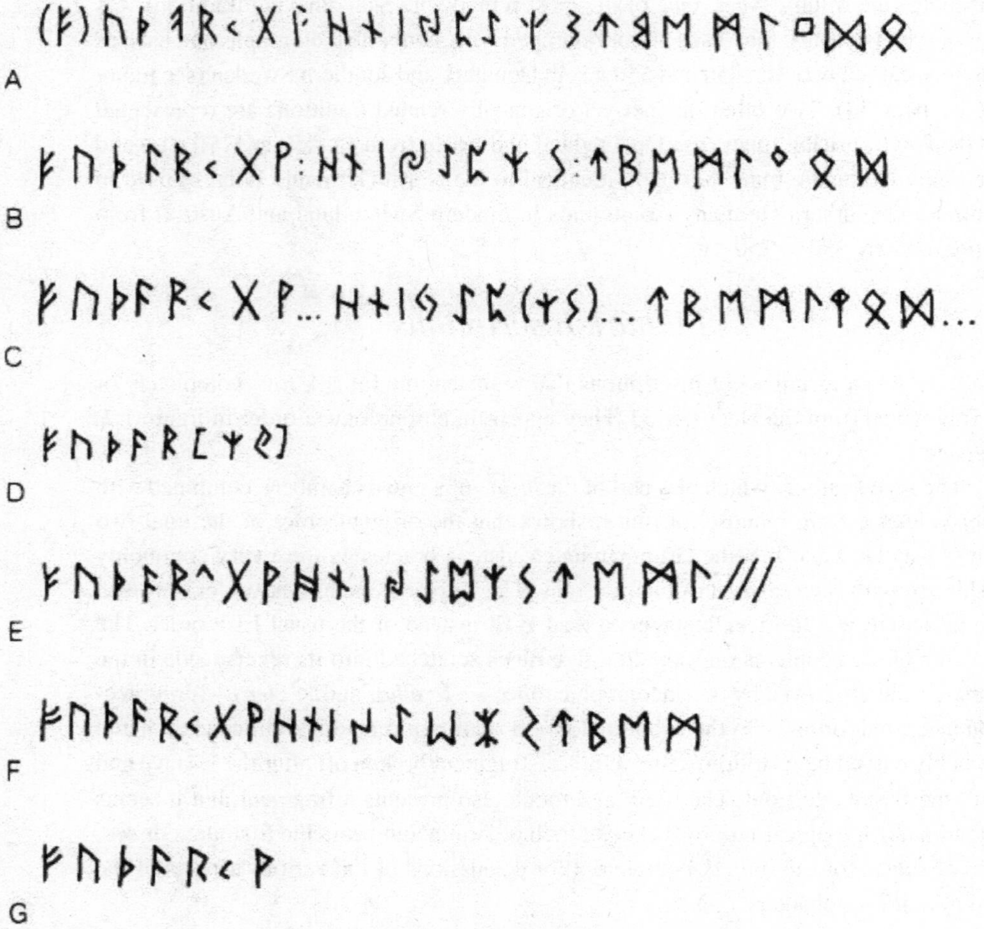

Figure 1.2. The Elder Futhark inscriptions: a) The Kylver stone, ca. 400; b) The Vadstena/Motala bracteates, ca. 450–550; c) The Grumpan bracteate, ca. 450–550; d) The Beuchte fibula, ca. 450–550; e) The marble column of Breza, ca. 550; f) The Charnay fibula, ca. 550–600; 8) The Aquincum fibula, ca. 550.

Mobile Objects

Runes are found carved on a wide variety of objects: weapons (swords, spearheads and shafts, shield bosses), brooches (also called *fibulae*), amulets (made of wood, stone, and bone), tools, combs, rings, drinking horn statuettes, boxes, bracteates, buckles, and various metal fittings originally on leather or wood. Most of these had magical functions.

The runic spearheads belong to one of the oldest magico-religious traditions among the Indo-Europeans, and they are among the oldest known inscriptions. The blade of Øvre-Stabu (Norway) was, until the recent Meldorf find, the oldest dated runic artifact (ca. 150 C.E.). On Gotland, the spearhead of Moos dates from 200 to 250. Farther south and to the east, we find the blades of Kovel, Rozvadov, and Dahmsdorf (all from ca. 250). There is also the blade of Wurmlingen, which is much later (ca. 600).

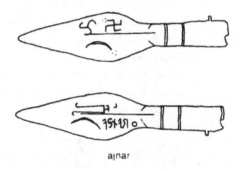

Figure 1.3. Spearhead of Dahmsdorf.

All but Kovel (plowed up by a farmer) and Wurmlingen were found in cremation graves. The Wurmlingen blade is from an inhumation grave. However, their primary function was not funerary; they probably were clanic treasures of magical import that were burned and/or buried with the chieftain. The magical use of the spear in the warrior cult is well known in the Germanic tradition. Hurling a spear into or over the enemy before a battle was a way of "giving" them to Odin, that is, of sacrificing them to the god. Odin himself is said to do this in the primal battle described in the "Völuspá" (st. 24):

> Odin had shot his spear
> over the host

This practice is also known from saga sources.

As an example of these powerful talismanic objects we will examine the blade of Dahmsdorf (found while digging the foundation of a train station in 1865). It is now lost. The blade is made of iron with silver inlay and is probably of Burgundian origin. It is especially interesting because it bears many other symbols besides the runes, as figure 1.3 shows. On the runic side we see a lunar crescent, a *tamga* (a magical sign probably of Sarmatian origin); the nonrunic side shows a triskelion (trifos), a sun-wheel (swastika), and another crescent. The runic inscription reads from right to left: *Ranja*. This is the magical name (in the form of a noun agent) of the spear itself. It is derived from the verb *rinnan* (to run); hence, "the runner." Its function was, in a magical sense, "to run the enemy through" and destroy them.

The brooches, which were used to hold together the cloaks or outer garments of both men and women, were in use from very ancient times (see *Germania*, chapter 17). As such, they were very personal items and ideal for transformation into talismans through the runemaster's craft. And indeed it seems that the majority of the twelve major inscriptions in this class (dating from the end of the second century to the sixth) have an expressly magical function. In six cases this includes a "runemaster formula" in which a special magical name for the runemaster is used. The magical function is either as a bringer of good fortune (active) or as a passive amulet for protection.

For an example of this type of inscription we might look at the brooch of Værløse, which was found in a woman's inhumation grave in 1944. This gilded silver rosette fibula dates from about 200 C.E. The symbology of the object also includes a sun-wheel, which was part of the original design, whereas the runes were probably carved later; at least we can tell that they were carved with a different technique. The inscription can be read in figure 1.4.

Figure 1.4. Værløse inscription.

Figure 1.5. Numerical analysis of the Værløse formula.

The Værløse runes are difficult to interpret linguistically. Perhaps it is an otherwise unknown magical formula made up of the well-known *alu* (magical power, inspiration; which can be understood in a protective sense), plus *god* (good). The meaning could therefore be "well-being through magical power." It also could be a two-word formula; for example, "*alu* [is wished by] God (agaz)," with the last word being a personal name making use of an ideograph to complete the name. However, the magical formulaic dynamism contained in its numerical value is clear, as we see in figure 1.5.

The numerology of the Værløse formula is a prime example of how numbers of power might have been worked into runic inscriptions. Here we see a ninefold increase of the multiversal power of the number nine working in the realm of six. See chapter 11 for more details on runic numerology.

The bracteates were certainly talismanic in function. Well over 800 of them are known, of which approximately 250 have runic inscriptions. These were not *carved* but rather *stamped* into the thin gold disks with the rest of the design, most commonly an adaptation of a Roman coin. The iconography of these Roman coins, which often show the emperor on a horse, was completely reinterpreted in the Germanic territory, where it came to symbolize either Odin or Baldr, his son. It is quite possible that the bracteates represent religious icons of the Odinic cult. They were produced and distributed in and around known Odinic cult sites in what is today Denmark.

The bracteate depicted in figure 1.6 comes from a German find near Sievern (a total of eleven bracteates). The iconography of the Sievern bracteate is also interesting. According to medieval historian Karl Hauck, the curious formation issuing from the mouth of the head is a representation of the "magical breath" and the power of the word possessed by the god Odin. This can also be seen in representations of the god Mithras. The inscription was badly damaged but probably reads as interpreted in figure 1.7. This reading can be understood as *r(unoz) writu,* I carve the runes, a typical magical formula for a runemaster to compose.

As an example of a wooden object preserved by this process we might take the yew box of Garbølle (on Zealand, Denmark) found empty in 1947. It is designed like a modern pencil box with a sliding top and dates from around 400 C.E. The inscription can be read in figure 1.8. The runes are generally interpreted *Hagiradaz i tawide*: "Hagirad ["one skillful in council"] worked [the staves] in [the box]." The five vertical points after the staves indicate that the reader should count five staves back from there to discover the power behind the runes (:ᚠ:).

There is also a whole range of fairly unique objects that are difficult to classify. Many of them are tools and other everyday objects that have been turned into talismans, whereas some, such as the famous horns of Gallehus and the ring of Pietroassa, are interesting works of art.

The ring of Pietroassa (ca. 350–400) makes a suitable example for these unique objects. It is (or was) a gold neck ring with a diameter of about 6 inches that would be opened and closed with a clasp-like mechanism. The ring, along with twenty-two other golden objects (some with jewels),

Figure 1.6. Runic bracteate of Sievern.

Figure 1.7. Sievern bracteate inscription.

Figure 1.8. Garbølle formula.

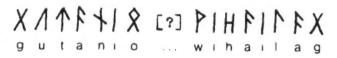

Figure 1.9. Formula of Pietroassa.

was found in 1837 under a great limestone block by two Romanian farmers. Unfortunately, almost all of the artifacts have since disappeared or have been heavily damaged. Of the ring, only the portion with the inscription itself survives, and that in two pieces. These objects seem to have been the sacred ritual instruments belonging to a pagan Gothic priest-chieftain (perhaps even Athanaric himself?). A neck ring was the insignia of sovereign powers in the pre-Christian Germanic world. Figure 1.9 gives the runic forms as we can now read them. They are to be interpreted as *Gutani* : ᛆ : *wih-hailag*. An unclear sign between runes seven and eight is probably a triskelion, and the eighth rune itself is probably to be read as an ideograph (= *othala*, hereditary property). Therefore, the translation of the whole formula would be something like "The hereditary property of the Goths, sacrosanct." For more about this treasure and the Gothic spearheads, see *Mysteries of the Goths* (Rûna-Raven, 2007).

Fixed Objects

Essentially, there are three types of fixed objects in the elder tradition, all of them in stone but of differing kinds and functions. There are first the rock carvings, cut directly into rock faces, cliffs, and the like. Then there are the so-called *bauta* stones. These stones are specially chosen and dressed and then moved to some predetermined position. The final group is made up of *bauta* stones that also have pictographs carved on them.

Four rock carvings date from between 400 and 550, and all are on the Scandinavian peninsula. They all seem to have a magico-cultic meaning and often refer to the runemaster, even giving hints as to the structure of the Erulian cult.

All of the inscriptions serve as a kind of initiatory declaration of power in which the runemaster carves one or more of his magical nicknames or titles. This type of formula can be used to sanctify an area, to protect it, or even to cause certain specific modifications in the immediate environment.

Figure 1.10. Veblungsnes formula.

The simplest example is provided by the rock wall of Veblungsnes in central Norway (see figure 1.10), which dates from about 550. In words, the Veblungsnes formula would read *ek irilaz Wiwila*: "I [am] the Erulian *Wiwila*." (Note that ᛗ : is a bind rune combination of : ᛗ : and : ᛉ :.) The formula consists of the first person pronoun "I," the initiatory title *irilaz* (dialect variation of *erilaz*), the Erulian (widely understood simply as "runemaster"), and the personal name. This name is, however, not the normal given name of the runemaster but a holy or initiatory name. It means "the little sanctified one" or "the little one who sanctifies." It might be pointed out that the name *Wiwilaz* is a diminutive form of *Wiwaz*, which is also found on the stone of Tune, and it is related to the god name *Wihaz* (ON Vé. "sacred"). In this formula the runemaster, or Erulian, sanctifies an area by his magical presence. He does this by first *assuming* a divine persona and then acting within that persona by carving the runes.

Bauta stones are the forerunners of the great runestones of the Viking Age. Such stones date from between the middle of the fourth century to the end of the seventh, but they continue to develop beyond this time.

Inscriptions of this kind are almost always connected with the cult of the dead and funerary rites and/or customs. As is well known, this is an important part of the general cult of Odin and one with which the runes were always deeply bound. Sometimes the runes were used to protect the dead from would-be grave robbers or sorcerers, sometimes they were employed to keep the dead in their graves (to prevent the dreaded *aptrgöngumenn* ["walking dead"], and sometimes the runes were used to effect a communication with the dead for magical or religious purposes.

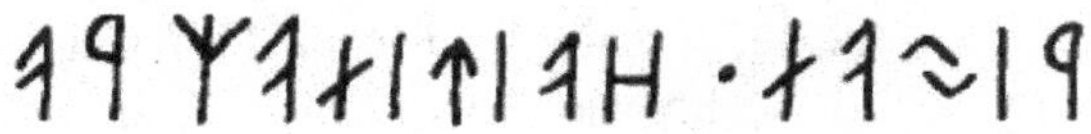

The stone of Kalleby, the formula of which can be seen in figure 1.11, is an example of the runemaster's craft to cause the dead to stay in their graves, or at least

Figure 1.11. Kalleby formula.

to return to the grave after having wandered abroad for a while. These conceptions are common in many ancient cultures. In the Germanic world, the "undead" were often reanimated by the will of a sorcerer and sent to do his bidding.

The Kalleby formula is to be read from right to left *thrawijian haitinaz* was: "he [the dead man] was ordered to pine [for the grave]." The use of the past tense is very often found in magical inscriptions for a twofold technical reason: (1) the basic magical dictum "do as if your will was already done," and (2) the fact that the ritual that ensured the will of the runemaster had already been performed *before* the actual effect was called upon. These conceptions are fundamental to the Germanic worldview concerning the ultimate *reality* of "the past" and its power to control what lies beyond it. The Erulian *uses* this effect his will.

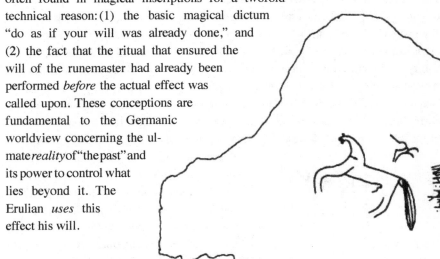

Figure 1.12. Stone of Roes.

The pictographic stones combine runic symbology with pictographic magic. This is especially clear in two of the stones, Eggjum and Roes, both of which have schematic representations of horses (see the E-rune). The tradition of combining runestaves and pictographs appears to be very old, since the oldest of the four inscriptions dates from about 450 and the last (Roes) from about 750. The technique would eventually flower into the great pictographic runestone tradition of Viking Age Scandinavia.

Perhaps the best example of the combination of the runes and the horse image is seen on the Gotlandic stone of Roes (see figure 1.12). This hefty talisman (a sandstone plate 22 by 30 by 3 inches) was found under the roots of a hazel bush during the nineteenth century. The actual runic formula can be read in figure 1.13. Its interpretation is not without controversy, but the best solution seems to be one that makes the complex figure a bind rune of U + D + Z, so that the whole could be read *ju thin Uddz rak*: "Udd drove, or sent this horse out." But what is this supposed to mean?

Old Norse literature provides us with a good clue to the significance of this symbol complex. In *Egil's Saga* (chapter 57) we read how Egil fashioned a *nídhstöng*, or cursing pole, out of hazelwood and affixed a horse's head atop it. This pole of insult was intended to drive Erik Blood-Ax and his queen, Gunnhild, out of Norway—and it worked.

Before leaving the inscriptions of the Elder Futhark it seems proper to say something about the language they employ. It was at about the time that the runestaves began to be used in writing that the Germanic languages really began to break up into distinct dialects. The language of the period before the breakup is called Proto-Germanic (or Germanic). There also seems to have been an early differentiation in the north that can be called Proto-Nordic or Primitive Norse. The Goths who began migrating to the east (into present-day Poland and Russia) from Scandinavia around the beginning of the Common Era developed the East Germanic dialect (which played an important role in the history of the early runic inscriptions). On the Continent to the south a distinctive South Germanic linguistic group developed what eventually came to include all German, English, and Frisian dialects; whereas in the north Proto-Nordic had evolved into West Norse (in Norway) and East Norse (in Denmark and Sweden). In the first few centuries of the elder period all of these dialects were mutually intelligible; and besides, the

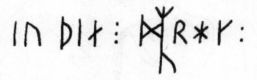

Figure 1.13. Roes formula.

runemasters had a tendency to use archaic forms in later inscriptions because they were often ancient and long-standing magical formulas. It has been supposed that there was even a pan-Germanic "sacred" dialect used and maintained by runemasters.

Anglo-Frisian Runes

There are as many reasons for keeping the English and Frisian runic traditions separate as there are for looking at them together. The Frisian tradition is only sparsely known, but it is filled with magical practice; the English is better represented yet less overtly magical in character. However, there are striking similarities in the forms of individual staves, and this fact, coupled with the close cultural ties between the English and Frisians throughout early history, leads us to the conclusion that there was some link in their runic traditions as well. Unfortunately, we have no complete Frisian Futhork.

First let us examine the rich English tradition. The oldest inscription yet found in the British Isles is that on the deer astragalus of Caistor-by-Norwich. It probably dates from the first real wave of Germanic migration during the latter part of the fifth century. But it is perhaps in fact a North Germanic inscription that was either imported or carved by a "Scandinavian" runemaster. This possibility must be considered because the northern form of the H-rune (:ᚺ:) is used and not the English:ᚻ:. The dating and distribution patterns of English runic monuments are difficult because the evidence is so sparse and the objects are for the most part mobile. In all, there are only about sixty English runic artifacts, mostly found in the eastern and southeastern parts of the country before 650 C.E., and mainly in the North Country after that time. The epigraphical tradition (i.e., the practice of carving runestaves), which must have begun in earnest as early as 450 C.E., was extinct by the eleventh century. The runestaves found another outlet in the manuscript tradition. These are valuable for our study but are rarely magical in nature.

The history of the English runic tradition can be divided into the two periods mentioned above: (1) pre-650 (in which a good deal of heathen ways survive), and (2) 650 to 1100 (which tends to be more Christianized, with less magical or esoteric practice in evidence).

The English Futhorc

The only futhorc inscription that remains is on the somewhat faulty Thames scramsax, which dates from around 700 C.E. It is actually a sample of fine Anglo-Saxon metalwork in which the craftsman inlaid silver, copper, and bronze into matrices that had been cut into the iron blade. The order and shape of the runestaves can be seen in Runic Table 2 (Appendix I). This futhorc is followed by a "decorative" pattern and then comes the personal name Beagnoth—probably that of the swordsmith, not the runemaster. As can be seen, there are a number of what seem to be formal errors as well as ones of ordering. All of this is due, no doubt, to Beagnoth's miscopying of a model. It is fortunate that we have more, if later, evidence that shows that in fact the English runic tradition was both well developed and very close to the Continental one. This evidence comes from the manuscript tradition. The most informative document is, of course, the "Old English Rune Poem" (see chapter 8).

The "Old English Rune Poem" contains a futhorc of twenty-eight staves; the codex Salisbury 140 and the St. John's College MS 17 also record Old English futhorcs of twenty-eight and thirty-three staves, respectively. Another manuscript, the Cottonian Domitian A 9 even records a futhorc divided into aettir, or families. Here, it is significant that the aett divisions are made in the same places as those of the Elder Futhark. This demonstrates the enduring nature of the underlying traditions of the Germanic row.

It seems that the oldest runic tradition in England was the Common Germanic row of twenty-four runes, which was quickly expanded to twenty-six staves, with a modification of the fourth and twenty-fourth runes: (4): ᚠ : [a] became: ᚩ : [o]; (24): ᛉ : had the phonetic value [œ] and later [ē]. In addition, the stave-form: ᚠ : was relocated to position 25 and named aesc (ash tree). These changes took place as early as the sixth century. As the English language evolved and changed, so did the Old English futhorc. This is the normal way an alphabet develops. As a sound system of a language becomes more complex, so does its writing system.

The use of English runes can be divided into three main classes:

Loose objects

Fixed objects (e.g., stones)

Manuscripts

The loose objects represent the broadest category. They are generally the earliest type of inscription, yet they also persist to a late date. Unfortunately, many of them are fragmentary or damaged to such an extent that exact readings are almost impossible. Most of the mobile objects have the runes scratched into metal, bone, or wood; however, some represent the staves by more intricate techniques of metalwork (see the Thames scramsax) or fine wood/bone carving (e.g., the famous Franks Casket). The Old English runestones mostly date from the Christian period and seem to represent a pseudo-Christian adaptation of the tradition, but they may still have magical, and certainly religious, import. Most of them are actually memorial stones or stone crosses and were carved by skillful stonemasons.

There is no Old English manuscript entirely written in runestaves, but they are nevertheless widely represented in the literature, where they serve both cryptic and pragmatic ends. Two runes were adapted by the English for writing with pen and parchment in the Roman alphabet; they were the p <: ᚦ : [th] (*thorn* [thorn]) and the P <: ᚹ : [w] (*wynn* [joy]). From there this orthographic practice was taken to Germany and to Scandinavia.

The Caistor-by-Norwich inscription mentioned above is a good example of the loose type of object from an early period. Its runes appear in figure 1.14. This bone was found with twenty-nine other similar ones (without runes), along with thirty-three small cylindrical pieces, in a cremation urn. It is possible that the objects were used as lots in divinatory rites. The inscription itself is difficult to interpret, but it may mean "the colorer" or "the scratcher" and be a holy name of the runemaster.

Figure 1.14. Caistor-by-Norwich inscription.

An explicit example of magic used by the Odinic runemasters is hard to come by in the English material, but the scabbard mount of Chessel Down (see figure 1.15) is probably one. The inscription was scratched on the back of the fitting and is thus invisible when in place. It might be translated as "Terrible one, wound [the enemy]!" If this is so, then *æco* (terrible one) would be the name of the sword, and *sœri* (wound [!]) its charge.

æ c o   s œ r i

Figure 1.15. Chessel Down formula.

An interesting example of a magical runestone from the pagan period is provided by the seventh-century Sandwich stone. It probably represents the name of the runemaster, Ræhæbul, and was originally part of the interior of a grave. The text, as best it can be made out, can be read in figure 1.16.

Among the manuscript uses of the runes, the one most approaching magical practice is the concealment of secret meanings in texts through the use of runes. One such text is found in Riddle 19 of the *Exeter Book*,[1] which translated from OE would rsead:

r æ h æ b u l

Figure 1.16. Sandwich inscription.

> I saw a ᚻᚱᚠᚾ (horse) with a bold mind and a bright head, gallop quickly over the fertile meadow. It had a ᛏᚠᛗ (man), powerful in battle, on its back, he did not ride in studded armor. He was fast in his course over the ᚠᚷᛗᚹ (ways) and carried a strong ᚻᚠᚠᚠᚳᚾ (hawk). The journey was brighter for the progress of such as these. Say what I am called . . .

Here, the runes spell out words, but they are written *backwards* in the text. So the runic words read *hors* (horse), *mon* (man), *wega* (ways), and *haofoc* (hawk). However, and this is a remarkable and mysterious thing, the individual *rune names* were to be read in the order as written so that the poem would have its proper alliteration.

Frisian Runestaves

No Frisian Futhork exists, but we do have a small body of interesting inscriptions. There have been about sixteen genuine Frisian monuments found so far (there are also a number of fakes). They date from between the sixth and ninth centuries. These inscriptions are generally found on wooden or bone objects that have been preserved in the moist soil of the Frisian terpens (artificial mounds of earth engineered in the marshes as an early form of land reclamation).

Frisian runic monuments seem to have a distinctly magical character, but many of them are difficult to interpret. We can be sure that they occur in a solid pagan context because this conservative region, often under the leadership of heroic kings such as Radbod, resisted the religious encroachment of the Christians—along with the political subversion of the Carolingian empire—until the late seventh century. We can even safely assume a period of reluctant religious compliance until long after that.

One of the most interesting, if difficult and complex examples of these Frisian pieces is the "magic wand" or talisman of Britsum (figure 1.17), which was found in 1906 and which dates from between 550 and 650. The wand is made of yew and is about 5 inches long. Side A of the inscription reads from left to right: *thin ᛏ a ber! et dudh*; side B can be read from right to left: *biridh mī*. The damaged part of the piece cannot be read. The whole formula is translated "Always carry this yew [stave]! There is power [*dudh*] in it. I am carried. . . ." It might be pointed out that the seven-point dividing sign on side B indicates the seventh rune following the marker; that is, :ᛁ: (in this inscription) =:ᛇ: yew—the power contained in the formula.

Figure 1.17. Wand of Britsum.

Chapter 2

VIKING AGE RUNES

(800-1100 C.E.)

As with all historical epochs, the Viking Age was not a sudden development but rather the result of a long, continuous process that had begun in the last centuries B.C.E. with the first movements of the Cimbri and Teutones from Scandinavia—that "Womb of Nations," as the Gothic historian Jordanes called it.

In the years around 800 Scandinavia was undergoing a number of internal changes and taking new directions. Sweden (especially Gotland) had already begun to develop the trade routes to the east among the Slavs, routes that would eventually reach Byzantium, Baghdad, and Persia. In Denmark powerful kings (Godfrid and Horik) were beginning to shape the Danish "nation" by mustering vast armies and mighty retinues. Norway, however, in its isolated and geographically fragmented condition, held to more local institutions and conservative ways. Although part of Sweden (Uppland and Gotland) and certain areas in the Danish archipelago had long been wealthy, the rest of Scandinavia was just beginning to accumulate wealth and to grow in new ways at this time. The first Viking raid was carried out by Norwegians in 793 on the monastery at Lindisfarne (Northumbria), followed by raids on Monkwearmoth (794) and Iona (795), all of which heralded the dawn of the Viking Age.

Just as the historical Viking Age was the result of a long process, so too was the evolution of the Younger Futhark from the older one. An examination of Elder Futhark inscriptions and alternate forms of elder runes will show that stave forms that were to become standard in the Younger Futhark were already in use from about 600 C.E. The evolution from the elder to the younger tradition took place at a fairly rapid pace during the eighth century, so that by 800 the new, systematically formed Younger Futhark, reduced from twenty-four to sixteen staves, had been completed, institutionalized, and disseminated throughout all of the Scandinavian lands.

The Younger Futhark is a purely Scandinavian cultural phenomenon, although many inscriptions are found outside Scandinavia, mainly in the British Isles and in the east. All of these inscriptions were carved by Nordic runemasters.

It is quite certain that all of this development took place within a traditional cultic framework—otherwise the older alterations and the eventual reformation of the row would not have taken place in such a uniform fashion and be spread with such speed and precision over such a wide expanse. In many ways the history of the younger reformation runs parallel to the original formation of the elder tradition. One of the major contrasts, however, is the way in which staves of the Younger Futhark were quickly altered (in some cases drastically) in certain regions. This may point to an increased fragmentation in the tradition, but the fact that it held on to its internal system of order (number), phonetic values, and aett divisions, as well as to the traditional modes of use (i.e., *carving*, not writing), testifies to the strength of the deep-level tradition.

We can suppose that the original, reformed "Common Nordic" rune row appeared in the form we see in figure 2.1. However, the final and most standard version of the futhark appeared in the slightly different form that we see in figure 2.2.

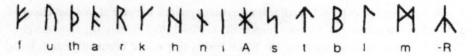

Figure 2.1. Common Nordic Futhark.

The development of this futhark was dependent on a combination of linguistic and magical criteria. But in discussing the role of linguistic change in the evolution of the younger row, it must be noted that the evidence shows this to be strictly secondary. The elder row could have been adapted easily (as indeed it has been earlier) to any sound changes that might have occurred in the language. But this was not done. Instead, as the language developed a more complex sound system, it simplified its writing system—an unheard-of event in the history of orthography. This is accounted for by the fact that the reformation took place for extralinguistic, magico-religious reasons.

Before we get into the traditional evolution, it is important to recount some of the major linguistic changes and how they were reflected by the staves, so that a "grammar" of the inscriptions will be clearer. To begin with, the phonetic value of : ⌄ : had always been uncertain, and it rarely appeared except in magical formulaic inscriptions. Also, : ⟨ : alternating with : ✳ : changed its phonetic value at an early date (ca. 600) in the north because an original initial *j* was generally lost in Nordic at that time. A neat example of this rule is provided by the rune name itself, where Germanic *jēra* became Primitive Norse *jār*, which developed into Old Norse *ár* : ⼁ :. Hence, the phonetic value of the stave goes from [j] to [a]. In addition, : ⼁ : went from [a] to a nasalized form [ą]. It is also important to notice the new ambiguity of the whole writing system, where many staves now have to represent two or more sounds (see Table 3 in Appendix I.)

The traditional elements indicate the continuity of the two systems, both elder and younger. These elements clearly show that the transition from one system to the other was carried out within a cultic framework and that the developers of the younger row had knowledge of the elder row and its traditions. This conclusion is bolstered by the fact that all of this took place in what was essentially a nonliterate society. For although the runes were a form of writing, they had not yet been generally put to the task of simple and profane interpersonal communication. For one human being to be informed about a complex system of any kind (e.g., runelore) he had to be told about it by another human being. In those days the would-be runer could not go to a library and pick up a dusty tome about a long dead tradition and reanimate it.

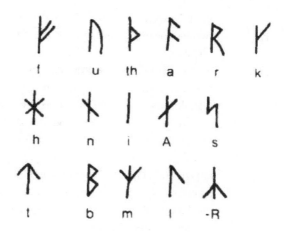

Figure 2.2. Standard Nordic Futhark.

The first element in this system is the continuity in the linear order of the staves, especially the first six: F-U-TH-A-R-K; otherwise, none of the staves of the Younger Futhark is displaced from its relative position in the elder row. Certain elder staves are dropped, and a new order emerges. The one exception to this rule is: ᛣ : [-R], which is moved to the end of the whole row. This is perhaps due to the fact that it occurred only at the ends of words, but it also may have something to do with a conscious effort to preserve certain elements of the ancient aett system. As we saw with regard to the elder period, the aett system was an integral part of the elder tradition. (See chapter 9 for more esoteric aspects.) The continuity of this unusual feature is more evidence for the conscious manipulations of a cultic institution. The first aett of the younger row is made up of the first six staves of the elder, in an unaltered order. It is also important that the second and third aettir begin with the same two staves as in the elder period, i.e., H–N and T–B, respectively. This, combined with the necessity of a symmetrical division following the mandatory sixfold first aett necessitated the movement of: ᛣ : [-R] to the end; otherwise it would have caused the third aett to begin with: ᛋ:. In any event, the continuation, and indeed strengthening, of the threefold grouping is a truly remarkable characteristic.

Simpler correspondences are nonetheless amazing. The level of continuity of stave forms is noteworthy: eleven forms remained unchanged, and three changed staves actually represent older alternate forms (i.e.,: ᚲ :/: ᚡ :,: ᛟ :/: ᚻ :) and the virtually interchangeable: ᛤ :/: ᛉ :, which originally developed from a: ᛜ : form. That leaves only two that pose any problems at all; : ᛗ : became: ᛉ :, and : ᚻ : became: ᛉ :. These are explicable on formal grounds. The younger row generally made all double staves into single ones, so that by moving the head staves together, the new forms: ᛉ : and : ᛏ : would emerge. The: ᛏ : was already an old unaltered form, so the modification: ᛉ : was preferred. This latter form is also explicable on esoteric grounds (see chapter 10).

Another remarkable element is that of the continuity of the rune names and hence their primary phonetic values. Although we do not have any sources for the elder rune names, a combination of the comparative study of the languages in which the names do appear (i.e., OE, Go., and ON and the study of the *ideographic* use of the elder runes (see, for example, the ring of Pietroassa, on page 15) indicate that the later names are indeed a continuation of an age-old system. The Old Norse tradition preserves the names in rune poems (see chapter 8). The only apparent divergence is in the [-R] : ᛤ : *ýr*, "yew" (bow), from [-R] : ᛉ : *elhaz*, "elk." However, the elder alternate form : ᛜ : has been interpreted as originally having to do with tree symbolism (see the four cosmic harts [= elks?] in the limbs of Yggdrasill). Also, the second rune,: ᚼ :, has received a secondary meaning, "drizzling rain," which is explicable on mythical, cosmogonic grounds (see chapter 10).

It seems necessary to assign an original homeland to the Younger Futhark because it would be difficult to account for two simultaneously developing identical systems in both Norway/Sweden and Denmark. Based on the evidence, the most likely location for this phenomenon is extreme southern Norway and the adjacent Swedish region, where runic activity had remained strong through the end of the elder period. The time of this formation would have been the closing decades of the eighth century. From this location it quickly spread to Denmark. There it fell on fertile ground and began to revivify the runic tradition in the Danish archipelago. In Denmark it was slightly modified and became the most influential model for future runic development. This situation sprang from the general growth in Danish cultural and political influence in the region at this time.

All of this leads us to a discussion of the most common forms of the futhark actually codified in Viking Age Scandinavia. Despite the variations in the shapes of individual staves, they maintained a consistent inner structure and organization.

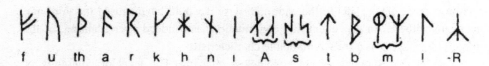

Figure 2.3. Danish Futhark.

THE BIG BOOK OF RUNES AND RUNE MAGIC

From the original codification in and around southern Norway and Sweden, the Younger Futhark spread to Denmark, where the codified forms were generally those found in figure 2.3. This Danish row was to become the most common of all futharks. It lasted from the ninth century to the eleventh and was the model for even later developments.

The Danish Futhark was, however, quickly reformed in some areas on the Scandinavian peninsula. By 850, in southern Norway and in Östergötland, Sweden, a simplified row was developed, which can be seen in figure 2.4.

Figure 2.4. Rök Futhark.

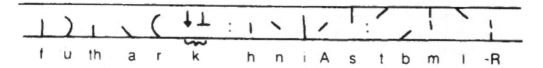

Figure 2.5. Hälsinga Futhark.

This is generally known as the Rök row after the most famous inscription in this futhark, the Rök stone. These particular stave forms lasted only until the latter half of the tenth century, when they were again replaced by the more standard Danish type.

Besides these two main futhark styles in use during the Viking Age in Scandinavia, in Sweden there was the sporadic use of a radically simplified stave system, later called the Hälsinga runes (after the province in which they are found). These are generally formed by removing the head or vertical stave from the form. A futhark of such staves is shown in figure 2.5.

This row is rare in inscriptions, and it has been speculated that it was actually a runic shorthand used in more profane communications and for legal affairs. It might have been in use as early as the tenth century, but the most famous inscriptions date from the middle of the eleventh. Although the Hälsinga runes were never more than a local convention, it is noteworthy that they remained a part of the ancient tradition.

Viking Age Inscriptions

We can, for the most part, find every kind of inscription in the younger period that we found in the elder one, but the type that comes to predominate in the evidence we have is that of the memorial stone. This is due in part to its durable character. However, talismans of various kinds remain an important part of the record as well. To date, around 5,000 younger runic monuments of all types have been found, but this number continues to grow as more Viking Age settlements are excavated.

Runic Memorial Stones

The tradition of carving, first, gravestones (very often found *within* the grave with a direct magical function), and later, memorial stones with apparent magical import dates back to the elder period. The *bauta* stones were, of course, closely connected to the grave. The younger tradition seized on this idea and made it a mainstay of its work. In the younger period such stones were not necessarily so closely associated with the grave itself, and therefore they are better referred to as memorials. They were often put in areas where travelers would pass by and where men capable of reading them could see them. This tradition began in Denmark around 800. It should be noted that this new bursting forth of revivified runic practice coincided with the reception of the reformed futhark and historically in connection with the ideological threat from Christianity in the south.

A famous example of an ancient form of gravestone, which actually represents the transition between the *bauta-* and memorial-stone types, is found on the stone of

Figure 2.6. Snoldelev stone.

THE BIG BOOK OF RUNES AND RUNE MAGIC

Snoldelev (see figure 2.6). This stone, which dates from between 800 and 825, was probably originally placed within the grave mound, but its formula bears some resemblances to the later memorials. It is also interesting to note that the stone was used for cultic purposes as early as the Bronze Age (ca. 1500–500 B.C.E.). We know this because a sun-wheel sign is still barely visible (with proper lighting) on its face (see dotted lines on figure 2.6). Its inscription is to be transliterated:

kun uAltstAin sunaR
ruhalts thulaR asalhauku (m) [?]

which can be translated: "Gunvald's stone, the son of Rohald, the *thulr* [= cultic speaker in the cult of Odin] at Salhaugen."

Snoldelev is especially interesting for its testimony concerning an official title within the Odinic cult (the ON *thulr* and the OE *thyle*), which has to do with the role of the magician/priest as a cultic reciter of law, incantation, mythic song, and the like—and the powerful holy signs, the three interlocked drinking horns (a symbol of the Odinic cult) and the solar-wheel/swastika. (Note the relationship between the later solar wheel and the older sun-wheel sign.)

A more classic example of the memorial-stone tradition is provided by the great Strö stone from near the village of Strö in southern Sweden (Skåne). The stone dates from about 1000 and was originally part of a grave-mound complex of seven stones (two with runic inscriptions). Although the mound has since fallen in, this was one of the first runic monuments to be described by Ole Worm in 1628.

The staves, which can be read in figure 2.7, are executed within a zigzag, serpentine ribbon.

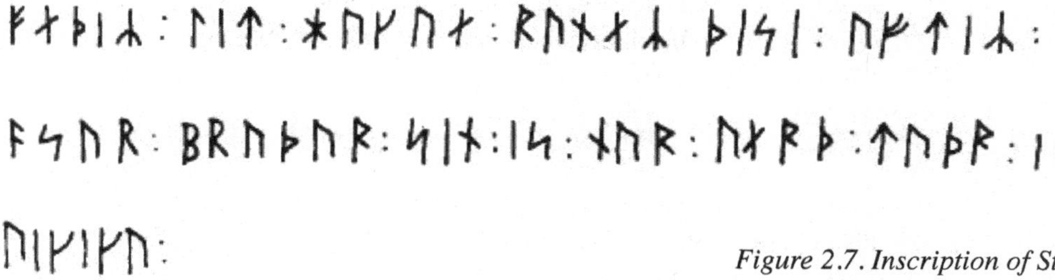

Figure 2.7. Inscription of Strö.

This inscription would be rendered in Old Danish as *Fadhir lét hoggva rúnaR thessi øftiR Azzur bródhur sínn, es norr vardh dødhr í vikingu* and translated: "Father had these runes cut after [= in memory of] his brother Asser, who died up in the north while a-viking."

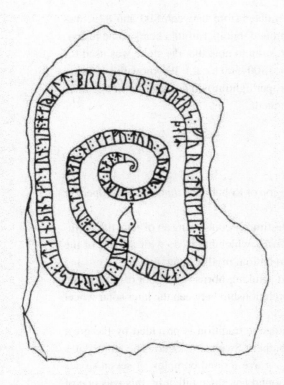

Figure 2.8. Gripsholm stone.

The Strö stone clearly shows the memorial characteristics of these monuments. A few technical observations are in order also. Note that often double letters are not indicated by the staves (ᚼᚢᚴᚢᚾ = *hoggva*); : ᚭ : can stand for -*ng*- , as well as other ambiguities in the orthography of the inscription.

This stone shows us how these monuments were carved in memory of Viking raiders who died in foreign lands, which apparently was quite common. It also gives testimony to the fact that (professional?) runemasters were engaged for the carving of the staves.

A possible mytho-magical example of such a memorial stone is magnificently provided by the stone of Gripsholm. This stone commemorates a "brother of Ingvarr" who fell with the mythic hero (Ingvarr) while in the east. The outlines of the Gripsholm stone, which dates from the middle of the eleventh century and measures 6 feet by 4 feet 6 inches, are given in figure 2.8. Its inscription, beginning at the head of the serpent, should be transliterated as follows:

tula: lit: raisa: stain: thinsat: sun: sin: haralt: bruthur: inkvars:
(thaiR) furu: trikila: fiari: at: kuli: auk: a: ustarlar: ni: kafu: tuu:
sunar: la: asirk: lan: ti.

The latter part of the formula is in verse, and the whole may be translated:

Tola had this stone raised for his son Harald. Yngvarr's brother.
[They] fared boldly
far away after gold
and in the east
they gave [food] to the eagle;
they died in the south
in Serkland.

(Note that the double-point dividing signs, which usually indicate the divisions between words, are sometimes used within words. There may be some magical encoding at work here.)

More than thirty stones from this region (around Lake Mälar) and time period refer to men dying in the east with Yngvarr. Here we are probably dealing with a ritualized mythicizing of the deaths of men who fell in Russia and beyond during the later Viking Age. The Yngvarr to which these stones refer is a historical figure who launched a great expedition against the Islamic world in the east—Serkland—around 1040. ("Serkland," which means either "shirt land" or "silk-land," is sometimes more narrowly identified with Persia.) His expedition ended with the disappearance of the men off into Central Asia departing inland from the east coast of the Caspian Sea. All of this, coupled with the fact that this Yngvarr (sometimes spelled Ivar) had the same curious nickname (*vídhfadhmi* [far-traveler, or wide-fathomer]) and the same theater of demise (Serkland) as a semi-mythical Yngvarr (who would have lived in the sixth or seventh century) tend to make us believe that at a certain point all of those slain in the east were ritually said to have "fallen with Yngvarr," a heroic figure from the mythicized past. The mythical Yngvarr is mentioned in the *Heimskringla*, and a whole medieval Icelandic saga is devoted to him.

The poetic lines of the inscription are interesting because they testify to an ancient and sacred formula—*erni gefa* (to give [sacrifice] to the eagle)—as a way of expressing the sacral nature of battle in connection with the Odinic cult.

Talismanic Objects

A wide variety of object types continued to be transformed into talismans in the Viking Age and beyond. Many were pure talismans (see figure 2.11 on page 33), whereas others were utilitarian objects turned into talismanic ones by means of loading them with rune might.

The famous ship burial of Oseberg (late-ninth-century Norway), perhaps the grave of queen Asa, included two runic inscriptions—one on a bucket and one on a round stake (beechwood, about 8 feet long) of uncertain function. It was probably part of the steering mechanism of the ship. The inscription, which is executed in Norwegian/Swedish (Rök) runestaves, can be read in figure 2.9.

This formula requires a good deal of runic knowledge to read. Nevertheless a literal meaning can be extracted:

ᛚᛁᛏᛁᛚᚢᛁ᛬ᛁ   *Litil(l)-víss m(adhr)*

The last stave is used ideographically to stand for its name, and the entire text can be translated: "[the] man is little wise," or "[a] man [who] knows little," the significance of which is to ward off the uninitiated from the deeper meaning of the inscription.

This deeper meaning is concealed by the common technique of stave scrambling. In this case it hides the famous magical formula *mistil*, which shares significance with the word *mistletoe* (ON *mistilteinn*), the twig of the little mist. Note that the latter part of the *mistil* formula is repeated twice, as is the other part of the formula, *vil* (= ON *vél* [craft]).

<pre>
l i t i l u i s m -and- l i t i l u i s m
9 8 4 5 6 7 2 3 l   6 5 4 8 9 7 2 3 l
</pre>

Figure 2.9. Oseberg formula.

Figure 2.10. Lund weaving temple formula.

So the secret inscription would read:

mistil-til-vil-il or simply *mistil-vil*

In standard Old Norse this would be *mistil-vél*, the craft of the little mist—the magical powers over life and death. References to this magical mythos can be found in the story of the death of Baldr.

Another talismanic inscription on a utilitarian object is found on the weaving temple of Lund (Sweden), from about 1000 C.E. This interesting runic text gives us a sample of the curious mixture of love and curse magic, and the common blending of

THE BIG BOOK OF RUNES AND RUNE MAGIC

the two in Nordic sources. For other examples from the literature, see the "Skírnísmál" (stanzas 25–36) in the *Poetic Edda* and the confusion between the two forms found in *Egil's Saga*, chapter 72. The runic text of the temple can be read in figure 2.10.

In more standardized form: *Sigvarar Ingimar afa man min grat*, which can safely be translated "Sigvör's Ingimarr will have my sorrow," is then followed by an eight-stave magical formula: *aallatti*. The effect of the inscription is strengthened by the hidden numerical pattern of twenty-four staves in the main formula and eight in the auxiliary rune *galdr*. The purpose of the inscription is clear: it is to cause the husband (or fiancé?) of Sigvör (who is named Ingimarr) to have the runecarver's lovesickness; that is, he will lose Sigvör in some manner so that the runer can have her.

The final example of a talismanic object from the Viking Age is the copperplate (about 2 inches square) of Kvinneby (Öland), which dates from the late eleventh century. This is a truly remarkable amulet, the complexities of which we cannot fully explore in this space. Its fairly long text (144 staves) is inscribed in nine rows of *boustrophedon* (as one plows a field; i.e., from left to right and then back from right to left, etc.). This was a continuous practice in runic inscriptions from the elder period. The text is preceded by six magical bind runestaves (the first of which has been obliterated). These bind runes can be seen in figure 2.11. These signs are followed by the runic text itself, which can be translated as follows:

Figure 2.11. Kvinneby bind runes.

> Glory to thee I bear,
> Bofi. Help me! Who
> is wiser than thou? And bear all
> in evil from Bofi. May Thor protect
> him with that hammer that from
> the sea came, (it) flew from evil. Wit
> fares not from Bofi. The gods are
> under him and over h-
> im.

This is followed by a schematic drawing of a fish.

What is important to notice in the surface meaning of this talisman is the use of mythic imagery to shape the magical charge. In this case it is the protective power of Thor —his hammer, Mjöllnir—which always returns from the source of "evil" once it has hit its mark. Also, the image of the gods surrounding the shielded man, above and below, is significant in that it shows the gods present below as well as above. The Old Norse word that is usually translated as "evil" is *illr*, which keeps to its original primary meanings "ill, oppressive, difficult, mean (things)," and so on, rather than its later Christian meaning that indicates an absolute moral force.

Runic Technology

An often-ignored aspect of runology is that of the materials and techniques used in the actual production of runic objects. This is one area where "experimental archeology" can be of great value, which in turn can lead to a deeper understanding of the inner realms of the runes. Most of what is said here is valid for both the elder and younger periods.

We know certain things about the way in which they were executed by the runemasters from the runic inscriptions themselves. For example, besides the obvious physical evidence, we know from the runic terminology that runestaves were *carved* into the surfaces of various substances. The most common term in regard to this is Germanic *wrītu* (I carve), which eventually becomes Primitive Norse *ristan* (to carve). These terms are related to the English "write." However, the original sense was that of carving or cutting.

The tools with which these carvings were made are generally unknown to us, so we can only guess at their nature. The famous stone of Eggjum tells us that it was not scored with an iron knife (*ni sakse stAin skorin*). Therefore, we know that for certain purposes there was probably a prohibition against using iron in cutting runes, but we also know that many objects must have been carved with iron knives. Here we are most certainly dealing with the elemental science of runecraft. The great runestones of the Viking Age were surely carved by means of a hammer and chisel after they had been dressed with a pick and/or ax. Some inscriptions may have even been executed by means of a pick hammer, tapping away at the surface along the lines of the staves. The stone of Snoldelev seems to have been done in this way. Other kinds of tools used in magical inscriptions were knives (see *Egil's Saga*, chapter 44) and needle-like objects (which must have been used to cut inscriptions such as the Kvinneby amulet). Some of these needles may have been crafted from nonferrous metals (bronze, copper, etc.) or from nonmetallic substances (e.g., bone or stone).

The physical evidence also bears ample witness to the substances into which runes were carved. Furthermore, the epigraphic and literary terminology of runelore gives us clues to the relative frequency with which various materials were employed. Wood was clearly the medium of choice among the runemasters. Terms for the runes themselves generally revolve around wood and not any other runic medium. Very often the word *stave*, which literally means "stick" or "staff," is used as a synonym for rune. We get our English word *stave* from the plural form of *staff* (ON *stafr*). This points to the fact that originally the figures representing the mysteries were carved onto small wooden sticks (used in magic and divination) and that a shift in meaning took place in which the most popular mode of representing the rune became a synonym for the concept itself. Although this connection must go back to the era of runic origins, the oldest example of "stave" standing for "rune" is on the now lost stone of Gummarp (ca. 600 C.E.), which reads:

HAthuwolAfA
sAte
stAbAthria
ᚠ ᚠ ᚠ

This can be translated as "Hathuwulf set three staves : ᚠ ᚠ ᚠ."

Not only did the "stave" come to stand for the sign of the rune, but it eventually took on all the meanings of the word *rune* itself, so that in Old Norse we find *stafr* (more usually in the plural, *stafir*), meaning not only "staff, stick, post" but also "lore, secret lore, wisdom, magical sign."

Runic terminology was so well entrenched in the languages that in many dialects the vocabulary of Latin letters was reshaped by it. In Old Norse, written letters are referred to as *stafir*, and even the complex magical signs (ON *galdrastafir* [magical staves]) use this term even though they are sometimes drawn with pen and ink. Old English *stæf* (letter, writing) and Old High German *stab* (stave, letter) are also examples of this. Note the modern German word for "letter" Buchstabe vs. Stab (stick, stave, wand).

Another often neglected yet essential aspect of runic technology, which is nevertheless important to modern runecraft, is that of coloring the staves and the objects on which they are carved. Again, the elder inscriptions themselves tell us that the staves were indeed colored, by frequent use of the verb *fāhidō* (I colored, or painted). The later Old Norse vocabulary continued to use the descendant of this Germanic verb form, *fá*, in the same context. Moreover, we know that the most popular color for the runes themselves was red (made with red oxide of lead, minium, or most often, ochre). This was generally a magical substitute for blood (see *Egil's Saga*, chapter 44). Comparative historical linguistics gives us good evidence for the magical importance of the color red for the Germanic peoples. The Old English *teafor* is an old term for red ochre, but the word is also found in Old High German as *zouber* (magic, divination) and in Old Norse as *taufr* (talismanic magic, talisman). It seems that one of the old ways "to do magic" was "to make red [with ochre]" some symbolic object in conjunction with a transference of magical might. This technique is made very clear in the passage from *Egil's Saga* cited above.

Other colors that were used, especially on later runestones, were black (made with soot) and white (a lime solution), as well as blue and brown. Traces of some of these have been found on the stones themselves. The Viking Age runestones were not originally the gray objects we might see today but brightly colored blazing beacons on the landscapes of all the worlds.

The coloring was used in a variety of ways. Its original function was undoubtedly magical. However, this was multileveled. The runes were stained a different color from the background (often red on white or black), which made the stave stand out. Furthermore, colors were used to make word divisions, with every other word (or part of speech) in a different color. There is also evidence that some runes were not actually cut into the stone but only *painted* in place! This opens up the possibility of an enormous number of forever lost runic documents that were just painted on the surfaces of rocks or wooden objects—all long since washed or blown away.

The language of the Viking Age inscriptions is generally referred to as Old Norwegian, Old Swedish, or Old Danish, depending on the dialect area in which it was produced. However, those with a knowledge of the literary forms of Old Norse, coupled with some basic runology, would have little trouble in deciphering runic texts found on Viking Age runestones. This is because the Norse dialect remained quite homogeneous until around 100; then East Norse (Swedish and Danish) and West Norse (Norwegian and Icelandic) began to develop. But even then the changes remained relatively minor through the close of the Viking Age.

Chapter 3

MEDIEVAL RUNES

(1100-1600 C.E.)

The Viking Age was drawing to a close around 1050, and by 1100 the period characterized by the vigor of the Viking raids was over. Christianity was becoming the official cult of the court and eventually of most of the people. But we know from historical sources for this complex period that the Christianity they practiced was in many cases not really orthodox, and in fact their religion represented a kind of mixed faith of Asatru and Christianity.

Denmark had officially become Christian in the late tenth century; and although the Norwegians maintained a long struggle against the alien creed and political structure, Norway was officially secured by the Christian camp by the early eleventh century. In Sweden the story is more complex. There apparently had been a number of Christians in Sweden (Irish slaves who did not abandon their ways) from the early Viking Age, and various missionary expeditions sent into the country during the eleventh century exposed pagan ideas to many Christian formulas that found their way into heathen practice. But Sweden did not officially become Christian until around 1100.

In this period of tenuous and irregular beginnings much of the organized tradition of the runic cult was destroyed along with its larger religious framework. However, a number of factors, such as the comparative lack of Christian indoctrination of the Scandinavian clergy, a historically tolerant attitude, and the remoteness of the whole region compounded by the inaccessible outback districts, combined to make fertile ground for the survival of runic traditions among the farmers and lesser nobility.

For an in-depth look at the culture of the Germanic world and how the old pagan forms survived the Christianization process see *The Northern Dawn* (Arcana Europa, 2018). It is too often thought that either the old ways were entirely destroyed by the Christianization process, never to be recovered, or conversely that the ancient customs continued unbroken in some secret enclave. The truth is more complicated, and more fascinating than either of these extremes.

During the Catholic period the runes were brought into the service of the Church itself—or so it would seem. However, this was somewhat of an unholy alliance because the medieval runemasters were still largely in possession of the elder lore, albeit in a fragmented state. Magic was still their principal function, although they were also increasingly used in profane communication. But without an organized cultus in support of the runic tradition, it steadily declined throughout this period. However, the kernels of the tradition were preserved through rote formal learning of names and forms, sometimes in the context of profane writing. This process was carried out unconsciously in all parts of what had been greater Germania, and we will see evidence of this throughout our discussions. Besides this disparate formal survival—guided by the webwork of wyrd—the indwelling runic pattern survived as the "blood" of the ancient Erulians still coursing in our veins. The mysteries are virtually encoded in the pattern of what might be called our "collective unconscious."

The Reformation, which began in Sweden in 1527 and officially a bit later in Norway/Denmark in 1536, brought both blessings and a terrible curse. The blessings generally came about because of the growth in Swedish nationalism in the middle of the sixteenth century that promoted all aspects of indigenous culture. The doctrines of *storgoticism* were formulated from widespread beliefs by the last Catholic archbishop of Uppsala, about 1554. The curse came with the wave of intolerance that followed after the Protestant wave had been absorbed. This resulted in the persecution of all practitioners of the old ways, especially those of the peasant class and country folk.

The ambiguity of the sixteen-stave row developed in the Viking Age posed little difficulty to the initiated runemaster and served very well for esoteric practices because it remained organically within the systematic runic structure. However, as the level of training slipped, the ambiguity of the sixteen-stave row was somewhat altered by the introduction of "dotted runes" (ON *stungnar rúnar*) beginning as early as the end of the tenth century in Denmark. At first this was an occasional addition of a point to clear up any possible ambiguity in the inscription. Although this practice makes it obvious that "profane" interpretations of the runes were assuming more importance, for at least two hundred years more the sixteen-stave row, sometimes in the "dotted" form, was the rule.

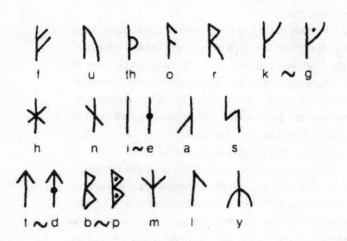

Figure 3.1. Dotted futhark.

These dots were placed on or near the stave to distinguish it phonetically from its contrasting opposite in a natural class, for example, b:p, t:d, k:g (distinguished from one another by *voicing*). The oldest dotted runes with their phonetic values appear in figure 3. 1.

This development became more "Latinized" until it was finally codified during the reign of Valdemar the Conqueror (1202–1241), when a true "runic *alphabet*" was formulated. That is, a stave was given for every letter in the Roman alphabet as it had been adapted for writing the contemporary Scandinavian dialects.

Figure 3.2. A runic alphabet.

In Norway the thirteenth and fourteenth centuries saw the runic alphabet shown in figure 3.2 in general use. A similar thing happened throughout Scandinavia, including Iceland, during the Middle Ages, where a little after 1100 Ari inn Fródhi and Thóroddur Rúnmeistari created an expanded standardized *Futhorkh* to compete with the Latin script.

Medieval Inscriptions

In this epoch we begin to see many more different uses and depictions of runes and rune magic. Many of the old traditions continued in some conservative areas, while new uses of the runes, often replacing Latin letters, were introduced. Also, stories about runes and rune magic abound in thirteenth- and fourteenth-century Iceland, where we can be sure the runes were indeed used in arcane arts.

The memorial runic *bauta* stones continued to be a lively tradition on Gotland until after 1700! And although they were superficially Christianized, there remained much in them, both in their symbology and in their deeper structure, that reminds us of the old way. It is probable that those with knowledge of esoteric runelore were also not unwise concerning their hidden meanings at this time.

Figure 3.3. Solar wheel/cross sign.

The "holy signs" (ideographic symbols) that would appear on these stones often seemed to have a mixed significance. The cross was usually equal-armed and sometimes appeared with a solar wheel in its midst, as shown in figure 3.3.

This motif, and elaborations on it, was continued until the end of the period in question. It has been speculated that this kind of cross was a substitute for the *ægishjálmr*

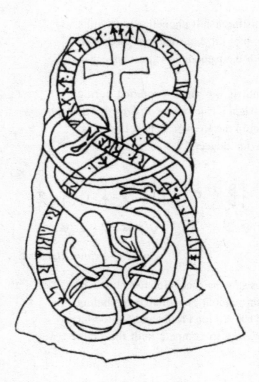

Figure 3.4. Morby stone.

(helm of awe) sign that had appeared in similar contexts in the heathen period. A typical example of the post-Christian *bauta* stone is provided by the Upplandic Morby stone (figure 3.4). It follows a peculiar tradition that developed at this time (early in the Christian period, ca. 1050–1150) of building a bridge for the dead relative and raising a memorial stone that also makes reference to the bridge—all of this being done for the sake of the dead one's soul (ON *önd* or *sál*). The staves of the Morby stone can be transliterated:

khulu lit kira bra f(u)rant kilau[h]a tatur sin[a]
uk sum ati ulfr ubir risti

These runes are easily translated: "Gudhlaug had this bridge built for the soul [ant = *önd*] of Gillaug her daughter whom Ulfr had married. Øpir carved [the runes]." The stone is "signed" by Øpir, one of the most famous runemasters of history.

The practice of making runic talismans (*taufr*) continued into the modern era, and they were certainly popular throughout the medieval period. But because they were often carved in wood (and usually on very small pieces) and increasingly were being written on parchment, very few of them survive. Also, runemasters sometimes would destroy the talismanic objects once their work was done, and many were destroyed because of the post-Reformation persecutions of magical runemasters.

An example of a magical talismanic object from the medieval period is provided by a rib bone (ca. 30 inches long) that was found in the old church at Särkind, Östergötland, Sweden, and which dates from the fifteenth century.

This bone probably functioned as a *göndr* (magical wand), and it bears the complex inscription seen in figure 3.5 on page 41.

The first part of side A is to be transliterated thaet tae refen (this is the rib bone). The second complex is made up of a manifold bind rune of uncertain meaning. It could conceal the name of the magician, or it could be a combination of certain runes for magical effect. This side of the inscription is concluded with a bold *hagall* rune, which in the esoteric school of this period would have had well-developed cosmic significance as the image of the World Tree and the seed of the multiverse. The three R-staves on side B are intended to formulate and guide the magical power generated by the vitki, as is clear from the esoteric lore surrounding the :R:.

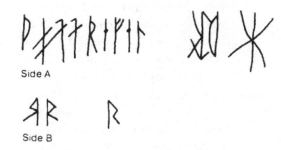

Side A

Side B

Figure 3.5. Wand of Särkind.

Besides these archaic and sacred uses of the runes, they were also being employed in new and profane ways in common communications. We know that this was increasingly the case throughout the thirteenth and fourteenth centuries as the late saga literature often mentions the sending of runic messages on *rúnakefli* (rune sticks). *Hákons saga Hákonarson* in the *Heimskringla* mentions this several times. But the greatest evidence for "runic correspondence" was found in the excavations of the dock district in Bergen, Norway, where dozens of these messages were actually found. Some are as simple as a "note" from a wife telling her husband to come home from the local tavern and some are as intriguing as an example that dates from the early thirteenth century, which may be translated as follows:

> I want to ask you to leave your party. Carve a message to Olaf Hettusveinn's sister—she is in the nunnery at Bergen—and ask for advice from her and from her kinsmen, when you want to come to terms. You are surely less stubborn than the earl. . . .

This is followed by a set of staves that have not yet been satisfactorily interpreted but may be transliterated: atu:kena:nu:baetu. It is possible that the message carries an encoded secret meaning; however, on the surface this is clearly an appeal from a member of one party or faction to a member of another, asking the recipient to leave his side and come over to that of the sender, but this is to be done secretly through a third party (the woman in the convent).

Runestaves were also increasingly finding their way onto the written page. At first this was part of an effort by some (such as Ari and Thóroddur, mentioned above) to develop the runes as an alternative to the Roman alphabet. There were probably many manuscripts written in runestaves, but only one lengthy one remains to us, the so-called *Codex Runicus*. The staves, or runelike signs, also were used ideographically in some manuscripts, standing either for the rune name or for some other symbolic quality. In the *Codex Regius* (the MS that contains the *Poetic Edda*): Ψ : is often used as a substitute for the word *madhr* (man). There were also many manuscripts that contained lines written in runestaves and several treatises on runes—for example, the one by the German scholar/monk Hrabanus Maurus. Also, the important evidence of the *Galdrabók* cannot be forgotten because it represents runes and runelike "staves," secret runes, and the like, firmly within a magical context.

The rune poems are prime examples of the use of runestaves in manuscripts, but we will examine them separately in chapter 8.

It is only in the manuscript of the Laws of Skaane (*Skaanske Lov*)—or as it is more descriptively known, the *Codex Runicus*—that any surviving attempt at a substitute of runestaves for Latin letters is found. The manuscript probably dates from the fourteenth century. Later attempts to "revive" the runes as a utilitarian script were carried out by antiquarians, some of whom were quite serious and virtually "neo-pagan" in their beliefs (see Johannes Bureus, on page 44).

Besides these uses, the runes were widely employed in the construction of "primstaves" or "rim-stocks," which worked as perpetual calendars. These seem to have the nominally Christian function of computing festival days, but the fact that runes were almost exclusively used in the construction of these objects from at least the fourteenth century all the way into the eighteenth shows the eternally living nature of runelore in the Scandinavian lands.

Chapter 4

MODERN RUNIC HISTORY

(1600-1945)

T his age is, in the beginning, historically closely connected with the Age of the Reformation. However, there was also a growing and more formal difference evolving between the knowledge of the scholar, who consciously attempted to rebuild the structure of older lore, and that of the folk, who in constantly changing form preserved the lore unconsciously. The distinction between revival on the one hand and survival on the other was growing. Each hold their advantages and disadvantages.

Revivalists, even in this early time, went back to material from the Elder and Viking Ages and thus *could* have come into contact with the "purest" and most traditional forms; whereas the folk tradition was (as the *Galdrabók* shows) always ready and willing to assimilate foreign features and thus lost sight of the original system (e.g., Latinization in the runic "alphabet"). But the folklore was directly bound, unconsciously and imperfectly as it might be, to the seed forms of the ancient worldview, an advantage not enjoyed by the revivalist scholars. The latter had been educated in the "classical" tradition, indoctrinated with Judeo-Christian ideas, and initiated into a largely Hermetic school of magic. Therefore, their attempts at revival of the old way were inevitably shaped by their backgrounds in the newly established traditions. But the potential for going beyond this, directly to the oldest levels, was eventually made possible by their efforts and groundbreaking work.

The first great homeland of runic revival, after it had been relegated to the most remote rural regions and deepest level of the cultural hoard, is Sweden. Around 1600 Sweden was an emerging world power with great pride in her past and great plans for her future. The combination of the intellectual freedom granted to the Swedish intelligentsia (but certainly not to the folk) by the Reformation and the growing nationalism led to the canonization of an ideology known as *storgoticism* (megleogothicism). This ideology is probably rooted in concepts that reach all the way back to ancient times, and it first raised its head in the late 1200s, within a century after the "Christianization" of the Swedes. *Storgoticism* is wrapped up with the almost mythic proportions attained by the people called Goths. This has continued in many ways as the word and concept

Goth or *Gothic* have taken on many different meanings. The first documented reference to this latter-day "Gothic mythology" in Middle Ages occurs in the records of a Church Council held in Basel in 1434, where the Spanish claimed precedence in a matter over the English because they (the Spanish) were identical with the Goths and therefore the elder nation. To this the Swedish replied that in such case Sweden held precedence because they were the original Gothic people and the main stem of that nation.

Storgoticism was eventually codified by Johannes Magnus, who was the last Catholic Archbishop of Uppsala, in his book *Historia de omnibus gothorum sveo-numque regibus* (1554). As Johannes Magnus formulated it, storgoticism was firmly bound to Hebraic mythology. It was thought that Sweden was the first land to be settled after the Deluge by the descendants of Japhet. This type of mythology was common in Great Britain at the same time. Essentially, Magnus's mythic history was a preconditioned fantasy in which, for purposes of prestige, he connected the Swedes to the Hebrews and claimed that all of the wisdom of ancient times (such as that possessed by the Greeks) was actually taught to the world by the Swedes. Also, it was believed that the runic "alphabet" was the oldest script in the world (with the possible exception of Hebrew).

This mythology influenced the next generation of storgoticists, which was contemporary with the Reformation in Sweden and the development of that nation into a world power. The great reformer of *storgoticism* was Johannes Bureus or Johan Bure (1568–1652), who was a tutor and advisor of King Gustavus Adolphus. *Storgoticism* had become a virtual religion by that time, and the historical aspects had been refined by Johannes Messenius in his *Scandia Illustrata*. But our main interest is with Bureus.

Bureus was the first great runic revivalist. His scholarship was considerable, and one of his most important tasks was the collection and recording of runic inscriptions from all over Sweden. By the end of his life he had transliterated about one-fourth of the then known inscriptions. Bureus was made Antiquary Royal in 1630, after having had the chair in history at the University in Uppsala. In 1620 it was declared that all future holders of this chair were bound to learn "runic" (i.e., the old language that the runes were used to represent) and how to interpret the signs. Between 1599 and 1611 Bureus wrote three books on runes, including a small illustrated edition of inscriptions, his *Runarafst*, and a runic primer. Although Bureus's scientific work was considerable, it was largely superseded in his own lifetime by the Dane Ole Worm. But this scholarly work was only part of the importance of the runes for Bureus.

Soon after 1600 Bureus began to develop a system of what he called "adulrunes." In this system he began to use the runes for mysto-magical purposes. Although it is said that he originally learned of the runes from the peasants of remote Dalarna, Bureus evidently was not content with building on the folk tradition, and he began to apply runelore to the magical teachings with which he was already familiar—"Christian

Kabbalism." The adulrune system was simply developed by analogy with the Hebrew lore of the *Seper Yetzirah* (which we know he read). It is still unclear how much the indigenous Germanic traditions (such as runelore) influenced the shape of "mainstream" medieval magic, but in any case by this time there was a basic theoretical framework that must be described as Christian and that was to a large extent distinct from the folk traditions. Bureus's main sources were Paracelsus and pseudo-Paracelsian writings (e.g., the *Liber Azoth* and the *Arbatel*), early Rosicrucianism, and the works of Agrippa von Nettesheim. His principal runic technique was a variation of *temura* (a Kabbalistic procedure involving the permutations of letters in a word to give a new, "revealed" meaning). Bureus believed that all knowledge had originally been *one*, and since the lore of the Goths represented by the runes was the oldest of all lore, he could gain access to inner knowledge by acquiring the ability to grasp the adulrunes. Bureus did not, however, consider himself to be a neo-pagan. Quite to the contrary, he considered himself a "true" Christian, and he believed that the worship of God and the mastery of the power of prayer were essential to success in his system.

In 1613 Bureus became more deeply engrossed in the esoteric aspects of his studies and was especially enthralled by apocalyptic speculations. By the early 1620s the local church authorities began to look askance at Bureus's heretical theories, but his royal connections protected him from any prosecution by the Church. He believed in the approaching Judgment Day so strongly that he divided all of his property among the poor in 1647 — the apocalyptic year according to his calculations — and lived five more years supported by royal aid.

Bureus's work is important in two areas: (1) it was the beginning of scientific runology, and (2) it again used runes in sophisticated magical and philosophical work. But the predictable and unfortunate shortcomings of his effort in the latter field are obvious.

The whole *storgoticism* movement had far-reaching political ramifications. On its tide of nationalism Gustavus Adolphus broke with the Catholics and began his nationalistic programs justified by the ideas of *storgoticism*. In the area of religion there seems to have been an elite gathered in high circles for whom the Reformation was a cover for the development of a "Gothic Faith." The office of the Antiquary Royal was the center of this new national religion, headed by Bureus and supported by the king.

The runes played an important role in the inner workings of this system, but they also were being touted for more practical reasons. Bureus developed a cursive runic script with which he hoped to replace the Latin. During the Thirty Years' War a Swedish general, Jacob de la Gardie, wrote communications to his field commanders in runes as a kind of code.

As the power of Sweden waned and the Age of Enlightenment began, the doctrines of *storgoticism* and the theories of men such as Bureus lost favor with the establishment, and they again slumbered in darker and more remote corners.

The next breakthrough of runic investigation began in the European Romantic period began about one hundred years later, in the late eighteenth and early nineteenth centuries. Again its strongest representative, as far as genuine revivalism was concerned, was Sweden. There, in 1811, the *Gotiska Förbundet* (Gothic League) was formed by the poets and social reformers Erik Gustave Geijer and Per Henrik Ling. Their movement was essentially grounded in literature, although it was a serious attempt to quicken the ancient spirit.

On the other side of the coin, there was the continuing folk survival of runelore throughout Germania and her colonies. This was especially vigorous in Scandinavia, where runes and runic writing continued to be used for both everyday affairs as well as magical spells.

In Scandinavia and the North Atlantic isles, the runic alphabet survived as a writing system well into the twentieth century. This is especially true in remote regions such as Dalarna, Sweden, and Iceland. The runic alphabet remained purely runic until the middle of the eighteenth century, when Latin letters began replacing staves and it became a mixed script. Besides this writing system, the runes also were used in the construction of prim-staves or rim-stocks. These are perpetual calendars introduced into Scandinavia in the Middle Ages and were always carved into wood or bone. These calendars were a common form of time reckoning in the North well into the nineteenth century.

Knowledge of the runes was kept vigorous by folk traditions, and the lore and craft of the runes was preserved along with their more mundane uses. In more remote parts of the Scandinavian peninsula there were runesingers who could perform magical acts through *galdr*, or incantation, and in Iceland magical practice involving runes and *galdrastafir* (often runelike magical signs) continued at least into the seventeenth century. At this folk level, as well as at the scholarly level, as we have just seen, elements of "establishment magic" (i.e., Judeo-Christian) quickly spread throughout the system and was happily syncretized into it. But those who have studied the sixteenth-century *Galdrabók* (which was used and added to in the seventeenth century as well) will know that the underlying methods remained virtually the same as in the native tradition. The text of the *Galdrabók* and many other examples of Icelandic magic are contained in *The Galdrabók* (Rûna-Raven, 2005) and in *Icelandic Magic* (Inner Traditions, 2016).

In the southern Germanic areas there is some hard evidence for a similar tradition of runic survival. One of the most interesting examples of this is found in the Black Forest region of Germany in the so-called *Heidenhäuser* (heathen houses!). These are very old farm buildings in which the threshing floor and other parts of the house are decorated with magical ideographs, some of which are of undoubted runic origin. Some of these are single runes, for example, ◇ ◁ ⋈ ೪ ⁑ ⋏ ⋏ ↑, whereas others are bind runes or holy signs, for example, ⋏ ⴼ ⊗ ⴲ ⴲ ⟑ ⋔ ⊠ ᛘ. The buildings in which these signs appear mostly date from the late sixteenth to the early eighteenth centuries. It is probable that the signs were carved by a certain group of "initiates" who still knew the symbols and how to work their magic. Similar magical signs have been found in the Harz region of Germany, and if we can believe some investigators, a wide range of medieval symbolism had its roots in runic shapes. But not only did the mere shapes survive—so did the essential lore surrounding them. However, as far as Germany and most of the rest of northern Europe are concerned, the events of 1914 to 1918 and 1939 to 1945 destroyed much of the remainder through death and the rending of the social fabric. The darkest hour is before the dawn.

Not only do we find survivals of this type in Europe but America also is not without her runic heritage. Here we are not speaking of the highly controversial "American runestones" but rather of the living magical traditions of the Pennsylvania "Dutch" (Germans). In the eighteenth century these settlers brought a rich magical heritage, the major tool of which is the "hex sign." This term is perhaps derived from an early misunderstanding of the German *Sechszeichen* (six sign), so called because the earliest and most common signs were designed around the sixfold star or cross in the form seen in figure 4.1.

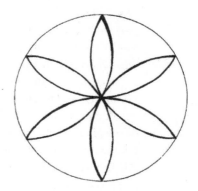

The word *hex* could be just as old because this term comes from the old Germanic sacred vocabulary and originally had to do with the "sacred enclosure" and the people (especially women) who practiced their arts there.

Such hex signs are virtual Germanic *yantras* and are used for every possible magical purpose. The sign is painted in bright colors on a round disk (usually of wood) and placed in locations significant to the working—out-

Figure 4.1. Hex sign pattern.

side on a barn or house, inside a house, or even carried on the person as an amulet. Again we see an important social aspect to this tradition. Hex signs can be effectively made only by an initiated *Hexenmeister*, and the work must be accompanied by an incantational formula. One formula known in South Carolina even calls on Thor! There are indeed many dark and little-known corners of this aspect of American history that deserve more work in our field. Some practical hints about how to use and construct these signs are included in the book *Northern Magic* (Llewellyn, 1992, 1998).

Practitioners of the folk tradition remain unconscious of the historical details of their past and continually re-create the system according to their needs and conditions. This process is indeed the natural and healthy one; but when the folk tradition becomes "tainted" with an ideology hostile to it, this process becomes less effective as the life is slowly drained from it. Due to these circumstances it became necessary to develop new tools to dig out the lost life and lore of the elder heritage. The spirit necessary to this task was reborn in the early nineteenth century in northern Europe under the banners of literary Romanticism and academic philology.

When it was discovered in the late eighteenth century that the languages of India and Europe were somehow organically related, a great school of thought arose in northern Europe, especially in Germany, that sought to put the study of these languages and cultures on a scientific basis. This came in the Age of Romanticism—which in many respects is a misnomer because in northern "Romanticism" people generally were looking more to Germanic models and away from those of classical antiquity. Perhaps a better term would be "German-ticism." In any event, serious interest in things Germanic, their origins, and their relationships to the greater Indo-European world grew rapidly. The greatest contribution to this area was made by Jacob Grimm, who, along with his brother Wilhelm, set about studying a wide range of manuscripts and collecting folk tales. In the process they virtually founded the disciplines of historical linguistics, comparative religion and mythology, and folklore. By means of what is now called "Grimm's Law" it was shown how Germanic was regularly derived from Indo-European, and its relationship to other dialects in that group (e.g., Sanskrit, Greek, Latin) was demonstrated.

Together with linguistics, the religions expressed in the texts being studied—the Eddas, the Vedas, Homer, Irish sagas—and the names of the gods were being compared; and schools of thought concerning the ways to interpret the mythologies were developing. As might be expected, many of those theories seem rather naive today, but the road to reconstruction is by its very nature fraught with pitfalls. The details of this historical process are much too complicated to go into here, but we must mention two theories held by older investigators. One was the tendency to go for "naturalistic" interpretations, to see mythology as a pure reflection of natural phenomena, which we now know to be only a part of the mythological function. The second tendency, or controversy, was the oscillation between considering mythology to be the creation of an ancient priesthood or sovereign class and the idea that it was essentially an outgrowth of the tales of the simpler folk tradition. The recognition of this dichotomy was astute, and it was later to become an important concept.

The importance of this pioneer work is that it put the investigation of such matters on a scientific basis, which has as its foundation the careful study of existing evidence of all kinds. If this work is carried out in an objective yet sympathetic manner, the veils of negative (Christian) psychological conditioning are lifted, and the possibility of penetrating to the most archaic levels of ideology is offered.

The Magical Revival

It was not until the first years of the twentieth century that a magical runic revival began, but this revival had manifold roots and was itself many-faceted. The late nineteenth century also saw the emergence of spiritualism and occultism in popular culture. The most influential branch of this phenomenon was Theosophy, as formulated by Helena Petrovna Blavatsky and promoted through the Theosophical Society. Concurrent with this new interest in the occult was a strong revival of Germanicism, which also might be called Neo-Romanticism. This was coupled with the growth of political Pan-Germanicism following the unification of the German Empire in 1871.

All of these factors began to work together with the latest theories concerning mythology, religion, science (especially Darwinism), and philosophy. From this mighty mix emerged the heterogeneous *Deutsch-Bewegung* (Teutonic Movement). In every aspect the adherents of this movement had a practical bent. They were not out to philosophize from ivory towers, but rather it was their intention to alter the world in which they lived. They wanted to bring society back to its traditional (pre-Christian) roots — at least as they saw them. Even those who formally wished to think of themselves as "Christians" rejected most of what had traditionally been thought of as the Christian heritage and replaced it with Germanic mythology and folk tales. This branch of the movement generally went under the banner of the *Deutsch-Christen* (Teutonic Christians). But other, perhaps more honest, members of this social revolution rejected the Christian tradition and again took up the standard of the All-Father.

As far as our central purpose of runic revival is concerned, the great figure of the age was *der Meister*, Guido von List (1848–1919). List was born into a well-to-do Viennese family with business interests. Although young Guido had a deep interest in the mystical and natural world from an early age and wanted to be an artist and scholar, he followed in his father's footsteps. Partly out of a sense of duty, it seems, he entered a career in business. It is said that when he was a boy of fourteen, he stood before a ruined altar in the catacombs of St. Stephen's Cathedral in Vienna and declared, "*Wenn ich einmal gross bin, werde ich einen Wuotans-Tempel bauen!*" ("When I get big, I will build a Temple to Wotan!")

During those early years, in the time he had free from his professional duties, List explored the alpine regions from his native Lower Austria to Switzerland. But in 1877 his father died, and he began to pursue more intensely his work as an artist, mystic, poet, and prophet. The years between 1877 and 1889 were difficult and obscure ones for List, but in the last of these years his two-volume novel *Carnuntum* appeared. This is a historical novel depicting the struggle between the Germanic and Roman cultures along the Danubian frontier — a favorite theme in his works. It was both a critical and a popular success.

During the next period of his life (1889–1891) List apparently devoted himself to study and inner work, for in the last year of this period a new phase began that shows evidence of initiatory insight. In 1891 he published his two-volume *Deutsch-Mythologische Landschaftsbilder* (Teutonic-Mythological Landscape Formations), which is a kind of geomantic investigation of the megalithic monuments, tumuli, earthworks, castles, and other sacred sites in Lower Austria; and a virtual catechism of his philosophy called *Das Unbesiegbare: Ein Grundzug germanischer Weltanschauung* (The Invincible: An Outline of Germanic Philosophy). Both of these works show signs of the elegance and ingenuity of his more systematic thought yet to come.

In German-speaking countries throughout these years the ideology expressed by Theosophy was quite influential, and although List's own relationship to the Theosophical Society itself is somewhat vague, he does seem to have been influenced in the direction of its philosophy and cosmology. *Der Meister* was, it seems fair to say, at least the equal of Madame Blavatsky in matters of this kind. It is a fact that many of the prominent Theosophists of the day were also followers of List.

Between 1891 and 1902 List's literary career was coming to a close—he had bigger things ahead of him—but this was his most successful period in literary endeavors. He produced several dramas and his second major novel, the two-volume *Pipara*.

The year 1902 was, however, the great turning point in the evolution of List's thought. In that year he underwent surgery for cataracts on both eyes. For eleven months he was virtually blind. During this time List seems to have undergone an initiatory experience, one that opened his inner eye to the secrets of the runes as expressed through the "Rúnatals tháttr Ódhins" in the "Hávamál" (see chapter 8). He began to investigate the Germanic past and its secrets with this newly won (or refined) ability. The years between 1902 and 1908, when the first book appeared in what was to become an encyclopedic series of works outlining his elegant system, were filled with great inner and outer activity. List was well connected with leading Pan-Germanic political figures and ideologies (e.g., Dr. Karl Lueger, the *Bürgermeister* of Vienna) as well as with many wealthy industrialists, all of whom supported his investigations into and actualization of the ancient Germanic mysteries. So in 1905, the Guido von List Gesellschaft (Society) was formed to underwrite the work of "the Master." In conjunction with this exoteric branch an esoteric inner group called the *Armanen Orden* was planned for initiatory work and the teaching of more occult practices.

In 1908 List's first book in his investigation series appeared, entitled *Das Geheimnis der Runen* (*The Secret of the Runes*), in which he postulates that the primal futhork was an eighteen-rune row. The original row was made up of a series of staves to which certain formulaic "kernel words" were attached. These kernel words, and variations on them, could then be used to decode any other word, ancient or modern, to get back to their original meaning in the "primal language" (*Ursprache*) itself.

Although there was a whole magical system attached to List's runic revelations, it remained largely secret until after his death—and much of it remains so today.

The rune book was followed in that same year by a general two-volume work—*Die Armanenschaft der Ario-Germanen* (The Armanism of the Aryo-Germanic People)—that outlined the ancient social structure and religion and pointed the way to its rebirth.

Also in that year *Die Rita der Ario-Germanen* (The Sacred Law of the Aryo-Germanic People) appeared. (Here, *rita* is a term borrowed from Sanskrit *rta* or *rita*, cosmic order, law.) With this work List attempted to reestablish, on a religio-cosmic foundation, a Germanic basis for law and political structure.

The next year, 1909, saw the publication of *Die Namen der Völkerstämme Germaniens und deren Deutung* (The Names of the Tribes of the People of Germania and Their Interpretation) in which List applied his theories concerning the investigation of hidden significance in names and words through an analysis of the kernel syllables.

In 1910 he published *Die Bilderschrift der Ario-Germanen: Ario-Germanische Hieroglyphik* (The Symbol Script of the Aryo-Germanic People: Aryo-Germanic Hieroglyphics), which concentrated on the investigation of the esoteric significance of a wide range of symbol forms, including runes, glyphs (holy signs), and especially coats of arms. This work was compared to Blavatsky's *Secret Doctrine* by the famous theosophist (and member of List's group) Franz Hartmann in his journal *Neuen Lotusblüten* with the words, "The author has lifted away the thick veil, which covered the history of Germanic antiquity, and has given us deep insight into the Secret Doctrine of the ancient Germans and the meaning of their symbology."[1]

The most complex and comprehensive book in the series was *Die Ursprache der Ario-Germanen und ihre Mysteriensprache* (The Primal Language of the Aryo-Germanic People and Their Mystery Language). This did not appear in completed form until 1915, although sections of it had already been published as early as ten years before. The huge volume contains List's system of *kala*, of decoding words to reveal their hidden meanings. This system is a virtual science of folk etymology, which is very potent in magical practice but thoroughly disregards every rule of historical linguistics. The companion to this volume was to have been *Armanismus und Kabbala*. In this book List was to show the relationship between the two systems, and how the Kabbalah was actually *Armanen* wisdom that had been absorbed into Judeo-Christian thought and esoteric philosophy. However, in 1919, before the completed manuscript could be printed, List died, and the manuscript apparently was stolen—or kept secret by members of the *Armanen Orden*.

The grandiose ideology and religious philosophy expressed in List's works is far too complex to enter into in any detail here. But some of the principal ideas he articulated that have found their way into the runic revival in modern Vinland are (1) the "trifidic-triune triad," (2) the "bifidic-biune dyad" (*zweispältig-zweieinigen Zweiheit*), and (3) the historical concept of concealment of ancient lore and even sacred systems in apparently Christian or secular literature and symbology. A general overview of List's ideas can be found in the introduction to *The Secret of the Runes* (Destiny, 1988).

The idea of the bifidic-biune dyad resulted in the concept of a balance between spirit and matter and the idea that matter was actually condensed spirit.

However, List's formulaic use of three is the most prominent feature of his system. In many ways it prefigures the theories of G. Dumézil concerning the Indo-European tripartite socioreligious structure (see chapter 13). The kernel concept of List's triadic thought is the archetypal pattern of arising (birth), becoming/being (life), and passing away to new arising (death/rebirth). This paradigm is applied to a number of concepts to form an elegant religio-magical philosophy. First of all, it is applied to cosmological principles. But perhaps one of the most interesting applications is to a system of tri-level interpretation of myths or of any concept or symbol. In this system a concept is seen on (1) a common level—a popularly understood form, (2) the level of exoteric symbolism, and (3) the esoteric level. This puts any word or concept through a spiral of semantic permutations to reveal inner truths and hidden relationships.

The Guido von List Gesellschaft continued to flourish after the death of *der Meister*, as did dozens of other Neo-Germanic groups (not all of them having anything to do with rune knowledge). In the years before 1933 other investigators, such as Friedrich Bernhard Marby and Siegfried Adolf Kummer, began to teach some of the more practical aspects of runecraft (especially the use of runic postures—so-called "runic yoga"—and talismanic magic).

In order to understand the National Socialists' relationship to runelore, one must first realize the level of popularity such things had reached in the late nineteenth and early twentieth centuries. Runes and runelike forms had again become symbols (but often very "common" ones) of *Deutschtum*. Runology was not only a beloved topic of academicians, it also became a topic in which the layman could immerse himself.

The idea of a non-Judaic religious revival was also strong, and it ran the gamut from the "Teutonic Christians" (who replaced the Old Testament with Germanic lore and "Aryanized" Jesus) to the largely pagan organizations such as the Guido von List Society.

The roots of National Socialism are manifold, and we cannot enter into them in too much depth here. However, we can point to some of the uses and misuses to which the Nazis put the runes. We must also preface these remarks with the statement that whether it is runes or religion of which we speak, the *party-line* Nazi doctrine is usually anathema to the essence of true Germanic concepts and often the antithesis of kernel pattern of Odian philosophy and practice. There were, however, secret cells within high levels of the *Schutzstaffel* (SS) gathered around Heinrich Himmler, especially at the Castle of Wewelsburg in Westphalia, in which more open experimentation was practiced. Some of the inner teachings of this world are explored in the book called *The Secret King* (Feral House, 2007).

There can be little doubt that certain elements within these cells had a genuine interest in the establishment of a Germanic religious worldview; however, the highest party leadership seems to have shown little real interest in this direction.

But they were all masters of the magical forms of mass manipulation that involves the stimulation and activation of popular images and engineering them in such a way as to work one's will on the mass population. (Today we call it advertising or branding, among other things.) One of the important steps one must take in using this process is the establishment of what might be called a meaning shift (or semantic shift) with regard to symbols.

✳	*Lebensborn* (Spring of Life) program for racial eugenics.
↑	*Hitler Jugend* (Hitler Youth) used this sign as a part of their badge.
⚡⚡	In tandem stood for the *Schutzstaffel* (SS), the "Protection Detachment."

Table 4.1. Runic symbols used by National Socialists.

This is most effective when one takes an archetypally powerful symbol (e.g., ✚ or 卐) and fills it with a personalized significance (Jesus and Hitler, respectively). Some of the more common runic symbols used in the National Socialist movement are shown in table 4.1.

Soon after 1933, when the Nazis came to power, the various groups involved in the Germanic Renaissance outside the structure of the Party itself were outlawed. All of the work done by dozens of organizations and individual leaders was either absorbed into official Party doctrine, liturgy, and symbology or was submerged. F. B. Marby himself spent ninety-nine months in the concentration camp at Dachau.

What had not been destroyed in the years of consolidation of Party power between 1933 and 1938 was subsequently further damaged by the war itself. Not only did the war destroy individuals of great knowledge—it also ripped apart the social fabric all over Europe. The mass displacement caused by the hostilities and the socioeconomic revolutions that followed in Western Europe were probably the final blow to any vestiges of the folk tradition in many rural areas.

Indeed, it always seems that the darkest hour is before the dawn, and that holds true for the rebirth of our traditional ways. After the willful destruction of the traditions by the Church, and the often misguided distortions of political movements, the way is hard to bring the runic secrets back into the fabric of our culture—but this is a heroic challenge of our time.

Chapter 5

CONTEMPORARY RUNIC REVIVAL

(1945-PRESENT)

In the aftermath of World War II, interest in Germanic religion and in the runes was frowned upon in Germany, and to a certain extent even in academic circles, which had not gone untouched by "NS-runology." Although German esoteric runology within the context of Germanic religion had been virtually eliminated, it did find a new home in the more eclectic branches of Western occultism and in that most prestigious lodge of German occultism, the *Fraternitas Saturni* (Brotherhood of Saturn). Runic work based on the theories and practices of Guido von List, Friedrich Bernhard Marby, and Siegfried Adolf Kummer became a part of the magical curriculum of the Fratenitus Saturni chiefly under the guidance of Frater Eratus (Karl Spiesberger). Spiesberger's efforts, largely outlined in his two books *Runenmagie* (1955) and *Runenexerzitienfür Jedermann* (1958), led esoteric runology in the direction of universalism and away from the *völkisch* interpretations. There is also a heavy admixture of Hermetic-Gnostic ideas, a trend already evident to a lesser extent with earlier rune magicians.

F. B. Marby, after his release from Dachau at the end of the war, again became active. But he was never able to gain the same level of achievement as he had during the earlier part of the century.

Runology in the context of a general Germanic revival began slowly. Around 1969 Adolf and Sigrun Schleipfer reactivated the *Armanen Orden*. They also took over the leadership of the Guido von List Gesellschaft, which also had been dormant since the war. The new Grand Masters set about making the *Armanen Orden* a real working magical order with a foundation in Germanic mysticism. Other Neo-Germanic groups active in Germany do not show practical interest in rune magic. Through the 1970s and 1980s there developed in Germany a sort of dichotomized universalist or semi-universalist esoteric runology (represented by Karl Spiesberger, Werner Kosbab, and others) and a tribalist-nationalist esoteric runology (represented by the *Armanen*). All of the groups in Germany use the eighteen-rune Futhork.

The runes have always held a special mystique for those interested in the Germanic way. As a general Germanic Renaissance again began to spread (apparently almost spontaneously from around 1970) in Europe and North America, the runes often figured prominently in the imagery and symbolism of the various groups; for example, the ritual of the Discovery of the Runes used by the Odinic Rite in England, or the name of the journal published by the Ásatrú Free Assembly, *The Runestone*, with its runic masthead. However, no in-depth esoteric runology was undertaken in the early years by any of these organizations.

In the summer of 1974 I came across the book *Runenmagie* by K. Spiesberger[1] in the university library. This occurred after I had received a flash of illumination that consisted of one "audible" word, *RUNA*, just a few days before. From that day forward I worked in the runes. My studies in magic, after having begun well in daimonic splendor, had taken a philosophically uninspiring turn into the morass of Neo-Kabbalism. The runes, and the Way of Woden that is shown through their might, were to set me back on the road to that great power. At the time I was ignorant of the contemporary Germanic revival and remained so until 1978. By the summer following the discovery of Spiesberger's book, after I had worked intensively with the philosophy and practice of the *Armanen* Futhork, I produced a text of my own that was largely a compilation of material from concepts contained in the books of such authorities as K. Spiesberger, Guido von List, and R. J. Gorsleben. This is the unpublished *Runic Magic of the Armanen* finished in August of 1975. This esoteric activity simultaneously led me to a deep academic interest in Germanic religion and magic. By the next year I was a graduate student learning Old Norse and investigating the Way of Woden on an intellectual level as well.

This interest in things Germanic had not begun suddenly in 1974, however. The year before, the book *The Spear of Destiny*[2] had sparked my imagination. It also fired my investigative zeal, and I set out to find the original texts on which its edifice was built. Later I found that many of these texts had been misused, or interpreted incorrectly. Still earlier, the words "The ravens of night have flown forth . . ." had rung in my mind as well.

I continued to develop my hidden path in solitude until the summer of 1978, when I made contact with the Ásatrú Free Assembly and began a period of close cooperation with Neo-Germanic groups. At the same time I was completing work on the restoration of the esoteric system of the Elder Futhark of twenty-four runes, which in 1979 resulted in the text of *Futhark: A Handbook of Rune Magic*.[3] Intellectual studies had led me to the realization that in order to know the runes as they truly are, one must work with the ancient archetypal system as it truly was.

During this same time, but unknown to me, a fellow traveler, David Bragwin James, was working in similar directions in a similar personal situation in New Haven, Connecticut.

It was soon apparent that no group in the English-speaking world was privy to any deep-level runelore, and therefore the burden fell to me to quicken the knowledge of our folk mysteries in a coherent and communicable fashion—no easy task. This work eventually led to the independent formation of the Rune-Gild for the practice and teaching of runework and runecraft. This institution was originally conceived of as an organic part of certain Neo-Germanic religious groups, but this proved quite impossible. It seems the runemasters are in some ways a Gild of Outsiders, and as such they remain largely outside other natural, organic structures. It is the purpose of the Rune-Gild to expand the level of knowledge and interest in the genuine Germanic Way and to carry out runework systematically, providing a reliable stream of basic rune skill and rune wisdom to all and giving a way of entry into the Gild Hall to the few. Subsequent to these early developments, the Rune-Gild matured to a viable organization with a published curriculum of runic instruction known as *The Nine Doors of Midgard* (The Rune-Gild, 2016, 5th edition).

Chapter 6

HISTORICAL RUNE MAGIC
AND DIVINATION

Too many modern rune-magic schools have been forced, either by their ignorance of the timeless traditions or by their inability to gain access to the traditional mysteries, to ignore or to forget the true runic sources handed down to us in lapidary splendor by our ancestors. In this chapter we shall explore the actual runic corpus for evidence of rune magic as it was practiced by the ancients.

The hoary documents carved in stone and metal are but the visible fossils of a living process of runecraft. The literary accounts help us flesh out this process to a great extent, but to understand it one must ultimately plumb the depths of runelore.

Inscriptions

Runic inscriptions represent messages—sendings—of a mysterious nature. They are complex and symbolic communications, which are only sometimes "legible" in the sense of natural language. More often their messages are far more obtuse. However, through a careful analysis of the evidence we may come to some meaningful conclusions on some of the ways rune magic was practiced in days of yore.

As far as operative magical acts are concerned, we can divide the types of runic formulas into seven categories: (1) messages in natural language, (2) symbolic word formulas, (3) futhark formulas, (4) magical formulaic words (e.g., *luwatuwa*), (5) runic ideographs, (e.g., *galdrastafir*), (6) numerical formulas, and (7) the runemaster formulas.

Sendings in Natural Language

Because the runes enabled them to communicate directly with that other (objective) reality, the runemasters could simply write runic messages in natural language to effect some alteration in the environment. These were often magico-poetic vocal formulas symbolically given objective reality through the carving ritual. The most famous of these have been the curse formulas (to prevent the desecration of a grave or holy site) and formulas intended to hold the dead in their graves. "The walking dead," or *aptr göngumenn*, were a real concern for ancient Northmen. What is sometimes forgotten about this phenomenon is that these corpses often were actually reanimated through the will of some magician and sent to do damage to the community.

In the elder period some of the most noteworthy examples of this kind of magical working are the curse formulas found on the stones of Stentoften and Björketorp in southern Sweden (both from around 650 C.E.). The texts are closely related, so here we will give only the clearer Björketorp example, which reads: *ūtharba-spā! haidR-rūnō ronu falhk hedra, gina-rūnaR, ærgiu hearma-lausR, ūti ær wela-daude sāR that brÿtR.* This formula can be translated: "Prophecy of destruction! A row of bright runes hid I here, magically loaded runes. Through perversity, [and] without rest, on the outside, there is a deceitful death for the one who breaks this [stone monument]." By means of the runemaster's will, and by the power of the runes to communicate that will into objective reality, the legalistic curse formula simply says that whosoever breaks down or disturbs the holy site is cursed unto death by the deceptive power (*wela-*) of the runemaster. (See also the discussion of the Lund talisman on page 32.) Because no judge or executioner is present—and the potential wrongdoer was certainly not literate—the death sentence is carried out purely by magical means. (The stone setting of Björketorp is still intact, by the way.) This triangular arrangement of stones was apparently a ritual and legislative site, as no grave has been found in the area.

Word Formula Sendings

Another, more terse form of magical communication was effected by single formulaic words packed with great and multilevel symbolic powers. In the elder period some of these words were *alu* (ale, ecstatic psychic force),[1] *laukaz* (leek),[2] *ehwaz* (horse), *lathu* (invocation), *auja* (good luck), *ota* (terror), and perhaps even *rūno* (rune), secret lore itself.

Many times those words would be inscribed in isolation on various objects in order to invoke the power of the concept the word embodies into the object, or more generally, into the vicinity of the object. Each of the words mentioned above carries with it enormous psycho-magical force and meanings that were very close to the surface for our ancestors but now perhaps lurk in the archetypal depths within us. *Alu* comes from an ancient Indo-European concept of ecstatic power and the magic performed by means of that power. It is undoubtedly related to the Hittite term *alwanzahh*, "to enchant." This basic meaning was then transferred to the sacred, ecstasy-containing substance of the holy ale used in the sacrificial and magical rites of the Germanic folk. In ancient times *laukaz* was a general term for many plants belonging to the genus allium (garlic, onion, leek, etc.). These plants hold great health-giving and preserving powers. Also, the leek is especially known for its fast-growing, straight, green stalk—a magical symbol of increase and growth in force and vitality. The magical power of the "horse" concept in Germanic lore is well known and complex (see the E-rune). As a runic word formula it is a sign of transformative power, a symbol of Sleipnir, Odin's eight-legged horse, and of the vital strength of the horse in the horse/man relationship (:ᛗ:).

Each of the foregoing symbol words has a physical counterpart in the natural world. However, there is also a series of concepts that are more abstract. It might be best to consider *rūno* and *lathu* together. Both may ultimately refer to a vocal activity on the part of the magician—that is, the vocally performed incantations (*galdrar*) that were intended to call magical forces into objective reality and that were certainly secret in nature and kept hidden from the non-initiate. The word *lathu* is ultimately related to the English term to load, and it can be understood in the dynamistic sense of a loading of magical force into an object, or the "invitation" (see German *Einladung*) of divine beings into the area. As another example of the fact that *rūno* was *not* understood to be synonymous with letters or written characters, we can present the reading of the simple runemaster formula on the Freilaubersheim brooch: *Bōso wræt rūno* (Boso carved the rune [singular]). There are other examples that show that the word *rune* was used collectively to mean "secret lore" or "magical incantation" throughout the elder period. The term *auja* refers to a concept very similar to that of *hailagaz* (holy), as it generally means "to be filled with divine or holy power" and hence the well-being and good fortune derived from that state. The opposite side of magical might is referred to by the rather obscure formula *ota*, which is derived from the archaic form *ōhtan* (awe, fear, dread; related to ON *ægi-* in the name of the magical *ægishálmr* [the helm of awe]). These terms, formulated in staves and therefore subject to ritual manipulation, are thought to be the magical media through which linkage was made between the complex subjective reality of the runemaster and his gild and the objective reality, thereby bringing about conditions in accordance with the will of the "master of the mysteries."

Futhark Formulas

One of the most conspicuous types of rune-magic formulas is that of the complete or abbreviated futhark (see the examples from the elder tradition in chapter 1). Such inscriptions also were common in the Viking Age and especially in the Middle Ages. In some rare cases it may be that the futhark was carved for teaching purposes, or merely "for practice." However, this certainly could have been more readily accomplished in other, less time-consuming ways. But for the most part the futhark appears to have had a magical function. The symbolism of the rune row is at least twofold: (1) it is the collection of all *essential things*, and (2) it is in a special, set *order*. It is the symbol of the order of essential things. Bringing order (cosmic, natural, or psychic) to a given environment (subjective or objective) is certainly a common enough motive for the performance of magic.

Rune Formulas and Magical Formulaic Words

If the futhark formula is a symbol of order, then the so-called nonsense inscriptions are symbols of disorder, or of a non-natural order of some kind. We call rune formulas those sequences of staves that seem random and unpronounceable or repetitive. Examples of this kind of formula are especially plentiful on bracteates. There are also those sequences that are pronounceable but that form no known word in the Germanic vocabulary of natural language. These "words" may indeed be from the "language of the gods," a non-natural language received directly from another world. Famous examples of such words are, *luwatuwa*, *suhura-susi*, *anoana*, *salusalu*, *foslau*, and later *suf-fus*. Some may be "decoded," some not. These are but the few remnants of a non-natural, magical language shared by Odin and his earthly Erulians—a language to which access must again be won. Such words were probably first received and spoken by magicians (*seidhmenn*) in trance states and subsequently passed on in the tradition as a part of the vocabulary of magic. Their use in runic formulas is again understandable in terms of the "objectifying principle" of the runes.

Ideographic Runes

In theory the only kind of character that could qualify as an ideographic rune is a stave of the futhark that stands for its name (i.e., a logograph) or for a word within its field according to scaldcraft. However, there are also certain types of *galdrastafir* (magical signs) that were originally made up of bind runes (staves superimposed one on another) and often highly stylized. We have already met with examples of these on the Sievern bracteate, the Pietroassa ring, the Gummarp stone, and the amulet of Kvinneby. These ideographic runes actually represent a kind of alternate encoding of secret meanings to conceal them further. But the motive for this concealment, this *hiding*, was not to make the text more difficult for other humans to read—few inscriptions, especially the elder ones, were ever meant to be "read" at all. Quite to the contrary, it was intended to make the text more pleasing to and more empathetic with the hidden realms. The more meaning that could be concealed in a terse manner, the more powerfully empathetic the magical message of the runemaster was for the objective, but hidden, other reality of the eight outer worlds.

Number Formulas

The topic of runic numerology will be addressed in great detail in chapter 11. At present, let it suffice to say that numerical pattern is another form of concealment, with the same motive as other forms of "magical hiding" in the Germanic tradition.

Runemaster Formulas

Any nonmagical interpretation of the many runemaster formulas seems absurd. It is clear that when the runemaster carved the staves of the formula *ek erilaz fāhidō rūnō* (I the Erulian [= runemaster] colored the rune) he was not merely performing some elaborate form of graffiti (although certain psychological processes may be common to both acts). Runemaster formulas represent documents of transformative magical acts in which the rune magician assumed his divine aspect for the performance of some working. It is quite possible that with runemaster inscriptions we are dealing with the remains of but one fraction of a more elaborate ritual process. A runemaster formula could give force to a rite working together with the formula, or it could be the whole of an operant working in itself. In the latter case one will usually find that the runemaster designates himself with various magical names (which are often very similar to some of the holy names of Odin). One of the most famous examples of this is provided by the Järsberg stone in central Sweden. It reads: *ek erilaz rūnōz wrītu. Ūbaz haite, Hrabanaz haite*, "I the Erulian carve the runes. I am called the Malicious-one (= Ubaz), I am called the Raven." This stone, not attached to any grave and probably originally part of a ritual stone arrangement, is then charged by the force of the runemaster in this threatening aspect of "the malicious one" and "the raven." Through the linkage of these foreboding aspects with the site, he is able both to fill it with magical force and protect it from desecrators.

Literature

Without the written sources, especially in Old Norse and Latin, we would have a difficult time scientifically determining the nature of historical rune magic as practiced from about 100 C.E. onward. These accounts, and certain words used in them, give us a key to the structure of runic ritual and provide contexts for certain types of magical acts with runes. There are, however, limits to this evidence. First of all, the texts in question begin to be common only in the Middle Ages, and although they surely represent much older material and reflect archaic practices, we should be aware of this time discrepancy. Second, the saga accounts are, after all, integrated into narrative tales and may have some degree of literary convention built into them. But both of these points are minor when viewed in the broad scope of the tradition. Rune-magic acts apparently were common enough in the Viking and Middle Ages that they form natural parts of the sagas, and they are presented in what might be for some a surprisingly matter-of-fact way.

Runecasting

In part three of this book we will explain in some practical detail how the modern runer can engage in runic divination. It is our purpose here to explain something of the history of the art and craft.

When the Germanic peoples began writing in the same manner as the Greeks and Romans, they called the graphs with which they performed this task "runes." Each rune represented a mystery, and a certain principle of esoteric lore was attached to it. (This is not surprising since the people who developed and maintained this system were also the custodians of other intellectual and religious material in the culture.) Beyond this, the system itself could be used to represent natural language and thus phonetically preserve the magical formulas themselves. These runes—or runestaves—became "whisperers of secrets." Through them—silently and over great spans of time and distance—communication could be effected. Symbolically, this could also be said of their ability to effect communication between the very realms of existence—from gods to humans, from humans to gods and even to the natural realms.

The importance of this should be obvious to anyone who is interested in either magic or divination. The runes, although not a language in the usual sense of the word, do constitute a *metalanguage*. A metalanguage is a symbolic system through which meaning can be transmitted above and beyond that of which the natural language is capable. Poetry also does this. Indeed, classic Germanic poetry very likely grew out of runic divinatory practices.

By means of this metalanguage the runecaster can carry out a meaningful dialogue with his or her environment—inner and outer. This aspect is at the root of the real meaning of the word "rune." Also, all this makes much more sense when understood within the ancient Germanic cosmology of multiple worlds—and their psychology of multiple souls.

Runecasting in History and Literature

Without the written sources, especially Old Norse and Latin texts, it would be difficult to determine the nature of historical runecasting in any scientific way. These accounts, and certain words used in them, give us many clues to the structure of runic divinatory ritual and provide contexts for acts of divination in general. There are, however, limits to this evidence. First, these texts only became common in the Middle Ages, and although they surely represent much older material and reflect archaic practices, we should be aware of this time discrepancy. Second, the saga accounts are integrated into narrative tales and may have some degree of literary convention built into them. Both of these points, however, are minor when viewed in the broad scope of the tradition.

There are no clear examples in the archaeological record of runestaves carved for divinatory purposes, but most likely this is due to the fact that they were scratched on perishable materials. Or, perhaps, they were ritually destroyed after use as a matter of normal procedure. It is another surprising fact that there are no direct, non-mythological references to the act of runecasting in Old Norse literature. Despite all this, and chiefly based on linguistic evidence and parallel accounts in historical texts, we can be fairly certain that the practice was known.

Linguistic evidence is rich and is of two kinds: words for the tools of runecasting and terms that originally must have been characterizations of the results of runecastings.

Actual pieces of wood on which individual runes or runic combinations were carved (and usually colored with blood or red dye) were known in Old Norse as *hlaut-teinar* (sg., *hlaut-teinn*; lot twig) (also known by Snorri Struluson as blood twigs), and *hlaut-vidhar* (lot woods). The original use of the Germanic term *stabaz* (stave, stick) perhaps had to do with the fact that runes were carved on pieces of wood that were most probably used in divinatory practices. The terms *rūno* and *stabaz* were so intertwined by this practice that the words became synonymous. An interesting piece of corroborating evidence is found in the Old English word *wyrd-stæf* (stave of wyrd or weird) — an obvious reference to divinatory use.

Old Germanic dialects are full of compound words that refer to various types of runes/staves. Some are technical descriptions (ON *málrúnar* [speech runes], ON *blódhgar rúnar* [bloody runes], Old High German *leod-rūna* [song rune], etc.); whereas others give an indication of the reason for which they are to be worked (ON *brim-rúnar* [sea runes — to calm it], *bjarg-rúnar* [birth runes — to help in it], etc.). However, among these there are some designations that seem to classify the results of a runecasting. Some are auspicious (ON *líkn-stafir* [health staves], ON *gaman-rúnar* [joy runes], ON *audh-stafir* [staves of riches], ON *sig-rúnar* [victory runes]); whereas others seem inauspicious (ON *myrkir stafir* [dark staves]; ON *böl-stafir* [evil staves]; OE *beadu-rūn* [conflict rune]; ON *flaerdh-stafir* [deception staves]). Of course, in many cases the passive readings of these terms could be turned around to active workings.

As far as the actual practice of runecasting is concerned, the best description is provided by Tacitus writing in chapter 10 of the *Germania* (about 98 C.E.). Formerly, there might have been a debate as to whether the *notae*, signs, mentioned by him actually could have been runes, since the oldest inscription was thought to date from about 150 C.E. The discovery of the Meldorf brooch (about 50 C.E.), however, provided hard evidence that the runes were known from before the time when the *Germania* was written. The account by Tacitus may be translated:

> To the taking of auspices and drawing of lots they pay as much attention as any one: the way they draw lots is uniform. A branch is cut from a nut-bearing tree and cut into slips: these are designated by certain signs (Latin *notae)* and thrown randomly over a white cloth. Afterwards, the priest of state, if the consultation is a public one, or the father of the family, if it is private, offers a prayer to the gods, and while looking up into the sky, takes up three slips, one

at a time, and interprets their meaning from the signs carved on them. If the message forbids something, no further inquiry is made on the question that day; but if it allows something, then further confirmation is required through the taking of auspices.[3]

In *The Conquest of Gaul* (Book I, 53) Caesar, writing in about 58 B.C.E., also mentions "consulting the lots three times" *(ter sortibus consultum),* so this must have been an important aspect of Germanic divination.[4]

Three Eddic passages also give significant magical—and rather cryptic—insight into runic divinatory practices. All occur in mythic contexts. In the "Völuspá," st. 20: "(the Norns) scored on wood, they laid laws, they chose lives, they spoke the 'fates'" (ON *ørlög)*. While in the "Hávamál," st. 80, we are told that "it is proven when you ask of the runes, which are sprung from the gods" (ON *regin,* divine advisors). In the "Hávamál," st. 111, there is the instructive passage:

> *It is the time to sing*
> *on the stool of the theal*
> *at the well of Wyrd—*
> *I saw and I thought*
> *I saw and I spoke*
> *heeded the lore of Hár*
> *of runes I heard it spoke*
> *nor thought I of readings*
> *at the hall of Hár*
> *in the hall of Hár*
> *so I heard it said.*

This passage not only gives indication of the objective picture of what the ritual procedures were—as Tacitus the outsider also could do—but it also gives us insight into the subjective, inner processes within the mind of the runecaster. This is something only an insider, only someone who was actually skilled in runecasting, could have done.

There are other historical accounts by Christian observers which tell us little more than that the number three was of great importance.

Magic (Galdr)

The runes were of course also widely used for operative magical purposes. A verbal derivative, Old Norse *rýna* (to work magic with runes, or to inquire), shows the close link between illuminative and operative acts. Also, terms that often may seem to indicate the coming to pass of certain events (e.g., *sigrúnar* [victorious outcome]) also can be used to bring about this state through operative action. "Victory runes" are carved and/or spoken to inject objective reality with their power.

At this time perhaps a word should be said about the true and exact meaning of such terms as "victory runes," "ale runes," "birth runes," "sea runes," and the like found in abundance in Old Norse, Old English, and Old High German. Many lay investigators (and some scholars) have generally sought to identify such terms with specific runestaves for example, victory runes: ᛏᛏ: and/or: ᛋᛋ:, the former based on the famous Eddic passage in the "Sigrdrífumál," stanza 7 (where Sigurdhr is told to "call twice on Tyr for victory"), and the latter on the "skaldic link" between Old Norse *sig* (victory; or modern German *Sieg* for that matter)—and the S-rune. Both suppositions have some merit, and their appeal is not to be denied. However, they do not delve deeply enough into the complex lore surrounding the word *rune* to be able to explain the ways these terms were used. If we always keep it in mind that the old Germanic word *rūno* primarily means mystery and that it is derived from a vocal concept (whisper, roar, etc.), the possible breadth of such terms becomes clearer. *Sig-rúnar* are not *only* runestaves that either signify or bring about victory but also the *galdrar*, or whole poetic stanzas, that work to the same ends. From this the use of these terms developed to indicate normal speech that might have the same effects; for example, Old Norse *gaman-rúnar* (joy runes) became an expression for merry talk, and Old Norse *flaerdh-stafir* (deception staves) became a way of saying seductive words. That into late times the ideas of *rún* (rune), *stæf* (stave), and *galdr* (incantation) were sometimes virtually synonymous is shown by the Old Norse pairs of compounds *líkn-stafir* (healing stave), *líkn-galdr* (healing spell), and *val-rúnar* (death runes)/*val-galdr* (death dirge).

Actual runic carving rituals are depicted several times in Old Norse texts. The saga accounts have the advantage of showing us how the runes were used by magicians in everyday situations, and some cryptic Eddic passages give clear indications of the mytho-magical pattern on which these rites were based.

The "Hávamál," stanza 142, provides a representation of the process of a runic risting (carving) rite as archetypally performed by the Great Runemaster, Odin:

> Runes wilt thou find
> and read the staves,
> very strong staves,
> very stout staves,
> that Fimbulthulr [= Odin] colored
> and made by the mighty gods
> and risted by the god Hroptr [= Odin]

The greatest account of a human runemaster which has survived is that of Egill Skallagrímsson (*Egil's Saga*). Once Egill detects poison in his drinking horn (chapter 44):

> Egill drew out his knife and stabbed the palm of his hand, then he took the horn, carved runes on it and rubbed blood on them. He said:
>
>> I carve a rune [sg.!] on the horn
>> I redden the spell in blood
>> these words I choose for your ears. . . .
>
> The horn burst asunder, and the drink went down into the straw.

Later in the same saga (chapter 72) Egill heals a girl of sickness caused by ill-wrought runes. The *laun-stafir* (secret staves, i.e., coded runes) were carved by a peasant boy trying to cure her, but it only made her sickness worse. The whalebone on which the characters were carved was found lying in the bed!

Egill read them and then he whittled the runes off and scraped them down into the fire and burned the whale bone and had all the bedclothes that she had thrown to the winds. Then Egill said:

> "A man should not carve runes
> unless he knows well how to read:
> it befalls many a man
> who are led astray by a dark stave;
> I saw whittled on the whalebone
> ten secret staves carved.
> that have given the slender girl
> her grinding pain so long."

> Egill carved runes and laid them underneath the pillow of the bed, where she was resting; it seemed to her that she was well again. . . .

The possible nature and identity of the *laun-stafir* are discussed in chapter 7. One of the most remarkable uses of runes is in the preparation of the *nídhstöng* (cursing pole). Details on its preparation are given in at least two sagas. Again *Egil's Saga* (chapter 57) gives one example:

> . . . Egill [came] up on to the island. He picked up a hazel pole [ON *stöng*] in his hand and went to a certain rock cliff that faced in toward the land; then he took a horse head and set it upon the pole. Then he performed an incantation

[ON *formáli*] and said: "Here I set up the niding-pole, and I direct this insulting curse [ON *nidh*] against king Eiríkr [Bloodax] and Gunnhild the queen"—then he turned the horse head in toward the land—"I turn this insulting curse to those land-spirits [ON *land-vættir*] that inhabit this land so that all of them go astray, they will not figure nor find their abode until they drive king Eiríkr and Gunnhildr from the land." Then he shoved the pole down into a rock crevice and let it stand there; he also turned the horse head toward the land and then he carved runes on the pole, and they said all the incantation [*formáli*].

This may be compared to the description of the *nidhstöng* given in the *Vatnsdæla Saga* (chapter 34):

The brothers waited until three o'clock in the afternoon, and when it had come to that time, then Jökull and Faxa-Brandr went to Finnbogi's sheep stall, which was there beside the fence, and they took a pole [ON *súl*] and carried it down below the fence. There were also horses that had come for protection from the storm. Jökull carved a man's head on the end of the pole and carved runes in the pole with all those incantations [*formáli*] that had been said before. Then Jökull killed a mare and they opened it up at the breast and put in on the pole, and they had it turn homeward toward Borg. . . .

Another famous account of rune magic is found in the *Grettir's Saga* (chapter 79) where we read:

[Thuridhr] hobbled . . . as if guided to a spot where there lay a large stump of a tree as big as a man could carry on his shoulder. She looked at it and asked them to turn it over in front of her. The other side looked as if it had been burned and smoothed. She had a small flat surface whittled on its smooth side; then she took her knife and carved runes on the root and reddened them in her blood, and spoke spells over it. She went backwards and widdershins around the wood and spoke very powerful utterances over it. Then she had them push the wood out into the sea, and said it is to go to Drangey and Grettir should suffer harm from it.

One clear example of rune magic performed by a god is also present in the *Poetic Edda* ("Skírnismál," or "För Skírnis," st. 36):

A *thurs*-rune I for thee,
and three of them I scratch
lechery, and loathing, and lust;

off I shall scratch them
as on I did scratch them
if of none there be need.

Here, of course, the divine messenger of Freyr, Skírnir (the Shining-one), is threatening Gerdhr the etin-wife with a curse if she will not agree to become a bride of his lord. This whole poem has many Odinic elements in it; for example, the viewing of the worlds from Hlidhskjálfr, Odin's high seat, by Freyr and the traversing of the worlds on a horse by Skírnir. Certain interrelationships between Freyr and Odin are explored in chapter 13.

From the historical examples given thus far it is clear that runes could be used to heal as well as to harm. But aside from the mysterious and shamanistic initiatory ritual, were there any other forms of wisdom magic or rituals for self-transformation? The answer is yes. But because of the natural preoccupation with *conflict* in the sagas—they are, after all, stories intended as much to entertain as to recount "historical" events—such rituals are rarely mentioned. When looking at this question, one must remember that the primary purpose of illuminative runecasting was such a transformational process. The runecaster is literally in-*formed* by the communication and is not merely a passive and objectified receiver. That is why true runecasting should not be treated as a profane "game" or done casually by noninitiates. The most remarkable runic ritual of wisdom working is found in the "Sigrdrífumál," which after recounting the twenty-four mythic locations for runes to be carved (sts. 15-17), gives us this invaluable formula in stanza 18:

All [the runes] were scraped off,
that were scratched on,
and blended into the holy mead,
and sent out upon wide ways.

This gives the actual ritual formula for the draught of wisdom, which can be performed imitatively or symbolically.

Although we could wish for more details and examples of the performance of runeworkings in the old Germanic literatures, we must take heart in the fact that so much exact information has been left in the fragments we do have. There is enough to enable us to reconstruct with great historical accuracy the physical circumstances of operative runeworkings and to some extent illuminative (divinatory) ones.

The operative formula was a threefold process of (1) *carving* the staves, (2) *coloring* them (with blood or dye), and (3) *speaking* the vocal *formáli* that accompanies the graphic forms. This latter step may take many forms, for example, the intoning of rune names, words of power related to the working, the actual words represented by the inscribed staves, or similar poetic forms. The fourth aspect of the operative process is the *scraping off* of the staves from their material medium in order to destroy or transfer their force. This is the simplest form of the ritual we have in explicit representations. However, that more complex ritual forms were sometimes involved in runeworkings is strongly suggested by the "Hávamál," stanza 144:

Knowest thou how to carve [*rísta*]?
Knowest thou how to read [*rádha*]?
Knowest thou how to color [*fá*]?
Knowest thou how to test [*freista*]?
Knowest thou how to ask [*bidhja*]?
Knowest thou how to offer [*blóta*]?
Knowest thou how to send [*senda*]?
Knowest thou how to sacrifice [*sóa*]?

The terminology of this stanza is clearly connected to runeworkings, but only the first three technical terms are purely runic—to carve, to color, and to read (i.e., to interpret runestaves in divinatory workings). The other five terms are more usually designations for processes in sacrificial rites. In Old Norse, *freista* means to test, to put to the test, or to perform. This testing may be the search for signs or omens to corroborate or confirm the results of illuminative workings common to the practice of Germanic divination. Bidhja indicates the mode of correctly requesting divine action or "feedback," and the last three terms refer more directly to the modes of actually sending sacrifice to the god(s). All of this leads us to believe that sacrificial rites were sometimes performed as an integral part of a runeworking.

As far as the ritual form of runecasting is concerned, the Old Norse texts are rather silent. The Northmen, of course, knew a variety of illuminative techniques, many of which are classed as seidhr (shamanic, i.e., trance-inducing rites). Runecasting is more analytical and *galdr*-oriented. Because it is known that runes were in evidence in the Germanies during the first century C.E, and because the account given by Tacitus in chapter 10 of the *Germania* is so detailed and contains elements confirmed by later, more fragmentary descriptions, we can be virtually certain that in that passage we possess an authentic formula for runecasting. The basic structure of the working would have been:

1. Cutting and scoring of staves.

2. Calling on the Norns (or other gods).

3. Casting the staves (onto a white cloth).

4. Calling on the gods.

5. Choosing of (three) staves.

6. Sitting on the theal's chair.

7. Reading of the staves.

8. Confirmation by omens, etc.

Seidhr

In the annals of ancient Germanic magic there is an alternate form of magic known as *seidhr*. In later times this acquired a sinister reputation, but this is probably mainly because it was primarily (but by no means exclusively) practiced by women. In the mythology it is said (*Ynglinga Saga*, ch. 7) that Odin learned this skill from the Vanic goddess Freyja. Virtually everything we objectively know about the practice of *seidhr* is summarized in *A Source-Book of Seidhr* (Lodestar, 2015). It is not our purpose in this book to outline the practice of *seidhr*, as we are focused on runic practice. But it is worthwhile discussing the basic idea of *seidhr* due to is general importance.

The etymology of the word *seidhr* is uncertain. Its etymology certainly has nothing to do with the idea of boiling (seething). It most likely refers to some sort of vocal performance. A review of all of the literary references to this practice shows that a vocal performance—either singing of certain songs to attract spirits or magical songs (*seidhaeti*) meant to cause direct effects—is a prominent part of the tradition.

Perhaps originally those kinds of magic that later came to be classified as *seidhr* were traditions practiced in the so-called "third function" of the Indo-European culture and religion. This magic belonged to the farmers and herdsmen, of the craftsmen and smiths, of the musicians and even entertainers. Their magic was powerful and unique, and evidence generally shows that it was dominated by female practitioners. As the Indo-Europeans moved into Europe several millennia ago, this type of magic was assimilated to local forms of magic belonging to what has been called the people of Old Europe.

This field of Germanic esoteric tradition is not very well documented. It is for this reason that anyone trying to revive its practice should take special care to make use of what is known about it. It is especially tempting to fill in the gaps of the unknowns with ready-made solutions from other cultures. This method can cause many treasures to be lost.

An analysis of the material we have shows that trance was induced by songs sung by assistants, and the performance usually took place on top of a high platform or elevated space. Any percussion was perhaps done by striking a wooden box, which contained the practitioner's talismans and holy objects. The practitioner enters a trance state and remains silent while in this state, which involves the loss of normal waking consciousness. Upon return to normal consciousness the *seidhkona* or *seidhmadhr* (seid-woman or seid-man) then soberly recounts the information gained from the entities while in the trance state. This generally describes the process of sooth-saying by means of *seidhr*.

Chapter 7

RUNIC CODES

One of the most remarkable aspects of the complex "runic system" (see chapter 9) is the possibility of creating various runic codes. The aett system itself makes this complexity possible. This system essentially consists of dividing the entire futhark into three sections or rows. In the elder period there were three rows of eight, as seen in figure 7.1.

It is also known from evidence found in five manuscripts that the Old English Futhorc could be divided into these groups, plus a fourth group of four staves, as shown in figure 7.2 on page 73. The Old English system clearly shows that the first twenty-four runes in the rows were considered an organized whole to which the extra four (five or more in later times) were "eked out."

There is also the later Norse system of aett divisions. Here things get quite curious. The reduction of the rune row from twenty-four to sixteen made an equal division into three groups impossible. So two rows had five and another had six. The row was initially divided in the manner indicated in figure 7.3 on page 73. However, for the construction of runic codes in the Viking Age, this order was usually altered to that shown in figure 7.4 on page 73. Such reordering for cryptic reasons may also have been an archaic practice inherited from the older time.

The basic idea behind most runic codes founded on the aett system is a binary number set, one which represents the number of the aett (in the case of the elder system a number between one and three), and the other which represents the number of the runestave counted from the left (for the elder period a number between one and eight). A simple example would be 2:8 = : $\mathcal{S}$: (second aett, eighth stave). There are many methods for representing this binary code; in later times the only bounds seemed to have been those in the imagination of the runemaster.

Figure 7.1. Aett divisions of the Elder Futhark.

Although it was in the Viking and Middle Ages that the art of runic cryptology seems to have reached its peak, the system was certainly known from the beginning of the tradition. The Vadstena/Motala bracteates are the oldest representations of the Elder Futhark divided into aettir, but there are also perhaps as many as six elder inscriptions that seem to have some kind of runic code in them.

The ring of Körlin bears the symbol: ↑ : along with the inscription: ᚠ᛭᛭ :. The latter is clearly a reversed *alu* formula, while the former could be a runic code for 2:1 (i.e., second rune of the first aett = :ᚢ:). The stave as it stands is, however, also a bind rune of A + L. This combined with encoded form renders another *alu* formula. This gold ring dates from 600 C.E.

So any method of graphically representing two numbers could be used to write cryptic runic messages. But of course, the "reader" must be familiar with the aett system and all of its intricacies to be able to interpret the message. Other possible runic codes of this kind in the older period are seen on the stone of Krogsta (ca. 550 C.E.), part of which appears: ᚤ᛭ᚼᛁᚼᛏᛊ :, to be read from right to left as SIAINAZ. This makes no linguistic sense. But if we read the :↑: rune as a code stave for 1:1 =:↑: (with reordered aettir, then it makes sense as *stainaz* (stone). This identifies the object, or it could be the name of the runemaster.

In the inscriptions, code runes are also rare in the English tradition. We do know of the special aett divisions and one inscription, the stone of Hackness (carved sometime between 700 and 900 C.E.). The formula resulting from its decipherment, however, makes no linguistic sense.

Among the most widely practiced of the dozens of known forms of cryptic runes are the *isruna*, *is*-runes. These are known from a medieval German manuscript written in Latin, called the "Isruna-Tract." An example (figure 7.5 on page 74) of this runic code system, which spells out the name Eiríkr, is found on the Swedish stone of Rotbrunna in Uppland.

Figure 7.2. Aett divisions of the Old English Futhorc.

Figure 7.3. Aett divisions of the Younger Futhark.

Figure 7.4. Cryptic reordering of the aett division of the Younger Futhark.

Figure 7.5. Is-runes of Rotbrunna.

This latter system may be the key to the passage on rune magic quoted from Egil's Saga (chapter 72) on page 66. There Egill speaks of "ten secret staves carved," which were supposed to be scratched in an attempt at a healing working. A good ideographic formula for such a working would be : ᚠᚢ:, *fé* and *úrr*, for energy and vital force. A way of putting these into cryptic, and therefore more magically potent, form in is-runes is shown in figure 7.6a. But the unskilled farm boy carved one too many staves, and the resulting formula (figure 7.6b) was hurtful. Figure 7.6b gives *fé* (energy, heat) to *thurs* (gigantic, destructive force)—a formula inappropriate for a healing rite, to say the least. Note also the traditional effect of the TH-rune on women alluded to in the Old Norwegian Rune Poem and Old Icelandic Rune Rhyme! By carving one too many staves in this cryptic formula, the uninitiated rune carver caused the opposite of the willed effect: *Skal-at madhr rúnar rísta, nema rádha vel kunni. . . .*

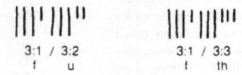

Figure 7.6. Left: Reconstructed healing formula in is-runes *(a total of nine staves); right: Farm boy's* is-rune *formula (a total of ten staves).*

Besides the aett cryptograms, there are a variety of ways to conceal the natural language message of a runic formula. Phonetic values could be shifted along the futhark order, so that : ᚾ : = F, : ᚦ : = U, : ᚱ : = TH, and so on. Single runes could be used logographically for their names; for example, in the *Poetic Edda* the stave : ᛘ : is sometimes written as a substitute for ON *madhr* (man). Single key words also can be abbreviated in various ways. When a single rune stands for a word other than the rune name, we get a glimpse of the hidden lore of the esoteric system of alternate rune names, a subject of ongoing research in the Rune-Gild.

Other common ways to obscure or alter the natural language message are (1) leaving out certain runes (e.g., all of the vowels), (2) scrambling individual words, (3) inscribing the whole text, or just parts of it, from right to left (although this is sometimes so common that it seems to be a regular option), (4) substitution of special non-runic signs for certain staves, and (5) use of elder runes in younger inscriptions.

The magical (operative) effect of these runic codes is clear. They were not meant (originally, at least) to confuse human "readers." They were intended to hide the runes, and what is hidden has effect in the hidden, subjective realms. Thus, an operative link is made between the subjective and objective realities, within the god-sprung framework of the lore of the runes.

Chapter 8

RUNE POEMS

Besides the primary lore of the rune names, shapes, order, and aett divisions, the oldest systematic lore attached to the staves is embodied in the rune poems. There originally were perhaps several of these poems in the tradition, but there can be little doubt that they all belonged to the same sacred body of lore. In this chapter we will present the three major rune poems, along with a little-studied piece of apparent doggerel that may teach us something. All of the poems are translated with a minimum of commentary or internal interpretation. In addition to the rune poems proper—which are essentially series of explanatory poetic stanzas, each beginning with the rune name/ stave of a rune row—there are a number of stanzas in the *Poetic Edda* directly relevant to runelore, and we will provide some esoteric commentary on the significance of these sections of the *Edda*. The original purpose of these works may have been to help the runemasters hold certain key concepts in mind while performing runecastings, or they may have just been traditional formulations of the general lore of the runes. In any event, we will later make use of this poetic material when interpreting runecastings in part three of this book.

The texts of the rune poems in their original languages and a full glossary of the words used can be found in *The Rune Poems* (Lodestar, 2018).

The Old English Rune Poem

"The Old English Rune Poem" records stanzas for the twenty-nine-stave Old English Futhorc. This is especially valuable because it is a source for the lore of the staves of the Elder Futhark not present in the younger row. The drawback is that some of its stanzas seem to have been altered for a Christian audience. But it is wise to remember that the "Christianity" of the English court society of the early Middle Ages was hardly an orthodox one, and it certainly preserved much of the old heathen culture.

For the text of this poem we are dependent on a transcription made by Humfrey Wanley that was subsequently printed in the *Thesaurus* of George Hickes in 1705. The manuscript of the poem was destroyed in the fire that ravaged the Cottonian library

in 1731. Although the manuscript from which the transcription was taken dated from
around the end of the tenth century, it is probable that the original version of the poem
dates from as early as the late eighth or early ninth century:

ᚠ [Money] is a comfort
to everybody
yet every man ought
to deal it out freely
if he wants to get a good judgment
from the lord.

ᚢ [Aurochs] is fearless
and greatly horned
a very fierce beast,
— he fights with his horns —
a famous roamer of the moor
he is a courageous wight.

ᚦ [Thorn] is very sharp;
for every thegn
who grasps it; it is harmful,
and exceedingly cruel
to every man
who lies among them.

ᚩ [God/Mouth] is the originator
of all speech,
the mainstay of wisdom
and a comfort to the wise ones,
for every noble warrior
hope and happiness.

ᚱ [Riding] is easy for every warrior
while he is in the hall
but very hard
for the one who sits up
on a powerful horse
over miles of road.

ᚺ [Torch] is to every living person
known by its fire,
it is clear and bright;
it usually burns
when the athelings
rest inside the hall.

ᚷ [Gift] is for every man
an ornament and praise,
help and worthiness;
and to every homeless adventurer
it is a benefit and substance
for those who have nothing else.

ᚹ [Joy] is experienced
by the one who knows few troubles
pains and sorrows,
and to him who himself has
power and blessedness,
and a good enough house.

ᚻ [Hail] is the whitest of grains,
it comes from high in heaven
gusts of wind hurl it,
then it turns to water.

ᚾ [Need] is constricting on the chest
although to the children of men it often becomes
a help and healing nevertheless,
if they heed it in time.

ᛁ [Ice] is very cold
and exceedingly slippery;
it glistens, clear as glass,
very much like gems,
a floor made of frost
is fair to see.

⌘   THE BIG BOOK OF RUNES AND RUNE MAGIC

ᛃ [Year/Harvest] is the hope of men,
when god, holy king of heaven,
causes the earth to give forth
her bright fruits
to the noble and needy alike.

ᛇ [Yew] is on the outside
a rough tree
and hard, firm in the earth,
keeper of the fire,
supported by roots,
joyously on the estate.

ᛈ [Lot box] is always
play and laughter
among bold men, in the middle
where the warriors sit
in the beer hall,
happily together.

ᛉ [Elk's] sedge has its home
most often in the fen,
it waxes in the water
and grimly wounds
and reddens ["burns"] with blood
any warrior
who, in any way,
tries to grasp it.

ᛋ [Sun] is by seamen
always hoped for
when they fare far away
over the fishes' bath
until they bring the brine-stallion
to land.

↑ [Tir] is a sign,
it keeps faith well
with athelings,
always on its course
over the clouds of night
it never fails.

ᛒ [Birch] is without fruit
but just the same it bears
limbs without fertile seed;
it has beautiful branches,
high on its crown
it is finely covered,
loaded with leaves,
touching the sky.

ᛗ [Horse] is, in front of the earls
the joy of athelings,
a charger proud on its hooves;
when concerning it, heroes—
men wealthy in war-horses—
exchange speech,
and it is always a benefit
to restless men.

ᛗ [Man] is in his mirth
dear to his kinsman;
although each shall
depart from the other;
for by his decree the lord
wants to commit,
that poor flesh
to the earth.

ᚱ [Water] is to people
seemingly unending

THE BIG BOOK OF RUNES AND RUNE MAGIC

if they should venture out
on an unsteady ship
and the sea waves
frighten them very much,
and the brine-stallion
does not heed its bridle.

ᛝ [Ing] was first
seen by men
among the East-Danes,
until he again went eastward [or "back"]
over the wave;
the wain followed on;
this is what the warriors
named the hero.

ᛗ [Day] is the lord's messenger,
dear to men,
the ruler's famous light;
mirth and hope
to rich and poor,
of benefit to all.

ᛟ [Estate] is very dear
to every man,
if he can enjoy what is right
and according to custom
in his dwelling,
most often in prosperity.

ᚨ [Oak] is on the earth
for the children of men
the nourishment of meat;
it often fares
over the gannet's bath [= sea]:
The sea finds out
whether the oak keeps
noble troth.

ᚠ [Ash] is very tall,
[and] dear to men,
firm on its base;
it holds its place rightly
although it is attacked
by many men.

ᛡ [Yew bow] is for athelings
and warriors alike
a joy and sign of worth,
it is excellent on a horse,
steadfast on an expedition—
[it is] a piece of war-gear.

✳ [Serpent] is a river fish
although it always takes
its food on land,
it has a fair abode
surrounded by water,
where it lives in joy.

ᛉ [Grave] is loathsome
to every warrior
when steadily
the flesh—the corpse—
begins to grow cold
to choose the earth
palely as a bedmate;
fruits fall
joys pass away,
pledges are broken.

⊠   THE BIG BOOK OF RUNES AND RUNE MAGIC

The Old Norwegian Rune Rhyme

"The Old Norwegian Rune Rhyme" dates from between the end of the twelfth century and the beginning of the thirteenth. It is clearly part of the same tradition as "The Icelandic Rune Poem," although it is contaminated by some Christian elements. The structure of each stanza is compact and actually twofold: a half-line with two alliterating staves, followed by a half-line containing a single alliterative stave. In the original the two half-lines rhyme. The ideological content of the two half-lines is *seemingly* unrelated; however, the second is actually an esoteric comment on an aspect of the first, which is emphasized in the whole. These stanzas, in an illuminative sense, work much like Zen *koans*:

ᚠ [Money] causes strife among kinsmen;
the wolf grows up in the woods.

ᚢ [Slag] is from bad iron;
oft runs the reindeer on the hard snow.

ᚦ [Thurs] causes the sickness of women;
few are cheerful from misfortune.

ᚬ [Estuary] is the way of most journeys;
but the sheath is [that for] swords.

ᚱ [Riding], it is said, is the worst for horses;
Reginn forged the best sword.

ᚴ [Sore] is the curse of children;
grief makes a man pale.

ᚼ [Hail] is the coldest of grains;
Christ* shaped the world in ancient times.

ᛁ [Ice], we call the broad bridge;
the blind need to be led.

ᛅ [Good harvest] is the profit of men;
I say that Fródhi was generous.

ᛉ [Sun] is the light of the lands;
I bow to the decree of holiness.

ᛏ [Tyr] is the one-handed among the Aesir;
the smith has to blow often.

ᛒ [Birch twig] is the limb greenest with leaves;
Loki brought the luck of deceit.

ᛦ [Man] is the increase of earth;
mighty is the talon-span of the hawk.

ᛚ [Water] is, when it falls from the mountain, a waterfall;
but gold [objects] are costly things.

ᛇ [Yew] is the greenest wood in the winter;
there is usually, when it burns, singeing [i.e., it makes a hot fire].

The Old Icelandic Rune Poem

"The Old Icelandic Rune Poem" dates from as late as the fifteenth century but preserves lore from a much older time, as do all the rune poems. The rhyme gives a complex body of information about each alliterating half-line, followed by an independent internally alliterating single half-line, all of which is followed by two words: 1) a Latin "translation" of the rune name, which is often an esoteric commentary, and 2) an alliterating Old Norse word for "chieftain," which also acts as a further key to deeper meaning. Here the Old Norse word is "etymologically" translated into English:

ᚠ [Money] is the [cause of] strife among kinsmen,
and the fire of the flood-tide,
and the path of the serpent.
gold   *"leader of the war-band"*

ᚢ [Drizzle] is the weeping of clouds,
and the diminisher of the rim of ice,
and [an object for] the herdsman's hate.
shadow [should read *imber*, shower?]   *"leader"*

THE BIG BOOK OF RUNES AND RUNE MAGIC

Þ [Thurs] is the torment of women,
and the dweller in the rocks,
and the husband of Vardh-rúna [a giantess?]
Saturn   *"ruler of the thing"*

ᚠ [Ase = Odin] is the olden-father,
and Asgardhr's chieftain,
and the leader of Valhöll.
Jupiter   *"point-leader"*

ᚱ [Riding] is bliss to the one who sits,
and a swift journey,
and the toil of the horse.
journey   *"worthy man"*

ᚴ [Sore] is the bale of children,
and an attack of battle,
and the house of rotten flesh.
whip   *"king" = descendant of good kin*

✳ [Hail] is a cold grain,
and a mighty snowfall,
and the sickness [destroyer] of snakes.
hail   *"battle-leader"*

ᚾ [Need] is the struggle of the bondmaid,
and an oppressive condition,
and toilsome work.
trouble   ON nfflunger, *"descendant of the dead?"*

ᛁ [Ice] is the river's bark,
and the wave's roof,
and a danger for fey men.
ice   *"one who wears the boar-helm"*

ᛄ [Good harvest] is the profit of all men,
and a good summer,
and a fully ripened field.
year   *"all-ruler"*

ᛋ [Sun] is the shield of the clouds,
and a shining glory,
and the life-long sorrow [= destroyer] of ice.
wheel   *"descendant of the victorious one"*

ᛏ [Tyr] is the one-handed god,
and the wolf's leftovers,
and the ruler of the temple.
Mars   *"director"*

ᛒ [Birch twig] is a leafy limb,
and a little tree,
and a youthful wood.
silver fir   *"protector"*

ᛘ [Man] is the joy of man,
and the increase of earth,
and the adorner of ships.
human   *"generous one"*

ᛚ [Liquid] is churning water,
and a wide kettle,
and fishes' field.
lake   *"praise-worthy one"*

ᛦ [Yew] is a bent bow,
and brittle iron,
and Farbauti [= a giant] of the arrow
bow, rainbow   *"descendant of Yngvi"*

The Abecedarium Nordmanicum

Because the *Abecedarium Nordmanicum* is such a curious piece and is usually not treated in texts on rune poems, we will give it some special attention here. The poem is found in a St. Gall (Switzerland) manuscript, the oldest manuscript of any rune poem, dating from the early 800s. However, its contents do not seem to belong to an ancient heathen tradition. It is written in a mixture of High and Low German, with some Norse characteristics. The manuscript probably was put together by Walafrid Strabo, who studied under Hrabanus Maurus in Fulda from 827 to 829. Hrabanus, who was in turn the student of the Saxon Alcuin, was the greatest single collector of runelore in the Middle Ages. Although all three men were Christian clerics, and their rationale for collecting this material might have been intelligence gathering for missionary work among Asatru Norsemen, they inadvertently gathered a great deal of genuine lore of Germanic troth.

ᚠ fee first.

ᚢ aurochs after.

ᚦ thurs the third stave.

ᚨ the Ase is above him.

ᚱ wheel is written last.

ᚴ then cleaves cancre:

ᚼ hail has ᚾ need

ᛁ ice. ᛅ year. ᛋ and sun.

ᛏ Tiu. ᛒ birch ᛘ and man in the middle

ᛚ water the bright.

ᛦ yew holds all.

This "poem" represents the younger Norse runes, but it was composed in the social context of those with knowledge of the Old English Futhorc and its traditions. This is clear from the Old English glosses made in the manuscript (not shown). For the most part, and at first glance, it seems that the words of this poem merely serve to knit the rune names together in proper order (as a mnemonic). But in at least four instances the phrases are esoterically meaningful: (1) "the Ase is above him" (= the thurs)—apparently a theological comment; (2) "and man [is] in the middle"—clearly is not a spatial but cosmo-psychological statement—man is in Midhgardhr; (3) "water [is] the bright one"—this is the shining water of life (see reference to gold in the "Old Norwegian Rune Rhyme"); and (4) "the yew holds everything"—the World-Yew contains the essence of the multiverse.

Comments on Runic Stanzas from the Poetic Edda

Besides the rune poems above, there are three lays of the *Poetic Edda* directly relevant to the runic tradition. These are, however, different from the futhark poems. The Eddic poems may delineate, in order, a series of *galdrar* clearly attached to runes, but the exact runic formula may remain hidden. Each stanza is not necessarily attached to a single runestave, although it is usually illuminating to classify the meanings in futhark order. Some of these stanzas are clearly meant to be teaching tools. The three lays of the *Poetic Edda* in question are the "Rúnatals tháttr Ódins" (= "Hávamál" 138–165), the "Sigrdrífumál," and the "Grógaldr" (= first half of the "Svipdagsmál").

"The Rúnatals Tháttr Ódhins"

The "Rúnatals tháttr" is a key document in the Odian tradition. It should be read and studied in detail by all runers. The lay is essentially made up of three parts: (l) the rune-winning initiation (138–141), (2) the teaching of technical runelore (142–145), and (3) a catalog of eighteen rune-magic songs (146–164). In the first part Odin is initiated (or initiates himself) into the wisdom of the runes by hanging himself in the branches of the World-Tree, Yggdrasill ("the steed of Yggr" [= Odin], or "the yew column") with its nine worlds, where he is "wounded by the spear." This is a typical shamanistic initiatory theme in which the initiate is subjected to some sort of torture or mock execution (in a cosmologically significant context) in order that he might come face-to-face with death. To hang the victim in a tree and stab him with spears in *the* traditional way of making human sacrifice to Odin, known from early Roman reports to Viking Age saga accounts. Here Odin gives (sacrifices) his Self to himself—"given to Odin, myself to myself." These words contain the great Odinic rune of *gebo*, the true nature of Odian Self-sacrifice. The Odian does not give his Self to Odin, but rather he learns the Odian path and gives his Self to himself.

In this process Odin descends into the realm of Hel (Death); and in that twilight between life and death, in the vortex of intensified opposites (:ᛉ:), he receives the flash of runic initiation, in which the runes are shown to him, and he becomes whole with the essence of the universal mysteries. From this realm he returns to the world of consciousness—the worlds of gods and men—in order to communicate these mysteries to the essences of these realms and to certain beings within them. That the substance of these runes is also contained in the poetic mead is emphasized in stanza 140.

This initiatory myth actually describes not a historical "event" but a timeless process in which "inspired consciousness" (*wōdh-an-az*) melds with the "universal mysteries"—not to be controlled by them but to gain mastery over their use. Its technical aspects give a ritual pattern (one among many) for human workings.

In stanza 141 Odin declares the effect of this on consciousness; it causes it *to become*—to evolve, grow, and thrive. The last two lines show the complex, transformationally linguistic nature of Odin's work within himself and among the gods and men. In the "moment" of runic initiation he "takes up the runes screaming"—that is, the melding with the universal mysteries is accompanied by a vibratory emanation, the vocalized *sound*. Hence, the primal link of "mystery" and "sound." In this vortex natural language fails to express the essential totality of the experience, but it is from this vortex that magical scaldcraft is born.

The second part of the "Rúnatals tháttr" contains essential technical runelore, in albeit cryptic form. Stanza 142 instructs us first to "find" and "read" the mysteries, that is, master passive knowledge of them. Learn to understand and interpret the great and mighty staves. Then we are to use them actively: to color, fashion, and carve, to do active workings with them. The next stanza, which has already been discussed in detail (page 69), is a list of technical terms, each a skill to be mastered by the would-be runer. This section is concluded with the injunction not to "oversacrifice"—best results are derived from correct proportion. The last two lines frame the whole:

> Thus did Thundr [= Odin] carve
> before the doom of man;
> there he rose up,
> when he came back.

This makes the primordial, non-historical nature of the text clear, and tells us that his "falling back" from the World-Tree was truly a *rising up*. The symbolism of this formula alludes to the Odinic transformational path, which is an oscillation between extremes, and to the idea that the World-Tree has not only branches but roots through which Odin wends his way.

Individual runestaves can be ascribed to each of the stanzas. This illuminates their essence. The rune row in question would be the Younger Futhark of sixteen staves, to which would be added (for esoteric reasons) the old E-rune and G-rune. The magical aim of each verse is usually self-evident: (1) help in removing distress and conflict of all kinds (through "wealth": ᚠ: ; (2) removal of disease, healing (through "vital force": ᚾ:); dulling of enemies' weapons (through "destructive force": ᚦ:); (4) removal of bonds and fetters (through "ecstatic magical force": ᚨ:); (5) deflection of enemy weapons through direct magical gaze (by the magical directing: ᚱ:); (6) reflection of a magical curse to its source (through redirection of energy: ᚲ:); (7) control of wild combustion (fire) (through cold ordering force: ᚺ:); (8) removal of conflict (through willed reversal of the effect of stress factors: ᚾ:) ; (9) calming of wild seas (through constricting force: ᛁ:); (10) confusion of destructive agents (through overloading of magical stream in willed direction: ᛅ:); (11) protection of warriors (through loading with the shield of "good speed [= luck]": ᛋ:); (12) learning of the secrets of the dead (through carving of *helrúnar*—raising the dead along the *axis mundi*: ᛏ:); (13) protection of a warrior at birth (by an endowment of invulnerability through magical enclosure: ᛒ:); (14) illustrative wisdom magic for knowledge of gods and other worlds (through calling up of the divine and cosmic heritage in man: ᛘ:); (15) sending of power to the other worlds (through increase in vital power: ᛚ:); (16) erotic love magic of attraction (through filling with powers of lust toward blending with the opposite: ᛤ:); (17) erotic love magic of binding (through the force of combination of paired opposites: ᛖ:); (18) dynamically erotic magic of exchange (through sex magical initiation: ᚷ:).

It is to be noted that the eighteen magical songs seem to be divided into two groups of nine, with the first nine being songs of magical drawing away of energy and the latter nine being songs of magical increase of energy. Thus, is it always in the magical ebb and flow of the bipolar Odinic worldview.

"Sigrdrífumál"

As a runic document, the "Sigrdrífumál" is the most complex in Old Norse literature. It is made up of many sections, each a whole but perhaps artificially linked together. There are three sections in the lay in which Sigrdrífa/Brynhildr, the *valkyrja* and "higher self" of Sigurdhr, gives systematic rune-rede to the hero. The first is in stanzas 6 to 14. Here she catalogs various runic genres: stanza 7—*sigrúnar*, victory runes, by which one gains victory; stanzas 8 and 9—*ölrúnar*, ale runes, by which one gains protection through higher consciousness and power; stanza 10—*bjargrúnar*, help-in-birth runes, by which one brings things forth into being; stanza 11—*brimrúnar*, sea runes, by which one calms natural disturbances; stanza 12—*limrúnar*, limb runes, by which one heals sickness; stanza 13—*malrúnar*, speech runes, by which one gains eloquence; and stanza 14—*hugrúnar*, mind runes, by which one gains intelligence.

In the second rune-rede section (sts. 17–19) Sigrdrífa indicates twenty-four things on which Odin "carves runes." The mythological nature of these objects (and the number of them!) shows this to be a working of cosmic shaping through the mysteries of idea–form–vibration on the part of the primal world consciousness—*Wōdh--an-az*. The three stanzas are actually attributed to the Mímir aspect, which communicates primal wisdom (see chapter 13.) The first lesson to be learned from these three stanzas is that twenty-four is the cosmological "key number" of wholeness, and that this whole system is consciously "vivified" by the will of Odin expressed through the runes.

The third section (stanzas 24–39) consists of a list similar to what we met in the "Hávamál" and will find again in the "Grógaldr." But this one is more didactic in the style of the earlier stanzas of the "Hávamál" and less "magical." The number of concepts systematically categorized is *eleven* (the number of *sól* in the younger row—ethical force).

As a whole, the three runic sections of the "Sigrdrífumál" have the function of imparting to the hero operative magical, cosmological, and ethical wisdom. These are depicted as having their source in the "higher" *fylgja-valkyrja* self.

"Grógaldr"

The "Spell of Gróa" is a poem of a type similar to the "Völuspá" in that a dead seeress is summoned from her slumber in Hel to give needful wisdom. The seeress Gróa (from Welsh *groach* [witch]) sings nine magical songs to her son, Svipdagr, who called upon her to give him magical aid in his quest for the etin-wife Menglodh. The magical intent of the nine songs are as follows: (1) to steady one's true will (:ᚠ:) ; (2) to protect one from malicious spells (:ᚾ:); (3) to provide safe passage through dangerous water, and maintenance of consciousness in the dark realms (:ᚦ:); (4) to give control over enemies' actions (:ᚱ:); (5) to liberate from bonds (:ᚱ:); (6) to still stormy seas (:ᛁ:); (7) to provide the life-heat of fire (:ᚢ:) ; (8) protection from malicious undead (:ᛂ:); (9) to make conscious link with the creative realm of eloquence (:ᚱ:).

Two things should be noted when reading the catalog stanzas of the "Rúnatals tháttr," "Sigrdrífumál," and "Grógaldr": (1) they do not necessarily follow in the futhark order, and (2) it seems that the magical songs themselves are often not overtly recorded (but rather what we find are descriptions of their purposes and effects). The keys to these encoded forms are given in Rune-Gild work.

Part Two

HIDDEN LORE

Chapter 9

INNER RUNELORE

In part one of this book we hoped to establish the firm *traditional* basis in exoteric aspects of runelore with insights into hidden and timeless lore. In part two we will continue to base ourselves as much as possible in the solid traditional framework. Emphasis on verifiable tradition (i.e., historical runic systems, old Germanic literatures, ancient histories) is important if we are to avoid being forced to accept one man's (or one group's) "revelation."

But of course, we will go well beyond the necessarily and properly limited academic/scientific aspect and delve into the practical application. We quicken the wooden forms of academic findings with the inspiration of Odin, but we remain forever open to new findings and conclusions reached through purely intellectual means as well. Ideally, the systematic collection of data and the logical analysis of those data to form rational conclusions, the intuitive understanding of the multiversal mysteries and the inspired use of those mysteries to transform or shape reality should work in tandem, each feeding the other. Hidden doors are thereby opened in both directions. This is the work of the Rune-Gild on all its levels.

"Rune" is in and of itself a magical formula. Paradoxically, as a word, the more we refine the definition of *rune*, the broader its meaning becomes. This is why the ambiguous "translation" as "secret" or "mystery" is suitable. (It is perhaps worth repeating that the term *rune* only secondarily refers to the letter forms [staves] commonly called runes.)

As a magical word, *rune* must be understood from self-created viewpoints, and as such its true "meaning" cannot be communicated through profane, natural speech. As a magical word it is "whispered in our ear" by the Odin within.

Starting points on this road are the realizations that, on a cosmological level, runes are focal points of energy/substance in a complex implicit cosmic framework, and on a "psychological" level they are "points of reference" at which cosmic intelligence interacts with human intelligence. Knowledge of this level concerning the character of the runes must be allowed to go with you in all runic investigations; only so armed will the atheling be able to find his way in the complex realms of runelore.

Runelore Tables of the Elder Futhark

The surest way for runers to expand their own fields of meaning for the runes is to meditate on their shapes, sounds, and names, but most of all on their corresponding rune poem stanza (if any). It must be constantly kept in mind that the lore of each individual runestave is only part of the mystery; the rest is in the hidden ways in which the runes are woven together in a multidimensional webwork of being. Therefore, the lore of the following twenty-four tables must be read within the context of sections on the runic system and rune worlds (chapter 10). It is of the utmost importance for true runic understanding that the vitki know not only what makes *fehu fehu* but also how *fehu* is bound to other runes in the system and how hidden lines of connection may be discovered. Each stave is internally suggestive of wider vistas, and each points outward from its center to interconnections with the essences of other runes. The would-be runer's main task with these tables is the acquisition of a basic and instinctual "feel" for the meaning of each rune as a category but a category surrounded by a kind of semipermeable membrane that allows interchange with sympathetic energies and essences but acts as insulation against antipodal concepts.

Here we will especially concentrate on what might be called in our modern language the mythological, cosmological, and psychological aspects of each mystery. Each of the sections can be seen as esoteric commentaries on the relevant rune poem stanzas as well.

Mythologically, the F-rune is bound to the three great deities whose names begin with its sound—Frigg, Freyja, and Freyr. These divinities derive some of their power from the mystery of *fehu*. From the numinous fire of *fehu* Frigg and Freyja receive their gifts as seeresses. From this common source runecasters derive their ability to "read the runes aright" in divinatory work.

Fehu is the mystery of *gold*. That is, it is the numinous power of that which is called money or wealth in our society (which is now dominated by these "pecuniary mysteries"). This rune exists in a great ecological system of power or energy. The rune must be *yielded* into receptive fields—: ◇ : —in order to be increased. It increases in power through circulation, and it is transformed from one shape to another. This must not, however, be done blindly but rather with foresight and wisdom.

The *fehu* power naturally belongs in the hands of the true athelings, and it is their responsibility to see that it is properly used. Those who do not do so face the natural withering process ruled by "the lord" as a representative of the gods. Abrogation of such responsibilities leads to strife.

In the cosmology this is the true outward force of the primal cosmic fire—the expansive force that answers to contraction and solidification in ice (:I:). This is a fire generated out of water and in the dark depths of the multiverse—and in the dark corners of the self.

It is within the self that the power of the *fehu* is most important to the runer. The F-rune is a force that lies hidden in most souls—like a wolf in the woods—yet can be raised along the path of the grave-fish (serpent). From death shall come life; from darkness, light.

In the mythology *uruz* is to be identified with the original cosmic bovine Audhumla (see chapter 6). This is the undomesticated "wild" force of formation, the concentrated will-to-form. As such, *uruz* is the mother of manifestation. It is the process of ordering substance (Ymir), which leads to the shaping of the world in its manifold multidimensional form.

Uruz is the most vital of energies. It is a fire blended with the waters of life, a vital fire that can remove all weakness—all the dross (such as Audhumla's tongue!)—and transform the weak into the strong. If, however, this vital energy is spent in the wrong direction, unguided by wisdom, it can become destructive to the individual or to society.

URUZ

The will-to-form is a powerful deep-seated instinct in man (hence, it is "on the moors")—as is the instinct to transform with which it must work in tandem. Part of the will-to-form is the desire to defend the form, practically at any cost—to defend the security of the "homeland" (:ᛉ:) of the soul.

The horns of the "beast" mentioned in "The Old English Rune Poem" are of extreme importance. Both of them point upward naturally but downward in the runestave. This twofoldness indicates manifestation in the objective universe and the ability to penetrate into other dimensions by the force of will.

The :ᚦ: is the sign of pure action, potency, and instinctual "will" devoid of self-consciousness. It is the embodiment of directed cosmic force in the multiverse as a combination of polar energies projected in a straight line.

This form of raw power is held, on the one hand, by the thurses (giants) and is directed against the consciousness embodied in the Aesir. However, the Aesir are able to combat this power, and match might with might, through their defender, the warder of Asgardhr—Thor.

THURISAZ

The TH-rune is therefore not only that of the thurses but also of the thunder and its god, Thor. This is due to their common origins as the result of the clash of polarized forces (see chapter 10) and also shows their common methods and motivations. Each is a reactive force. The thurses respond to the expansion of consciousness in the Aesir, and Thor responds with Mjöllnir to the resistance of the thurses. Thus, a balance is achieved but a precarious balance.

Thurisaz (3) is an assimilation of the potential energy contained in any two polarized extremes and the kinetic expression of them. Through this mystery the TH-rune is also the power of regeneration and fertility. As the thunder heralds the crop-bringing rains, so *thurisaz* breaks down opposition and releases energy so that new beginnings can be made. Here it is closely related to one of its formal correspondences: ᛒ :, but: ᛒ : is the "releaser" and: ◇ : the "container."

This tension is perceived by most individuals as a source of stress, but to the few (athelings or Erulians) it is a source of strength.

The "thorn is not only a symbol of the phallus but also of the whole psychosexual impulse used by athelings to transform the self.

It is rather clear that on one level the TH-rune is an expression of the combination of the F- and U-runes: fiery energy organized and directed, force and formation combined and directed.

ANSUZ

The A-rune embodies the powers of synthetic, Odian consciousness in the multiversal structure and in the psychological complex of humanity. It is the rune of consciousness, especially that which successfully integrates the right and left hemispheres of the brain. This rune is the magico-ancestral power innately transmitted from generation to generation since the dawn of mankind. *Ansuz* is the name for an ancestral sovereign divine being. In the singular this usually refers to Odin as the god. This link between the consciousness of the gods and the mind of man remains unbroken. The thurses and their "gods" seek to break it.

The powers contained in: ᚨ : were given (and these are their only gifts) by the Odinic triad of Odin, Vili, and Vé (or in another version Odin, Hoenir and Lódhurr) at the shaping of humanity (see chapters 12 and 13). These powers are received by humanity as the agents by which it can transform itself through the quest for knowledge and the expression of that knowledge in word and work, guided by the Odinic model.

On a cosmological level *ansuz* describes an ecology of energy. It is the medium through which power is received, the receptacle of that power, and the power itself when expressed through the inspired mental state. This is the rune of the magical word and breath, of the synthesis of linguistic thought with nonlinguistic, image-forming power in the poetry of the Erulians and skalds.

Raidho is the symbol of the cosmic law of right ordering in the multiverse, in mankind, and in the soul. It is a mystery the outward face of which we experience each day in the rising and setting of the sun and in the cycles of activity and sleep. All rhythmic action is ascribed to *raidho*—dance, music, and poetic forms.

It is by the might of this rune that institutions of all types are organized: states, religious bodies, guilds, and so on. When those natural laws are broken, the power of raidho rebalances them—sometimes violently.

The R-rune is the vehicle ("wagon") for and the pathway (the whole "ride") along the journey of *becoming* in the rune worlds. This path is hard and difficult at times—often in hostile social or natural environments—and a strong vehicle (= mental powers) and horse (= spiritual substance; see *ehwaz*) are needed in order to be successful.

This is the path of rightly ordered action—ritual working. It is the network of roadways between the worlds and an important part of the equipment needed to traverse these paths.

Raidho rules mathematical (geometrical) proportion, interval, and logical reckoning of all kinds. It is the rune of cognition. This is the might by which tally-lore works—active harmonization of forces appropriate to a willed end.

One of the great mysteries of the R-stave is its relationship to the idea of "wheels" within the psychophysical complex of man (see the Latin gloss *iter* [wheel] in "The Old Icelandic Rune Poem"). It is on these "wheels" that the magical journey of initiation is made.

The flow pattern of force in *raidho* is always directed, but it has a spiraling effect as well, which actually *concentrates* the force to a given aim. Its usefulness as a working tool should not be overlooked.

This is the rune of creativity—or more accurately, in Germanic terms, of the *ability to shape*. This is symbolized by controlled fire—the torch—but also by the fires of the hearth, harrow (= altar), forge, and pyre. Each serves the human will to shape and reshape itself or its environment. In a person this is the bright light that all recognize as "charisma." Although this is ever-present within the runer, it is most awake in "working states," that is, when inspiration is high but physical activity is restive.

Kenaz is the root of all technological knowledge, the rune of the craftsman and the crafty one—Wayland (ON Völundr) and Loki. It is also the mystery of the deep connection between sexuality and creativity that is so characteristic of the Odinic path.

The hidden root concept behind *kenaz* is dissolution, whether by organic means (see the Norse rune name *kaun* [ulcer, sore]) or by fire (torch). This dissolution is necessary for reshaping to take place in accordance with a willed plan. In a sense this is the *solve* portion of the alchemical formula *solve et coagula* (dissolve and coagulate). Here :ᛗ: would be the *coagula* portion—the recombination of forces in a transformed, self-aware essence :ᛁᚢᛁ.

In many ways the K-rune is a culmination of the process begun in the A-rune and working through the R-rune: inspiration rationally crafted.

GEBO

This is the rune that signifies the Gift of Odin in his triadic forms (see chapter 13)—the gifts of consciousness, life-breath, and form.[1] Here the emphasis is on the exchange of power—the flow of force from one system into another to be transformed and returned to its source.

Within human society this is most evident in the economic field— the process of giving and receiving, the object of which is *fehu* and/ or *othala*. Such an exchange builds strong bonds within society, and the same process is carried out between gods and men to build strong bridges between the worlds. *Gebo* is the rune of sacri-fice (or "making sacred")—of giving to the gods and their obligatory return gifts to man. This is the mystery of the interdependence of gods and men. The power of this mystery is exalted and internalized within the runer in the E-rune.

The :ᚷ: is the sign of the "magical (or alchemical) marriage." This again finds expression in ᛁˣᛁ (*mannaz*), where the process is brought into full manifestation, and in ᛁᚷᛁ (*dagaz*), where the process is absolutely internal and eternal. The most powerful example of this magical union is found in the *Völsunga Saga* where Sigurdhr, mounted on his otherworldly steed, Grani (see :ᛗ:), pierces the ring of flames and ascends the mountain Hindarfjell (Rock of the Hind) to awaken the sleeping *valkyrja*, Sigrdrífa (or Brynhildr).

Here we have what is perhaps the most archaic version of the "Sleeping Beauty" tale. On this mountaintop he ritually exchanges vows with her and receives runic wisdom from her. This process describes the attainment of communion with the "higher" or "divine self" of the runer.

The ecstasy of :ᚷ: is of a serene type—the quiet balance of perfectly harmonized inner concentration of flowing vital forces.

The W-rune is the harmonization of elements or beings of common origin (nations, tribes, clans, families) and the magical power to recognize hidden affinities between sympathetic entities. The *wunjo* describes the inner, subjective feeling one attains when in a state of inner/outer harmony—with self and environment. This is an *active* willed harmony toward specific evolutionary goals. The *wunjo* marshals diverse but sympathetic forces and/or beings to a common purpose. This is why it is the mystery that rules the bind-rune-making process.

"The Old English Rune Poem" gives specific guidelines for the winning of such *wunjo*. There we learn that the runer should separate the self from most woe of all kinds (but keep a little), and further have three things: (1) OE *blaed* ("prosperity": the inflow and outflow of energy); (2) *blyss* ("bliss": to be filled with a sense of meaningfulness and joy); and (3) *byrg geniht* ("a good enough enclosure": a good house of the soul). One needs vital breath, a psychological sense of meaningfulness, and a healthy body—after cleaving away negative influences detrimental to the concentrated work.

WUNJO

Wunjo also comes when the runer is able to make such a blend-work in the objective world—to bind and marshal forces to do his will.

This is the sign of the primal reunion of cosmic fire and ice—the poles of the multiverse—in the energized, yeasty seed form: the cosmic hailstone, or "hail-egg," that gives rise to Ymir (see chapter 10).

Hagalaz is the framework of the world, the pattern upon which the multiverse is fitted out by the triadic root of consciousness—Odin-Vili-Vé. The H-rune contains the complete model of absolute potential energy, as it holds the full dynamism of fire and ice in its form. From this harmonious balance of all-potential, an internal evolution can take place within its space.

HAGALAZ

Numerical symbolism is very important for *hagalaz*. Nine is the number of completion, fruition, and dynamic wholeness in the Germanic system. All of this comes together in : Ⲛ : (9). Nine is the number of worlds in the branches and roots of the World-Tree, Yggdrasill, which is the innate pattern present in both the seed and the full-grown tree.

The H-rune is the pattern of completion implicit in the seed of every evolving or growing thing. As the whole yew is contained in a hidden genetic code in the berry, so too is the completed, transformed cosmos held in the world-seed. *Hagalaz* is the code—the pattern of becoming and completion. This is the hidden form of perfection toward which all conscious shaping (creation) is directed.

The "hailstone" is the rune mother; all runes are held, and can be read, within its form when contained in a solid (see figure 9.1). This is ultimately a multidimensional model, also present in the Yggdrasill pattern discussed in chapter 10, page 125.

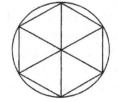

Hagalaz is the unification of all opposites into all-potential. Within its mystery is contained the power of transformation,

Figure 9. 1. Mother rune of the hailstone.

of the evolution from form to form along a consciously or mythically determined pattern.

Hail also has its destructive aspects, which can be turned to the advantage of the runer if they are directed outward in a protective way.

As the rune poems show, the N-rune can be experienced in unpleasant ways by those who do not have the understanding to *use* its power. *Nauthiz* is the force of cosmic resistance to the will and its actions. This is the source of the accumulation of layers of psychic substances that are the essence of what the Norse called *ørlög* (see the P-rune). But this "need" imposed from outside the consciousness can be the source of salvation for the runer who knows how and when to use it (see "The Old English Rune Poem").

The N-rune is resistance to actions, a cosmic friction between substances. This internal stress can be transformed into strength through the mystery of the need-fire (fire made by friction between two inert materials). Once the flame is kindled, the cold of need is alleviated. But without "need" the fire would never have been discovered in the first place. In this rune can be seen the root of the proverb "Necessity is the mother of invention."

As we look deeper into the mystery of the need-fire, we see that it is a self-generated flame. In the realm of consciousness this is to be understood as a certain tension or friction between aspects of the psyche. This leads to the kindling of the flame of higher consciousness that is attainable only through these means.

Because of the absolute necessity for resistance in the cosmos before manifestation can come about, the N-rune is both the mystery of cause and effect and of the Nornir (Norns). The three Norns (see the P-rune) came forth out of Jötunheimr and thereby established the law of cause and effect and its resistance to the will of the Aesir. This brought about the laws of entropy, and thus the seeds of cosmic destruction were sown. Whenever anything is brought forth out of becoming into being, the laws of the Norns and those of the N-rune are activated. This particular law must be kept in mind in all operant forms of runework. It is the rune of "coming forth into being."

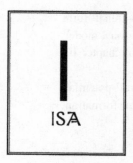

The "ice" in the I-rune is not to be identified with that of Niflheimr but rather with the ice stream that flows out of that cold world toward the fire of Muspellsheimr. It is an extension of a concentrated force of absolute contraction or an absolute stillness or lack of vibration. The power of *isa* attracts the fire toward the "center" and makes what we call "matter" possible by formulating the hailstone (:✳:). The I-rune is a kind of *prima materia* (or the force of density that makes such a substance possible). It is the absolute power of inward-turning force that is as de-

THE BIG BOOK OF RUNES AND RUNE MAGIC

structive as fire (expressed in : ᚠ :), but each balancing the other is the state sought by the conscious forces in the multiverse. When nonconscious forces gain supremacy, the pattern goes out of balance, and the destructive aspects of fire and ice are unleashed. It must be remembered, however, that this ebb and flow is to be expected in an evolving universe. The periodic release of the destructive forces is necessary to real change.

In the individual *isa* makes possible the manifold, polypsychic *omniego* (all-I), that is, ego awareness of all aspects of the whole psychophysical complex (see chapter 12). It holds these aspects together in a harmonious, preset pattern and is most evident when the mind is totally stilled and concentrated. The I-rune acts as a sort of psychic bonding material that can hold the self together through the stressful initiatory process. Unbalanced by the dynamic mysteries, this static bonding material leads to dullness and stupidity.

The : ᛁ : is the mystery of the concentrated point and of its first extension—the line. These two images are used as bridging tools in gaining conscious access to other dimensions outside Midhgardhr. *Isa* is the solid floor on which the consciousness can make transitions, but it is sometimes only as wide as a hair and does not make for an easy journey.

The J-rune is the sign of the solar year of twelve months; its mystery refers to the "summer" half of the year, when crops are sown, grown, and harvested. (The old Germanic calendar only had *two* seasons, summer and winter. "Spring" and "fall" refer only to short intervals at the borders of these tides.)

The central power of this rune lies in its *cyclical* nature. It is the rune of "eternal return." *Jera* embodies the idea of arising, becoming, and passing away to new beginning present throughout the rune row; and its position as a *core rune* (with : ᛃ :) shows its central importance.

It is the dynamic dyad and the ominpresent circumference.

Jera actually means "the fruitful year," or "the harvest." This is the reward reaped after a cycle of hard work within the natural (and numinous) laws. The symbolism of the agricultural process makes the meaning of *jera* clear. The seeds do not ask who planted them or why, only how they were planted. If the planting has been done *right*, the harvest *should* be good (see : ᛜ :). *Jera* is the reward for right work.

The mystery of the J-stave is fundamentally linked to the first and last staves, as symbols of peace, prosperity, and freedom.

The J-rune is the cosmic millstone, the cosmic axis of which is the EI-rune.

EIHWAZ

The EI-rune is the omnipresent center axis of the cosmos—the *omphallos* of the world—and is the second in the core dyad of the rune row.

This is the vertical axis of the World-Tree, Yggdrasill, the channel along which the cosmic squirrel, Ratatöskr, like an electric arc, spreads discord between the eagle at the summit of the tree and the great serpent, Nidhhöggr, at its roots.

The EI-rune synthesizes extreme opposites—life/death, day/night, summer/winter—in a dynamic way (see the TH- and D-runes and note the numerical correspondences: 3-13-23). This rune penetrates through the three realms: the heavens, middle-earth, and underworld— Asgardhr/Midhgardhr/Hel. It is the path of transformation of essences in any of these realms into essences of any of the others. "Material" objects can be made "spiritual" by this mystery.

The EI-rune is the latent, self-contained, transformational fire from within (activated by the N-rune and manifest in the K-rune). This is the hidden and immortal fire of the will that can remain vital in death (winter)—the hard spirit of perseverance.

It is along the "column of the yew" within the individual that the transformative magical fire is to be generated, rising *and* descending through the "wheels" of the body (see the S-rune). It is to this great mystery that the rune poems refer.

PERTHRO

This is the most guarded of the runes. It is the cultic symbol of the secret of *ørlög*—the mystery of wyrd. This is the power of the Nornir and one that complements the force of consciousness present in the Aesir. The runer must learn to investigate the way of wyrd that he may understand it and, when need be, overcome it. (This is the great Odinic accomplishment at Ragnarök.)

The P-rune is a sign of the path of the investigation of *ørlög* through the methods of runecasting. Perthro is the cup or framework from which, or into which, the runestaves are cast in divinatory workings. This is a symbol of the Well of Wyrd—the Urdharbrunnr (Well of Urdhr, the first and eldest Norn).

In *perthro* we find a synthesis of the laws of cause and effect (x causes y, which sets z in motion) and the laws of synchronicity (x, y, and z occur [significantly] together). Causality is a law of the horizontal (mechanical) plane, synchronicity of the vertical axis of consciousness. The synthetic element is the psychic dimension of time. This force, in conjunction with that of the N-rune and the B-rune, is the principal agent of change, or becoming, in the multiverse.

The idea of wyrd (and of *ørlög*) also partakes of this synthesis of horizontal and vertical reality. Wyrd actually means "that which has 'become' or 'turned.'" So it, like *ørlög*, which means "primal layers (of action)," has the mystery of past time bound up with it. This "pastness" is of vital import in the Germanic way of thinking. Only the "past" and

THE BIG BOOK OF RUNES AND RUNE MAGIC

the "present" have any objective reality. The "future" is a mass of undifferentiated all-potential for becoming. It is to be shaped by a combination of forces—cyclical laws, organic streams of life-force and tradition, the pattern of consciousness existing in the gods and other entities, and the will of man (especially that of runers). Nowhere is this more apparent than in the names of the three great Norns—Urdhr (that which has become), Verdhandi (that which is becoming), and Skuld (that which *should* become). Linguistically, the words *urdhr* (ON) and English wyrd (weird) are identical (the loss of the initial *w* is the result of the same regular rule that turns *Wōdhanaz* into Odin).

Elhaz is the divine link between a man and his fetch (see chapter 12). The Z-rune describes the power of attraction between the mind of man and its psychic counterpart, the "divine self." This force of attraction works together with the mystery of *sowilo* to generate the magical will. It is a symbol of the *valkyrja*, the protective aspect of the fetch-wife, which is often magically attached to a sword or other symbolic weapon. (This is the hidden meaning of "The Old English Rune Poem," stanza 15: elk-sedge = sword.) This symbolic link between horn and sword is nowhere more evident than in the myth of Freyr. After surrendering his sword in exchange for the etin-wife Gerdhr, it is said that he had only a horn with which to do battle.

The: Y :also describes the rainbow bridge, Bifröst, again a symbol of the link between Midhgardhr and the realms above and below.

In the Z-rune we see the force of protection that can come only with a linkage with the "personal divinity." This is the entity that the Greeks knew as the *daimon* and the Romans called the *genius*. In runelore the fetch or *valkyrja* is the source of this inspiration as the most direct link between the individual and the ultimate source of inspiration, Odin.

The image of the stave: Y :is one of the most potent in Germanic symbology. It indicates the splayed hand (= protection, humanity), the horn of the solar hart lifted to the heavens in pride and potency, the swan in flight (a reference to the *valkyrja*), and the Germanic arm posture for prayer and invocation. Some of this makes clear why this form was eventually used for the younger "man"-stave.

The loading with magical, numinous, or spiritual force effected through this rune implies a person or place with so much force that it becomes sacred, set apart and protected by divine power.

Also, there is a natural, underlying connection between this rune and the: ⋏ :— the yew-stave. This is expressed in many ways; most graphic, however, is the formal relationship. The probable original stave form was: ⋏ :, and in time: ⋏ :became the younger yew-stave (which is an alternate form of the elder *elhaz* as well).

SOWILO

The sun is the guiding beacon on the roads of becoming. It is the light of consciousness—and its pattern which stands in the objective universe for all of those who seek to transform themselves to see. The archetypal sun, and its counterpart the "night sun" (= the Pleiades), guide the "seafarer" from one zone of consciousness to another, from one "land" to another. This is the goal that gives motivation to the will. In skylore this is "the star" of the elliptic (the Pleiades), which at night travels the same path as the sun does by day.

In ancient Nordic symbolism the sun is seen as a wheel or as a shield. That is, it has transformative and protective, nurturing aspects. As a wheel, *sowilo* is a sign of the wheels along the path of the yew column, Yggdrasill, by which the runer consciously evolves. *Sowilo* is the shield of the consciousness and provides it with greater significance toward which to strive. One who has developed the will by the light of the S-rune (in *all* of its aspects) is blessed with honor and success.

The sun describes a counterbalance to the power of :|:. In the row, however, both are necessary to a stable whole development of the world and of the runer. The S-rune also has been connected with the serpentine mysteries of the north, which involve the centers at which flows of heavenly and chthonic forces converge at a point on the surface of the earth. The power of the :ᛋ: breaks down psychological or cosmic inertia and transforms it into a vital, dynamic force.

TIWAZ

The *tiwaz* is also a guiding beacon; but unlike the dynamic circular pathway of the S-rune, the T-rune is a beacon of a much more distant, deep, and serene force—that of the Lodestar, Pole Star, or North Star (Polaris). It is also called "the Star" by the ancient Germanic sailors—the axis star that keeps its troth, and around which all other stars revolve. (See also "the Star" at the circumference of the elliptic in :ᛋ:.) The North Star is a visible symbol of the god-force of *tiwaz* as the summit of the world column—the *Irminsūl*.

The cosmogonic force of Tyr is expressed in the initial process necessary to the shaping of the multiverse: the separation or polarization of the cosmic substances that allows for the vital glories of manifestation between the poles of fire and ice. The T-rune describes the aspect of the cosmic column that keeps these separate, holding cosmic order.

This is the essence of the god Tyr (English Tiw). (Significant aspects of the T-rune are discussed in chapter 13.) It is the power of detached, transcendent wisdom at the center of things. This contrasts with the wide-ranging multiformed essence of the A-rune.

In the human realm, with this rune the god Tyr rules over the *thing* (legal assembly) of the Germanic peoples. He measures out justice in accordance with the law (see also *ørlög*, "or-law," in this regard). The T-stave is a sign of "law and order" in both the cosmos and the world of men.

It is meaningless to attempt to identify the natural tree to which "The Old English Rune Poem" refers under this stave. The B-rune is a numinous reality, not a botanical organism.

BERKANO

Berkano is the great and many-faceted "Birch Goddess," who rules over the process of human and earth transformations; for example, the critical human rites of passage—birth, adolescence, marriage, and death—and the seasonal round of agricultural year. The B-rune rules the cyclical process of arising (birth), becoming (life), passing away (death) to a new arising (rebirth).

As "The Old English Rune Poem" clearly, if symbolically, indicates, the power of *berkano* is self-contained. It can grow independent of outside forces, but no growth can take place in the natural world without the aid of the self-generated process of the B-rune. *Berkano* takes seed substance, hides or conceals it in its enclosure, breaks the enclosure, and bears the transformed substance forth. It is structurally linked to, though independent of, the NG-rune.

The symbol of the B-rune is the birch rod, the magical instrument through which its powers (of fertility, transformations, eroticism) are evoked in the earth and in humanity.

Cosmologically, : ᛒ : is a "unit of becoming." It is that *moment of being* (a single "micro-cycle" of arising-becoming-passing away) on which all *becoming* is based—the eternal now. The B-rune also describes the principle of phenomenological randomness in the multiverse—chance in the evolutionary process.

Berkano is a conserving, protective force and rules over concealing enclosures (especially those used in transformational rites).

The B-rune also conceals the great mystery of the "alchemy of the word," the power by which words are woven into meanings beyond their concrete definitions. In this, *berkano* is closely allied with *ansuz*. This is understandable because of all goddesses, Freyja is mistress to *all* aspects of the B-rune.

This is the rune of the symbiotic relationship between any two systemically distinct yet harmoniously working beings. In ancient times this was most directly perceived in the relationship between a man and his horse, especially among the Indo-Europeans who were the first to train these powerful creatures. *Ehwaz* is the mystery of the dually arrayed and sympathetic forces: man/horse, horse/chariot, and so on.

EHWAZ

The E-rune is the *living* vehicle of the runer's journeys in self-transformation: the rune of the *fylgja* itself (not just the force of its attraction: Y :) as a controlled or cooperative entity. That this symbolism is deep rooted is demonstrated by the Old Norse formula *marr er manns fylgja* (the "horse is a man's fetch"). The "horse/man symbiosis" as a metaphor for true human existence (or that of the atheling or Erulian) is shown by the bind rune: M : $(e + m\ (+k), I$ am). Perhaps most central to the mystery of *ehwaz* is the steed of Odin, Sleipnir (an offspring of Loki). The level of identity between Odin/Sleipnir is indicated by riddle (no. 72) recorded in the *Saga of Heidrek the Wise*:

> Who are those two,
> that have ten feet,
> three eyes
> and one tail?

> (Answer: Odin riding on Sleipnir)

Ehwaz is the force on which the runer "slips" from one world to another. It is a sign of great loyalty, especially between men and women, and it is a symbol of lawful marriage.

The archetypal force of this rune is still vibrant around us even in popular culture, especially once one realizes that unconsciously the "horse" has become *motorized*. The man/horse/woman "triangle" is virtually cliché.

MANNAZ

This is the structure of (divine) consciousness in mankind, imparted there through a genetic link with the unified god of consciousness. This is possessed in varying degrees by humans as described in the "Rígsthula" in the *Poetic Edda*. The link is there because ultimately humans are *descendants* of the gods; that is, the relationship is genetic not *contractual*. Hence, it is actually unbreakable.

A god with the name *Mannus* was worshipped in the time of Tacitus (first century C.E.), as there we have the earliest parallel to the Rígr/Heimdallr version of the origin of human society recorded in the "Rígsthula." (See the *Germania*, chapter 2.)

Mannaz is a god made flesh, not as a unique historical event, as Christians would have us believe, but as a great biological, sociological, psychological process of consciousness becoming manifest. This is the mystery underlying the rune poem stanzas having to do with this stave.

The M-rune is the harmonious combination of the "mind" and "memory." In the M-rune Huginn and Muninn speak freely to one another and inform the whole-self of the god Odin (see chapter 12). This is the man made whole, the initiate of the Odinic cult (Erulian). In Jungian terms it is the individuated self.

THE BIG BOOK OF RUNES AND RUNE MAGIC

Mannaz is the rune of the moon, and of its tripartite nature: dark ● — becoming ◑ — light ○. In Germanic lore the moon is masculine (the *man* in the moon) and a transformational essence. It is the synthesis of the intuitive and rational (measuring, analyzing) intelligences in man. Its very name means "the measurer" (of time). As with Odin, his face is always changing, yet it remains always the same.

This *laguz* is the primeval cosmic water that wells up from Niflheimr — containing all life-potential — which is transformed into cosmic ice and energized by the fires of Muspellsheimr. It is the ultimate medium for life-containing forces. (See "Cosmogony" in chapter 10.)

LAGUZ

Laguz-force "falls" into the realm of manifestation from extradimensional realms (Útgardhr). This downward flow of energy complements the upward flow described in the alternate name of the L-rune, *laukaz* (leek). For this reason, the waterfall is a potent symbol of the dynamic mystery of this rune. It should be noted that the original place of the golden hoard of the Nibelungs was under a waterfall; it is to this myth of mysteries that the second half-line of "The Old Norwegian Rune Rhyme" refers.

The L-rune describes the layers of the laws of life, the layers with which *ørlög* works to form the wyrd of the cosmos and of individual elements within it.

Laguz is the rune of organic life and the passage to and from that state. This "water" is the main element in the mixture (ON *aurr*) that the Norns draw up out of the Well of Urdhr (Wyrd) to preserve the organized life of the World-Tree. At birth the Germanic child is reintegrated into the organic life of its clan through the rite of *vatni ausa* ("sprinkling with water"). Here the noun *aurr* and the verb *ausa* are derived from the same root. Also, the old Germanic funeral rites are often connected with water symbolism (ship burial, ship cremation, burial or cremation within ship-formed stone settings, etc.). The entryways into Hel are conceived of as rivers, with Odin often seen as the ferryman of the souls.

As a rune of life and vital power, *laguz* is closely related to the mystery of *uruz* (by the laws of skaldcraft *uruz* became connected to the concept *aurr*).

The L-rune manifests the unknown, dark depths of the watery, primeval state and that of death. If the runer (seafarer) is fitted out with an unsuitable vehicle (ship), he will fear the ebb and flow of this force. The "brine-steed" must be controlled in order to fare well.

INGWAZ

The *ingwaz*-force is that which is released to give the plentiful year (: ◇ :). This is demonstrated in the relationships between their stave shapes. The force that breaks it open is that of *berkano* (: ᛒ :). The NG-rune is the nourishment, the seed energy needed during the period of gestation. The cosmic food is contained and consumed by *berkano* and borne forth through its power to replenish energy lost in the cyclical process.

It should be noted that the NG-stave was originally made smaller than other staves in the row and separate from the sometimes imaginary bottom line of the other staves. It is withdrawn into a hidden and independent realm for the secret exchange of energies that leads to transformation. In the NG-rune is contained the mystery of the transformational process of withdrawal–transformation–return. This process is useful in initiatory rites but is actually a powerful aid in any transformational operation (see figure 9.2).

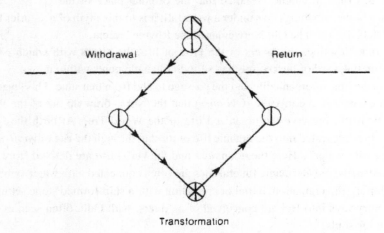

Figure 9.2. Process of transformation.

This process is often experienced intellectually when an idea that is somehow incomplete or imperfect is "put on the back burner" for a while, allowed to gestate in the unconscious (or perhaps better said, in the "hyperconscious") to be brought forth as a completed and perfected concept. The aspect of submersion into hidden realms is made quite clear in "The Old English Rune Poem." "Going to the east" is always a code for faring into the realm of the etins, the dark preconscious forces of the cosmos.

The D-rune is the process that takes place at the edges of extremes. As the day and darkness merge in the twilight and the beacons of that tide, the morning and evening stars (for which *Dagaz* [ON *Dagr*] is a name) shine into the realm of Midhgardhr. It is a sign of the light of consciousness born by Odin-Vili-Vé to mankind by their gift.

DAGAZ

In "The Old English Rune Poem" a synthesis between the powers of the drighten (lord = Woden or Odin) and the metod (measurer = Tiw or Tyr) is indicated, a synthesis between the right and left brain thinking that is the hallmark of inspiration.

Dagaz is the "Odinic Paradox"—the sudden realization (after concerted conscious effort of the will) that perceived opposites are aspects of a third idea that contains them both. This is the mystery of hyperconsciousness central to the Odinic cult, the Germanic cult of consciousness. In the light of the D-rune the pathways between extremes are seen clearly. An Odian does not seek the mystery of *dagaz* at the center but rather at the extreme borders. This is the simultaneous, bidirectional will that is almost unique to Germanic magical lore. The search ends when the contents of the extreme borderlands fall into a vortex of single pointed wholeness in the "center" (actually an extradimensional concept).

In : ᛞ : we see the extradimensional models such as the Moebius strip and the toroidal vortex (see figure 9.3), where in becomes out and out becomes in. This is of ultimate importance when considering the nature of the Odian mission in the world.

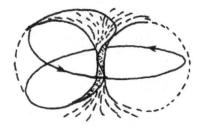

Figure 9.3. Toroidal vortex: Dagaz.

Othala is the sacred enclosure. In it is embodied the central concept of Midhgardhr and of the whole idea of "in-sidedness" and "out-sidedness" so prominent in Germanic (and Indo-European) thought. The O-rune describes the ring-wall, the symbol of the enclosed land separated from all that around it and thereby made sacred (ON *vé*). It is a sign of the site set apart for sacred purposes, the fane or hall. For the most part the *othala* force acts as a selective barrier. It prevents forces detrimental to the health of the interior form from entering, but it actually conducts beneficial energies into its interior.

OTHALA

In the often highly mobile society in which the runestaves were developed this concept quickly took on an abstract meaning, that of the spiritual heritage of the clan or tribe of which the odal-enclosure had been a symbol. As such, the O-rune is a sign of the *kynfylgja* (kin-fetch)—the sum of the spiritual heritage of a group. These kin-fetches are inherited from one generation to another and attach themselves to tribal or national leaders (see Runic Psychology, chapter 12). This is a metagenetic concept, and as such cannot as yet be fully explained in physical or purely organic terms. It is a hidden genetic code governed by laws of heredity active in families, clans, tribes, nations—but it goes beyond them as well.

Forces held by the ring of the O-rune must be well ordered and harmonious, following the path of right (:ᚱ:). With this state the common good is provided for, and peace and freedom reign. To this *in*-side, Odin turn his All-fatherly face—but he also faces outward into Útgardhr whence the Odian oft draws power and inspiration to serve himself and the good of the folk. But for the non-Odian to be thrust into the outside world—to become outlawed—is tantamount to a death sentence. This is because the non-atheling does not have a sense-of-self developed to the stage where he could survive such a psychological shock. Deprived of human context he is obliterated. The O-rune contains all aspects of this mystery.

Othala describes the essence of the mystery of the ebb and flow between states of order and chaos—the great cosmic state of flux. However, it celebrates the state of balance obtained when forces of consciousness have established their enclosures (Asgardhr and Midhgardhr) interacting with the powers of the exterior darkness (Útgardhr). Odin and his Erulians seek to maintain this balance. All-father is wise enough to know the ultimate outcome—but sly enough to know how to overcome it.

The Runic System

After studying the foregoing rune tables, the reader will be impressed with the degree to which the runes seem to interrelate. Runes weave in and out of one another in a great serpentine interlace of meaning. Indeed, their heritage is as much one of poetry (skaldcraft) as of "science." As in poetry, linkages are made between "words" (here, ideas) through associations on various levels: sounds (rhyme, alliteration, etc.), spatial arrangements (meter), and mythic allusion. Skaldcraft sprang from runecraft, so the similarity in practice is not surprising. It is the intention of the runic system to break down barriers in the consciousness and to reveal the hidden meanings within the worlds. It does this through a sometimes tangled webwork of words and images, each reverberating off the other. Each rune is bound to the other as surely as it has its own unique identity. Certain obscure aspects of the ways the runes relate to each other are explored in the section "Runes" in chapter 10; however, here we will deal with the secrets contained in the most traditional yet mysterious arrangement of the runes in the three aettir ("families" or "eights").

There is no "logical" or linguistic reason why the runestaves should be arranged in three groups of eight. This is a feature the Elder Futhark shares with ancient Greek, and there may be some Indo-European mystery of "twenty-four-foldedness" shared from the remote past at work here. Also, even among scholars there is no commonly agreed on reason as to why the runes have actual *meaningful names*. The Greek and Roman alphabets have only nonsensical names, like our letter "names." The idea of having meaningful words as letter names is a feature shared with the Celtic ogham and the Hebrew alphabet.

What is known is that the runes remained an organized body of lore that went far beyond the amount of information necessary to keep a simple alphabet system intact for more than a thousand years. When all is said and done, the whole of runelore is summed up in table 9.1.

ᚠ	ᚢ	ᚦ	ᚨ	ᚱ	ᚲ	ᚷ	ᚹ
f-ehu	u-ruz	th-urisaz	a-nsuz	r-aido	k-enaz	g-ebo	w-unjo
1	2	3	4	5	6	7	8
ᚺ	ᚾ	ᛁ	ᛃ	ᛇ	ᛈ	ᛉ	ᛋ
h-agalaz	n-authiz	i-sa	j-era	ei-whaz	p-erthro	elha-z	s-owilo
9	10	11	12	13	14	15	16
ᛏ	ᛒ	ᛖ	ᛗ	ᛚ	ᛜ	ᛞ	ᛟ
t-iwaz	b-erkano	e-hwaz	m-annaz	l-aguz	ing-waz	d-agaz	o-thala
17	18	19	20	21	22	23	24

Table 9.1. Synthetic rune table.

To unlock this table, we are faced with a double problem. First we must delve into the innate mysteries themselves, but before we can do that we must know a good deal about the basic meanings of these names and configurations. Through comprehension of the ancient lore, knowledge of the timeless mysteries will grow.

The deep-level structure of the multiversal mysteries (runes) is precisely reflected in the outer form of the system of the staves (= runes). This runic system is a complex, sometimes extralinguistic framework of lore that includes

1) individual stave shape

2) phonetic values of staves

3) names of staves

4) explanatory poetic stanza

5) order of staves (= number)

6) tripartite division of staves (aettir)

Only the second element of this system is truly necessary for a simple, linguistically functioning alphabet system. All of the rest is there for some other, more mytho-magical reason. In this section we hope to begin to instill in the aspiring runer some of the depth of this system, which underlies all formations and transformations of the runic tradition throughout history.

Stave Shapes

As far as the actual shape of individual runestaves is concerned, there seem to have been some variations. However, only rarely did these go beyond what might be called "typological" variants. For example, in the elder period, the S- rune could be represented by forms such as: ⟨ ⟩ ⟨ ⟨ ⟨ ⟨ ⟨ ⟨ —but they all belong to the zig-zag or serpentine type. These principles should be kept in mind when intuitively exploring the inner meaning of the stave shapes. Through history, some never change, whereas others do. There is a hidden significance in this development or lack of it.

Phonetic Values

The sound value of each stave shape is also relatively fixed, with only certain systematic shifts. This second element in the system is actually totally dependent on the third.

Stave Names

These ideologically and culturally loaded names are acrophonic; that is, they indicate the sound value of a stave through the initial sound in the name of the stave, for example, *f-ehu* = [f]. The *names* themselves, however, are to be interpreted on three levels. As the runer will come to understand, this multilevel approach is basic to all illustrative runic work. These three levels are (using *uruz* as our example): (1) the "fundamental" or literal (aurochs—a large and powerful, wild four-legged beast), (2) the esoteric or metaphorical, oft socio-mythological (aurochs—the primeval bovine of formation); (3) the runo-Erulian, often runo-psychological (aurochs—the circulation of vital forces in consciousness and the capacity to understand).[2]

The name contains the idea and the sound. It is highly probable that there existed in ancient times a complex system of names, and that each rune had a group of words (possibly three) that could be used as its names. The Rune-Gild is slowly recovering these, but here we deal with the primary names and their meanings, shown in table 9.2.

Anyone with an active interest in the runes will want to begin to make certain associations among and between runes on all levels. What shapes are related to what other shapes and how? What names are related to what other names and on what levels? On this last point it will be noticed, for example, that these primary rune names are drawn from certain areas of life: (1) the superhuman realms: *ansuz, thurisaz, tiwaz, ingwaz,* and perhaps *berkano*; (2) organic nature: *fehu, uruz, eihwaz, elhaz,* and *mannaz*; (3)

inorganic nature: *hagalaz, isa, jera, sowilo, laguz*, and *dagaz*; (4) technology: *raidho, kenaz, perthro*, and possibly *nauthiz*; and (5) cultural realms: *gebo, wunjo*, and *othala*. These categories can be further analyzed and recombined to give deeper meanings.

fehu (f)	domesticated cattle , livestock, unit of monetary value, FEE
uruz (u)	AUROCHS, wild horned beast
thurisaz (th)	THURS (primal giant), thing of great strength
ansuz (a)	an ancestral sovereign god (the Ase. Odin)
raidho (r)	wagon, RIDE
kenaz (k)	torch (secondary name , *kaunaz* [sore])
gebo (g)	GIFT, hospitality
wunjo (w)	oy , ecstasy
hagalaz (h)	HAIL(stone)
nauthiz (n)	NEED, necessity; need-fire
isa (i)	ICE
jera (j)	(the good) YEAR; harvest
eihwaz (ei/i)	YEW
perthro (p)	lot cup
elhaz (-z)	ELK (secondary name, *algiz* [protection])
sowilo (s)	sun
tiwaz (t)	(the god) Tyr (OE Tiw)
berkano (b)	the BIRCH (goddess)
ehwaz (e)	horse (see Latin *equus*)
mannaz (m)	MAN
laguz (I)	water (LAKE)
ingwaz (ng)	(the god) Ing
dagaz (d)	DAY
othala (o)	ancestral (ODAL) property

Table 9.2. Stave names and meanings.

[Words in capitals indicate modern English cognates, i.e. words that are directly derived from the ancient terms.]

Runic Arrangements

The ordering of the twenty-four runes gives each stave a numerical position in the series 1 to 24, and the division of these twenty-four into three segments results in groupings of eight. These numerical formulas are innate in the runic system. When the system was reformed in the Viking Age, it was done by a systematic reduction of these numerical formulas.[3]

All runes came into being simultaneously, and each is linked to the other on different levels. The most obvious linkages are seen in the ordering and aett divisions ("airts"). Indeed, on one level, *fehu* is related to *uruz*, which is linked to *thurisaz*, and so forth in a straight line 1 to 24. This line is divided into three in such a way that each group of eight (aett) also shares certain characteristics, and in addition this results in eight groups of three runes vertically arranged (e.g., :ᚠ:/::ᚺ::/:ᛏ:) that are also bonded in a special way. It should also be noted that even on the horizontal 1 to 24 series, groups of three (1–3, 4–6, etc.) are significant. For the active runer these can serve as excellent subjects of meditation and contemplation.

The underlying meanings of the three airts are clear. The first airt delineates the mysteries the runer must learn and master before setting out on the difficult path of the Odian. This airt shows the establishment of the basic talents and characteristics of the runer: energy, understanding, action, inspiration, ritual, controlled will, generosity, and fellowship. It corresponds to the dreng. The second airt is twofold and full of trial and tribulation. H to J outline the process of overcoming objective confrontations and gaining the good harvest from them, and EI to S describe the subjective conflicts and the pathway to success. This corresponds to the work of the thegn. The third airt (of Tyr) describes the realm in which the Erulian, or runemaster, works. Established at the summit of the world column (:ᛏ:) and able to generate his own power internally along the pathways of the tree (:ᛒ:), the runemaster, in tandem with his self-created and integrated divine "ego" (:ᛗ:), is able to pass through all layers of existence (:ᛚ:) to become the independent, self-contained, and ever-evolving Erulian god-man (:◇:) enlightened by the "light" of day (:ᛝ:), ever interacting with the world "outside" while remaining above and beyond the fray (:ᛟ:). This is the work of the drighten.

As the next chapter will make clearer, the runes actually belong to a fourth-dimensional reality, and therefore all attempts to represent them or their relationships must fall short. Ultimately, the runes can be seen clearly only in the "light" of *dagaz*. Through weaving the great webwork of mysteries, and thereby "worming" along the ways toward conscious realization of hidden realities, the runer will emerge and wing his way toward the Gard of the Gods.

THE BIG BOOK OF RUNES AND RUNE MAGIC

Chapter 10

ESOTERIC COSMOLOGY

(BIRTH OF THE WORLDS)

Under the heading of *cosmogony* we will also discuss theogony (birth of the gods) and anthropogony (birth of man), each in its turn. In the *Gylfaginning* (chapters 5–9) we read in great detail how the world was wrought. The description given there tells of the watery realm of Niflheimr (Mist-World) in the north, out of which flowed the ice streams loaded with yeasty venom, and of Muspellsheimr (Fire-World) in the south, out of which flew fire and sparks. These two extremes of energy flowed toward each other through *Ginnungagap* (Magically Charged Space). The extremes on either side brought about a harmonious condition in the center of Ginnungagap; and as the sparks and hot air of Muspellsheimr hit the ice, it quickened the yeast within it, and a form was shaped from the union of these energies—Ymir (the Roarer).

From Ymir are descended the rime-thurses. As a bisexual being, Ymir engendered a male and female thurs under his left hand, and one of his feet engendered a son with the other foot.

As a part of the same process in which Ymir came about, Audhumla, the cosmic bovine, was shaped as a coagulation of the dripping rime. She gave nourishment to Ymir with the milk that flowed from her udders. She, in turn, was fed directly from the frozen drizzle, by licking a salty ice block formed by it. From this block, she licked the form of a being named Búri. Búri, an androgynous entity, engendered a son called Borr, who subsequently married an etin-wife named Bestla, the daughter of an etin named Bölthom (Evil-thorn). From the union of the proto-god Borr and the etin-wife Bestla, the divine triad Odin-Vili-Vé was born.

This godly triad then set about to kill (sacrifice) Ymir. This they did and took his form to the middle of Ginnungagap, and from this substance they fitted out the framework of the multiverse. They gave shape to the world and set the mechanisms of the world in motion within the context of the four quarters. The heavens were shaped from Ymir's skull, at the four corners of which the gods set four dwarves—Nordhri, Austri, Sudhri, and Vestri. At the very center they built a stronghold from the brows of Ymir, which was called Midhgardhr (the Middle-Yard).

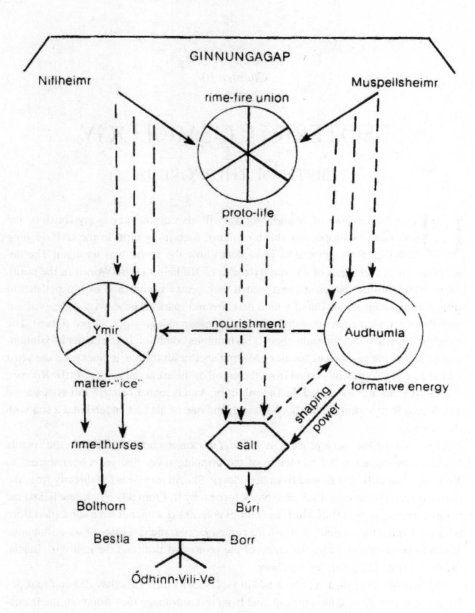

Figure 10.1. Cosmogonic process.

⊠   THE BIG BOOK OF RUNES AND RUNE MAGIC

Now the divine triad set about shaping mankind. This was done as Odin-Vili-Vé were in Midhgardhr near the sea, where they found two trees. To these already living beings Odin gave *önd* (spirit, the breath of life), Vili gave *odhr* inspired mental activity), and Vé gave form, speech, and the senses. This process is also described with the divine triad Odin-Hoenir-Lódhurr in the "Völuspá" (sts. 17–18) in the *Poetic Edda*. The male being was called Askr (ash) and the female Embla (elm).

This text should be read by all students and meditated upon deeply. It contains many runic mysteries.

The whole cosmogonic/theogonic proto-process is schematized in figure 10.1, which conceptualizes the entire primordial evolutionary complex as seen by the ancient Germanic peoples. This can be only an approximation, however, because the actual process is multidimensional.

Ginnungagap is a space charged with a field of proto-energy. Niflheimr and Muspellsheimr constitute that energy in a highly polarized and intensified state, which then interacts with itself in the center, where a new form modeled on innate multiversal pattern is manifested. This is symbolized by: ✳:, which is the pattern of the World-Tree as an ultimate crystallization of this seed pattern. It is also the snowflake pattern which demonstrates the nature of these unmanifested images to become visible once they are fed with the proper energies and substances. The fiery realm is a manifestation of the light energy of maximal vibration, whereas the icy realm is a solidification of the dark energy containing the elemental kernel of the mysteries of life and death—yeast, salt, and venom.

Once this proto-seed form is shaped, it splits into another polarization of proto-matter (Ymir) and proto-energy (Audhumla), but some of the energy from the proto-seed falls into Ginnungagap and is recrystallized as the ice block from which the proto-energy exercises its shaping power to form the androgynous proto-god/etin, Búri. Búri contains the pure pattern from the direct union of fire and ice but is shaped by the forces of proto-energy itself (and gives of itself in a form of self-sacrifice to the cosmic bovine). Ymir, the mass of raw cosmic material and the innate cosmic form or pattern contained in the "seed of ice"—the hailstone (*hagall*: ✳:)—is ultimately sacrificed by a triad of divine beings (i.e., the forms of primal consciousness). These three beings—truly a whole—are the first conscious, and therefore divine, beings because they can comprehend dualities and shape their environment due to the innate synthetic consciousness that results from their descent from a triple source: (1) the primal seed union, (2) Ymir, and (3) Audhumla. The triad of consciousness dissolves Ymir, and out of its matter reshapes the static cosmos into a dynamic, living, and conscious organization, according to the *right* (i.e., innate) patterns already contained in the matter itself (Ymir) and in the primal seed.

Humanity is a further shaping by the conscious divinities. But again, humanity is a part of the whole of the cosmos, not something *created* (*ex nihilo*) by the "gods."

Askr and Embla were already living beings (organic: here symbolized as plants), and the complex artificially expanded consciousness was imparted to them (co-equally and simultaneously) as a part of the non-natural evolution of consciousness in Midhgardhr.

Runes

The runes themselves define the pattern of existence and of consciousness; therefore, they are at work throughout the cosmogonic process. Before the sacrifice of Ymir, those patterns are unmanifested, and only in a rudimentally differentiated state. Only the biune duality between the murk runes (ON *myrkrúnar*) and the shining runes (ON *heidhrúnar*) was manifest. The runes bloom forth into an independent and isolated state upon the birth of Odin-Vili-Vé (when the murk and shining runes are entirely resynthesized into a whole coherent system). The runes, as we can begin to know them, are manifested in divine consciousness and in world being. When the triad of consciousness sacrificed Ymir (the crystallized seed of runic pattern) they *shaped* this primal substance according to the inherent runic structure. They arranged it in the shape of the nine worlds of Yggdrasill (see figure 10.7 on page 126).

It must be born in mind that these "events" take place in dimension(s) beyond our three, and as such, processes that we must discuss in a sequence may be "synchronistic." So it is with "events" of the birth of Odin-Vili-Vé, the sacrifice of Ymir, the manifestation of the runes and the world (Yggdrasill), and the rune-winning initiation of Odin (see Runelore of the Gods, chapter 13). On different levels these events all describe one face: consciousness enters the organic order from outside that order.

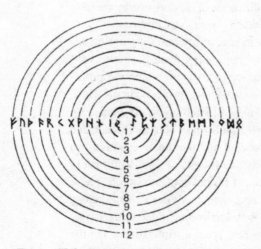

Figure 10.2. Diagram of the futhark pattern of manifestation.

As far as the (re)birth of the runic system is concerned, this manifests itself through the processes of (1) the blooming forth of the runes from a central point in a bidirectional or twofold spherical pattern (see figure 10.2) and (2) the wrapping of the resulting sequence around an eightfold plane (see figure 10.3). This gives the runes an organization that is comprehensible and communicable. It provides order and orientation.

The first unfolding from a central point begins with the two kernel, or "core," rune forms of cyclical (:ᛃ:) and vertical (:ᛇ:) force—the cycles of becoming and the axis of being. Thus, according to the pattern of the mystery of twenty-four, the runes manifest within a twelvefold sphere; each rune aligns with another according to a "law" of sympathy/antipathy as the spheres expand. The numerical sequence 1 to 24 is crystallized upon the application of the ordering force of consciousness that organizes the runes from left to right (in the *natural* order, i.e., along the pathway of the sun). It must be remembered, however, that runes could be carved in any direction—left to right, right to left, or back and forth. These facts show the way to a deeper understanding of the hidden meanings behind this practice. The spherical ordering of the futhark is graphically represented in figure 10.2. The significance of the dyadic parings of the runes that result from this pattern of "blooming forth" shown in figure 10.2 is indicated in table 10.1.

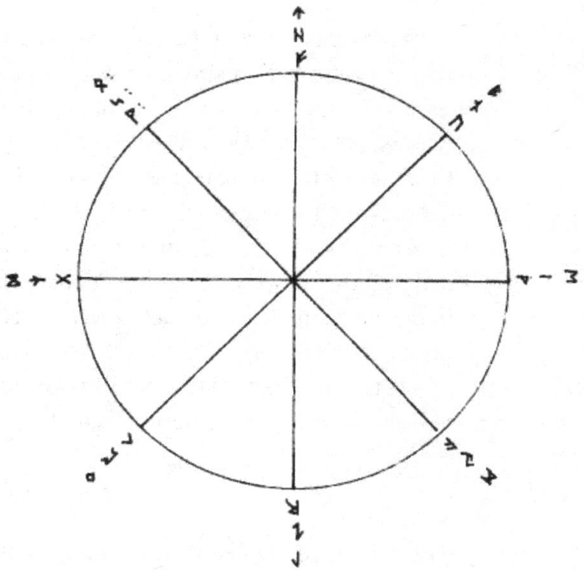

Figure 10.3. Eightfold division of the futhark.

Sphere Number	**Rune Forms**	**Cosmogonic Characteristics**
1	ᛃ:ᛇ	orbit/axis
2	ᛁ:ᛈ	contraction/evolution
3	ᚾ:ᛉ	resistance/attraction
4	ᚺ:ᛊ	seed form/light crystal
5	ᚹ:ᛏ	harmony/order
6	ᚷ:ᛒ	exchange/retention
7	ᚲ:ᛖ	ability/trust
8	ᚱ:ᛗ	cosmic order/human order
9	ᚨ:ᛚ	transformation/growth
10	ᚦ:ᛜ	breaker/container
11	ᚢ:ᛞ	formation/paradox
12	ᚠ:ᛟ	mobile power/immobile power

Table 10.1. Runic dyads.

From the previous chapter it is known that the harmonious arrangement of the runes in aettir is a significant mystery in and of itself. As the runes are ordered in their sequence 1 to 24, they emerge into the horizontal plane of existence from the "north" (that is, out of the doorway to other worlds) and, like a serpent, wrap themselves three times about the circular plane around Midhgardhr. In the Germanic tradition, planes are divided into eight segments in order to gain a position or orientation on that plane. These eight segments or divisions are called aettir (which can mean *both* "families" and "eights," i.e., the "eight directions"). (The archaic Scots dialect word *airt* survives in this meaning.) It is probably from this cosmological pattern (see figure 10.3) that the primary significance of the airt divisions of the futhark was derived.

Yet a third basic "arrangement" of the runes, one which emphasizes the multidimensional reality of the mysteries in the branches of Yggdrasill, will be discussed later.

Runic Elements

The subject of elements in the runic context has been one of the most hotly pursued areas of speculation and inner work among those dedicated to the Odinic path. This in large measure is due to the prominent role played by the four elements of air, fire, water, and earth in the Hermetic/Neo-Platonic school of occult philosophy to which the runic is often compared, or out of which it loosened itself in more recent times. These Neo-Platonic elements may very well derive from some formalization of Indo-European patterns, and these may indeed have been shared by the Germanic peoples. The elements are essentially basic classes of substances occurring in nature that evoke certain subjective psychic responses when meditated on. They are classificatory tools for the psychophysical complex. As such, it seems most beneficial to explore the runic ideology to extract from it directly, through runic investigation (a combination of lore learning and "wizardry"), the nature of the mysteries of *runic elements*. Here a note must be interjected: Although what follows is based on traditional sources, it is not intended as a dogmatic rule. Other interpretations may be possible. It is hoped that this work will open some doors and at least broaden somewhat those doors that have long stood wide.

As far as the lore is concerned, the secrets of the Eddas have for too long been ignored. In them is housed a great wealth of hidden knowledge if one will only open one's eyes to it. The cosmogonic myth explored at the beginning of this chapter holds the keys to the secrets of the ancient and complex science of runic elements.

The polarized primary elements are two in number: (1) fire and (2) ice, and the secondary ones are (3) water and (4) air. Further elemental building blocks of life are also described in the *Gylfaginning* in the *Prose Edda*: (5) iron (slag and the "sparks" from Muspellsheimr as its heat reaches the center), (6) salt, (7) yeast, (8) venom. These are all synthesized in the final element—(9) earth. All of these elements work on the "plane of manifestation"—the horizontal plane—not on the vertical axis of consciousness. These elements are meaningfully diagrammed in figure 10.4. A short description of the nature of each element, read in conjunction with the cosmogonic myth, and with comprehension of the runic system will help in the understanding of this complex:

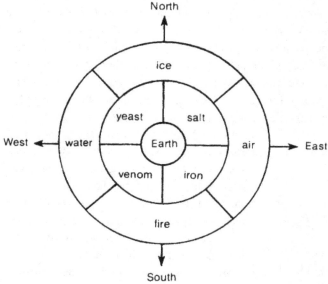

Figure 10.4. Runic elements on the horizontal plane.

Fire: Total expansion, all-vibration, heat, light, dryness, proto-energy—dynamic.

Ice: Total contraction, non-vibration, coldness, darkness, proto-matter—dynamic.

Water: Stillness, evolutionary being, wetness, matrix for form—static.

Air: All pervasiveness, formless space, warm, matrix for consciousness—static.

Iron: Primary synthesis, hot/cold, hard, dynamically penetrating, inert matter.

Salt: "Stuff of life" and substance of organic life, maintainer of form.

Yeast: Dynamic "livingness," organic movement, growth, health.

Venom: Latent dissolution, corrosiveness, organic dynamism (negative evolutionary factor—destruction necessary to reshaping).

Earth: All-potential, manifestation, final elemental synthesis.

These must not be interpreted as "emanations" of one another. All elements are real and latent in the whole, in the universe (omniverse), before they are manifested in the multiverse.

The primary dyad fire:ice interacts across the expanse of the *gap* (filled with *ginnung*, proto-consciousness, which will "solidify" in the vertical axis), and those dynamic all-extremes call forth the balancing, mediating factors of the secondary dyad water:air. The interaction of these elements gives rise to the whole of the organic processes. At the most direct, least mediated contact point between fire and ice, primal iron is forged in the cosmic crucible, and its primary and most purely "elemental" synthesis of fire:ice interacts like a lightning bolt with the latent organic mixture of yeast/salt/venom within the matrix of fire:ice/water:air. This spark of life first quickens the yeast, causing the organic birth process to be set in motion. This is eternally maintained by the salt of life, which holds the process together. However, the latent venom ensures the continued dynamism and evolutionary nature of the process because it is continually dissolving life so that it may be reshaped in ever more complex forms by consciousness. Here we see the origins of the material aspects of the "high-holy-three" (trifidictruine dyad)—birth-life-death to rebirth (as in figure 10.5).

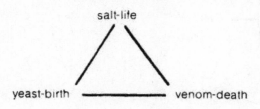

Figure 10.5. Elemental cycle of becoming.

All of these factors go into the formation and quickening of the center of the horizontal plane, the middle of the *gap* where all conditions are ideal for ultimate development and reproduction of the whole—the *earth*. This is also the center point of the numinous vertical axis of the world, which completes its potential for the realization of the whole.

These seem only to constitute a first level of runic elemental wisdom. Actually, the elemental factors could probably be multiplied and refined more and more (as they have been by the physical sciences) to construct a veritable "periodic table" of runic elements. The roots of such a system are shown in figure 10.6.

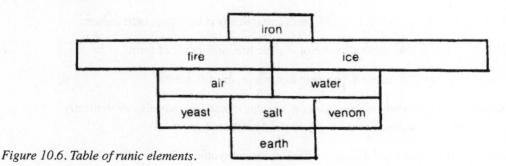

Figure 10.6. Table of runic elements.

THE BIG BOOK OF RUNES AND RUNE MAGIC

The employment of "elemental thinking" in the development of a true philosophy—which takes into account not only consciousness but also the natural world and the building of symbolic and psychological bridges between the two—is of invaluable aid. This is because the conscious analysis, categorization, and experience of readily apparent physical phenomena leads to an internalization process with regard to the environment, so that nature can indeed become a loremaster in a living way and the path toward the whole will become clearer.

Yggdrasill

Once the gods have shaped the cosmos from the primal substance according to its pattern and set the whole in motion, so that it becomes a living, organic, evolving thing, the whole is viewed as a cosmic tree—Yggdrasill. The descriptions of the world structure given in the Eddas does not always provide a totally consistent picture, but we do not expect one in a multiversal system. The enigma and mystery housed in metaphors show us that these are observations of the travelers in the supraconscious, the true shamans, and not the dogmatic constructs of rationalistic philosophers. However, at present we have need and use for these schematizations to help us unwrap some of the enigma enshrouding the cosmos. Therefore, we must now explore the esoteric analytically before delving into the uncharted waters of Niflheimr. The approximations of such schemata must always be borne in mind.

From the *Prose Edda* and our knowledge of the nine worlds of Yggdrasill, we can build a primary structure of the cosmos. But in and around these worlds (ON *heimar*; sg., *heimr*) there are many dwellings, and the Eddas speak of them in many passages.

We know that Midhgardhr (the manifested "material" world) is in the *middle* of Ginnungagap; that is, it is not, as some occult philosophies would have us believe, at the bottom of the universe. To the north is Niflheimr, to the south, Muspellsheimr; to the east lies Jötunheimr (Etin-World), and to the west is Vanaheimr (Vanir-World). Along a central (but omnipresent) axis—the Irminsûl—running through the center of Midhgardhr, the realms "above" and "below" Midhgardhr are arranged. It must be remembered that these directions are symbolic of eternal and omnipresent mysteries. Below Midhgardhr is Svartálfheimr (Black-Elf [= dwarf]-World), and below that is Hel (= enclosure of death, the hidden place, the stead of stillness). Above Midhgardhr is Ljóssálfheimr (Light-Elf-World, or simply Elf-World), and above that is Asgardhr itself (the enclosure of the Aesir). These nine worlds are thus arranged along the plan of Yggdrasill and the three-dimensional snowflake pattern. Figure 10.7 gives a detailed description of the mysteries of Yggdrasill. This pattern consists of a horizontal plane, described by Muspellsheimr-Niflheimr-Vanaheimr-Jötunheimr-Midhgardhr, and a vertical axis described by Midhgardhr-Ljóssálfheimr-Svartálfheimr-Asgardhr-Hel.

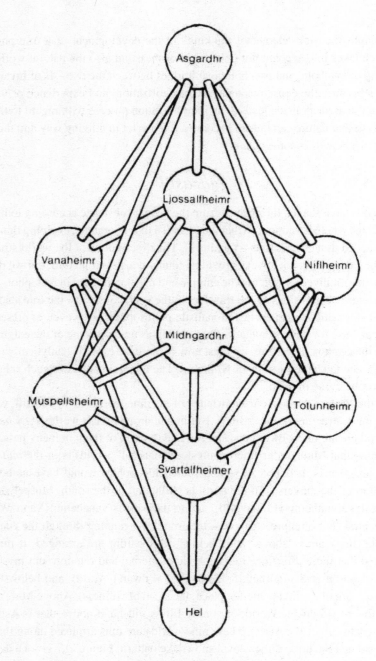

Figure 10.7. Yggdrasill.

⊠   THE BIG BOOK OF RUNES AND RUNE MAGIC

Actually, the center plane should be tilted in the imagination so that Niflheimr is on the nether-edge and Muspellsheimr is on the higher one. We know that this is an old conception because linguistic evidence shows that the root word from which "north" is derived (*ner-*) originally meant "under." Above Midhgardhr is the realm of light—"the heavens"; below is the world of darkness—"the nether world." And the Irminsūl, the cosmic pillar of Yggdrasill, connects them all. M. Eliade's book, *Myth of the Eternal Return*, speaks most eloquently of this mystery. The vertical column or axis defines the psychocosmic bisection between the conscious and unconscious, between light and dark, just as the horizontal plane defines the bisection between the expansive, electric energies of fire and the constrictive, magnetic energies of ice. The horizontal is energy and the plane in which "physical" energy is found; the vertical is the psychic pattern of consciousness and being. All meet in potential harmony in Midhgardhr. This potential can be activated by the runer.

Asgardhr	Realm of consciousness that is in and of itself complex, with many enclosures and halls within it, among them Valhöll (Walhalla), Hall of the Fallen. The abode of the fetch, and the house of the spirit (ON *önd*).
Ljóssálfheimr	Broad expanses of light (which also contain other subplanes). The abode of mind and memory—the intellect.
Midhgardhr	Middle-Earth. In the Cosmos this is material manifestation—*earth*. In the makeup of man this is the body, but also the all-potential of the self. In Midgardhr all the worlds meet.
Svartálfheimr	Abode of the *hamr* (shape or hide). A "subterranean" world of darkness where shapes are forged. Realm of the emotions.
Hel	Realm of the instincts. Abode of stillness and inertia—unconsciousness. The final resting place of the soul of the non-Erulian.
Niflheimr	Realm of mist becoming ice, abode of contraction and magnetism. The force of antimatter, a point constantly pulling in on itself, like a "black hole."
Muspellsheimr	Realm of fiery sparks, abode of expansion and electricity. The force of pure energy constantly expanding away from itself.
Vanaheimr	Realm of organic patterning and coalescence—water. Abode of forces in fruitful and static balance.
Jötunheimr	A realm in constant motion, seeking to oppose and give resistance to whatever it meets. Force of dissolution and deception. Reactive power of destruction (necessary to evolutionary change).

Table 10.2. Keys to the worlds of Yggdrasill.

It will be noted that between these nine worlds there are *twenty-four* pathways. This has two meanings. It indicates that the mystery of twenty-four helps shape and hold the entire cosmos together (as it formulates the structure of the runic system itself), and on a certain level it indicates that runestaves could be ascribed to the various roads as keys to unlock conscious access to them. Experience has shown that there may be no objective one-to-one correspondence between a runestave and a roadway, although speculative exercises in this direction have always proved meaningful. The universal truth seems to be that the structure of Yggdrasill and that of the runic system are shaped by the same twenty-four-fold force and that each pathway contains an entire potential futhark within it. In the ebb and flow of energies within the system one rune may dominate a certain roadway, but that does not mean other runes are not to be found there. As is usual with the runes, much is dependent on the state of being of the runer—the observer of the mysteries.

As far as analyzing the essences of the worlds is concerned, table 10.2 on page 127 provides the fundamental esoteric lore necessary to the runic comprehension of the realms of Yggdrasill.

These worlds and enclosures interact with one another in a cosmic ecology of energy and essence. The eight realms outside Midhgardhr each oppose and balance a counter realm: Asgardhr balances Hel, Ljóssálfheimr balances Svartálfheimr, Muspellsheimr (fire) counters Niflheimr (ice), and Vanaheimr counters Jötunheimr. The "material world," Midhgardhr, stands in the midst of all—the realm of all-potential. From it the runer can reach out in all directions and ascend to the realms above or ride down to the worlds below. However, it should be noted that there is a special relationship between Asgardhr, Midhgardhr, and Hel, which are properly called "the three realms"—heavenly, earthly, and chthonic. There is a similar bond among those six realms properly called *heimar*, which "surround" Midhgardhr. Access to realms beyond these six into the outermost two is difficult, to say the least.

Collectively, the pathways between the worlds are known as Bifröst, the Rainbow Bridge. The structure is a model of the world, but it is also the pattern of the "world within"—the microcosm of man, if you will. This is made abundantly clear in the skaldic language of the north in which humans are often paraphrased in terms of trees; for example, a warrior will be called "the oak of battle." These "kennings" are derived from the mythic fact that humans were "shaped" from trees (i.e., already living, organic substance) by the triad of divine consciousness. (Compare this to other mythologies in which humans are fashioned from inert matter.) In the Yggdrasill pattern we have the ancient Germanic (and perhaps even Indo-European) model of the subjective universe and a model for its linkages to the objective universe. Here continues to be hidden a rune of great power.

Chapter 11

RUNIC NUMEROLOGY

If one has access to the voluminous scholarly works on rune magic, one is at once struck by the abundance of numerological interpretations. Underlying these studies seems to be the assumption that mere numerical patterns (real or imagined) are enough to indicate the "magical" nature of an inscription. The weakness of these works lies in the fact that the authors never tell us *how* these patterns are magically effective, nor do they tell us much of the indigenous Germanic number lore that would be necessary to understand these inscriptions in this way. From a purely historical point of view, it even seems doubtful that runes were ever used as numerals at all. No clear example of such usage exists, and when numbers are expressed in the inscriptions, they are always spelled out in words. (This is not to say that there was no sacred or magical tradition of number lore that was a thing altogether separate from the use of "profane" numbers.) The runo-numerological scholars believe that the runemasters of old used both rune counts (counting the total number of staves in an inscription, line, or phrase; e.g.,: ᚠᛏᚢ := 3) or rune totals (counting the total of the numerical values assigned to the staves by virtue of their positions in the row; e.g.,: ᚠᛏᚢ := 4 + 21 + 2 = 27).

The question arises: are these practices legitimate in view of the general lack of historical evidence for them? The answer is yes on two grounds: (1) the historical evidence generally has been handled badly, and the scientific case (especially for rune counts) needs to be kept open; and (2) in the spirit of living innovation consistently expressed by the elder runemasters, we new runers should feel free to incorporate and develop tally lore in our system regardless of its historical position. It is not our aim merely to copy older practices but rather to extend them in ways harmonious with the tradition. Our treatment of runic numerology, or tally lore, is informed by deep knowledge of the uniquely Germanic number lore (usually ignored by earlier scholars in favor of foreign systems) and by the spirit of intuitive innovation.

Tally Lore

Numerical patterning makes an inscription more effective in the realms corresponding to those indicated by the key number. This is simply a part of the laws of systemic empathy necessary to magical working in general. The willed act of consciously shaping operative communications on ever more subtle levels has a powerful intrinsic effect for magical work. In other words, for a magical working to be effective it must be in a form—a code if you will—that the object of the working will be able to "understand" and respond to. Numerical pattern is a subtle level of this encoding process. This is one of the more obscure parts of the answer to the Odian question "Knowest how to carve?"

On the other hand, there is an important passive side to this active aspect. One must also be able to answer the question "Knowest how to read?" That is, the runer must be able to understand the runes when they are presented to him—to the mind's eye, as well as to the body's eye. Therefore, skill at tally lore is also a tool for subtle, illuminative magical work (runecasting).

One thing that has always kept rune tally lore from becoming fully effective has been the general effort to try to make it fit into Mediterranean numerology as practiced by the Greeks, Hebrews, and others. Although the Germanic number system is similar to that used by the Greeks (both being ultimately derived from Indo-European), there is an important shift of emphasis from two to three and its multiples that results in a quasi-duodecimal system for the Germanic peoples. This is why we have "eleven" and "twelve" and not, as we would expect, something like "onteen" and "twenteen." There is an underlying system with an emphasis on twelve and its multiples in the ancient Germanic number system, one that also underlies the tally lore of the runes. When an ancient Saxon in England heard *hundred*, he thought of, in our terms, 120 "things"—*teontig* (ten-ty = 100), *endleofantig*, (eleven-ty = 110), and so on. This latter term even survives in some southern American dialects as "elebenty."

That number values were in some measure a part of the ancient runic tradition is obvious from the nature of the systems of runic codes (see chapter 7). The runic system, as discussed in chapter 9, and the whole of runic cosmology have a strong numerical basis. Within the runic system certain key numbers stand out. Three and its multiples are obvious—the three airts (aettir) of the runestave, for example. Three is an essential cosmic binding number on the vertical numinous axis, a formula that connects what is "above" and "below" with the here and now. Three and all of its multiples contain this root value.

Four and eight have a similar effect on the horizontal plane of nature. The symbolism of these number groups is already clear when one looks at the airt arrangement of the runestaves.

In a spherical and multidimensional sense, the numbers twelve and thirteen are of central importance (see chapter 10). These are at the core of the runic system, and each contains a unique and distinct mystery. In other words, thirteen is not merely twelve plus one. The essence of thirteen is something independent of twelve (this is the central "breaking point" in both the runic system and in the Germanic number system).

The ultimate number of wholeness is twenty-four. It contains a sense of entirety, although it is also subject to significant multiplications. In this regard, the formula 24 x 3 = 72 seems to be of particular import. This value of wholeness for twenty-four was even retained once the system had been reformed. One of the greatest testaments to this fact is the mysterious "twenty-four things" on which runes are to be carved in Sigrdrífa's instructions to Sigurdhr (see the "Sigrdrífumál" in the *Poetic Edda*).

Essentially, there are four systemic key numbers: thirteen, sixteen, eighteen, and twenty-four. Each expresses an aspect of totality. In addition, all prime numbers—those that are independent, free, and isolated unto themselves—express an aspect of the magical will of the runer.

Nordic Number Lore

To some extent the runic tables of interpretation[1] reveal a good deal of lore concerning the meanings of number and numerical relationships among the runes. However, as a detailed reading of the oldest texts of Germanic lore shows, there are certain specific powers of characteristics of numbers that the aspiring runer should know. These characteristics are quite often different from those of Mediterranean numerology.

One (1) is the number of beginnings of root causes and solitary force. It is rare in operative runecraft and in mythological references.

Two (2) is the number of cooperation of the redoubled working of tandem forces. In operative work it is sometimes used to strengthen, especially physically. In mythological lore it shows the power of teamwork between complementary pairs: Huginn/ Muninn, Geri/Freki (Odin's wolves), Árvakr/Alsvidhr (team of horses that pulls the Sun's wain), or the divine tandem Odin /Loki.

Three (3) is a "holy number" that is vastly represented in lore. It indicates a complete functioning process *process* and is the root force of dynamism. In runecraft, three is used to complete and to quicken things—to move things to action. In the mythic lore threes abound; for example, Urdhr-Verdhandi-Skuld, Odin-Vili-Vé, the three "roots" of Yggdrasill, and the three containers of the poetic mead, Ódhrœrir -Són- Bodhn.

Four (4) is a number of stasis, of solidity and waiting. It contains power, and this is one of its chief operative uses. In myth we learn of the four harts that chew the leaves of Yggdrasill and of four dwarves Nordhri-Austri-Sudhr-Vestri at the four cardinal directions.

Five (5) is the number of ordered time and space. The ancient Germanic week was five nights long—called in Old Norse a *fimmt*—which was also the interval of time one had to respond to a legal summons. It is rarely found in mythological lore, but for operative purposes it is a powerful invocatory formula.

Six (6) is the number of vibrant life and strength. This can be used to create or destroy. It is rarely found in mythic contexts.

Seven (7) is the number of death and passive contact with the "other worlds." A seven-night interval (ON *sjaund*) is traditional between death and the performance of funeral rites. Not often seen in mythology. Some mythic occurrences seem to have been influenced by astrological lore.

Eight (8) is the number of complete manifestation of wholeness and perfect symmetry. Its chief significance can be found in the eightfold division of the heavens (see chapter 6). It is the number of spatial ordering. Eight is abundant in mytho-magical lore, mainly as a way to list things, for example, the eight woes and their remedies. ("Hávamál," 137), the eight runic operations ("Hávamál," 144), and the eight "best things" ("Grímnismál," 45). All of these texts are to be found in the *Poetic Edda*.

Nine (9) is the "holiest of numbers" and the root of psycho-cosmic powers. It lends its force to any purpose. It is the number of life eternal and death unending. Nine transforms what it touches, yet it remains eternal within itself. Its use abounds in myth and magic. Just to name a few of many examples of the use of nine: nine are the worlds of Yggdrasill, nine are the nights Odin hangs upon it and is thereafter taught nine mighty songs, nine is the number in which the *valkyjur* often appear to the Erulian.

The two main ways in which runes may be manipulated as numbers are outlined in an operative context in *Futhark* (especially on pp. 102–104). These two methods involve computing the rune count (by adding the number of runestaves) and the rune total (by adding the numerical values of each of the runestaves). For example, one side of a famous and complex runic formula from around 500 C.E. (the Lindholm amulet) may be seen in figure 11.1.

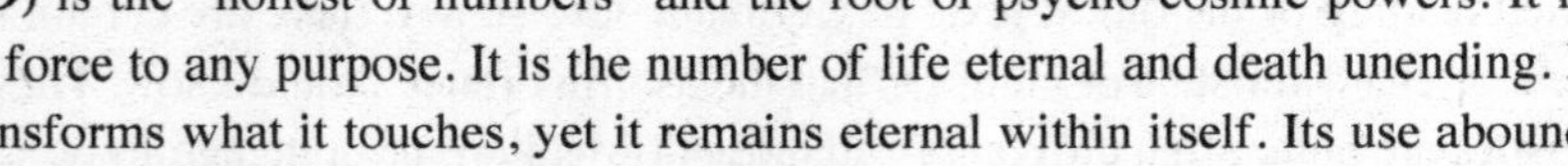

Figure 11.1. Side B of the Lindholm amulet.

The rune count usually indicates the realm in which the formula is to work, and the rune total shows the subtle aim or final willed outcome of the formula. These two numbers are further analyzed by adding their digits to come up with a "tally" key number (reduced to a number between one and twenty-four) and by finding multiple values to arrive at "multiple" key numbers. These numbers refine the values already demonstrated by the rune count and total, and show the "magical instruments" by which they work. For example, an analytical table for side B of the Lindholm amulet appears in table 11.1.

By using these subtle ways to "read the runes aright," we see that in the most esoteric terms the inscription in figure 11.1 expresses the pure ordered (5) will of an Erulian vitki (47) working with craft (6) within the whole objective universe (24) toward manifestation (10).

To conclude this chapter on number we must speak to the most mysterious example of numerical symbolism in Germanic literature: stanza 24 of the "Grímnismál" in the *Poetic Edda*, which reads:

> Five hundred doors
> and forty withall,
> I know to be in Valhöll:
> eight hundred lone-warriors [ON *einherjar*]
> go through a lone door
> when they fare forth to fight the wolf [= Fenrir].

Many scholars and mystics alike have been struck by this stanza. On one level the numerical analysis would seem to be 540 x 800 = 432,000—which just happens to be the number of years in the Kali Yuga in the scheme of Hindu cosmology. This has led historians to conclude that there may have been a good deal of borrowing of ideas from Indo-Iranian culture in the North, or that we are faced with an example of ancient Indo-European lore common to both cultures from prehistoric times.

Rune count	24	realm of working
tally key	6	
multiple key	4 x 6	way it works in realm
Rune total	235	aim of working
tally key	10	
multiple key	5 x 47	way it reaches its aim

Table 11.1. Numerical analysis of Lindholm amulet (B).

However, from an indigenous point of view, it must be remembered that when a Norseman said "one hundred" he had in mind 120 in our terms—therefore the formula from the "Gríminismál" would appear:

five hundred (= 600) and forty (40) = 640 (= 16 x 40)

eight hundred (= 960) (= 24 x 40)

and the multiplication of the two numbers would result in 614,400 (= 40 x 15,360). That two systemic key numbers (16 and 24) are present, and that there is an apparent instance of intentional multiples of forty, all seem to point to an independent and internally coherent Germanic number symbology. The final unlocking of this mystery is yet to come.

Chapter 12

RUNIC PSYCHOLOGY

The lore of the soul—psychology—is a complex but fundamental aspect of runic (esoteric) studies. The ancient Germanic peoples possessed a soul-lore as intricate and precise as any in history and far more complex than what we commonly have today. Much of this wondrous world can be recovered through the study of the words the ancients used to describe various soul conceptions and psychophysical processes. It is easy to see that when a group has a highly specialized or technical vocabulary in a given field it is because (1) they understand its intimate workings and need terms to distinguish various aspects of which they have knowledge, and (2) it is an area of life to which they attach a high level of importance. Besides the "souls," another idea that dominates Germanic thought is that of "fate"—wyrd. It cannot be fully understood apart from the lore of souls, and it helps to explain exactly *how* these souls are at work within us.

Forms of the Soul

It is somewhat of a misconception to separate a discussion of the "soul" from the "body" in runelore. They are intimately tied together, but, paradoxically, they may be consciously divided from one another through runework. Without such work this would naturally happen only at death. When speaking of the "whole person," it is perhaps most accurate to use the somewhat cumbersome terms psychophysical or psychosomatic (soul/body) complex. In any event, the soul is made up of various aspects—essences and/or substances that may lie more or less dormant in some individuals but in the runer are awakened to vital existence. It is hardly a wonder that once a people loses the terminology for an experience it soon fades from memory. Runelore and runework reawaken that memory.

Because the Norse were the last of the Germanic peoples to be "converted" to Christianity and because in Iceland the early phase of the conversion was of a tolerant nature, the Norse language and lore preserve intact the most complete runic psychology.

It is on this lore that the following analysis is based. However, it appears most likely that all of the other Germanic peoples—Anglo-Saxons (English), Germans, Goths, and so on—had equivalent systems.

There are nine psychological constructs (each more or less complex) that go to make up the "whole man."

1.   The physical vehicle is made up of several elements. The body itself (ON *lík*) is a complex of various substances (ON *efni*) such as "appearance" (a special ON term *lá* that may refer to the hair; also ON *sjón*, see *hamingja* below), movement (ON *laeti*), health or good complexion (ON *litr*). These are the original gifts of the god Lódhurr. The "substances" of the body are gateways to other aspects of the self, and they are the ultimate receptacles of magical work. Therefore, certain subtle substances in the body become focal points for the development of the self or the person of whole consciousness, aware of all aspects in an exalted ego state.

2.   The "shape-substance" (ON *hamr*) is closely associated with the "body." It gives the plastic foundation or subtle matrix to physical reality. However, it can be brought under the control of the will (in the mind; ON *hugr*) and cause first subtle, then more substantial forms to take shape in accordance with the will. This is the power of imagination. Taken to its extreme forms it can cause "materializations" of imaginary beings (natural or non-natural) into which the consciousness can be projected. Old Norse literature is full of such descriptions. Most typically, the vitki lies as if asleep or dead, and in another location he is able to materialize an animal shape in which he can fight or stalk his enemy. If this shape is injured, the vitki will receive the wounds as well.

3.   The faculty of ecstasy (ON *ódhr*) is the gift of the god Hoenir. This is as much an experience, a state of mind, as anything else. It is the faculty—emotionally almost physically experienced—of rising up and out of the normal state of consciousness into a high level of energy and enthusiasm. *Ódhr* is the same root present in the name Odin, and it is by this power that magical force is manipulated. This is the active agent directed by the will. It is this power over which Odin rules.

4.   Closely linked with the ecstatic faculty is the vital breath (ON *önd*), which is the gift of Odin. (It must be remembered that the triad Odin-Hoenir-Lódhurr actually represents a triform Odin.) The *önd* is the "divine spark," the all-pervasive vital energy on which all life is based and which is the foundation of all runework. The concept is similar to the Indian *prāna*, and even the word itself is related to Sanskrit *ātman* (spirit, self). It is the bridge to higher levels of being.

5. The "mind" (ON *hugr*) is a complex entity indeed. It is actually made up of three faculties: (1) volition, (2) perception, and (3) cognition. This is the seat of the will, and as such it has the power to assimilate other aspects of the psychophysical complex to itself. This is why the term *hugr* is often used in Old Norse literature when other aspects might have been expected. It seems to "take over" the personalities of advanced runers because their evolution comes more and more under conscious control. By this faculty, persons do analytical thinking of a conscious sort. It is synonymous with the left brain functions.

6. Intimately linked to the "mind" is the "memory" (ON *minni*). These are the two psychic aspects represented by Odin's ravens: Huginn and Muninn (Mind and Memory). This faculty is indeed memory, but it is much more than what we commonly associate with this term. It is more than the simple recall of past events; it is the storehouse of all mysteries, the great rune-hoard. This is why, in the "Gríminismál" (st. 20), Odin says of the relative values of Huginn and Muninn:

> The whole earth over,
> every day
> hover Huginn and Muninn;
> I dread lest Huginn
> droop in his flight,
> yet I fear me still more for Muninn.

A coordination of the mind and the memory faculties is what gives "intelligence." The mind processes external stimuli (including that received from memory), whereas memory (*minni*) reflects on its own infinite material. *Minni* is analogous to the right brain.

7. The "soul" (ON *sál*) usually comes into play only after death. This is the shade—a subtle body in which the psychic aspects (or some of them) are focused after the death of the physical aspects. In life this is the part of the psyche that passively receives the record of one's actions and remains the negative space into which one evolves. It is analogous to Jung's "shadow" concept of the unmanifested aspects of the psyche, discussed in the next section.

8. The "fetch" (ON *fylgja*) is in many respects the bright side of the shade. In men the fetch is seen as female, and in women it is male. Actually, there are three fetches, or "following spirits": in human form, in animal form, and in geometrical form. Each image has its own function. The one in human form is attached for the duration of life and can be passed on from generation to generation, either along genetic lines or according to willed projection. The animal-shaped fetch is usually in a form that corresponds to the character of the person to whom it is attached—a wolf, an eagle, a horse, a fox, a

mouse, and so on. It can be separated from the vitki as a magical act. The vitki also may project his conscious will into the fetch in order to carry out magical workings. A geometrical shape is often seen by those with "second sight" going out *in front of* persons of great power. The *fylgja* is the repository of all of the actions of the persons to whom the entity was previously attached. It can be the source of great power but also of tremendous responsibilities and even hardships. This entity is the storehouse of *ørlög*—it can protect and it can doom. The fetch is closely related to, and in some cases identical to, the *valkyrja* or *dís* entity.

9.   The "luck" (ON *hamingja*) of a person is extremely complex and, in many ways, closely linked to the fetch. *Hamingja*, which is linguistically derived from *hamr* (i.e., *ham-gengja*, one who can go about in another shape) is essentially a *power concept* analogous to Polynesian *mana*, Iroquois *orenda*, and so on. It too has some anthropomorphic symbols and is conceived of as (1) "luck" (personal power), (2) guardian spirit (symbolically derived from that luck), and (3) shape-shifting ability (which is its original meaning). A wide variety of consciously willed actions develop this magical power. It can be transferred from one person to another (although its effects are only temporary unless it is attached to the fetch-wife). The *hamingja* is the collective might and main of the individual. It is fed by and feeds the fetch-wife with power so that during a man's lifetime we can speak of a *hamingja-fylgja* complex that works in harmony.

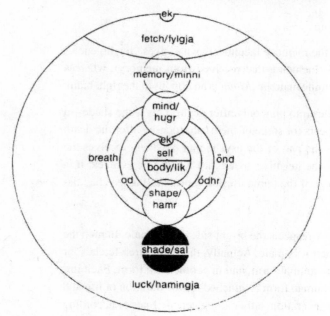

A schematic representation of the psychophysical complex (figure 12.1) perhaps gives a clearer image of just how these various concepts relate to and interact with one another. However, since the reality of this model, like that of Yggdrasill (figure 10.7 on page 126) is actually multi- or extradimensional, a two- or even three-dimensional model is somewhat inadequate.

Other structures that appear in the figure include the *ego*, or

Figure 12.1. Germanic structure of the psychophysical complex.

THE BIG BOOK OF RUNES AND RUNE MAGIC

"I" concept and the magical "ego" (or *persona*). The "I" (ON *ek*) is linked to, or identical with, the name or names of the individual. On the Odinic path the runer—as he or she develops stronger links with the fetch and strengthens the powers of the other psychic aspects—forms magical "I" concepts allied with the fetch. These alternate personae are usually of the same gender as the "natural body." Each of the personae has a name and can be evoked with the right formula. It is in these self-shaped magical forms that the runer carries out runeworkings. The magical personae can be quite numerous, but each embodies a part of the whole psychophysical complex; each is a hyper-aware entity. Ultimately, it is in these concepts that the essence of Odianism is to be understood. This also gives a key to the understanding of Germanic heroic mythology, and each of the runestaves speak to at least one aspect of this realm.

Runic and Jungian Psychology

The only modern theoretical psychological structure that comes close to encompassing the power of the ancient Germanic practical soul-lore is that developed by the Swiss psychiatrist C. G. Jung. Jung's psychology has been the subject of "occult" investigations before, but the Germanic system seems unusually well suited to his structure because it is particularly understandable in Jungian terms. Jung himself devoted some space to the Wotan archetype in an article in which he compared the half-forgotten archetype to a dry riverbed that awaited only the release of the waters of life to renew it, along its old patterns.[1] So too it is with concepts of the soul. As a culture, we have been impoverished with regard to the soul—cut off from our ancestral ideas about it (or them)—and given only hazy, often contradictory doctrines as replacements. The time has now come that the waters of life be restored to their ancestral beds, and the souls will again come alive.

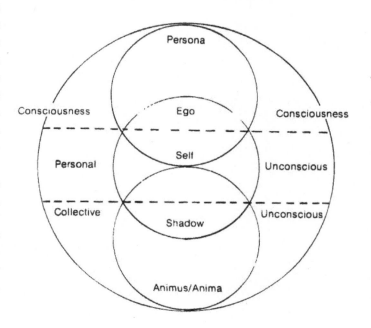

Figure 12.2. Jungian structure of the soul.

Jung's psychological scheme is characterized by certain structures, as figure 12.2 indicates. Jung's scheme, of course, lacks the overtly magical (practical) functions of the *hamingja-fylgja*, but their reflections remain in the process of the "alchemical marriage" between the animus and anima (the masculine and feminine sides of the soul). It is in the common process of a union between contrasexual aspects of the soul that the two systems are most alike on a practical level. Also, Jungian techniques designed to activate the "transcendent function" are of benefit in any effort to gain access to the fetch-wife or fetch of today.

In addition, the shadow bears a close resemblance to the "shade" function of the soul. Even gods have their shadows, for this is what Loki is to Odin. Perhaps the most prominent feature of Jungian psychology is the structure of the collective unconscious. This comes as close as anything—perhaps with the addition of theories concerning the bihemispherical brain—to defining the true nature of *minni* and the mysteries taught by the raven Muninn.

THE BIG BOOK OF RUNES AND RUNE MAGIC

Chapter 13

RUNELORE OF THE GODS

(ESOTERIC THEOLOGY)

Runelore is dominated by the figure of Odin. It is the path exemplified by him that the runer seeks to travel. However, as Odin has shown, other gods are also essential for the healthy workings of the cosmological, sociological, and psychological orders. We know—from a tale told by the monk Saxo Grammaticus in Book I of his *History of the Danes*—that it is the will of Odin to preserve and to promote the whole structure of the gods—the entire pantheon. In this tale, we read that Odin left his kingdom, and his place was taken by one called Mitódhinn. The name Mitódhinn may mean either "the one beside Odin" (Mit-Odin), or "the one who measures out" (Mitódh-in), related to an Old English word for "god," Meotod. In either case, it appears to be a name for Tyr. Mitódhinn tried to institute a separate cult for each of the gods. When Odin returned, he overthrew Mitódhinn and restored the common cult in which sacrifices were made (three times a year) to all of the gods and goddesses of the pantheon together. Mitódhinn's plan would certainly have led to fragmentation of the society, whereas Odin's restoration was aimed at maintaining a cohesive whole. As we will see, those two tendencies are what we should expect of Odin and Tyr.

Before delving into the Odinic archetype we should, being true to the Odian path, delineate the structure of the whole of the Germanic pantheon from a runic or esoteric viewpoint. In the twentieth century two investigators, working from two different perspectives, have again provided keys with which to unlock the ways the divinities relate to each other. C. G. Jung, with his theory of archetypes within the collective unconscious (see chapter 12), has given a workable basis on which to understand the linkage between the human psyche and the gods and goddesses of our ancestors. Georges Dumézil, a French historian of religion and an Indo-Europeanist, has added the key to the structure of the pantheon.[1]

The gods and goddesses have both subjective (i.e., *within* the psyche of the individual) reality and multiversal objective (i.e., *outside* the psyche of the individual) realities. These objective realities are essentially three: (1) within the national group (an inherited "metagenetic" divine pattern), (2) within the species *homo sapiens*, and (3) independent of humanity. Not all gods partake of all three objective realities. The first reality is the strongest objective link man can have with the divine. This metagenetic link is most powerful within close national/linguistic relationships, that is, ones that correspond to one's heritage (although all native English speakers will have absorbed a good deal of that nation's indigenous structures regardless of ethnic heritage). But "mega-nations" or linguistic groupings (e.g., Indo European, Semitic, Sino-Tibetan) will have significant impact as well. Only Odin, as the shaper of humanity, is independent of it.

What is a god or goddess? In runic terms a god is a living entity with some sort of existence independent of the individual psyche, although most gods may have had their ultimate origin there. It may be incorporated anywhere within the psychophysical complex; that is, it may have its origin in an instinctual, emotional, physical, mental, or spiritual pattern. A god, as most first perceive it, is a subtle tendency within the self, which then can be fed with psychic energy by means of myth, ritual, runework, and the like. The anthropomorphic shape of a god is a symbol. This is the simplest way for most people to grasp entities that have certain roles and complex interrelationships. The anthropomorphic symbol is not altogether arbitrary because the gods are essentially creatures of the great force of consciousness given by the All-Father to *mankind* alone. A part of the god is housed within the *minni* of an individual and is inherited metagenetically from the ancestors.

In the final analysis, there are as many conceptions of the divine as there are individuals. No two persons comprehend a deity or theology in exactly the same way, yet there are innate tendencies that are determined by living metagenetic forms. Of course, another method, used by the prophets of revealed religion, is that of dogma and coercion.

For the individual who may wish to understand the inner or outer reality of a god or goddess, a process of learning about the inner form and of linking that inner form with its external counterpart must be developed. This is a form of communication with the divinity and is a chief concern of religion. The task of the Odian runer goes somewhat beyond this, as we shall see.

The Great Gods of Aesir

The various Germanic divinities relate to one another in a way that is profound, archaic, and of great potency in the understanding of deep-level runelore. Table 13.1 on page 143 shows, in abbreviated form, the most important structural aspects of the oldest form of the Germanic pantheon. It amounts to a social structure of the pantheon and is essentially the Dumézilian restoration with additional runic insights.[2] On the other hand, the nonhuman elements of the multiverse extend beyond the realms of the Aesir and Vanir, and these worlds are represented in the pattern of Yggdrasill (refer to figure 10.7 on page 126).

Again, these relationships are to be found within individual psyches, within the national psyche of a people; they have their correspondences in the objective multiverse as well. To some extent these relationships give us the internal structure of the *minni* — the psychic "stuff' with which one is born. The dynamic interrelationships between these living inhabitants of this part of the psyche are the starting points for the great myths. Through various workings of a religious nature one may link the elements of one's own psyche with those in the objective world of the mythic tradition and become in-*formed* by them.

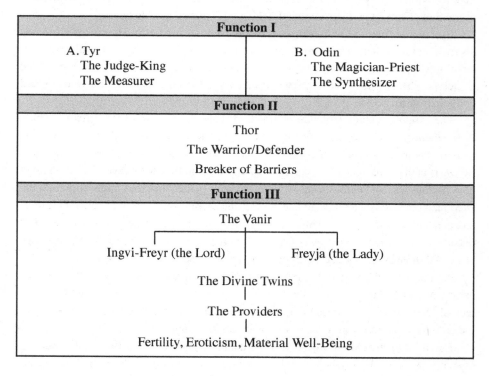

Table 13.1. Structure of the Germanic pantheon.

Odin

Although Odin will be discussed in depth throughout this chapter, here we will put this divinity in the context of the whole pantheon.

Odin is a god like no other. He is the Alfadhir—the All-Father. He is called this because he is the source of consciousness among the gods and mankind. His gift is the expanded human consciousness that allows the synthesizing self-concept to arise. It is for this reason that the active Odian does not so much seek to worship an external god-form of Odin as he does him-*Self* to embody and to develop the Self-concept and consciousness given by *the god*. Whereas other religious cults turn outward to the objective manifestation of the particular god, the cult of Odin turns inward and seeks a deification of the Self. The Odian does not worship his god—he becomes his god.

By his very nature Odin *synthesizes* everything around him. He makes all things his own and uses them according to his *will*, while remaining in an essential way apart from outside things. In the history of Germanic myth, this can be seen as the Odinic archetype absorbs the Týric aspect and takes upon itself aspects of the warrior and craftsman/farmer.

The essential Odinic structure is threefold. The oldest name of this tripartite entity is *Wōdhanaz-Wiljōn-Wīhaz* (ON Odin-Vili-Vé). The meanings of these names show us how this tripartite entity of consciousness works. *Wōdh-an-az* (master of inspiration [*wōdh-*]) is the expansive all-encompassing ecstatic and transformative force at the root of consciousness and enthusiasm. *Wil jōn* (the will) is the conscious application of a desired plan consciously arrived at, and *Wīhaz* (the sacred) is the spirit of separation in an independent sacred "space." This separation between consciousness and "nature" (that outside consciousness) must be effected before any transformations or "work" can take place. All three are necessary; all three should work together as a whole.

Although Odin is first and foremost the god of synthetic consciousness, this characteristic allowed him to assume the roles of the god of the dead, of poetry, and of intellectual crafts of all kinds (including runes). This latter aspect made him the favorite of the elite bands of innovative and aware warriors and kings.

Essential to the Odinic mystery is his manifold nature. He is the whole made up of many parts. In the mythology this is made clear not only by his tripartite appearances but also by his many "nicknames" (ON *heiti*). More than a hundred of these have been documented. A litany of a substantial number of them can be found in the "Grímnismál" (sts. 47–55). These range from names meaning Worker of Evil (ON *Bölverkr*) to Father of All (ON *Alfödhr*) and every quality in between. Perhaps one of the names sums up this quality—*Svipall* (the Changeable One), which indicates the ultimate transformational character of the god. This divine case of "multiple personalities" gives an indication as to why Odin is often misunderstood. Indeed, those who approach him from a non-Odian viewpoint will be disappointed, confused, or destroyed.

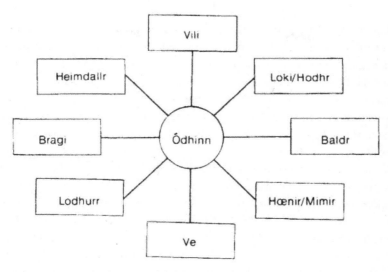

Figure 13.1. The eight great aspects of Odin.

If the *heiti* were not enough to confuse the non-initiate, the greater aspects (hypostases) have even confounded many experts. A hypostasis is an aspect of a god that seems to be an independent god-form but on closer investigation is shown to be a particularly well-developed functional aspect of it. Because of his many-sided character, Odin is especially subject to this mode of understanding. Figure 13.1 shows the eight great hypostases of Odin. Some of these are dual in nature.

Vili and Vé have been discussed and will be explained further in the "Odin: The Hidden God of the Runes" section below. The forms Lodhur and Hœnir are Odin's counterparts in the anthropogonic myth reported by Snorri in his *Prose Edda*. Hœnir also figures as a partner with another god named Mímir. When these two god-forms were given as hostages to the Vanir at the conclusion of the First War, Hoenir who was reputed to be wise, proved to be "empty-headed" unless advised by Mímir. This so angered the Vanir that they cut off Mímir's head and sent it back to the Aesir. Odin is said to preserve the head in order to learn hidden lore from it. At first glance this myth is baffling, especially when we see that Hoenir is otherwise depicted as a powerful intellectual force. In the "Völuspá" he gives Askr and Embla *ódhr*, and after Ragnarök he comes back as the chief diviner of the gods who can read the runestaves. But everything becomes clear when Hoenir/Mímir are understood as aspects of Odin. The fact that they never really act independently is one indication of this, but their *names* contain the key. Hoenir is derived from the same root as *hugr*, and Mímir is related to the same root as *minni*. Therefore, we have figures related to Odin in the same way as their zoomorphic counterparts Huginn and Muninn, the ravens of Odin. These are the cognitive and reflective functions of the god.

Bragi is the poetic aspect of the god and a name taken by an ancient skald who became identified with the elder god of poetry. Baldr is the young warrior aspect of Odin and also an aspect that relates to the initiation of the young warrior into the band of armed men. Heimdallr is the guardian aspect of Odin. He guards the Rainbow Bridge (Bifröst) against the coming of the rime-thurses, but he is also the aspect that continually communicates with mankind. It is Odin, in the form of Heimdallr and going by the nickname Rígr, that becomes the progenitor of human society. The mystery of Heimdallr is found in the M-rune.

The most puzzling hypostasis of all is that of Loki. In Loki, Odin contains the seed of his own destruction but also a necessary part of the process of his rebirth and transformation in the new age. Loki, as a name and as a separate entity, is a latecomer to the Germanic pantheon and is really found only in sources of Norse origin. But in most respects the characteristics of Loki correspond to the "darker" one of Odin as the sly, deceitful, perverse god. In a way, Loki is the objectified shadow-self of Odin. But he still works together with his "dark brother," and it is even said that they become "blood brothers" (see "Lokasenna," st. 9). Actually, they are of the same "blood."

Where Loki is most conspicuous is in his role connected to Ragnarök—the Judgment of the Gods. Once one realizes that the Ragnarök process is actually a model of transformation and that the central triadic figures of Odin-Baldr-Loki/ Hödhr can be understood as internal forces, the true meaning of the "dark brother" becomes clearer. The blind Hödhr (whose name means "warrior") is guided by the force of negation (Loki) to kill the Lord of Light, the bold Baldr (another name meaning "warrior"). Baldr is sent to the dark, still enclosure of Hel, informed by the greatest of secrets (runes) that Odin whispered into his ear as he was on the pyre before being sent Hel-ward. There he awaits Ragnarök to be reborn in the new age. Loki too is cast down and bound in the underworld as punishment for his murderous act. There he too awaits the "final conflict." This deed of the dark blood brother has set the process toward Ragnarök in motion. When the final hour comes, Odin, with his hosts of Valhöll and Asgardhr turn southward to face Loki and the forces of Hel and Muspellsheimr. The god of consciousness has turned to face his shadow-self. Heimdallr and Loki kill one another, and Odin is swallowed by the Fenris-Wolf (a son of Loki). In turn, Odin is avenged by his son Vídharr, who kills the Wolf by either splitting him open with a sword or ripping his jaws apart. Rune wisdom tells us that this means Odin too is "reborn," in a transformed state, into the new age. But in what form? He is Hoenir made whole, who will "handle the blood-twigs."

When viewed as a mythic paradigm of transformation, the Ragnarök process takes on meanings that are powerful and useful in runework, and it gives a deeper understanding of the function of Loki and of Odin's "dark side."

Before returning to Odin's meaning and might, we should explore the ways that the Odian views the other holy gods of the North.

Tyr

The essential mysteries of this god are embodied in the T-rune that is named after him. Tyr is the god of justice and of self-sacrifice for the good of society. This aspect is illustrated by the myth in which the gods capture the Fenris-Wolf by binding him with a fetter made of six things that indicate subtle mysteries, while Tyr holds his (right) hand in the jaws of the Wolf as a pledge of troth. When Fenrir finds he cannot escape, Tyr's hand is sacrificed to the jaws of the son of Loki (the Wolf). As a mythic figure, Tyr retreats into the realm of relative inactivity after this. However, in religious practice (especially that connected to *legal* matters) he remains a god of great importance. Tuesday is named after him. In German we have *Dienstag,* which is derived from an older form *Dings-tag*, day of the *thing* (legal assembly). So in one language we have the god; in the other we have the instruction over which he ruled.

As the overall structure of the psychocosmological aspects of the pantheon shows, ideally Tyr and Odin should work together in harmony as the left brain and right brain, respectively. In the process of shaping or creating anything, both forces are necessary. The Tyr aspect lays the plans, and the Odinic aspect puts the plans into action and makes them real. Tyr is the planner; Odin, the doer. The Germanic soul is essentially one of action and eternal motion. For this reason, the Odinic aspect was always at least slightly dominant in the pantheon; Odin is the high god and the All-Father. Odin's expansive transformational essence led to his aspect, largely synthesizing that of Tyr. Nowhere is this clearer than in the later legendary name of the North Star, Odin's Eye. The North Star is, of course, primarily identified with Tyr (see the T-rune), but in a sense Tyr becomes the all-seeing eye of Odin aloft on Hlidhskjálfr, the Gate-Tower. This is the eye that sees all over the worlds, whereas that which is pledged in Mímir's Well is the eye that sees "beneath" all the worlds, into their deepest secrets (runes).

The latent antagonism between Odin and Tyr is merely that which often occurs within systems composed of complementary aspects. An act of will is needed to cause them to work together harmoniously.

Thor

This god seems simple, yet he is complex. Great mysteries of Thor are contained in the TH-rune. Essentially, Thor is the ancient god of war. In later times, as Odin absorbed that function, he lost much of that attribute among men. Yet we note that he retains it among the gods themselves. He is their defender and the one who exercises his brute strength and power of his cosmic hammer, Mjöllnir, against the nonconscious or preconscious forces of Jötunheimr.

The Aesir—gods of ancestral consciousness and transformation—are faced with the forces of nonconsciousness and entropy pressing in from the east and south—out of Útgardhr. To oppose these forces the gods need a power very similar to that of the thurses and etins but loyal to them alone. This is Thor. Thor does little "thinking" for himself; he follows the orders given by the sovereign gods. Realistically speaking, there is, of course, superficial antagonism between the "Warrior" and the "Wizard" (see the "Harbardhsljódh" in the *Poetic Edda*), but ultimately the Warrior follows the guidance of the Wizard. The Wizard rules by wisdom; the Warrior rules by weapons. As long as Odin remains dominant, wisdom rules the weapon. It is Thor out of balance that leads to national catastrophe.

Freyja

Although the "theology" of runic practice is dominated by Odin as the great runemaster, another figure—Freyja—looms large in the practice of Germanic magic. She is even said to have taught Odin a form of magic known in Old Norse as *seidhr* (shamanistic trance-inducing methods). In many ways Freyja is the female counterpart of Odin. She is the magical archetype for women involved in magical pursuits, as Odin is for men. In her most basic aspects, Freyja is "the Lady" (this is the literal meaning of her name). Her companion is her brother/lover Freyr, "the Lord." However, it would be a large mistake, as we have already noted, to assume that Freyja is primarily a fertility goddess. Among the Vanir, it must be remembered, she is the one chiefly concerned with the numinous. In her very essence she embodies a profound relationship to the Odian pathways.

Like Odin, Freyja is known by many names. Some examples of these are Vanadís (the Goddess of the Vanir), Vanabrúdhr (Bride of the Vanir), Hörn (Mistress of Flax), Gefn (the Giver), Syr (the Sow—her solar aspect), Mardöll (the Sea-bright), and Gullveig (Gold-Greedy). These names tell us quite a bit about the range of Freyja's functions and her position. She is of great importance among the Vanir, perhaps in many places superior to her brother. She is indeed connected with prosperity and growth, and she gives her gifts (material and numinous) to humans. In her cosmic aspect she is connected to the sun (which is feminine in Germanic; see the S-rune) through her image as the "golden sow." The boar and sow are the animals of Freyr and Freyja, respectively. In Germany today, when the sun is very hot, they still say *Die gelbe Sau brennt* (The yellow sow is burning). The linkage with gold is made on many occasions, and on one level this is a further expression of Freyja's capacity as Vanic deity of prosperity and well-being. There is another level that is made clear in the mystery of *fehu*.

In the "Völuspá" we read how a certain sorceress named Gullveig came to the Aesir from the Vanir when those two groups of gods were at war. This is Freyja in another guise. We know this because, although Freyja is later found among the Aesir, she is *not* one of the Vanir (Freyr, Njördhr, and perhaps also Kvasir) who went over to the Aesir as hostages as a part of the truce between the two divine races.

Before we consider three of Freyja's myths in some detail, it might be well to remember how much of her lore is lost. At one time there was a vast body of mythic and cultic material connected with the goddess, but perhaps because of the erotic nature of her mysteries and myths they were especially singled out for eradication by the monkish missionaries to the north. Even in normally tolerant Iceland, her poetry—the *mansöngr* (love song)—was prohibited. And unfortunately, her cult could not recede into the protective confines of the chieftain's hall. But some of it was saved by the skald's art.

Heidh

During the First War—the war between the Aesir (first and second functions) and the (third function) Vanir—a sorceress named Gullveig came to the Aesir, into Odin's hall. The Aesir tried to kill her by piercing her with spears and burning her. But each time she was reborn. The third time she transformed herself from Gullveig into Heidh (the Shining One). This "thrice-born *völva* (seeress) is most probably Freyja, and it is in this form that she became Odin's teacher in the ways of *seidhr*. After her lore and her cult had been assimilated into that of Odin and of the Aesir, the lore of *seidhr* became an integral (but specialized) field within runelore (in the sense of esoteric studies).

Brisingamen

The necklace of the Brisings is much more than a pretty trinket. It is the all-encompassing fourfold cosmic ring, under the control of the great goddess Freyja. It is the magical equivalent of the Midhgardh Serpent that girdles the entire cosmos. *The Tale of Sörli* tells us how Freyja obtained this magical tool by spending a night with each of the four dwarves—the Brisings (descendants of the Shining Ones)—who forged the necklace. These four dwarves may be the same as Nordhri, Austri, Sudhri, and Vestri, who are stationed at the four cardinal directions of the world. It may have originally been that she had sexual relations with all four, simultaneously or over four nights. In any event, the result is the same: Freyja gains control over the fourfold cycle of the cosmos and its generative and regenerative powers. The object is said to be worn either as a belt or as a necklace, depending on how the goddess wished to use its power. At one point the mischievous god Loki stole the Brisinga-men from Freyja, and it was restored to her only after it had been recovered by the god Heimdallr. What is interesting here is that both Loki and Heimdallr are considered aspects (hypostases) of Odin—his dark and light sides, if you will.

Search for Ódhr

It is said that Freyja is married to a god named Ódhr, who is none other than Odin himself. The name Ódh-r simply indicates the force of ecstasy, of the magically inspired mind. To this, indeed, the goddess Freyja is wedded, and it too (as with Odin himself) is the chief aim of her strivings. As Ódhr wandered, so Freyja wandered after him, shedding tears of gold. Many have wanted to see in this mournful search a parallel with the search of Ishtar for Tammuz. However, the significance of this Sumerian/Akkadian myth and that of Freyja's search for Ódhr is quite different. Freyja's quest has nothing directly to do with fertility—she is seeking the "numinous inspiration" embodied in the god.

Each of these three myths indicates something of Freyja's primarily magical or numinous character. That fertility, wealth, well-being, and eroticism grow out of this character is perhaps secondary but nevertheless essential.

Another important fact about Freyja is that she receives one-half of all those slain in battle, according to her choice, to go to her otherworldly stronghold called Folkvangr (Field of the Warrior-band). The other half, of course, goes to Odin.

Like Odin, Freyja is a threefold divinity. She, as no other goddess is able to do, covers all three functions of the pantheon: (1) she is a magical figure, (2) she is a goddess of warriors, and (3) she is a Vanic deity with all the powers of that race of gods. She can bring things into being, can cause them to become, and can cause them to pass away toward new beginning. This magical power is at the root of her fertility function. Ultimately, the "marriage" between Freyja and Odin is a rather "modern" one. Freyja is *not* the "feminine side" of Odin (he carries that comfortably within himself—or in his "devilish" aspect, Loki); nor is Odin the "masculine side" of the Lady—she contains this as well. Perhaps Freyr even originally grew out of Freyja the way the masculine Njördhr grew out of the feminine Nerthus. In any case, we are dealing with two individuated deities drawn together by a common purpose. There are still a great many mysteries to be unraveled about this most powerful of goddesses.

Freyr

Of all the gods, the one most independent of Odin is Freyr, the God of This World (ON *veraldar godh*). Despite this independence, or perhaps because of it, there is little conflict between the Lord and Odin. In fact, it seems they *secretly* conspire with one another in many regards. Through runic investigation we find that besides Odin it is Freyr who is best represented in the ancient runelore. By this fact the runers of old acknowledge the importance of the Lord in the workings of the world.

Freyr is not the god's actual name but a title. This is not unusual. But in this case, we perhaps have the actual name of the god in the name of the NG-rune: *Ingwaz*. It is also possible that two gods are assimilated here, as the originally Aesiric Ing and the Vanic Freyr. The mysteries of the god are contained in the NG-rune. Yngvi is also a great progenitor of royal houses (especially in Sweden); the Ynglings are the greatest clan of the Sviar (Swedes).

Although Freyr is sometimes connected to the imagery of war, he is most often a figure of peace, prosperity, and pleasure. At Midsummer the Norse sacrificed to him for good harvest and peace (ON *til árs ok fridhar*). Another name of Freyr is perhaps Fró-dhi, who in the form of a legendary king ruled over a golden age of peace in the north called *Fródha fridhr* (Peace of *Fródhi*). Runically, this points us in the direction of *jera* (younger name, *ár*). Remember that for *ár* the "Old Norwegian Rune Rhyme" reads: "I say that Fródhi was generous." In Freyr, the Lord of the World, we see the force ruling over the organic processes that bind together the J- and NG-runes. The: ◇ : is the closed circle of the year, the cycle of gestation, and: ◈ : is the dynamic opening of the yearly cycle at harvest when the fruit is born forth.

Odin and Freyr work most harmoniously together in the *Völsunga Saga*. Yet this cooperation is largely hidden from the uninitiated eye. That Odin is the divine progenitor of the Völsungs and that he and his agents are responsible for the initiation of the members of this clan into the secrets of the gods is well known and obvious. But in his little-expressed warrior aspect Freyr is also present in the greatest of the Völsungs-Sigurdhr (or Siegfried) the Dragon-Slayer. In some versions of his myth Sigurdhr is raised by hinds in the woods and is later identified as a hart (which is his animal-fetch). Now Freyr is also closely associated with this high-horned beast, and after giving up his sword to gain the favor of the etin-wife, Gerdhr, he must fight with all that is left to him—the horn of a stag. This and other hidden associations show us that Freyr and Odin could work together in an independent fashion to form great initiates—Odin as progenitor and initiatory sponsor and Freyr as earthly provider.

Wights

Besides the high gods—Aesir and Vanir—there are a number of important beings that inhabit other dewllings in other worlds within the branches of Yggdrasill. Odin actively and fruitfully interacts with beings in all of these worlds. Odin himself is, after all, a synthesis of the pure streams of thurs-force and god-consciousness (see chapter 10), and his inherently expansive consciousness seeks wisdom in all realms and rejects nothing that might be instrumental in effecting his will.

Elves

The elves (ON *álfar*; sg., *álfr*) are a complex lot. They dwell in (Ljóss)álfheimr and are sometimes associated with Freyr. The word *elf* means "the shining-white one." These are entities of light (not always seen because they are exceedingly small in stature) that sometimes interact beneficially and sometimes maliciously with humans. Essentially, they are the collective lightbodies or "minds" (ON *hugar*) of the ancestors (in their female forms they are called *dísir* or dises or ides) that continue to have contact with the minds of humans. They have much lore and wisdom to teach. They are the mental faculties of the ancestors that have been reabsorbed into the cosmic organism.

Dwarves

The dwarves are also known in Old Norse as *svart-* or *dökk-álfar*, and they dwell "below" Midgardhr in Svartalfheimr. These entities too have much lore to teach, but their main function is that of *formulators*. They are the shapers of shapes that come into being in Midgardhr, especially those shapes capable of effecting the will of a great warrior or magician. That is why they are always said to be the forgers of magical weapons. They also can be considered the reabsorbed ancestral skills and crafts.

Rises, Etins, Thurses

The words most often translated as simply "giant" are actually three different words in the tradition. Old Norse *rísi* (ris) is a true *giant*, an entity of great size and perhaps even ultimately referring to the prehistoric inhabitants of the north. They are often said to intermarry with humans and to bear children with them. In addition, they are more often than not beneficent and often beautiful to look at. The etins (ON *jötnar*, sg, *jötunn*) are characterized by great strength and age, although size is not of particular importance. They can be vast as the worlds (Ymir) or virtually microscopic (the name of a certain beetle in Old Norse is *jötunuxi* [etin-ox]). Etins are vastly potent ageless entities who often embody the wisdom of the aeons through which they have existed. In regard to the eternal "battle" between the conscious and nonconscious, they are neutral. That is, some side with the Aesir and some with the thurses. What is certain is that they *exist*. Etins are non-evolving beings—they are now as they were in aeons past. It is for this reason that Odin often engenders children with etin-wives. The forces of nonconsciousness are embodied in the thurses (ON *thursar*, sg., *thurs*). They are, even in later tales, marked by their *stupidity*. Thurses too are of great age (see chapter 10), but they are actively antagonistic toward the forces of consciousness and seek to destroy it through their rime-cold entropy. The "sons of Muspell"—and their leader, Surt—who come out of Muspellsheimr to destroy cosmic order with fire are also ascribed to this group—the polar opposites of the rime-thurses. It is impossible, from an Odian point of view, to call these forces morally "evil" in the Christian sense; they are merely nonconscious natural forces of the mechanical or organic multiverse that eternally seek stasis. They are, however, entities contrary to the purposes of men and gods alike.

The lore of all of the gods and all of the wights throughout the multiverse is to be mastered by the Odian. Therefore, nothing lies outside his interest, and no path is closed to him. But before the ways of other gods are opened to the Odian, the deep essence of the road shown by the great god must be fathomed.

Odin: The Hidden God of the Runes

Odin must be known forever in his true nature as the *omnideus*, the whole-god of inner being/transformation and timeless mystery. Odin holds the holy words to open the doors of the new dawn, but he will not give them away; we must win them by our own wills. To do this the first step is the discovery of the character of his godhood.

What is meant by the formulation "Odin: Hidden God of the Runes"? First of all, let us restate and expand the etymology of the name Odin. The name occurs in most of the major Germanic dialects (OHG *Wuotan*, OE *Wōden*, as well as ON *Ódhinn*). The Germanic form of the name would have been *Wōdhanaz*, which is quite transparent in meaning. *Wōdh-* is a term for ecstatic, inspired numinous or mental activity; it is almost like a physiological response in the psychophysical complex to a high level of stimulation present in such phenomena as ecstasy, enthusiasm, outflowings of physical power, and the feeling of awe in the presence of the *numinosum tremendum* (the terrifying aspect of the "divine"). *Wōdh* is first and foremost a magical power concept. The element *-an-* regularly indicates the "master of" whatever concept it is attached to. (Other examples of this would be Old Norse *thjódh-inn*, the master of the people (= king), and Old Norse *drótt-inn*, the master of the warrior band. The grammatical ending *-az-* is already familiar to the reader from the rune names. In most cases this ending became an *-r* in Old Norse, but following an *-n-* it changed to an *-n* as well. Also, the loss of initial *w-* before a long *ó* or *ú* is already known from the relationship between Old Norse *Urdhr* and Old English *Wyrd*. Thus, *Odin* is just a regular development from *Wodhanaz*.

The Master of Inspiration is only one of many characterizing names (*heiti*) ascribed to this age-old and actually nameless, hidden god. The esoteric numen or archetype of the mysteries is not hidden by a veil as such, nor is it mainly occulted by its transcendence alone but rather by its omnipresence. That is the key to his many names. What makes Odin especially "occult" is his intense presence in paradoxical formulations. His co-equal presence as a binding force between opposites is an essential feature of his character, yet one that often baffles the human view that tends to understand things in a more dualistic-analytical way. But Odin comprehends through the whole entity expressed by polar constructs. Odin sees with the whole eye. This is the essence that hides him from our rational ("two-eyed") minds—he is the embodiment of the "suprarational-all."

Odin is a god because he serves (and has served for aeons) as an exemplary model for the expression, development, and transformation of human consciousness. This was for long ages institutionalized in a "national cultus" among the Germanic peoples, with each tribe holding its special versions of emphasis within a general traditional framework. Odin, by any name, served this function since the birth of Indo-European humanity, and hence cannot be extinguished except through the physical destruction of his people.

The runes are an integral part of the Odinic essence because it is through them and by them that he grows in power, becomes indestructible, and is able to communicate multiversal mysteries to his human kindred. Odin, the runes, and humanity form a matrix in which the conscious/ unconscious and existence/nonexistence meet.

To establish a traditional framework for the exploration and emulation of the Odinic archetype, it is wise to read what was composed about Odin's evolution in the nights when his ways were an established, institutionalized lifestyle, uncluttered by centuries of intervening ignorance. For this we must concentrate on the sources of Odin's wisdom and power as outlined in passages in Old Norse literature.

The primary Odinic initiatory myth is that of the self-sacrifice on Yggdrasill described in the "Hávamál," stanzas 138 to 165. This process must be understood as taking place in a realm beyond time, in that immense cosmogonic space before the advent of the Nornic Laws (see the N- and P-runes). The "birth" of Odin and the World-Tree self-sacrifice are essentially simultaneous—without it Odin is not Odin. In this process Odin gives his *self* to him-*Self* while hanging on Yggdrasill (the steed of Yggr [= Odin], or the yew-column). The subject has turned upon itself and has successfully made itself the object of its own work. Odin becomes omnijective. In this action Odin meets with the dark realm of Hel—the unconscious—and merges with it *while keeping his wits*. Thus, in a flash of inspiration he is infused with the entirety of the runic pattern. Because Odin is, by his tripartite essence, a conscious entity, this pattern is reshaped by his will into a *communicable* form. Through this central Odinic mystery the conscious is melded with the unconscious, the light with the dark, and it is made comprehensible by the supraconscious essence of Odin. The runes then begin to be formulated by Odin into a metalanguage contained in the runic system, in poetry, and in natural language, as "one word leads to another, and one work leads to another." The seed of Odin, his gift, is then the essence that makes this comprehension possible in his descendants: conscious humanity.

A complex source of Odin's secret wisdom is found in Mímir. As we have seen (page 145), Mímir is really the "memory" aspect of Odin and a counterpart to the Hoenir aspect. Mímir belongs, even on the exoteric level, to that generation of "first Aesir" sometimes identified as a wise Ase, sometimes as an etin. This twofold nature is due to the fact that Mímir is to a large extent the "ancestral memories" of Odin, whose ancestors are among the thurses and etins! Odin derives wisdom from this aspect in two ways: (1) from the severed head of Mímir and (2) from his eye, which he has hidden or pledged to Mímir's Well.

From the myth of the hostage exchange between the warring Aesir and Vanir (see page 145) we learn that Mímir's head was cut off by the angry Vanir because they felt cheated that Hoenir (Mímir's partner) was less intelligent than he had been represented to be. Odin preserved this head in herbs and spoke spells over it to keep it alive. It is

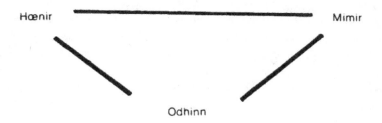

Figure 13.2. Odin-Hoenir-Mímir complex.

kept, with older wisdom, at Mímir's Well. The consultation with the "head of Mímir" is then a magical image in which the self is shown to have access to the *minni* aspect. But because it has been "severed" due to mistrust of it by noninitiates, it requires magical acts of will to keep the channels of communication open to it. When Odin gets rede from Mímir's head (memory), Hoenir (mind) is informed, and thus another threefold pattern is completed as shown in figure 13.2. Ultimately, "Mimir's head" is a metaphor that indicates the focusing of consciousness in the *minni*—in the Well of Mímir.

This Well of Mímir is said to be under a root of Yggdrasill (also called in ON *Mímameith* [Mímir's Tree]) that is over Jötunheimr. In order to gain and grow in wisdom, Odin desires to drink of the waters of this well, but Mímir's head asks of him one of his eyes—a part of himself—as a pledge or sacrifice. Odin "hides" his eye down in the column of vertical consciousness, down in the depths. There his eye remains active, always able to see, to "drink in," the wisdom of all the worlds. Thus, Odin always has two visions—one over "this world" (from Hlidhskjálf) and one in the "other worlds" (from the Well of Mímir). It also might be pointed out that Heimdallr also stores his *hljódh* (hearing, or ear) at this well; thus, he (Odin) is also able to hear in all the worlds.

In the myth of Mímir, the Odian recognizes the necessity for access to the realm of *minni*, the inherited storehouse of magico-mythic imagery, and the necessity for a synthesis of the various psychic aspects designated by the names Mímir and Hoenir. This is done through a magical act of will by means of a secret "technology" whereby the focal point (head) of this storehouse is obtained, preserved, and assimilated. One eye is focused downward into the well of "wyrd" (images), and the other is focused outward into the wide worlds of words and works. (Again, the functions of the bihemispherical brain seem indicated.)

Odin also gains knowledge from sources outside himself. The main source of this kind is Freyja. As we have seen, the Vanadís taught Odin the arts of *seidhr*. There is every reason to believe that this took place in some sort of sexual initiatory context in which certain secrets of what might today be called "sex magic" were originally passed from female initiates to males and from male initiates to females. In myth we see this reflected in the magical marriages between a warrior and his valkyrie or between humans and superhuman initiators. The "Rúnatals tháttr Ódhins" (see page 88) tells us that the eighteenth secret (probably here to be ascribed to the G-rune) is spoken to no one "except her who embraces me or who is my sister." It is in this cultic context that Odin and Freyja exchange occult secrets. The techniques of *seidhr* include trance induction for divinatory purposes, shape-shifting (which also can be done with *galdr*), the deprivation of others' souls, creation of illusions, and other arts more or less thought by some to be "shamanistic." It must be noted from the standpoint of the history of religion, however, that shamanism as such appears to be a distinctly different tradition. These techniques were often used in aggressive magic, which in part has led to its being thought of as an evil undertaking. But perhaps another trait led to its reputation as being "unmanly"; that is the practice of men transforming themselves into women in order to engender magical beings (often harmful ones) through sexual sorcery. In this fashion Loki becomes the mother of the steed Sleipnir.

Another of these quests assumes an importance second only to the Yggdrasill rite: the winning of the poetic mead from the realm of the etins. The poetic mead had been created from the blood of Kvasir, who was a linking being between the Aesir and Vanir when they made their truce. (In one version of the myth he is shaped from the spittle of the two divine races; in another he is simply one of the Vanir sent as hostage [see the *Skaldskaparmál* in the *Prose Edda*, chapter 1].) In any case, Kvasir was reputed to be the "wisest of all beings," but he is killed by some dwarves, who make the poetic mead from his blood. This liquid—the essence of the inspired consciousness of the Aesir and the organic unconscious of the Vanir—eventually came into the possession of the etins (by nature beings of the nonconscious realm). Therefore, the mead by necessity had to be won back by Odin "by hook or crook." This myth is described both by Snorri (*Skaldskaparmál*, chapter 1) and in the "Hávamál" (sts. 104–110). The process by which this is done is most significant. In the guise of Bölverkr (Worker of Evil) and by cunning and oath-breaking, he gains access to the mountain (*Hnitbjörg*—knit-mountain), where an etin-wife, Gunnlödh, guards the mead. He bores his way into the mountain in the shape of a serpent and remains in the interior for three nights, sleeping with the etin, after which he gets to drink down the mead in three gulps from the three vessels—Ódhoerir, Són, and Bodhn—in which the mead was held. Then he shape-shifts into an eagle and flies out of the top of the mountain and back to Asgardhr, where he spits out the mead into three vats—thus returning the mead to its rightful place among the Aesir and humanity. It is specifically stated that some of the mead dropped to the earth when Odin flew away, and this *anyone* can drink (if he or she happens upon it by accident). Thus, it is called the "fool-poet's share."

This myth is vital to the runic tradition. The sign of the Rune-Gild—three interlocked drinking horns—is derived from this tale. It describes the path of becoming, the pathway of transformational Odianism, and the essential mission of the Gild: to serve the larger conscious community of gods and men.

Figure 13.3 graphically shows the process of the rewinning of the poetic mead of inspiration. In this process we see the amoral force of Odin, obeying only his higher laws of will and service to the path of becoming/consciousness, gain access to the hidden realm that conceals the ill-gotten power by transforming himself into a serpent. He allies himself with the underworldly forces of dissolution to break through the mountain and to enable himself to traverse the exceedingly narrow etin-ways of dense reality. Here is hidden the significance of the serpentine aspect of the Odinic cult, well known from snake-bands on runestones and the famous dragon ships of the Vikings. While in the interior chamber with Gunnlödh—perhaps in conjunction with rites of sexual sorcery in which darkness and light are wedded (knit together; see the meaning of the name of the mountain)— Odin consumes all the mead from the three vats. The static force of the mead held by the etins, but useless to them, is now reassimilated to Odin who transforms himself into an eagle, the wide-ranging bird of prey that transmits the ecstatic force back to the world of the Aesir separate from the world of men and under the control of consciousness. There the mead is rearticulated into its threefold essence and returned to the three vessels: (1) Ódhroerir (the exciter of inspiration, which is also a name of the mead itself) (2) Són (atonement), and (3) Bodhn (container). The significance in the number of these vessels is in the threefold essence of the mead itself. Normally, this "triessence" of consciousness is only shared by Odin with the Aesir and with human initiates of his cult.

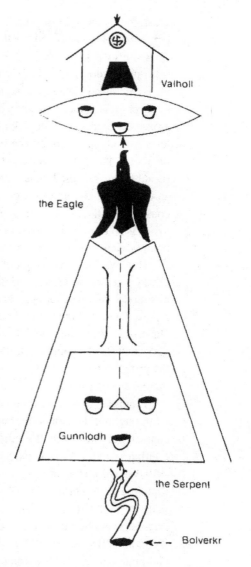

Figure 13.3. The rewinning of the poetic mead.

The path of the serpent leads to wisdom (:ᚢ:). In the mountain enclosure (:ᛒ:) opposites are wed (:ᛗ:) and inspiration is gained (:ᚠ:), to be returned by the flight of the eagle (:ᛦ:) to the enclosure of the gods and initiates (:ᛉ:), to be given (:ᚷ:) by the great god to those in his band. In this myth we see why Odin is considered both the Drighten of Darkness and the Lord of Light.

Odin's wisdom is derived from three continuous sources: (1) the Yggdrasill sacrifice (for rune wisdom), (2) Mímir's Well (the head of Mímir and the "hidden eye"), and (3) the poetic mead Ódhoerir. The mythic paradigms connected to these sources give shape to the process of the acquisition of runelore, rune wisdom, and runecraft. They also serve as psychic models that the runer follows in the Odinic pattern. The "god" Odin is on one level something separate from the paradigm of "that which comprehends opposites" at the root of the Odinic mystery. These aspects can be contained in the archetype concept (if not in the strictest Jungian terms). The archetype is not a personified thing but rather an impersonal pattern of action or pure consciousness. As this paradigm becomes more conscious in the human being, a "personification" of that pattern begins to emerge and to act as an exemplary model of consciousness and behavior—a "god." From the Odian point of view this is the process of all gods and goddesses.

Here we want to concentrate on Odin the god as a psychic model for the evolution of the runemaster, the role of the runes and their interaction with and assimilation to this model, and why Odin must ever remain the hidden god.

At the root of the Odinic archetype is the concept of wholeness within twofoldness. His origins show this quite clearly. He is born of Borr, son of Búri (of the race of proto-gods) and Bestla, daughter of the etin Bölthorn. Odin therefore represents a synthesis of the primal (preconscious) entities (see chapter 10). The bridging function is something that he eventually can give to his human kindred.

From this twofoldness comes the great manifoldness ("all-ness") that is represented throughout the Odinic literature by his unlimited names and shapes. This manifold character is most formally represented in Odin's all-pervasive number—three (and its multiples). Odin is again and again represented in triads of aspects, for example, Odin -Vili-Vé, Odin Hoenir- Lódhurr, Odin-Hoenir-Loki, and Hárr (the High)–Jafnhárr (the Equally High)–Thridhi (the Third). The oldest formulation of this type is certainly Odin -Vili-Vé, which dates from the common Germanic period. We know this because it was originally an alliterative formula. The Germanic forms of the names would have been *Wōdhanaz*, *Wiljōn*, and *Wīhaz*. An examination of the deeper levels of the formula will yield much of the hidden structure of Odin (see table 13.2).

Wōdanaz should be clear enough by now as that which integrates the many into a conscious whole and describes this entire process (hence, this is the most common name for the god). *Wiljōn* is the will that charges the process with a joyful dynamism. The idea of joy is expressed by this root in most of the ancient Germanic dialects, including Old English. This is the power of conscious willed direction. *Wīhaz* contains a root concept of separateness, "other-ness," which is absolutely essential to the threefold working of the god as it works in all of the worlds. This is bound up with the dichotomy of the "holy" as

Name	Meaning	Essence	Function
Wōdhanaz	inspiration	wholeness	integrative
Wiljōn	desire/joy/will	dynamism	transformational
Wīhaz	sacrality	separation	separative

Table 13.2. The structure of the Odinic triad.

expressed in Indo-European thought. *Wīh-* is that terrifying and mysterious aspect (the *numinosum* or *mysterium tremendum*)—the doorway between the worlds through which all who would transform themselves, gods or men, must pass. When seen from the outside, *wīhaz* can be terrifying, but once the runer becomes *wīhaz*, he sees for the first time and is therefore often feared, resented, or even hated.

Therefore, the whole describes an eternal process of evolution, of transformation—the power to shape and reshape. This process is the interplay between the two halves of the whole; and Odin is the embodiment and eventual conscious model of the oscillation between the fields of light and dark through a continuous process of separation from one field, merger with the other, there to undergo transformation, followed by reintegration with the first field. Thus, the fields of darkness are sown with the seeds of light, and the fields of light are sown with the seeds of darkness. All polar fields contain the seeds of their opposites.

All of this is done by means of a will, or consciousness, that is fundamentally separate from the process itself. This is most evident in the Yggdrasill initiation, where Odin binds together the realms of light and dark, life and death, conscious and unconscious. But he is not consumed by the process—he makes use of it. The other sources of Odinic wisdom also have elements of this binding of polar opposites and ultimate utilization of them by the magical Self.

For the modern runer this has many lessons to teach. The true essence of the lore is by its very nature impossible to express fully in "words," that is, in common natural language. But what can be said is that Odin's being teaches the way of the "whole-I," the "all-self," *as well as* the "higher self." This higher self is a supraconscious entity, the "holy self' or the magical ego of the runemaster. It can mingle with the natural, organic cosmos. It can mingle with the non-natural, numinous realms. It does so, however, in order that it may further its willed aims. It is the essence of the way of the true seeker, never resting, always searching in darkness and in light, high and low, in life and in death. But the process of synthesizing the polar fields is not one of neutralization but of maximization—a boring directly through to the kernel essences. Only in this way can the whole of the power be known and used.

The runes play a central role in all of these Odinic mysteries. It is through them that Odin comprehends these processes, through them that he formulates them so that he can master and eventually (in part) manipulate them, and through this formulation that he can communicate the mysteries to his human kith and kin.

The "cosmic runes" (ON *ginnrúnar*) are innate and eternal patterns in the substance of the multiverse, indestructible and ever-growing along eternal patterns. They cannot be fully comprehended, however, because when a part of them is comprehended (internalized by a conscious being), they at once grow beyond that comprehension; this process is also eternal. Odin, like the modern theoretical physicists who have followed him, knows this well and knows that his search for totality is a never-ending one. Yet he continues in his heroic struggle, as must his fellows. Those who find this prospect disheartening are not meant for the Odian path.

When Odin undertook the Yggdrasill working, the primal heroic deed of consciousness was completed. The very basic and elemental systematic structure of the whole was at once won and comprehended. These runes, divided into bright runes (ON *heidhrúnar*) and murk runes (ON *myrkrúnar*), now provide the road map for the unending exploration of the multiverse. The runes held by Odin may be won by humanity through following Odin's example and by assimilating, as he did, the pattern of his consciousness imprinted with the runic system. (The Odian does not seek "union" with Odin but seeks union only with that with which Odin sought union—the Self.)

These runes represent totality in its simplest yet most whole form comprehensible to the human psychophysical complex. But as Odin can never comprehend all of the cosmic runes, so humans can rarely fully comprehend all of the divine runes. However, because we are the children of the All-Father (i.e., conscious beings) and have received his primal (and only "free") gifts of consciousness (see chapter 10) we are able to ride the runeroads with the Aesir. The runes are the road map by which man can find selfhood and the gods, and in turn they provide the way through which Odin can chart the edges of unknown time and space.

It should now be evident why Odin is the hidden god. As popularly understood, the formulation "hidden god" indicates that unknown and unknowable "god beyond duality." No other archetype working in the realm of consciousness so perfectly represents the path to that state. The processes outlined above show how this god works; essentially, its function cannot be understood in the intellectual sense. It can be understood only through experience in magical workings of the "Odinic paradox." Even when this comprehension takes place, and you begin to open the runic secrets, Odin will still remain a hidden god, for in actual experience the intellect and the words of human speech fail because they are phenomena of only half of the whole to which the experience belongs.

Part Three

READING THE RUNES

RUNECASTING AND
RUNIC DIVINATION

Chapter 14

SITTING AT THE WELL OF WYRD

o communicate directly with a god, or the gods—that is what divination is
all about. The runes on their most mundane level are a writing system. On
both the mundane and the cosmic levels they are a system of *communication*.
They are tools for reading otherwise hidden truths. Runes are a sort of traditional code,
originally the gift of the god Odin, through which messages can be sent from one level
of reality to another, from one world to another. Whether in magic (*galdr*), where the
runer's aim is to cause the objective world to conform to subjective will, or in runecasting, where the runer's aim is to read the hidden truths of his or her own subjective being
or of the objective worlds, the runes are used as tools—as media—by which messages
may be sent and received.

In reality, of course, the true runes dwell within the soul of the runer—within *you*.
The runestaves are symbolic objects which act as a kind of magical mirror of your soul.
When you gaze upon the runestaves strewn on the holy cloth of white, you are truly
gazing deep within the Well of Wyrd. As a runecaster, the vitki approaches the level of
a priest or priestess (of a *godhi* or *gydhja)*, someone charged to deal with the gods and
to act as a communicator between the worlds of the gods and that of Midhgardhr. Most
important, however, is the fact that anyone who takes the time to become skilled in
runecasting will open unseen channels between the conscious and unconscious selves.

This "opening of channels" is won only after some effort and willpower have been
spent. The would-be runecaster must learn much and work much before great success
can be expected. In this book, you will find all that you will ever need to become an
effective "runic communicator."

This part of the book is intended to contain practical concrete indications of exact traditional lore and procedures; but it should not be taken to be overly restrictive.
Where the elder tradition is clear, we follow it, but in some technical matters we have
had to reconstruct some details. This was done in the spirit of the Germanic and runic
tradition. Each detail can be supported by some aspect or interpretation of the older tradition as it has survived in historical or literary sources. However, it is also an integral

part of the Germanic and runic tradition to innovate where necessary. The potentially great runecaster will not hesitate to invent new forms or rune readings, casting methods, etc. Most runecasters—and would-be experts on the subject—do not err on the side of innovation, but depend too much on unthinking, rote borrowing from some other (usually later, more "popular") system of divination. These borrowed elements then are shoved willy-nilly into the runic system.

Another problem often encountered in books on "runic divination" is that the writer is often totally ignorant of the actual tradition—and prefers to remain so. The quality of your runecasts will be greater if you invest the time and energy to learn something before you begin casting (much less writing!).

Runic divination needs to be practiced before you can become skilled. This will require that you make many castings which you will probably undertake with only a modicum of passion. You are urged not to make runecasting a profane form of "play" (for entertainment purposes); to this end the rituals should help. However, from a practical standpoint, how can you expect to become proficient if you only undertake runecasts on important occasions? In the beginning, daily practice should be observed, though it is probably wisest not to undertake more than one casting per day. In this balanced way, a healthy respect for the runes, along with initiated familiarity, will be gained in the shortest possible time.

Sometimes the runecaster poses a question to the runes, but the runes seem to be speaking to another point. The runes (i.e., your personal *inner* runes) tend to pick up the real question on your mind or in your heart. It is easiest to get accurate readings from these kinds of questions. More refined questions require more direction of the conscious will.

All in all, runecasting itself is perhaps the best method of "getting to know" the runes. Reading—even memorizing—what the elder tradition says is fine, but the direct method of runer to runes is by far the most powerful way of learning about the "mysteries." Skills in runecasting can be applied directly to all other aspects of runework and runecraft.

There is a great deal we have already said in part one of this book about the history of runecasting as it is found in literature and folklore. Here we move on to the more current story of the practice of runic divination and its actual applications.

The tide has turned and the time has come for all the kith and kin of Odin to gather at the Well of Wyrd again to read the ordeal of the gods and humanity and to handle the mighty blood-tines.

Runic Divination and the Magical Revival

In this century, many systems of runic divination have appeared in the world. Only one of them, that presented in *Rune Games*, by Marijane Osborn and Stella Longland,[1] has even come close to being a traditional system. However, in Germany, systems inspired by the trailblazing work of Guido von List (1848–1919) became a virtual neo-tradition within various schools of magic in the twentieth century.

Most of the major writers on rune magic in the early Listian tradition did not explicitly address matters of runic divination. The one exception was E. Tristan Kurtzahn, whose *Die Runen als Heilszeichen und Schicksalslose* [The Runes as Holy Signs and Lots of Fate] (1924)[2] included an appendix on specific methods of runic divination—which he indicates he was reluctant to include. After the Second World War, Karl Spiesberger's book *Runenmagie* (1955)[3] included a whole chapter on "RunenMantik" (to a large extent drawn from Kurtzahn's work). A sidelight to runic divination proper also was presented in 1955 by Roland Dionys Jossé in his *Die Tala der Raunen* (*Runo-astrologische Kabbalistik*),[4] the subtitle of which translates: "a handbook of the interpretation of the essence and path of a person on the basis of the runes of fate concealed in his name." This is a type of rune-numerology based on a modification of the Listian system. The most recent foray into runic divination in this tradition is the comprehensive treatment by Werner Kosbab in *Das Runen-Orakel* (1982).[5]

In the English-speaking worlds we have not fared so well. As early as the late 1950s runic divination seems to have been known in occult circles, but since that time, and for the most part, only what can be described as bastardizations of the runic traditions have found their way into print in English. Unfortunately, and perhaps typically, one of the "offenders" in this regard was also the one most widely distributed: Ralph Blum's *The Book of Runes*.[6] Several other "systems" have been generated within the Anglo-American occult mill (see bibliography), but I believe only one, *Rune Games*, is worth considering by readers interested in tradition or authenticity. Osborn and Longland present a picture of a system and a culture in transition—from the heathen to the Christian. This may be seen as a reversed image of the present situation as the cultural pendulum swings back. *At the Well of Wyrd* tries to present a totally traditional, pre- (and post!) Christian system for those who are ready to throw away their crutches.

Although this section contains a complete system of viable runic divination that can be used by persons of differing traditions, it remains a significant part of the work of the Rune-Gild to teach deeper, even more traditional methods of runecasting, and to continue research in this field. Divination is an important tool not only in runework (esoteric self-transformation) but also in runecraft (esoteric environmental engineering).

Chapter 15

RUNIC DIVINATORY THEORY

Understanding how runecasting works can be a relative thing. How we understand it may be different from the exact ways in which an Erulian runecaster of ancient times might have explained it. There are also various levels of understanding in our own times. So why even bring up "theory"? Why not just "practice" and not worry about such matters?

From the standpoint of true runework on any level these questions are, of course, absurd. It is in the character of the runer to inquire and act, to seek further into the runes. If the runes are to be more than a "fortune-telling" system—which they must be—then working through various levels of understanding of them can only be enhanced by constant attempts to understand them in ever more comprehensive ways. So, the question of "theory," or understanding, is actually a practical one.

Traditionally, runecasting is a true act of direct communication between humans and the divinities of the many realms, as described in chapter 6, "Historical Rune Magic and Divination." This communication takes place in the metalanguage of the gods (runes)—the outer form of the Gift of Odin. The runestaves and all the lore attendant to them as well as the ritual methods of consulting them also were known to be of divine origin. The first "runecaster" was Odin himself, and in casting the runes the diviner is actually participating in the divine process in an imitative way. This is the essence of the traditional theory of runecasting, at least from an Odian point of view. The non-Odian populace of ancient times would have seen the divinatory process as one in which "the gods speak to mortals," and in this they probably were encouraged by the Odians.

This exoteric understanding—as all true levels of understanding—is not at all incorrect. However, what this level fails to see is that in the context of the ritual act the runecaster has assumed the status of "a god." Actually, in order to communicate with the hidden transpersonal reality (the runes) the runer must assume this status in order to be totally effective. The results of the casting are then communicated to the runecaster's own human level of consciousness (and perhaps to that of others) through the runestaves and their lore. Therefore, runecasting is not a totally passive undertaking.

The runer's will, ability, knowledge, and level of being are very important. Without them the runes would remain forever hidden.

Another aspect of traditional theory involves the "divinities of fate," which are numerous and prevalent in Germanic lore. These can be roughly divided into three "functions" or characteristic realms of activity. First, the Great Norns (ON *Nornir*) Urdhr, Verdhandi, and Skuld give the overall context in which action and reaction, cause and effect, time, and synchronicity exist, and provide the context in which they can be comprehended. Second are the personal "bearers of fate." These are conceptualized as the entities who are attached to an individual and who carry that individual's fate (ON *ørlög*), thus influencing his or her life and actions. To some extent the runecaster is seeking knowledge of these entities and their contents. Entities that belong to this second group include the fetch (ON *fylgja*) and Nornir (lesser Norns), as well as in certain instances *valkýrjur* (valkyries) and *disir* (dises).[1] Third are the "guides." These entities are thought to manipulate the runelots to fall or to be laid out in certain ways. Guides may be Norns, dises, or even valkyries. It might be noted that from the Odian standpoint these entities are actually parts of the whole self of the Odian.

The Runes and Fate

The *perthro*-rune is fundamental to the understanding of the context in which runic divination works. This rune contains the secret workings of the three Great Norns — Urdhr-Verdhandi-Skuld. These are vast forces of the cosmos whose manifestation is synonymous with the origin of time (including synchronicity), motion (thus cause and effect), and all becoming. These are dark etin-forces according to "Völuspá," st. 8, in the *Poetic Edda*.

The essence of their mystery is contained in the meanings of their names. Urdhr (OE *Wyrd*) is simply the past participle of the verb *verdha*, to become; turn (OE *wyrd* is similarly formed from the verb *weordhan*). So Urdhr really means "that which has become or turned," — in other words, "the past." Verdhandi is the present participle of the same verb, and so means "that which is becoming or turning," i.e., "the present." Skuld obviously comes from another verb, *skulu,* meaning shall. It is essentially, or qualitatively, different from the other two, and means "that which shall (be)." In Old Norse this has connotations of duty and obligation, but in the most archaic levels when the term first arose it merely indicated that which should come to pass, given past circumstances.

It is also of the greatest importance to realize that the old Germanic idea of time was built on a past vs. non-past model. If you will notice, even our modern English does not really have a future tense (it needs the auxiliary verb *will* to form this tense). This is a feature common to the Germanic languages — German, English, Dutch, and the Scandinavian dialects. But we do have a real past tense. This is because to the Germanic mind the past is real, the future is only hypothetical and subject to change, and the present is an ever-becoming now.

If those concepts are fully understood, it will be easy to see the true nature of the Germanic concept of "fate" (ON *ørlög*). *Ørlög* is not a set and immutable thing—in fact, it is being transformed constantly by ongoing action. However, *ørlög* is a powerful force and one from whose grasp few can escape once certain patterns of action become ingrained. The well-known Germanic "fatalism" is, for the most part, an exoteric understanding of this process. Your "Skuld" is affected—even determined—by "Urdhr," your Wyrd. Wyrd is essentially "past action" which has been formulated and absorbed by your being. Now, if to this already vast webwork the idea of Germanic "reincarnation" (ON *aptrburdhr*, rebirth) is added, a truly complex image arises. Wyrd seems (indeed is) so compelling because its roots are usually hidden in their remote "pastness"; they are so deeply ingrained in us that they have become invisible. Also, the sheer complexity of the webwork of wyrd, all of the past actions and reactions on all levels of being throughout the entire time of your "essential existences," make sorting out the threads of wyrd enormously difficult. On the most elementary level the power of wyrd can be expressed in the phrase "Old habits are hard to break." Through runecasting, the vitki endeavors to get at the root or Wyrd-level of the matter under question.

Two technical terms mentioned above probably need further analysis. *Aptrburdhr* or rebirth (ON) is a process whereby the essential powers and characteristics of a person are handed down to, and inherited by, later generations. This usually happens naturally and along genetic lines; e.g., the grandson is the reincarnation of the dead grandfather. With this rebirth the grandson also "inherits" the fate *(ørlög)* of the grandfather and of his whole clan or tribe. The child is affected by its heritage.

Ørlög itself is a complex idea. The word literally means "primal layers" or "primal laws," and really indicates action that has been "laid down" in the past. But *ørlög* cuts two ways. It is both the past actions that we have dealt out (in this and perhaps in the previous existences of our essential selves), and that which others (or impersonal forces) have dealt out to us over the same span of time. In English the only survival of this concept is in the word *ordeal* (primal-deal), i.e., that which was "dealt out" in the past. Thus, trials by ordeal (in theory) merely objectively demonstrated the truth based on these concepts.

From what has been said above, it should be clear that the process the runer sets out to investigate through runecastings is not strictly one of cause and effect. The nornic process is one that formulates a set of probabilities based on a whole range of complex actions and reactions on many levels of being. The runecasting is an attempt to reproduce an image of this webwork of wyrd so that its contents can be analyzed and read.

The theory that comes closest to fitting the Germanic model is that of synchronicity, originated by the Swiss psychologist C. G. Jung.[2]

A *synchronicity* is a meaningful coincidence, when outer events (happenings) coincide with a psychic event (an awareness of meaning). These are moments in which the eternal fields of meaningfulness open up and touch upon moments in cyclical (natural) time. These are moments when our souls and all the world around us can be reshaped to some extent—if we are aware of them.

Acts of runecasting are not so much attempts to predict future events as they are attempts to arrange inner and outer circumstances (the soul and the lay of the runestaves) in such a way that the center of the webwork of wyrd is made legible. From this center we are able to interpret the shape of much of the rest of the warp and weave of the world around us. We may even be able to see the whole world: past and "present," archetypal and mundane. Those who can read the runes will be able to expand their vision in such a way that all the conditioning factors of any situation are clarified. Lines in the webwork of wyrd can be extended in consciousness—and thus the realm of probabilities surrounding events yet to happen can come into view.

If the vitki considers the Yggdrasill pattern shown in chapter 10 on pg. 126 as a four-dimensional webwork, and the act of runecasting as a way of expanding consciousness out along all the wide ways into the nine worlds, then runecasting can be seen as a method of expanding awareness from a center point (Midhgardhr). But just as Midgardhr is the final fruit of the coming into being of the worlds of Yggdrasill, so too is it the seed from which new growth springs. Runecasting can give us the probable patterns for this new growth.

Finally, something needs to be said about the "experience of the wyrd." In our colloquial language the term "weird" has come to be synonymous with strange. This is an unfortunate turn of events. The word comes from the Scots language, the Germanic tongue of the Lowland Scots, northern English and northern Irish, a language in which many archaic concepts survive. In former times, a "weird" experience was one which seemed to have its origins in the numinous, in the world of the gods. A weird experience caused the hair to rise on the back of the neck, and it was felt to be highly significant. Such events and feelings were more synchronistic than anything else. Things became palpably clear, sometimes causing a fearful reaction. It is hoped that this book will help in some way to rescue this word from the oblivion of meaningless modern usage.

Chapter 16

RUNIC SYMBOLISM AND DIVINATORY TABLES

In the first chapters of this book we concentrated on absorbing the esoteric lore of the runes; in the latter part we will engage in actively using runes to cause alterations in ourselves and in the environment. But before the student seeks to make changes or *write* in the warp and weft of the world, the student must learn to *read* the runes aright. Here I will offer the basics of the skill of runecasting. It must be emphasized, however, that the keys presented here do not exhaust the possibilities of runic readings. Each vitki ought to keep careful records of every casting so that personal trends in interpretation may be noted and utilized. Just as no two people really speak the same language (each of us uses grammar and vocabulary uniquely), the way in which "you and your runes communicate" also will be unique. This is why learning the runes is actually tantamount to learning to know the self.

The following tables, however, are based on traditional associations essentially drawn from insights into the rune poems and other aspects of ancient runelore (associations of names, number, etc.). Also, some advantage has been taken of the divinatory vision of the German Armanic system in which a great deal of runecasting has been practiced successfully for decades.

These tables will delineate the runic readings on three levels: (1) general lore, (2) "positive" or birth/life levels (under the heading "Bright-stave"), and (3) "negative" or death level (under the heading "Murk-stave"). The first is necessary to give a general orientation to the runic symbolism and to provide a context from which the runer will be able to expand personal readings.

The "bright" reading of a rune is really its "normal" reading, the one it has in isolation and outside the context of other runes. This is by no means always "positive" in the sense of "beneficial." Take, for example, the runes *thurisaz, isa, nauthiz,* or *hagalaz,* all of which can be detrimental on their own in their "positive" aspects. The "negative" or murky reading of a rune is determined by its relationship to other runes or by the position in which it lands in a casting. This negativity is actually an expression of one of two possible patterns: (1) cataclysm, or (2) obstruction. When a rune is cataclysmically juxtaposed to another it indicates that change is in the offing, change that will perhaps be uncomfortable, but change that may lead to a new beginning. Obstruction of one runic force by another is the worst of possibilities; it suggests stasis and stagnation of the forces. Ways of determining the relative brightness or murkiness of a stave in any given reading will be discussed in detail in chapter 19.

Each table shows the stave shape, its numerical and phonetic values, its Germanic name with translations from various cultural and historical contexts, and the modern English word ultimately derived from it (or a reconstructed name). This English word can be used as an alternate modern name for the stave. Stanzas of the "Old English Rune Poem" (OERP), the "Old Norwegian Rune Rhyme" (ONRR), and the "Old Icelandic Rune Poem" (OIRP) that are relevant to each of the elder staves are also included. There are only sixteen runes in the younger system used by the "Old Norwegian Rune Rhyme" and the "Old Icelandic Rune Poem," so only those sixteen of the twenty-four runes of the elder system have stanzas from these two works.

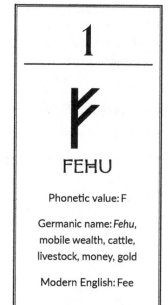

OERP

 (Money) is a comfort
to everybody
although every man ought
to deal it out freely
if he wants to get approval
from the lord.

ONRR

 (Money) causes strife among kinsmen;
the wolf grows up in the woods.

OIRP

 (Money) is the (cause of) strife among kinsmen,
and the fire of the flood-tide
and the path of the serpent.

Lore

This is the principle of mobile power—within nature, within the self, and within society. *Fehu* is a power that flows outward like fire from its course and must be circulated in order to be beneficial. This circulation of fire must be handled by the athelings with wisdom and foresight so they do not destroy themselves or others. The F-rune is a sign of the first vital fire of life and movement which ensures continuing change in the world.

Bright-Stave

Foresight is needed. Wealth may be in the offing, but it must be used with wisdom and shared generously to avoid conflict. If used properly, social success will be won. This is also true of the "inner wealth" of knowledge. Share and your power will grow. The origin of this power of well-being is outside your present consciousness; the power is just welling up from below the surface. Ethical behavior based on wisdom and tradition is called for. There may be travel in the offing. Great energy is indicated as well as new beginnings and new life. Erotic renewal. This rune could signify a person who works with animals or finances.

Murk-Stave

Greed can cause you to become an outcast in society, and to suffer inner alienation from the self. Discord may be in the offing, discord based on a lack of circulation of the power of *fehu*. Excess of *fehu* can cause you to "burn out" your creative energies. Control them and use them with wisdom. There may be a proclivity toward offensive aggression. Obstruction leads to a blockage or atrophy of vital energies. Failure and poverty are in the offing.

Keywords for Fehu

Bright: Social success, Wealth energy, Foresight, New beginning

Murky: Greed, "Burnout," Atrophy, Poverty, Discord

OERP

ᚢ (Aurochs) is fearless
and greatly horned
a very fierce beast,
it fights with its horns,
a famous roamer of the moor
it is a courageous animal.

ONRR

ᚢ (Slag) is from bad iron;
oft runs the reindeer on the hard snow.

OIRP

ᚢ (Drizzle) is the weeping of clouds,
and the diminisher of the rim of ice,
and (an object for) the herdsman's hate.

2

ᚢ

URUZ

Phonetic value: U

Germanic name: *Uruz*,
aurochs; drizzle, slag

Modern English: Urox

Lore

This is the principle of vital organic life energy, original procreation, and organic transformation. *Uruz* is the primal cosmic bovine-force that shapes manifestation and defends that manifested form. The aurochs was a wild and powerful large bisonlike longhorned bovine that roamed Europe until it became extinct. The beast was known for its power, ferocity, and tenacity. The medieval rune poems use different meanings: (1) a purifying fire that removes dross elements, or (2) water that is forced from the clouds in a similar process.

Bright-Stave

Vital strength is its essence. There is an emotive up-welling and out-pouring of energy. This energy leads to strength if it is tenaciously held on to and controlled. Properly this strength should be used to defend your "homeland," be that the physical home or the "hall" of the self (i.e., "defense mechanisms"). Strive toward inner goals and more power will result. Use the strength to burn away weakness and dross. Be constant and vigilant. The organic essence of the rune will lead to knowledge and understanding, health and general luck. (The horseshoe as a symbol of luck was derived from the:ᚢ: stave.) This rune could signify a physician or someone in the crafts.

Murk-Stave

Obsessive protectiveness and possessiveness. Misdirection of energy ruins or destroys other beneficial aspects. This can indicate strength used in the wrong way or time ("rain on the hay"), or strength used by the wrong people whose only desire is to control others ("shepherd").

Uncontrolled enthusiasm leads to mania. A blockage of *uruz* leads to sickness, inconsistency, and ignorance.

Keywords for Uruz

Bright: Strength, Defense, Tenacity, Freedom, Form, Health, Understanding

Murky: Weakness, Obsession, Misdirected force, Domination by others, Sickness, Inconsistency, Ignorance

3

THURISAZ

Phonetic value: TH

Germanic name: *thurisaz*, giant (thurs); thorn

Modern English: Thurs or thorn

OERP

(Thorn) is very sharp;
for every thane
who grasps it; it is harmful,
and exceedingly cruel
to every man
who lies upon them.

ONRR

(Thurs) causes the sickness of women;
few are cheerful from misfortune .

OIRP

(Thurs) is the torment of women,
and the dweller in the rocks,
and the husband of Vardh-rúna (a giantess?)

Lore

The thurs is a reactive force in brute nature. It is a reaction to the clash of two polarized forces and the transformation of that force into kinetic energy. This occurs in nature in the form of the thurses (unconscious forces), but also the Ása-Thor makes use of an analogous force—Mjöllnir—to combat the encroachment of unconsciousness. The TH-rune is a sign of the psychosexual symbolic response, which in unconscious beings leads to compulsion but in conscious ones to transformation.

Bright-Stave

Reactions to your deeds may be dangerous. Take care in passively engaging or blindly grasping the "outside world" (i.e., outside yourself, home, etc.). Do so with knowledge. Danger may be present in the outside world. This is an erotic vital force. An intensification of erotic expression may be in the offing, but this may be mixed with pain. Correctly applied, this power can be protective and lead to evolutionary change and regeneration. This is the rune of crisis for good or ill, a catalyst for change. It may represent an unskilled brutal person.

Murk-Stave

Unwisely approached, the TH-stave betokens defenselessness and danger. Beware of enemies from the outside. It indicates reactive compulsion and misery in relations with the opposite sex. Betrayal may be in the offing. The thurs is an intellectually "dense" rock-like entity.

Keywords for Thurs

Bright: Reactive force, Directed force, Vital eroticism, Regenerative catalyst

Murky: Danger, Defenselessness, Compulsion, Betrayal, Dullness

OERP

(God/Mouth) is the chieftain
of all speech,
the mainstay of wisdom
and a comfort to the wise ones,
for every noble warrior
hope and happiness.

ONRR

(Estuary) is the way of most journeys;
but the sheath is (that for) swords.

OIRP

(Ase = Odhinn) is the olden-father,
and Asgardhr's chieftain,
and the leader of Valhöll.

4

ᚨ

ANSUZ

Phonetic value: A

Germanic name: *Ansuz*, the
Ase, Odin: sovereign
ancestral god of the intellect

Modern English: Ans

Lore

This is the principle of divine conscious power as embodied in the god Odin. Odin is the divine pattern or exemplary model for self-transformation, not a god with whom worshippers seek "union." This is symbolically shown in the analogies made in the ONRR: estuary/ship-journey, and sword/scabbard. *Ansuz* contains the mystery of the "meta-language" as it embodies all linguistic and symbolic systems. This is the rune of synthetic consciousness.

Bright-Stave

Skills involving language are indicated. The power of persuasion is great in the spoken word and the ability to imitate. Direct access to the source of consciousness and perhaps a transformative spiritual experience are in the offing. Learn the way of Odin, but do not worship him. Responsibility to ancestral ways and the promotion of the interests of the ancestors are indicated. It is necessary to synthesize, to bring together disparate elements in order to understand. Inspiration and intellectual achievement are present. The unexpected must be expected. Strive for the best and highest. This rune may indicate an intellectual or priestly person.

Murk-Stave

Without proper understanding, the *ansuz* may lead to delusion. Uncomfortable situations may be in the offing, as tests or catalysts to new understanding. Beware of attempts by others to manipulate you. Danger may come through a misuse of knowledge or from unwholesome influences. A blockage of this force leads to boredom and eventually to intellectual death.

Keywords for Ansuz

Bright: Inspiration (enthusiasm), Synthesis, Transformation, Words

Murky: Misunderstanding, Delusion, Manipulation by others, Boredom

OERP

ᛉ *(Riding) is in the hall*
to every warrior
easy, but very hard
for the one who sits up
on a powerful horse
over miles of road.

ONRR

ᛉ *(Riding), it is said, is the worst for horses;*
Reginn forged the best sword.

OIRP

ᛉ *(Riding) is a blessed sitting,*
and a swift journey,
and the toil of the horse.

5

ᚱ

RAIDHO

Phonetic value: R

Germanic name: *Raidho*,
riding, vehicle

Modern English: Riding
or Rowel

Lore

This is the principle of rhythmic and proportional dynamism or
energetic action. It is the cycle—but in spiral form—always governed by perfect proportion and
interval. As such, *raidho* is the rune of the long ride, the long, hard journey of growth and becoming in the world. This is a journey which must be governed by good rede (counsel) and a rational
process. *Raidho* is the practice of what *ansuz* has inspired.

Bright-Stave

An ordered change is indicated. Ordered ethical deeds are necessary. This requires planning,
preparation, and good judgment, however. Action is necessary. Gain experience in the "outside
world." The *fylgja* and *hamingja* must be strengthened. A journey or change in domestic situation
is in the offing. Logical matters may become a concern. Justice may be expected. Make use of
reason and good counsel. This rune may signify a person in the legal or transportation field.

Murk-Stave

Hard times are ahead. Spiritual crisis based on unpreparedness may be in the offing. Spiritual
boredom resulting from rigid routines could ensue. Beware of bad advice. A blockage of the
raidho force will lead to injustice, violence, stultification, or inappropriate irrationality.

Keywords for Raidho

Bright: Rationality, Action, Justice, Ordered growth, Journey

Murky: Crisis, Rigidity, Stasis, Injustice, Irrationality

6

KENAZ

Phonetic value: K

Germanic name: *Kenaz*, torch; or *kaunaz*, sore

Modern English: Keen

OERP

ᚲ

*(Torch) is to every living person
known by its fire,
it is clear and bright
it usually burns
when the athelings
rest inside the hall.*

ONRR

ᚴ

*(Sore) is the curse of children;
grief makes a man pale.*

OIRP

ᚴ

*(Sore) is the bale of children,
and a scourge,
and the house of rotten flesh.*

Lore

This is the principle of analysis (of breaking up things into their component parts) and of creativity or shaping things. *Kenaz* is the fire of divine inspiration under the control of human craft, which results in artistic creation. It is the fire of the torch, the hearth, the harrow (altar), the forge, and the funeral pyre.

Bright-Stave

Inner creativity and artistry, or general ability and aptitude are indicated. Rest and relaxation are necessary to allow it to arise. The creative fire is applied to the personality. Transformation is suggested, a shaping or reshaping of the present situation, enlightened by divine inspiration. A child may be in the offing. This rune may indicate a person in the arts or crafts.

Murk-Stave

Unwanted dissolution, perhaps in the form of physical disease or the breakup of a relationship. Problems with children may be indicated. Blockage of the *kenaz* force leads to inability and a lack of creativity or skill.

Keywords for Kenaz

Bright: Technical ability, Inspiration, Creativity, Transformation, Offspring

Murky: Disease, Breakup, Inability, Lack of creativity

OERP

 (Gift) is for every man
a pride and praise,
help and worthiness;
and of every homeless adventurer
it is the estate and substance
for those who have nothing else.

7

GEBO

Phonetic value: G

Germanic name: *Gebo*, gift, generosity

Modern English: Gift

Lore

This is the principle of the threefold Gift of Odin: consciousness, divine breath, and form. It is also the principle of giving and taking, of an exchange between any two beings or two realms. It is the sacrifice—or gift—made by people to gods in order to compensate or petition for divine favors. In human society this is reflected as simple hospitality.

Bright-Stave

Provide for hospitality and generosity with guests. Be prepared to accept it as well. A material or spiritual gift may be in the offing. You may expect great credit, honor, dignity—or you might be called upon to bestow these on another if you are in a position of power. You may have a magical exchange with a member of the opposite sex. A powerful and synchronistic (Wyrd) experience could be in the offing. This rune may represent a person who works for a nonprofit organization or charity, or someone in the hotel or restaurant business.

Murk-Stave

Take care not to give away all you have. Spend wisely. Do not become overly dependent upon gifts from others, for "aye does a gift always look for gain." An attempt to buy influence with gifts is possible; beware of financial enslavement. Things might get worse before they get better. Blockage of the *gebo* will cause greed and weakness, or poverty and loneliness.

Keywords for Gebo

Bright: Gift (giving), Generosity, Magical exchange, Honor, Sacrifice

Murky: Influence-buying, Greed, Loneliness, Dependence, Over-sacrifice

8

WUNJO

Phonetic value: W

Germanic name: *Wunjo*, joy

Modern English: Wyn

OERP

ᚹ *(Joy) is had*
by the one who knows few troubles
pains and sorrows,
and to him who himself has
power and blessedness,
and a good enough house .

Lore

This is the principle of ideal harmonization of entities or elements—especially those derived from the same source. From this, harmony, joy, and good cheer naturally arise.

Bright-Stave

Social and domestic harmony can be expected. Separation from pain or the ability to cope with it is indicated. Keep ideals in mind; strive for them. Either good physical health is indicated, or attention should be paid to it. Strive to bring together disparate elements in your life; organize things. Harmonize your inner and outer lives. New social relationships—not necessarily sexual ones—are likely. Material prosperity may result from business relationships. A person in social services may be signified by this rune.

Murk-Stave

Stultification of the individuality in the "group mind" is suggested. Blurring of individual efforts and minimalization of the individual ego can lead to loss of identity. Stoppage of the *wunjo* force results in poor relationships with others—strife and alienation—as well as inner alienation from the self and from the gods.

Keywords for Wunjo

Bright: Harmony, Joy, Fellowship, Prosperity

Murky: Stultification, Sorrow, Strife, Alienation

OERP

ᚻ *(Hail) is the whitest of grains,*
it comes from high in heaven
showers of wind hurl it,
then it turns to water.

ONRR

ᚼ (Hail) is the coldest of grains;
Christ[1] shaped the world in ancient times.

OIRP

ᚼ *(Hail) is a cold grain,*
and a shower of sleet,
and the sickness (destroyer) of snakes.

9

ᚺ

HAGALAZ

Phonetic value: H

Germanic names: *Hagalaz*, hail(-stone)

Modern English: Hail

Lore

"Hail" is a complex principle which involves the projection (from "above" or "beyond") of a hard and dangerous substance which is also the "seed of becoming," new creation, and transformation—sometimes through crisis. This is clear in all the rune poems which refer to "hail" as a form of "grain" or a seed. This is transformation within the framework of the cosmos, and the (re-)unification of polar opposites in a productive way. Like the number nine, it represents completion.

Bright-Stave

A change or transformation of your life situation. Perhaps crisis or trauma may be in the offing. The source of this impetus probably will come from beyond your present consciousness. Warning: Be prepared for crisis. This rune indicates self-ordering and inner harmony based on mythic models. (This is the only preparation possible.) Seek to develop pure—crystalline—ideals or principles. If change is undertaken from the impetus of crisis, a good outcome can be expected. A reshaping of your present situation modeled on higher forms or principles (archetypes) is indicated. This rune may indicate a mystic, magician, or priest.

Murk-Stave

Crisis leading to destruction of your vital powers and sources of well-being is indicated. There is lack of preparation. Change for the worse. Personal stagnation is an invitation to catastrophe. Blockage of the "hail" will result in total stagnation and lack of change in life. At first, this may seem beneficial, but crisis must be controlled, not avoided entirely.

Keywords for Hagalaz

Bright: Change according to ideals, Controlled crisis, Completion, Inner harmony

Murky: Catastrophe, Crisis, Stagnation, Loss of power

10

ᚾ
NAUTHIZ

Phonetic value: N

Germanic name: *Nauthiz*,
need, need-fire, distress

Modern English: Need

OERP

*(Need) is constricting on the chest
although to the children of men it often becomes
a help and salvation nevertheless,
if they heed it in time.*

ONRR

*(Need) makes for a difficult situation;
the naked freeze in the frost.*

OIRP

*(Need) is the grief of the bondmaid,
and a hard condition to be in,
and toilsome work.*

Lore

"Need" is the principle of resistance or friction in the universe. As with the "hail" rune, the source of this is outside the individual's control. This is the principle of the chain of causality—cause and effect. This is a root principle of *ørlög*—action and reaction in a chain of events. In the darkness and cold of the need-rune the need for fire is realized, but the fire must be generated from what you have within yourself. Thus the need-fire is kindled to banish distress.

Bright-Stave

Recognition of "need" leads to taking appropriate action to alleviate distress. Stress is turned to strength through consciousness. Resistance to the will leads to a strengthening of the will. Crisis forces original thought and self-reliance. A change leads to salvation from within the self. This rune may indicate a torrid love affair or a crisis in the present one. It also can signify a menial worker or bureaucrat—or a mystic/magician.

Murk-Stave

External circumstances constrain freedom. Beware a hostile environment. Your will is being resisted. The toilsome aspects of life are grinding you down. Friction is present in your inner and outer relationships. You are overly directed toward "outer" things—turn within. Blockage of the *nauthiz* leads to a lack of dynamic tension in life. There is a danger of being seduced to the "easy path" (the so-called "path of least resistance"). This would result in personal atrophy.

Keywords for Nauthiz

Bright: Resistance (leading to strength), Recognition of *ørlög*, Innovation, Need-fire (self-reliance)

Murky: Constraint of freedom, Distress, Toil, Drudgery, Laxity

OERP

| (Ice) is *very cold
and exceedingly slippery;
it glistens, clear as glass,
very much like gems,
a floor made of frost
is fair to see.*

ONRR

| (Ice), we call the broad bridge;
the blind need to be led.*

OIRP

| (Ice) is the rind of the river,
and the roof of the waves,
and a danger for fey men.*

11

I

ISA

Phonetic value: I

Germanic name: *Isa*, ice

Modern English: Ice

Lore

"Ice" is the principle of absolute contraction and stasis. It gathers all things around it into itself and tries to hold them in stillness, darkness, and coldness. This is the extension of the cosmic ice of Niflheimr which balances the all-dynamism of the fires in Muspellsheimr. This force acts as a bridge between worlds due to its "solidifying" quality. It is the bonding element in the cosmos. However, in its pure state it is a destructive and dangerous element.

Bright-Stave

Enhancement of self-consciousness and of ego awareness. Difficult situations are overcome with inner resources. Transition (not always easy) from one state of being to another. This rune may indicate a time to pull back into the self without separating from the world. You need enlightened action to guide your steps in the possible transitions. You possess self-control, the ability to influence others, unity of purpose and being. This element is not without the fascination of beauty. *Isa* also may represent a mystic, scoundrel, or dead man.

Murk-Stave

Out of balance, the "ice" can cause a freezing of life forces and an over-concentration in the ego center, leading to dullness and stupidity. There is a danger of becoming blind to the totality. Transitions bode dangers, though the dangers may be hidden by beauty. Your will may be weakened; or you may be controlled by others, by outside forces: A blockage of *isa* leads to a dissipation of forces and an inability to concentrate consciousness or activity.

Keywords for Isa

Bright: Concentrated self, (Ego) Consciousness, Self-control, Unity

Murky: Ego-mania, Dullness, Blindness, Dissipation

OERP

φ *(Harvest) is the hope of men,*
when god lets,
holy king of heaven,
the earth give her bright fruits
to the noble ones and the needy.

ONRR

ㅓ *(Good harvest) is the profit of men;*
I say that Frodhi was generous.

OIRP

ㅅ *(Good harvest) is the profit of all men,*
and a good summer,
and a ripened field.

12

JERA

Phonetic value: J (Y)

Germanic name: *Jera*, (good) year, harvest

Modern English: Year

Lore

Jera is the cyclical aspect of nature, the great wheel of the year.

When properly used, this natural cycle yields good fruits (rewards). The year is a mechanical/organic process, not a "moral" one. This concept of eternal cycle, or eternal return, is one of the core concepts of the rune row. The other is found in the axis of the yew-rune.

Bright-Stave

Rewards for right action. Plenty and a "good harvest" can be expected. You may be the recipient of the generosity of another. Peace and tranquility born of material well-being are in the offing. You experience the organic/material manifestations of your actions. Have patience to act at the proper time. This rune may represent a farmer or someone in financial affairs.

Murk-Stave

Enslavement to cyclical patterns. You are unable to get beyond repetitious behavior. Inappropriate timing or actions lead to negative results. Failure and poverty can result from wrong work. A blockage of the year-rune causes an inability to use cyclical, natural patterns. Ignorance of the ways of nature may lead to conflict with the self and with others as you attempt to compensate.

Keywords for Jera

Bright: Reward, Plenty, Peace, Proper timing

Murky: Repetition, Bad timing, Poverty, Conflict

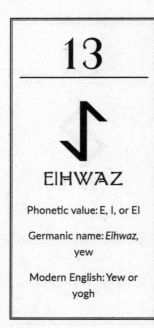

13

EIHWAZ

Phonetic value: E, I, or EI

Germanic name: *Eihwaz,*
yew

Modern English: Yew or
yogh

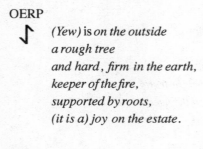

OERP

(Yew) is *on the outside*
a rough tree
and hard, firm in the earth,
keeper of the fire,
supported by roots,
(it is a) joy on the estate.

ONRR

(Yew) is *the greenest wood in the winter;*
there is *usually, when it bums, singeing (i.e.,*
it makes a hot fire).

OIRP

(Yew) is *a strung bow,*
and brittle iron,
and Farbauti (= a giant) of the arrow.

Lore

This is the principle of the vertical axis that penetrates into the world above and the world below and connects the human realm to the heavenly and chthonic regions. It is the synthesis of above and below, light and dark, life and death. The yew is a flexible force but also hard; it endures beyond all other things.

The yew is evergreen in the winter—life in the midst of death—and it is used to build fires, thus becoming the "sun within." This is the World-Tree Yggdrasill.

Bright-Stave

The "yew" promotes spiritual enlightenment along the vertical axis of consciousness. Mental toughness and flexibility are needed. The inner flame must be ignited through discipline. Seek independence from the natural/mechanical order of the cosmos. Controlled changes in consciousness are indicated (initiation). Realization of inner strength will protect you from outside dangers. Bring together the light and dark. This rune may also indicate a mystic or magician.

Murk-Stave

Eihwaz coming too early into the life of a person can cause deep confusion and consternation. The hot fires unconsciously ignited may cause "burn out," leading to death and decay. A stoppage of the "yew" principle in those who are prepared for it causes a profound sense of dissatisfaction, boredom, and meaninglessness. It also can soften your will and sense of self-discipline.

Keywords for Eihwaz

Bright: Enlightenment, Endurance, Initiation, Protection

Murky: Confusion, Destruction, Dissatisfaction, Weakness

OERP

ᛈ *(Lot-box) is always play and laughter among bold men, where the warriors sit in the beer hall, happily together.*

14
ᛈ
PERTHRO

Phonetic value: P

Germanic name: *Perthro*, lot-cup, device for casting lots

Modern English: Perd

Lore

Two things are necessary to understand the connection between the mirth described in the "beer hall" (i.e., a place where sacrificial drink is consumed) and the idea of divination or runecasting. First, you must understand that there was very little difference between the techniques and tools of runecasting and those of simple gambling. Second, you must realize that gambling was an absolute passion among the Germanic (and even Indo-European) peoples. (See the *Germania*, chapter 24.) Like war, gambling was a way to "test their luck"—which meant no less than the strength of their essential beings. This is the runic principle behind the process embodied in the three Norns—Urdhr-Verdhandi-Skuld—which results in *ørlög*, the ordeal of humankind. The mystery of *perthro* is what runecasting is about.

Bright-Stave

A source of joy to athelings (powerful, enlightened ones) who sit in the beer hall, i.e., a well of knowledge and ecstasy to athelings in a contemplative state contained within their psychosomatic enclosures ("hall") charged with the fluid ("beer") of Odian consciousness. This is generally a "good lot" to have and bodes well for runecasts. It portends good fellowship and happiness but indicates constant evolutionary change and growth. It may represent an entertainer or musician.

Murk-Stave

Too much of this force, an addiction to its pleasures, can cause chaos, destruction, and confusion. Unwise use of *perthro* leads to dissipation and squandering of vital forces. A stoppage of this force results in stagnation, loneliness, and withering of life's pleasures.

Keywords for Perthro

Bright: Good lot, Knowledge of *ørlög*, Fellowship and joy, Evolutionary change

Murky: Addiction, Stagnation, Loneliness, Malaise

15

ELHAZ

Phonetic value: Z

Germanic name: *Elhaz*, elk;
or *algiz*, protection

Modern English: Elks

OERP

*(Elk's) sedge has its home
most often in the fen,
it waxes in the water
and grimly wounds
and reddens ("burns") with blood
any man
who, in any way,
tries to grasp it.*

Lore

This, like the *thurisaz* rune (note the thematic similarities in the OERP), is a "two-edged" concept. The OE name "elk-sedge" is a kenning, or poetic name, for sword. Essentially, *elhaz* is the principle of numinous attraction and even union between the individual consciousness and the "higher self" embodied in the fetch of *fylgja*. (See Rune Poems, chapter 8.) This contact, of course, can be dangerous when attempted by one who is unprepared. As with the *eihwaz* rune, this also may be put into arboreal symbology to show the connection between the "roots and branches" of anything. Or it may take the shape of the "Rainbow Bridge" (Bifröst) which connects the human mind with the grandeur of the gods.

Bright-Stave

Except for the experienced atheling or runer, this runestave can bode danger. For those who know not to "grasp" the *elhaz* but to "become" it, however, divine realizations await. Do not barge in like a warrior, but rather approach with the craft of an Odian. This craft or awakening is foreshadowed. Divine communication is indicated. Also, this force can be turned around and used in an attack or to protect yourself. Generally, this rune does not signify persons, but rather divine forces.

Murk-Stave

Grave dangers lie hidden. Lack of preparedness leads to being consumed by awesome, archetypal forces and can result in injury to the self. Blockage of this force may be a blessing to most people. For athelings or Erulians, however, it means being cut off from an important well-spring of inspiration—the fetch (Greek *daimon*, Latin *genius*).

Keywords for Elhaz

Bright: Connection with the gods, Awakening, Higher life, Protection

Murky: Hidden danger, Consumption by divine forces, Loss of divine link

OERP

(Sun) is by sea-men
always hoped for
when they fare far away
over the fishes bath
until the brine-stallion
they bring to land.

ONRR

(Sun) is the light of the lands;
I bow to the holyness.

OIRP

(Sun) is the shield of the clouds,
and a shining glory,
and the life-long sorrow (= destroyer) of ice.

16

S

SOWILO

Phonetic value: S

Germanic name: *Sowilo*, sun

Modern English: Sun

Lore

This is the principle of the guide. It is also the goal after which the runer quests. It shines like a beacon attracting and encouraging those who seek it. *Sowilo* is the sun-wheel; it not only guides but also is itself a dynamically moving, spinning symbol, a counterbalance to the *isa*-rune. This is the rune of higher being. The S-rune is also a sign of the often ignored serpentine mysteries of the North which show the necessity of dealing with darkness to win true wisdom (see Odin's rewinning of the poetic mead, chapter 9).

Bright-Stave

There is reason for hope. Good guidance is being given. If you are "lost" you will find your way. Fixed concentration on your goal leads to success. This rune bodes well for any journey, especially those over water. Listen to higher rede (= counsel) from within the self or from others. The light of the "sun" burns away all external appearances ("ice"), leaving only the essential reality. This force will protect the runer from hostile powers. It will break cosmic or psychological inertia and help the journey along. *Sowilo* brings honor and luck. Educational undertakings may be in the offing. This rune also may signify a sailor or a teacher.

Murk-Stave

Bad counsel. This rune reveals an unthinking attraction to, and pursuit of, goals set by others. False success is gained by dishonorable means. There is a tendency to look outside yourself for answers to questions and for guidance. Gullibility. Blockage of the "sun" leads to loss of your sense of purpose and goals in life. Confusion and eventual defeat of your plans are due to a lack of direction.

Keywords for Sowilo

Bright: Guidance, Hope, Success, Goals achieved, Honor

Murky: False goals, Bad counsel, False success, Gullibility, Loss of goals

17

↑ TIWAZ

Phonetic value: T

Germanic name: *Tiwaz,*
the god Tiw (Tyr)

Modern English: Tue

OERP

↑ *(Tir) is a star,*
it keeps faith well
with athelings,
always on its course
over the mists of night
it never fails.

ONRR

↑ *(Tyr) is the one-handed among the Aesir;*
the smith has to blow often.

OIRP

↑ *(Tyr) is the one-handed god,*
and the leavings of the wolf,
and the ruler of the temple.

Lore

This rune is a threefold principle of (1) order (justice, law), (2) self-sacrifice, and (3) the world column. Each of these really derives from the unified principle of independent ordered existence, whose servants will sacrifice themselves for its sake. Its main cosmic function is the separation of the heavens and earth by the world column (Irminsûl) so that manifestation can take place in the "created" space. *Tiwaz* is the sign of the "pole-" or "load-star" used as a constant guide through the night sky.

Bright-Stave

This is the lot of *troth* (faith, loyalty) and trust that endures in the face of all hardships. Justice can be expected, and good judgment based on a careful analysis of the facts. Victory will be yours if you have acted wisely. Strive to order the environment in a rational way. The path to success may lie through self-sacrifice. Vigilance and hard work combined with knowledge are necessary. Reliability, loyalty, faithfulness must be practiced, and can be expected. Strive for exactitude and precision, and plan very carefully. Make your work methodical. Analytical models based on mathematical principles are indicated. The rune may indicate a scientist or academic.

Murk-Stave

You have a tendency to become bogged down in analysis and details, which may lead to a paralysis of action and a limitation in vision. You are always planning, never doing. Self-sacrifice is to the detriment of the ultimate interests—"sacrificing over much." A stoppage of *tiwaz* force leads to injustice, imbalance, confusion, a deterioration of rationality.

Keywords for Tiwaz

Bright: Troth, Justice, Rationality, Self-sacrifice, Analysis

Murky: Mental paralysis, Over-analysis, Over-sacrifice, Injustice, Imbalance

18

ᛒ

BERKANO

Phonetic value: B

Germanic name: *Berkano*,
birch, the birch goddess
or twig

Modern English: Birch

OERP

ᛒ *(Birch) is without fruit
but just the same it bears
limbs without fertile seed;
it has beautiful branches,
high on its crown
it is finely covered,
loaded with leaves,
touching the sky.*

ONRR

ᛒ *(Birch-twig) is the limb greenest with leaves,
Loki brought the luck of deceit.*

OIRP

ᛒ *(Birch-twig) is a leafy limb,
and a little tree,
and a youthful wood.*

Lore

The *berkano* principle is one of self-contained and continuous propagation or growth. It is the principle of birth itself which is never "born" but always is. This lot expands itself without losing its self-consciousness. It is a creative originator of being that extends into the heavens and into the nether regions. The Brune is a collector and conserver of energy and a sign of enclosure and shelter. The birch is the liberator of pent-up energies, which when released lead to new growth.

Bright-Stave

New beginnings based on old patterns are indicated. Gradual changes are on the way. Look for the importance of new things, things that might seem small at their birth. Spiritual growth comes within tradition. Domestic change occurs within a tranquil environment. New aspects are introduced into erotic relationships. Prosperity and beauty are indicated. Some elements of craft, deceit, or viciousness may be necessary to achieve goals. This rune may represent a mother or a whore.

Murk-Stave

Submersion into the "natural world" leads to a blurring of self-consciousness and awareness. There is a fascination with the sheer beauty of the world of appearances. Deceit is a danger. A blockage of the "birch" can lead to sterility of mind and body, and stagnation in all aspects of life.

Keywords for Berkano

Bright: Birth, Becoming, Life changes, Shelter, Liberation

Murky: Blurring of consciousness, Deceit, Sterility, Stagnation

OERP

ᛗ *(Horse) is, in front of the earls
the joy of athelings,
a charger proud on its hooves;
when concerning it, heroes—
wealthy men—on war-horses
exchange speech,
and it is always a comfort
to the restless.*

19

ᛗ

EHWAZ

Phonetic value: E

Germanic name: *Ehwaz*,
(war) horse; or *ehwo*,
the two horses

Modern English: Eh

Lore

This is the principle of "teamwork," especially in tandem. It represents two different, yet harmoniously working entities. In traditional Germanic culture this is most clearly experienced in the special relationship between rider *(mannaz)* and horse *(elhaz),* or by observing how a team of horses works. This is, then, a metaphor for the relationship of the self to the body and/or the special inner bond between any two entities or things that are directed toward noble endeavors.

Bright-Stave

Dynamic harmony with others is indicated, especially with a partner, mentor, husband, or wife. There is teamwork without loss of individuality. You understand the necessity of give and take and accept unique differences in the other. Good results are indicated. Develop a relationship with your fetch. Marriage or other formal partnership may be in the offing. Mutual trust and loyalty are necessary and present. The rune may represent your spouse or partner in some endeavor.

Murk-Stave

Loss of self in the partner is indicated. Too much "harmony" leads to sameness and duplication of efforts. A stoppage of the *ehwaz* results in mistrust, betrayal, disharmony, divorce.

Keywords for Ehwaz

Bright: Harmony, Teamwork, Trust, Loyalty

Murky: Duplication, Disharmony, Mistrust, Betrayal

20

MANNAZ

Phonetic value: M

Germanic name: *Mannaz*,
human being

Modern English: Man

OERP

*(Man) is in his mirth
dear to his kinsman;
although each shall
depart from the other;
for the lord wants to commit,
by his decree,
that frail flesh
to the earth.*

ONRR

*(Man) is the increase of dust;
mighty is the talon-span of the hawk.*

OIRP

*(Man) is the joy of man,
and the increase of dust,
and the adornment of ships.*

Lore

"Man" is the principle of embodied self-consciousness. This symbolizes humankind's earthly life as a heroic struggle, and points to the reality that we are only truly human when in the flesh. The stave refers to the origin of humanity (both Askr and Embla) as a result of the threefold gift of Odin-Vili-Vé, and to the origin of threefold human society (farmers, fighters, and rulers/magicians). Both myths show the shaping of people on earth (Midhgardhr) in the image of the divine—both in consciousness and in order. Our mortality—as that of the gods—ensures becoming.

Bright-Stave

This is the lot of humanity, of humanness with all its great nobility and power of spirit, as well as its weakness and mortality. Great intelligence born of divine or higher knowledge is indicated. Individuation of the self is needed. There is happiness in inner and social life, born of a realization of the truths of human existence. Blinders will be removed; you will see things as they are. Awakening. This rune could indicate any person, but especially seekers of all kinds.

Murk-Stave

Depression due to a perception of hopelessness is indicated. You dwell on mortality and weakness, fearing true knowledge. Relationships are based on lies and misperceptions. A blockage of *mannaz* leads to blindness, self-delusion, and a tendency to live in a fantasy world.

Keywords for Mannaz

Bright: Divine structure, Intelligence, Awareness, Social order

Murky: Depression, Mortality, Blindness, Self-delusion

OERP

ᛚ
(Water) is to people
seemingly unending
if they should venture out
on an unsteady ship
and the sea waves
frighten them very much,
and the brine-stallion
does not heed its bridle.

ONRR

ᛚ
(Water) is (that), which falls from the mountain;
as a force; but gold (objects) are costly things.

OIRP

ᛚ
(Wetness) is churning water,
and a wide kettle,
and the land of fish.

21

ᛚ

LAGUZ

Phonetic value: L

Germanic name: *Laguz*, water, lake; or *laukaz*, leek

Modern English: Lake or leek

Lore

This is the principle of cosmic water welling up from Niflheimr and containing the potential for life. This water is the great sea of dynamic forces into which you are thrust during your voyage of becoming. The deep can represent that vast sea of the world of which humankind is usually unconscious, and which can be threatening if you are voyaging in a "vessel" that is subject to disturbances on this "sea." A "downward" flow of vital energy is indicated. The alternate name "leek" indicates growth upward.

Bright-Stave

Stern tests in life are indicated, but you have the vital energies to stand these tests. The self evolves through the experience of true initiation. Transition from one state of being to another. Begin at once to act. Control of the self is most needed. Do not fear the journey. By "going under" you will gain the gold of well-being. Personal growth will occur through perhaps uncomfortable situations. A sailor, fisherman, or lawyer may be represented by this rune.

Murk-Stave

Fear of change, fear of the journey and of the unknown vastness within the deep self are present. There is a danger of "going around in circles," avoiding the path, avoiding life. Failing the test is indicated. A stoppage of *laguz* dams up the vital force and leads to stunted growth, withering, and poverty. Access to the deep self is blocked.

Keywords for Laguz

Bright: Life, "Water" journey, Sea of vitality, Sea of unconscious, Growth

Murky: Fear, Circular motion, Avoidance, Withering

22

INGWAZ

Phonetic value: NG

Germanic name: *Ingwaz,* the god Ing

Modern English: Ing

OERP

*(Ing) was first, among the East-Danes,
seen by men
until he again eastward (or "back")
went over the wave;
the wain followed on;
this is what the warriors
called the hero.*

Lore

This is the principle of contained, isolated separation, which is absolutely necessary to any transformational process. "Ing" is the stasis of being which forms a step along the path of eternal becoming. Entering into this principle is a movement "widdershins"—against the sun—"to the east" into the realm of darkness inhabited by the etins (giants). In this realm of darkness and solitude new growth arises.

Bright-Stave

"Ing" is the stave of rest, of active internal growth. There is a deep-level gestation of new power. Rest, let things "gestate," to be brought forth at the right time in full maturity. Have patience. Listen to yourself. This lot indicates concepts or aspects that have had the benefit of such a period of gestation. This is a time of stasis to be followed by fertile dynamism. Things are in a potential state awaiting activation. This rune may signify a farmer or a priest.

Murk-Stave

The misapplication of "ing" can lead to self-absorption and to a disassociation from the environment. You can become "bottled up" in the subjective world, unable to interact with objectivity. Paralytic stasis is indicated. This can be a seductive force, fooling you into thinking it is the "end" rather than a stage; thus it is the curse of many mystics. On the other hand, a blockage of the NG-stave can lead to a scattering of essence or a sense of meaningless motion—without stages at which essence can be gathered and consolidated. There is movement but without real change, and unbridled dynamism.

Keywords for Ingwaz

Bright: Rest stage, Internal growth, Gestation

Murky: Impotence, Scattering, Movement without change

OERP

(Day) is the lord's messenger,
dear to men,
the ruler's famous light;
(it is) mirth and hope
to rich and poor
(and) is useful for all.

Lore

This is the ultimate principle of bipolar creativity. It is a unique stave of consciousness as a developed, evolved form of the gifts of the god(s) Odin-Vili-Vé. In the light of day all seemingly polar opposites are brought together and understood. This is the rune of enlightened consciousness.

23

DAGAZ

Phonetic value: D

Germanic name: *Dagaz*, day

Modern English: Day

Bright-Stave

"Day" brings the boon of archetypal awareness, which can sometimes seem spontaneous. It is a source—really the only true source—of hope and happiness. The power of "day" can be known to all who seek it earnestly. A great awakening is at hand. True vision will be gained. This light may be found where you do not expect it. Seek the ideal. "Day" represents a true seeker.

Murk-Stave

It is difficult for "day" to be seen as a murk-stave in the active sense. The only detriment would be its manifestation in the life of someone who did not want it or who was not prepared for it. Of course, a blockage of the light of "day" means blindness, dullness, boredom, hopelessness, etc.

Keywords for Dagaz

Bright: Awakening, Awareness, Hope/happiness, The ideal

Murky: Blindness, Hopelessness

24

OTHALA

Phonetic value: O

Germanic name: *Othala,*
ancestral property

Modern English: Odal

OERP

*(Estate) is very dear
to every man,
if he can enjoy what is right
and according to custom
in his dwelling,
most often in prosperity.*

Lore

This is the principle of the "homeland" in its most ideal form. It represents the "inside" vs. the "outside." Psychologically, it is the self in all its complexity as distinguished from non-self. Socially, it is the group (be it family, clan, tribe, guild, order, etc.) distinguished from those outside that group. Right order must be preserved in this group for it to work. Although secure in the home, there is continued interaction—give and take—with the environment. It is the "home within," i.e., the ideal reality which is not attached to any particular "land." *Othala* is complete freedom. It is the active consolidation of all gains.

THE BIG BOOK OF RUNES AND RUNE MAGIC

Bright-Stave

"Odal" is the lot of stable prosperity and well-being. A solid and peaceful home-, family-, or group-life is indicated, and one that leads to continued growth. Attention must always be paid to customs and order within the group and to the vigilant defense of the group. There is true freedom stemming from a secure base. A new dwelling or a new allegiance may be in the offing. Productive interaction with "outsiders" is a continuing possibility. This lot may indicate a leader of some kind, or a whole group of people.

Murk-Stave

Again, this stave is difficult to see in an actively negative way. The only danger comes through not preserving right customary or traditional order within a group, thus limiting the powers of leaders. A misunderstanding of "odal" can lead to a totalitarianism that runs counter to the interests of the whole. All of this will lead to disaster. A stoppage of the O-stave, however, will end in slavery to outside forces, poverty, homelessness, and loneliness.

Keywords for Othala

Bright: A home, Group prosperity, Group order, Freedom, Productive interaction

Murky: Lack of customary order, Totalitarianism, Slavery, Poverty, Homelessness

Chapter 17

THE TOOLS OF RUNECASTING

As a method of divination, runecasting is remarkably flexible in the ways it can be used. Theoretically, all you need are twenty-four slips of paper on which the stave shapes could be written, for the magic is in the self of the runer, not in the objects. However, for most runers a permanent set of runestaves and a set of special runecasting tools are essential for maintaining the all-important sense of connection, dedication, and intensity.

The physical objects upon which the staves are carved may be left up to the runer. The "staves" can be made of wood, bone, stone, earthenware, or another material you like, and in whatever size and shape you prefer. The only thing I strongly urge is that you make your own runestaves. I suggested this for two reasons: (1) the runestaves are so simple anyone can easily make them (so take advantage of what is traditional), and (2) from a magical and talismanic viewpoint even slips of paper marked with a ballpoint pen are superior to mass-produced "rune cookies" since you put your own energy into the runestaves as you make them. This being said, it is still better to start working with quality manufactured staves than to put off too long the beginnings of actual work.

What kind of staves (or even "cards") the runer eventually will want to work with is largely a matter of taste or personal preference. I suggest a period of experimentation; see in practice which kind you prefer. In actual use, this may be different than what you preferred in theory. In ancient times, for readings of extreme importance, staves were prepared for the reading and then destroyed afterward, or the staves were then "sacrificed" by being burned or buried beneath the earth to decompose.

There are several types of runestaves: (A) small and round (of pottery, wood, or bone), (B) small rectangular slips of wood, (C) short, or (D) long rune tines, and even (E) cards. Examples of each of these types are illustrated in figure 17.1, shown in their approximately actual sizes.

Although different kinds of runestaves may be more suitable for certain types of castings or layouts, really any kind of stave can be used effectively for almost any method.

The small round stave may be made from tree branches (or even dowels) about one-half to three-fourths of an inch in diameter cut at intervals of about one-fourth of an inch. The result is a set of small disks on which you can carve the runestaves. This general type also can be fashioned from wooden beads—but spherical shapes can roll and thus prove unsuitable for some methods of runecasting.

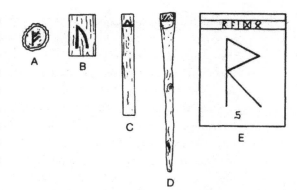

Small rectangular wooden slips can be made from carefully shaven and trimmed strips of wood, about one-sixteenth of an inch thick. This is probably the type Tacitus was describing. But they also can be fashioned from thin sheets of wood ve-

Figure 17.1. Various types of runestaves. Here we see examples of A) small round runestave—this one is of wood; B) runestave made of a small rectangular piece of wood; C) short and D) long runestave; and E) a "card" runestave.

neer. (These veneer sheets can be obtained in most hardware or hobby shops.)

Shorter runelots or runetines may be fashioned from short lengths (two to three inches) of twigs or from square strips of hardwood (about one-quarter inch wide). This kind and the rectangular wooden slips are most convenient for carrying in your pocket or purse.

The longer runestaves are perhaps the most traditional forms. Although no such examples have ever been found, ancient written descriptions seem to point in this direction. This type of runestave can be made easily from tapering twigs five to six inches long and one-quarter to one-half an inch wide at the top. They can be left rough, the bark still on them, with only a small surface smoothed at the large end on which the runestave can be carved.

Finally, for methods of divination that require laying out runic patterns, cards also can be fashioned. To these you might want to add information, such as the rune name or its numerical value, that could be helpful in your rune readings. These can be made easily from posterboard or blank paper cards of a size and shape that is pleasing to you.

The actual materials used in the creation of the runestaves can be of some importance. For the lots or staves themselves, organic substances, such as wood or bone, are preferred. Wood is, of course, the most traditional and the most widely used material for this purpose, but bone and even precious metals perhaps were also used for divination. The symbolism of the use of wood is clear in the Germanic cultural context. It reminds us of the World-Tree, Yggdrasill, at the roots of which lies the Well of Wyrd, and in whose roots and branches the runestaves shimmer as a mighty webwork. Use your intuition to decide what species of wood is best suited for your runestaves. Tacitus reports that fruit- or nut-bearing trees were used, but it is perhaps more important that you choose a wood that has special value or meaning to you. It is also possible to make the staves out of various kinds of wood, each one corresponding to the runestave carved upon it. The runer is urged to make use of intuition, but you also may want to consult Appendix III on page 294 for guidance.

The runestaves also will be colored. The traditional paint or dye used for this can be made easily from red ochre. (Other natural red pigments are also good.) Of course, the substance originally used was blood, but even in prehistoric times red ochre was being used as a substitute for blood. However, different colors—as determined by intuition—are also possible. White, however, as a color for the staves themselves, should be avoided since the cloth on which they will be cast is white.

One of the wonderful things about runecasting is that you can be as traditional or as innovative as you wish. It is relatively simple to include traditional elements with innovative techniques. For the ritual elements of the traditional shaping of runelots, see chapter 18.

The cloth upon which the lots are cast should be made of white material. Not only does Tacitus indicate this in his report, but this practice is borne out by the symbolism of white as a sign of the undifferentiated sum of magical light. It is upon this white field that the runes play out their interweavings of force. The cloth itself should be made of linen or some other natural material and should be between three and four feet square.

Some runers decorate their cloths in meaningful ways. Chapter 19 presents methods of runecasting that call for the runer to read certain significances into various fields on the cloth (see figure 19.9). This pattern could be stitched onto the cloth, or it simply could be envisioned with the *hugauga*—the magical eye. If the runer uses such lines on the cloth, they should be of dark blue or black and be as thin as possible. This latter point is merely a practical one for ease in making readings.

When not in use, the runestaves or runelots should be stored in a suitable container. A cloth or leather bag or a wooden box is ideal for this. Such a container is of the greatest importance if you have shaped and loaded your runelots as "talismanic creatures" with their own *ørlög*. Some runers like to cast their runelots from a lot cup (the wooden box can also serve this purpose). The lot cup can be made of horn, leather, or wood and can be any shape the runer determines. The only important factor is that it is large enough to hold all twenty-four lots easily and loosely. This cup, should it be treated as a *taufr* (talisman) itself, should be loaded with the *perthro* rune.

In very formal rites of runecasting, especially those of cosmic significance carried out by true Erulians, a three-legged stool painted gold is also needed. The runer sits upon this stool, called "theal's stool," before beginning to formulate a reading. (This, however, is not necessary for most runecasters' purposes.)

Other tools and equipment as needed in general runework are described more fully in chapter 21.

Chapter 18

RITES OF RUNECASTING

The use of ritual in every operation of runecasting is important for two reasons: to avoid the "parlor game" attitude that sometimes envelopes such sacred activity, and to help the runer reach a state of concentrated consciousness that will improve the quality of the casting and reading. Ritual work will put the runer in an altered state of mind that will direct his or her concentration to the question at hand, or to the general life situation of greatest importance at that time—thus opening the doors of communication between the runecaster and the realm of the Norns. After some time has been spent working with runecasting, the vitki will begin to feel that in certain operations he or she was more "in sync" than in others. To ensure this state on a regular basis is the function of inner ritual work.

Although the runer is free to create such ritual formulas as he or she sees fit, I urge everyone to carry out faithfully the example formulas a few times to see if the traditional methods are right for you. It is a great misfortune that the old Germanic tradition has been so neglected—especially since we have descriptions of the exact methods used for many centuries. After consulting all the traditional sources, the following complex ritual formula appears to have existed from the most ancient times:

1) Cutting and scoring of staves

2) Calling on the Norns (or other gods and entities)

3) Casting the staves (onto the white cloth)

4) Calling on the gods (or other entities)

5) Choosing staves (in threes or multiples of three)

6) Sitting on the theal's stool

7) Reading of the staves

8) Confirmation by omens, etc.

This would represent a complex and elaborate kind of runecasting, but elements from this great formula should be kept in mind as bases for experimentation.

Time

The season and the time of day the runer chooses to undertake runecastings, especially important castings, deserve some thought. Traditionally the runer takes into account (1) season (position of the sun in the yearly cycle), (2) moon phase, and (3) time of day (position of the sun in the daily cycle). Of course, the time chosen should conform to the kind of reading being undertaken, or the nature of the question. Inquiries involving new beginnings perhaps would be carried out most effectively at times associated with beginnings, during the yuletide for example (about December 21–January 2), at (Easter[1] or Ostara—the springtime festival at or around the spring equinox), nights just after the new moon, or just before the full moon at sunrise. The first three nights after the new moon, the fifth, seventh, eighth, ninth, twelfth, nineteenth, twentieth, twenty-third, and twenty-sixth nights of the moon are well suited to divinatory work, too. To find the correct night (or "day"),[2] count from the first night of the new moon. There are, of course, twenty-eight nights in the lunar cycle. Also, for consulting the runes on inner or esoteric matters, nighttime is preferred, while on exoteric or other mundane affairs the daylight hours are best.

It should be remembered also that these times are merely optimal ritual aids; from a fully Odian viewpoint they can be dispensed with.

Stead

For practical reasons, most runecasting will probably be carried out indoors, in your living quarters. For ritual effectiveness other runework should be done in the same area. One advantage to runecasting is that the vitki can carry the basic "holy stead" around in the form of the white cloth. However, for especially important castings other holy steads might also be considered. Most beneficial are sites under holy trees—oaks, beeches, yews, ashes—or near (south of if possible) a natural spring or an artificial well. Hilltops are also good places to do runework. Outdoors, the runecaster can follow the rede of the ancient tradition more effectively and look into the sky when picking the staves for the reading. The force can be especially powerful at night if you look directly to the Northern Star—into the eye of Odin—while choosing the lots.

Talismanic Creation of Lots

The physical objects or media upon which the runic characters are executed are referred to by various terms: staves (ON *stafir*), tines (ON *teinar*), or lots (ON *hlautar*), but all are *taufar,* talismans. Ideally, each runestave should be shaped and loaded according to the principles of talismanic creation. These are outlined in detail in chapter 21.

Runecasting

Not every runecasting or laying needs to be carried out with great solemnity; however, the more important the question, the more ritual the true runer will want to use. In a way, the ritual can be seen as a kind of "magical overkill"; the more ways in which communicative links between the inner and outer realms are forged, the more chance there is of gaining that special sense of "rightness," of being "in sync." From the traditional standpoint, such workings are seen as no less fundamental than the cast itself; it is a whole operation.

For a full ritual runecasting the white cloth should be laid out before the harrow (if one is used) with one flat side to the north. Depending on the type of cast or layout being done, the theal's stool (if one is used) should either be to the south of the cloth, or to the north of it in front of the altar or harrow as shown in figure 18.1. on page 206.

Opening: Perform a Hammer Rite of the kind described in chapter 21.

Call to the Norns: Facing north, in the *elhaz*-rune position, call out to the power of the Norns to help you cast and read the runes:

> Out of homes all-hidden
> out of the ways all-wide,
> need be I name the Norns,
> and deem the dises draw neigh.
> > *[Pause]*
> Urdhr-Verdhandi-Skuld.

With this verse the runer concentrates on engaging the "nornic forces" on two levels: (1) the personal Norns (with whose "help" the runic streams can be engaged) and (2) the Great Norns—as the impersonal dynamic matrix of constant change.

Question: Now concentrate for a period in silence on the question at hand. While doing this, shuffle the staves in your hands or shake them in the box or cup. Once it is felt that a firm link between the nornic forces and the question has been forged, repeat the formula silently or aloud.

> Runár rádh rétt rádh!
> > or
> Runes rown right rede!

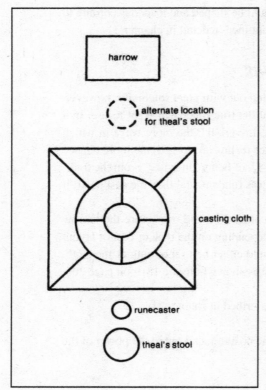

Figure 18.1. Configuration of elements of runecasting ritual.

Casting: Now, while gazing upward (to the Northern Star if you are outdoors) cast the runelots upon the white cloth spread out before you. As the lots are in the air, call out:

Urdhr-Verdhandi-Skuld!

NOTE: If a rune-laying [and not a runecasting] method is being used, questioning and casting are combined in such a way that while the lots or cards are shuffled or otherwise randomized, the question is being posed mentally. The process is then concluded with the "Runes rown right rede" and "Urdhr-Verdhandi-Skuld" formulas.

Call to Odin: After the lots have landed, and while still gazing aloft, the runer strikes the *elhaz*-posture and says:

Odin open my eye
that I may see the staves
and read the runes aright.
    [Pause]
Odin-Vili-Vé!

With this verse you engage your abilities to choose the staves with inner vision. (Note: Some may wish to substitute a verse to Frigga here.)

Choosing: (Skip this step if you are using a pure casting method in which the lots are read as they lie on the white cloth.) Now, with your eyes still directed upward, kneel down and blindly pick the right number of lots for the method being employed. It is, of course, very important to be sure to keep the lots in the proper order as chosen from the cloth. Lay them aside carefully—one at a time as you choose them. (Note: If a laying method is being used, the lots or cards should be laid out in their proper configuration at this time.)

Reading: If a theal's stool or chair is being used, the runecaster should sit down upon it now—still facing north—and lay the lots out in their right order according to the method being used, either on the harrow or on the edge of the white cloth. If a reading is to be made directly from the lay of the lots on the cloth, position the theal's stool to the south of the cloth and examine the configurations. Settle your mind at this stage, and before beginning the reading (especially when reading for others), intone this verse based on "Hávamál," st. 111:

> Time is come to sing
> upon the stool of the theal
> at the well of wyrd:
>
> I saw but said naught
> I saw and thought and thought
> I listened to the High One's lore.
>
> Of runes I heard it rowned
> rowning them within—
> in the hall of Hár,
> thus I heard them say,
> thus I read them aright.

Closing: After the reading is complete, close with the traditional words:

> Now the saws of Hár are said,
> in the hall of Hár!

You will, of course, always want to keep a record of your rune readings, so before returning the lots to their abode, make your records. Then place the staves in their container in silence.

Taking of Omens

If confirmation of the results of the reading are needed, omens should be taken. This is a traditional part of old Germanic (and Indo-European) divination—the necessity for "corroborating evidence" from another medium. The science of omens (ON *heilar*) is too complex to enter into in any great detail here. The simplest method is to sit in an open area out-of-doors; visualize an enclosed space in front of you (no smaller than ten feet square, but it can be much larger). Then wait for a bird or other animal to enter into, or fly over, that space. For a yes/no confirmation or denial of the validity of any given cast, dark-colored animals or birds (especially black, red, dark blue, or dark brown) mean "yes," and light-colored ones (especially white, light brown, light blue) mean "no."

Chapter 19

THE WAYS OF RUNECASTING

The almost two-thousand-year-old description provided by Tacitus gives us a good idea of at least one method of runecasting; however, there are many more based on traditional customs and on cosmological principles which have been used effectively by runecasters. In this chapter we will explore some of the most effective methods, ones that are also most deeply rooted in traditional concepts.

Runecasting, like any precise system of divination—I-Ching, Tarot, astrology—is based on the apparently random superimposition of "meaningful elements" over "meaningful fields." From the combinations and interrelationships of those combinations, the full interpretation is read. In runelore, the runestaves provide the elements of meaning, while the fields of meaning are provided by a number of key cosmological configurations. One of the weaknesses of previous books on runic divination is the general lack of traditional fields of meaning, for in order to know these it is necessary to have in-depth understanding of Germanic cosmology.

Each of the methods presented below may be suited to different kinds of inquiries or explorations as suggested. It is probably best to master one kind of casting first, however, before moving on to wider experimentation. Before setting out to do actual runecastings, you may wish to engage in some reading exercises that will begin to make the runes become more and more "your own."

Reading Exercise I

Lay out your runelots in the regular futhark order, arranged in the traditional aett pattern as in figure 19.1. Now, begin to make connections between neighboring runes. Go down the first ætt F through W, down the second aett, H through S, etc., and try to make a progression out of them. Then reverse this and begin with the third aett, O through T, then with the second aett, S through H, etc., again making meaningful interconnections between and among the runes.

Next, do a similar exercise with the vertical runes across the three aettir FHT, UNB, etc., going from top to bottom, and then reversing this from bottom to top. These exercises, which should be done in several different sittings, will strengthen your skills at reading runic contexts. They will also teach you about the living realities of the runic system in a way no book or other person could. This is direct runic learning. You also should begin to realize that the runes find their true meaning in that stead where the outer world runes come face-to-face with the inner runes of

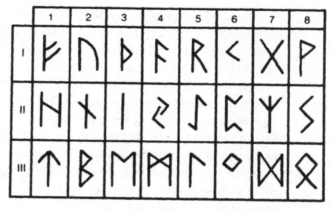

Figure 19.1. Elder Futhark in aett arrangement.

yourself. This process also begins to awaken your inner rune-life. Be sure to write down your results at each sitting.

Reading Exercise II

The next step in truly "making the runes your own" involves the personal expansion of the meanings of the individual runestaves. Take one runestave a day and meditate on it. Think deeply about it. Contemplate the relevant rune poem stanzas. Make your own interconnections and come to your own understandings of every rune. As in Exercise I, write down your results. Your finished notes will amount to your own personal and personalized versions of the Runic Tables in chapter 16. These should not be considered set in stone—allow them to grow as you get to know "your runes" better. Remember, these are your personal realizations and may not be valid for others. The Runic Tables were generated in a similar way over a period of some ten years of work informed by the esoteric runic tradition (both ancient and modern).

On Aspects

One matter crucial to rune reading is determining what aspect of a rune is to be interpreted. Should a lot be read as a bright-stave or as a murk-stave? That the negative aspects of the runes, called *myrkstafir* in Old Norse, were used in magic is beyond question. It also can be safely assumed that such interpretations were responsible for various negative terms presented in chapter 6. Some of the "positive" manifestations of the runes can be said to often have detrimental or dangerous consequences, especially the TH-, H-, N-, I-, and Z-runes. There is no shortage of dark aspects in the rune row. Remember, the runes are your inner advisors, and they must be able to warn you—before it becomes too late to overcome the force of Wyrd.

Aspects are determined in essentially two ways: (1) by the position a runelot falls in a casting (e.g., faceup or facedown; inside or outside a certain field), and (2) by the angle at which one runelot is juxtaposed to another. This latter method deserves a few introductory remarks. It will be noted that for the most part the runestaves are constructed with acute or obtuse angle combinations, and there are very few right angles in the shapes. Obtuse angles are known to have a dynamizing effect on the mind, while right angles generally have the opposite effect. (This was a matter of occult study in the late nineteenth and early twentieth century German orders, and is upheld by at least one working Order in America today.) In any event, it is clear that in the runic tradition obtuse or acute angles promote active, positive interaction between and among runes. Right angles create static, negative interaction—or they can block the flow of runic force altogether. They actually cross it.

Determination of Aspects

In casting, if a rune lands faceup it is to be read as a bright-stave; if it lands facedown it may either be disregarded in the reading or read as a murk-stave. The decision on how these lots are to be interpreted must be made before every casting. Also, each runer is encouraged to be consistent in this regard. The usual practice is to disregard them, however. In some casting, runes that fall outside the fields of meaning or off the white cloth also may be read as murk-staves. Again, you must determine how these are to be read beforehand.

When using angular aspects in castings, the runer must measure (at least approximately) the angle at which any two lots in question are juxtaposed. This is done by mentally drawing lines from the two lots through the center point of the cloth, and then determining the angle at which they are juxtaposed. An example of this can be found in figure 19.2. If the result is between 5° and 45°, or between 135° and 360° they are read as bright-staves; if they fall between 45° and 135° they are read as murk-staves. Exact measurements are unnecessary.

Probably the easiest way to see these relationships is by imagining a circle over the cloth that is divided into quarters and bisected by a third line that you will use to orient the rune in question to the others. Runes falling in the same quarter or in the quarter directly opposite are brightly aspected,

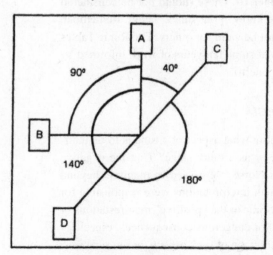

Figure 19.2. Sample angles for casting aspects.

while those in the quadrants on either side tend to be murky.

The closer a lot is to the bright angle the more positively it is to be read. Only those close to a 90° relationship should be read as "blockages." Juxtapositions approaching 180° also have a dark aspect, but one which will lead eventually to a positive outcome. In castings these aspects only refine what is already apparent in the reading of the rune and its field. (See Sample Reading 3 on page 211.)

Aspects of this kind are much more useful and easier to determine when using a rune layout method. To determine the relationship among runes in a layout, the runer can refer to figure 19.3, which essentially works on the same principles as the determination of aspects in casting. Let us take the example of *fehu* (F). Runes belonging to the same triad (e.g., F-H-T), or to triads on either side, or to the triads on the same axes as those adjacent to the "home triad" of *fehu* are to be read as bright-staves. Those in the opposite triad are read as murk-staves, but with a positive ultimate outcome. Those runes in triads at a 90° angle, those that cross the axis of the triad in question, are read as murk-staves, usually of a blocking variety. (See Sample Reading 1 on page 212 and Sample Reading 4 on page 221 for clarification of how this works in practice.)

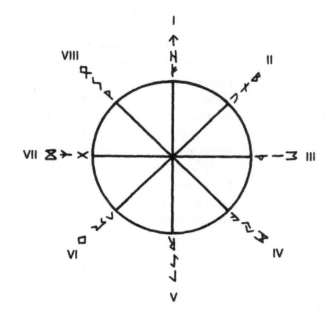

Figure 19.3. Aett aspectarian.

It also should be noted that there is a certain question of "aspect" with regard to the relationship of a given stave to the stead in which it falls or is laid. In the sample readings found below, practical indications of just how this might work are given for various methods. To a great extent intuition must guide the runer in these matters.

The determination of aspect is one of the finer points of the runecaster's skill and craft, and it is one that must be learned through personal experience because the runes will interact differently with different people. Fortunately or unfortunately, it is not a simple matter of reading reversed staves as "bad."

The Methods

These methods of runecasting are based on "models of meaning" used by the ancient Germanic peoples. It is strongly recommended that you seek to master one of these methods before you begin to work on the others. After a while, you can also begin to experiment with innovative casting or laying techniques. But the traditional modes themselves have something to teach about the "runic mind-set." Those who are experienced in other divinatory traditions with "fields of meaning," such as the Tarot or astrology, may wish to experiment with using runes in those contexts. However, they must realize that only part of the runic essence can come through in this manner.

The two classes of operation are casting and laying. The first method discussed here is really a combination of these two types. Castings, because the caster momentarily loses control of the lots, are most effective in reading things in the other world; layings, because the runer is always in control of the lots, are most effective in reading inner states. Both methods have their advantages and disadvantages. In a given casting you may have interest in a certain area of life, yet no lots will fall in that field (which may tell you something as well). On the other hand, with layouts, you will lay lots in steads that may or may not be of equal relevance to your situation—and it takes some skill to intuit which groups of lots are more significant than others.

I. The Nornic Runecast

This method is directly based on the account given by Tacitus in the *Germania*. The three-fold matrix he mentions is applied to the only obvious three-fold matrix of meaning for Germanic divination: the Urdhr-Verdhandi-Skuld formula.

The runer, following the ritual outline given in chapter 18, randomly casts the lots onto the white cloth, and with his or her eyes closed or diverted upward, blindly picks three lots which he or she lays out in order 1-2-3. To help the runer visualize their relationships, the lots should be laid out in the fashion illustrated in figure 19.4.

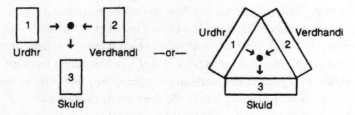

Figure 19 .4. Configuration of lots in the Nornic method.

Position (1) is the stead of Urdhr (Wyrd), which indicates what is really at the root of the question or problem. It tells what has come about in the past that has conditioned the lot in position (2)—the stead of Verdhandi—which is concerned with the present situation. It tells what is in the process of happening in the present. Both of these are synthesized into the third position—the stead of Skuld—which indicates what should come about in the future given the conditions of the first two positions.

In reading these runes, the vitki may wish to use the aspectarian to determine the quality of their relationships. Inverted or reversed lots may be taken into account; however, this is not necessary.

Reading the Nornic Runecast

Object of Inquiry: Situation surrounding the winning of a new job.

Reading: The layout is shown in figure 19.5. *Kenaz* in the Urdhr stead indicates that craft and creativity developed in the past are putting the person in a good position. The groundwork has been laid in a creative fashion. *Dagaz* in Verdhandi shows that the present situation is, however, in a state of flux. Things are now dynamic and malleable. The third stave, *uruz* in Skuld, is very hopeful; it indicates that the situation should be formed in accordance with the will of the job seeker. The final stave in this stead also advises "tenacity." The person should persevere with willpower to achieve the right outcome. *Kenaz* is well aspected to *dagaz,* which is in turn well aspected to *uru*—all of which indicate that the staves are working together smoothly. The *kenaz* is opposed to *uruz,* but because of the otherwise dynamic aspects it seems rather clear that this opposition will be one of a vivifying rather than stultifying kind.

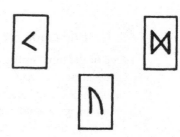

Figure 19.5. Sample Nornic runecast.

As a matter of fact, the person for whom the reading was done did get the job in question—certainly based on past performance, but also with a little help from magical agencies, and only with the utmost of perseverance.

• • •

The Nornic Runecast may be significantly expanded into the *valknutr* (knot of the slain). This is a sign of the god Odin's ability to bind and unbind fetters of all kinds—including those of "fate." It often is made up of three interlocking triangles (see figure 19.6). To expand the basic nornic reading into the *valknutr,* the runecaster picks three groups of three lots and lays them in interlocking triangles as shown in figure 19.7. The first triangle is an expanded analysis of the Urdhr stead, the second of Verdhandi, and the third of Skuld. This can give a more complete picture of what lies at the root of the question, what is happening in the present situation, and what the outcome is likely to be.

Figure 19.6. The Valknútr.

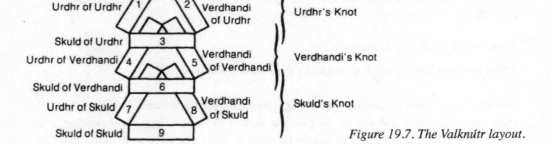

Figure 19.7. The Valknútr layout.

2. Casting Upon the Airts Method

One of the most well-established arrangements of space into meaningful fields known in the Germanic world is the division of the sky and the plane of the earth into "eighths," in Old Norse aettir, or in Scots dialect English "airts." In Old Norse these divisions are given the names indicated in figure 19.8. Although these names are of Norwegian origin, their inner sense of a fourfold division, expanded by cross-quarter points, fits with a continuing and timeless Germanic pattern. The names indicate that things to the east were more "close in," or earthly, and that things to the west were more "outer," or "far out," and that the main polarity is between north and south. It is no coincidence that the runes also are divided into "eighths."

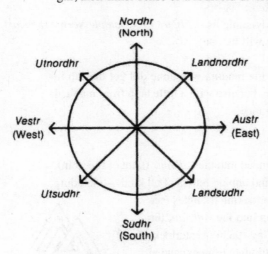

Figure 19.8. The Norse aettir of the heavens.

In runecasting this pattern is combined with the other most obvious division of "space," that of the nine worlds of Yggdrasill, to form the design used to divide the casting cloth into fields of meaning illustrated in figure 19.9. (The actual cloth should not have the names of the worlds on it.) In reality, this figure represents the "collapsing" of multidimensional space into a two-dimensional model—as do many sacred symbols of all kinds. The fields are names for the nine worlds of Yggdrasill and derive their meanings from these concepts as shown in table 19.1 on page 216.

Those lots falling within the inner circles made up of Midhgardhr-Asgardhr-Hel-Ljóssálfheimr-Svartálfheimr (which in the three-dimensional model make up the vertical column) give a reading of the subjective or psychological state of, or influences on, the person. Those of Ljóssálfheimr and Svartálfheimr are more "personal," while those of Asgardhr and Hel are more "transpersonal." The lots coming down in the outer fields of Niflheimr-Muspellsheimr-Vanaheimr-Jötunheimr (which together with Midhgardhr form the horizontal plane in the Yggdrasill model) clarify the state of the objective universe and how it affects the person in question. Note carefully the special synthesizing function of Midhgardhr—the center—where all potentialities are (or can be) manifested.

The runecaster may wish to decorate the cloth with the configuration of lines shown in figure 19.9. Or, you simply may visualize these fields if you are able. Such hidden keys are usually the basis of forms of divination that might seem random at first glance. If the cloth is decorated, it should be embroidered with dark blue or black thread.

Following ritual procedures outlined in chapter 18, the runer blindly casts the lots upon the cloth and then reads them (perhaps sitting on the theal's stool) as they lie on the cloth in their steads of meaning. According to personal custom, lots which land face-down may be read as murk-staves or they may be removed from the cloth and set aside. "Inverted" runes cannot be read as such in operations of this kind. Those that fall off the cloth altogether should be disregarded. (Note, however, what these lots are—they may be significant by their absence!)

Once the final configuration has been established, a complex picture may appear. This kind of casting is sometimes so complex that it cannot be fully interpreted at one sitting (especially by beginning runecasters). Therefore, be sure to draw out a record of the casting. You may simply make notes such as ":ᚠ: in Asgardhr," etc. Often the direction a lot is facing—it may seem to be "pointing to" another lot—gives subtle clues which

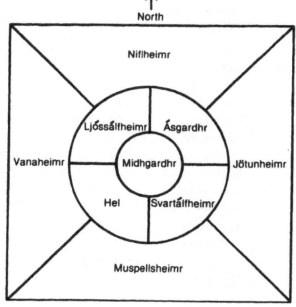

Figure 19.9. Casting cloth is divided into steads of meaning, and we can see the attribution of the nine worlds to the casting cloth.

Asgardhr:	Higher influences. Nature of relationship with the divinities. The veiled branches of the question. Matters of honor, positive (active) influences from past states of existence ("incarnations")—*ørlög*.
Ljóssálfheimr:	Mental influences. Family matters. Messages of Huginn—directions in which you should plan. What will help you. Paths to help you realize influences from Asgardhr.
Midhgardhr:	The way people come together to manifest themselves in life. The outcome in life. Ego consciousness.
Svartálfheimr:	Creative emotional influences. Money matters. Messages from Muninn—things you should reflect on. Paths to realize influences from Hel.
Hel:	Hidden or suppressed instinctual desires. Nature of automatic functions or behaviors. The hidden root of the question. Negative (passive, restrictive) influences from past states of existence—*ørlög*.
Muspellsheimr:	State of vital energies, that which vitalizes you. Active influences from outside. Things tending toward activity.
Niflheimr:	That which resists you. Passive or restrictive influences from the outside. Things tending toward dormancy.
Vanaheimr:	Promotes growth. Erotic relationships. Persons of the opposite sex. Balancing influences. Forces of continuity, structure, and well-being.
Jötunheimr:	That which confuses you. That which may be left to chance. Things that might test you. Forces pressing for change. Realm of crisis.

Table 19.1: Interpretations of the world-steads.

reveal nuances in the lot's interpretation. For this reason a sketched record is preferred. The true significance of the casting may not be realized until sometime later when you are contemplating the working record.

The pattern resulting from a casting upon the airts can be read in several ways. You may start from what is now manifesting itself in Midhgardhr and work out to the more remotely influential realms, e.g., from Midhgardhr to Ljóssálfheimr and Svartálfheimr, and from this pairing to Asgardhr and Hel, and from there to the outermost realms of Vanaheimr and Jötunheimr, and Niflheimr and Muspellsheimr. Or, you might reverse this process working from Niflheimr and Muspellsheimr back to Midhgardhr. Ultimately, no linear progression is really inherent in this pattern—it is rather an ultra-dimensional model. Therefore, intuition may be each runer's best guide.

✕

Sample Casting Upon the Airts

Object of inquiry: The progress over the coming year of an organization that is dedicated to the discovery and re-discovery of a potent form of magic.

Reading: The layout is shown in figure 19.10. General lack of staves in Vanaheimr indicates no organic tensions are present, while the lack of staves in Niflheimr indicates that there is really no outside pressure or resistance on this group (which is largely secret). The staves in Muspellsheimr, a murky *hagalaz* and a *thurisaz,* both indicate that there are active agents, probably within the consciousness of the various members of the organi-

zation, which have been retarding the activization of the organization's programs. These tendencies are, however, very weakly aspected and do not form a strong bundle. Therefore, it would seem that their influence is rather negligible.

A strong bundle is present in Jötunheimr. This indicates that the organization is in dynamic flux, and in many ways is searching for crystallized goals (*sowilo*). The crossing of *nauthiz* and *wunjo* in Jötunheimr suggests that some crisis of an interpersonal nature will lead to positive change. A second crossing between a murky *dagaz* and *kenaz* in Jötunheimr might indicate some confusion in technical matters.

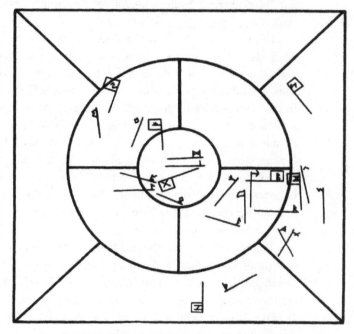

Figure 19.10. Sample airt casting. Note that square around stave indicates that the lot fell stave side down.

However, the favorable juxtaposition of *raidho* counteracts this and leads to a rational, ordered direction into the formative realm of Svartálfheimr. Thus the technical matters will be correctly ordered and put to positive use. The murky *eihwaz* in Jötunheimr is isolated, and therefore seems of little importance. However, it is negatively aspected with the murky *fehu* and *jera* in Ljóssálfheimr, which shows a continuing problem in bringing inspiration to solid fruition.

The bundle in Svartálfheimr would indicate that there will, however, be a great deal of upswelling inspiration which will find formative outlet. The general bundle of so many staves that are indicative of form, shape, and order *(uruz, tiwaz, raidho)* and divine connection and inspiration *(elhaz* and *ansuz)* in this one field of formative realization would seem to override other indications to the contrary. But, the other indications are reinforced by the presence of the murky B-rune in the midst of this bundle. This clearly indicates that although the formative force and inspiration are powerfully present, they are resisted. This is a warning to be vigilant. Each member of the organization must strive and seek in order for the promise of the A- and Z-runes to bear fruit.

In Ljóssálfheimr there is a loose complex of the E- and NG-runes, which indicates that intellectual development within the organization will be most effective if based on individual inner reflections and/or developed in pairs of persons working on special projects.

Ultimately, it is in the realm of Midgardhr that the outcome of this magical year is made clear. There are essentially two bundles here. *Mannaz* parallel to *isa* indicates a certain solidification of the archetypal social organization within the body in question. This is reinforced by the presence of the *othala* in the other bundle, which is closely linked with influences flowing from the dark depths of the hidden realm of Hel (i.e., influences from the past). This influence will be largely unplanned and spontaneous, as indicated by the P-rune, and it will be a truly transformative one, as indicated by the L-rune. Note that both of these lead out of Hel into Midhgardhr and from a bundle with the O-rune and with a murky G-rune. This G-rune, like the B-rune in the bundle found in Svartálfheimr, contains a hidden warning. In this case the warning is to be on the lookout for detrimental influences within the group that could easily arise due to this influx from suprarational realms.

To summarize, it may be said that this organization will be the subject of technical innovation by its members—innovation based on inner reflection and work done between pairs of members. This innovation will be of a highly inspired nature and it will lead to concrete organizational manifestation. However, all this will not come easily. In every instance there is a "thorn"—some active resistance which will require that all involved be of wakeful wills and hardened hearts.

3. Laying in the Futhark Method

The fixed runic order itself provides us with another traditional way of determining fields of meaning. The runestaves linearly arranged in their three-tiered aett configuration (as presented in figure 19.1) give the steads of interpretation shown in table 19.2.

23	21	19	17	15	13	11	9
7	5	3	1	2	4	6	8
10	12	14	16	18	20	22	24

Figure 19.11. Layout order of the Futhark method.

1	:ᚠ:	Money matters. Psychic energies.
2	:ᚢ:	Physical health. Vital energies.
3	:ᚦ:	What opposes you (perhaps physical).
4	:ᚨ:	Sources of inspiration and intellectual expression.
5	:ᚱ:	Travels—inner or outer.
6	:ᚲ:	Creativity. Erotic relationships.
7	:ᚷ:	What will be given to you.
8	:ᚹ:	Relationships, friends. What will give you happiness.
9	:ᚺ:	Area of possible crisis leading to transformation.
10	:ᚾ:	What resists you (psychically). Source of discontent.
11	:ᛁ:	What is constraining you.
12	:ᛃ:	Where rewards can be expected. Relationship with the natural environment.
13	:ᛇ:	Hidden influences, state of whole being. Relationship with the numinous environment.
14	:ᛈ:	How you will find joy.
15	:ᛉ:	Thing that needs attention. Way to the gods.
16	:ᛋ:	What will guide you.
17	:ᛏ:	Cognitive state. Legal matters. Ideals.
18	:ᛒ:	What provides growth and beauty.
19	:ᛖ:	With what or whom you should work. Erotic relations.
20	:ᛗ:	Overall psychic state. Attitude toward death.
21	:ᛚ:	State of emotional balance. What will test you.
22	:ᛜ:	What you should contemplate.
23	:ᛞ:	Area of unexpected synchronicity.
24	:ᛟ:	Greater family matters. National or community issues.

Table 19.2: Interpretations of the stave-steads.

The runer may cast the runes onto the cloth, and then take all twenty-four up one by one and lay them in the aett arrangement. Or, you may blindly draw them out of the lot box or bag and then lay them out one through twenty-four in the aett arrangement and in the order shown in figure 19.11 on page 218. Thus the futhark unfolds from its core and becomes fully manifest in the aett configuration. The result will be a complete reading in that all steads will be covered. Aspects may be determined by one of the usual methods outlined on pages 209–211.

Records of these casts are easy to make with notations such as: ᚷ:in:ᚠ:,:ᚲ:in: ᚺ:,:ᛜ:in:ᚦ:, etc. As always, the stead determines the area of life or existence in question, while the lot determines the quality being manifested in that area at the time of the casting or laying. This type of layout is useful for getting a complete reading of your present situation in life. It gives a holistic, synthetic picture, with no real emphasis on outcomes.

Sample Reading of Laying in the Futhark

Object of inquiry: General life reading to determine future directions.

Reading: The layout is shown in figure 19.12. *Fehu* in the first stead indicates financial affairs are in a state of prosperity. *Othala* in the second stead shows health and vital energies are under control and contained with no positive or negative factors indicated. *Laguz* in the third stead suggests a possible opposition by unconscious

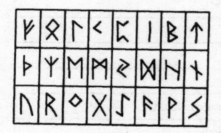

Figure 19.12. Sample of the Futhark layout method.

forces, while *kenaz* in the fourth stead demonstrates a certain inspiration from the creative fire (art). *Perthro* in the fifth stead indicates that travels undertaken will be of an inner kind—along the roads of time and space. The sixth stead occupied by *isa* bodes a shutdown of creativity by icy substance, or an inward turning of creativity to the ego level. *Berkano* in the seventh stead indicates a liberation of energies will occur. *Tiwaz* in the eighth stead points to relationships governed by reason and self-sacrifice (which will ultimately be a source of happiness). *Thurisaz* in the ninth stead points in the direction of a crisis of opposition by hostile reactive forces, while *elhaz* in the tenth stead indicates resistance from archetypal forces within. *Ehwaz* in the eleventh stead betrays an inner constraint. *Mannaz* in the twelfth stead indicates rewards in social stature in essential connections with the gods. (This seems to suggest that the crisis portrayed in the ninth, tenth, and eleventh steads will be overcome.) *Jera* in the thirteenth stead reveals a regular cyclical action in control of hidden influences, while the *dagaz* in the fourteenth stead shows that joy will be found in the experience of subjectivity. *Hagalaz* in the fifteenth stead indicates that attention must be given to the basics, to the seed concepts. (This also seems to relate to the crisis referred to in the ninth, tenth, and eleventh steads.) *Nauthiz* in the sixteenth stead may mean that the subject is being guided by crisis situations (probably through early recognition of the crisis of nine, ten, and eleven). *Uruz* in the seventeenth stead indicates that the cognitive state and ideals are dominated by bullish willpower. *Raidho* in the eighteenth stead shows regularity, rhythm, and motion at work, resulting in growth and beauty. *Ingwaz* in the nineteenth stead suggests that the subject should work alone, gestating within the self. *Gebo* in the twentieth stead indicates a willingness to give and take. *Eihwaz* in the twenty-first stead signifies a "vertical" emotional balance, i.e., emotions dominated by intellect with the likelihood of this tendency increasing. *Ansuz* in the twenty-second stead counsels the subject to meditate on Odin, or the personal divinity within. *Wunjo* in the twenty-third stead points to an unexpected synchronicity in the social field, while *sowilo* in the twenty-fourth stead demonstrates that the subject's current goals are in the social field itself.

The overall counsel of this reading to the subject is that in matters of basic security all is well. The principal opposition is within. This can be overcome by establishing firmer, more regular links with the personal divinity. If the subject develops inner connections he will be rewarded with outer successes.

4. The Seven Realms Laying

The ancient Norse often talked of seven realms of sentient beings from which information could be gained—if one but knew the "language" of that realm. This tradition is only imperfectly transmitted in the "Alvísmál" of the *Poetic Edda,* where seven realms are mentioned but only six are ever used in any one stanza. These stanzas were composed to reveal the secret poetic languages used in the realms of the Aesir, Vanir, elves, dwarves, etins, as well as among the dead, and among people in Midhgardhr. As Hollander notes in his introduction to the "Alvísmál," the poem represents a late and confused state of affairs. But it reflects an ancient cosmological order which only needs a slight adjustment provided by the Yggdrasill key to make it intelligible. Only seven of the nine worlds of Yggdrasill spawn sentient beings—Muspellsheimr and Niflheimr are devoid of consciousness as raw forces of "nature." The runes are one mode of communication between and among these sentient realms.

Note that the principle behind the layout pattern is that which underlies the cosmogonic process in Germanic lore: the continuing synthesis of polar opposites leading to transformation. This is superimposed upon the nornic process to give a picture of the layers of action or forces at work through time. Following your ritual procedure, draw twenty-one runes from the box or bag and lay them out in the order indicated in figure 19.13. These lots are then to be interpreted according to the key shown in figure 19.13.

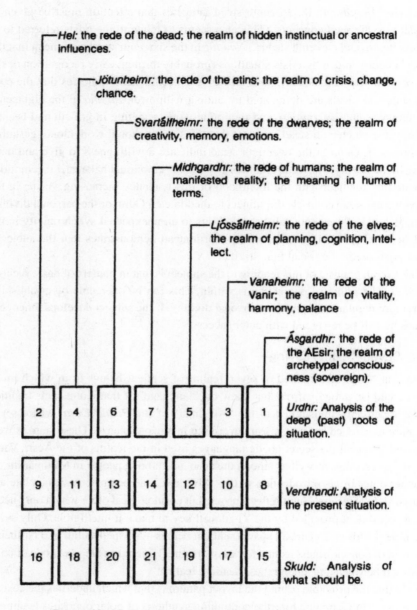

Hel: the rede of the dead; the realm of hidden instinctual or ancestral influences.

Jötunheimr: the rede of the etins; the realm of crisis, change, chance.

Svartálfheimr: the rede of the dwarves; the realm of creativity, memory, emotions.

Midhgardhr: the rede of humans; the realm of manifested reality; the meaning in human terms.

Ljóssálfheimr: the rede of the elves; the realm of planning, cognition, intellect.

Vanaheimr: the rede of the Vanir; the realm of vitality, harmony, balance

Ásgardhr: the rede of the AEsir; the realm of archetypal consciousness (sovereign).

Urdhr: Analysis of the deep (past) roots of situation.

Verdhandi: Analysis of the present situation.

Skuld: Analysis of what should be.

Figure 19. 13. Layout and key to the seven realms method.

This layout pattern is most useful for complete self-analyses, and in many ways represents a more "controlled" version of the method of casting upon the airts.

This kind of reading will be improved as you become more knowledgeable about the realms. Also refer to the discussion of these realms under the Casting Upon the Airts Method in chapter 6 as well as in chapter 18. Each lot stead is read quite simply as a bringing together of the nornic process with the realms of sentient beings. At each level the row is synthesized in the Midhgardhr stead, so that lot steads seven, fourteen, and twenty-one are the ultimate keys to the reading. The three lots excluded from the reading also may be significant by their absence.

Sample Reading in the Seven Realms Method

Object of Inquiry: Analysis of the ultimate effect of disruptive personality within an esoteric organization.

Reading: The layout is shown in figure 19.14. *Ehwaz* and *fehu* in the outer levels (Asgardhr and Hel) of Urdhr indicate that sexual energy and erotic relationships are at the ultimate root of the question. There is a general freezing of vital forces shown by *isa* in Vanaheimr. An intense level of emotional crisis and conflict is evidenced by *nauthiz* in Jötunheimr. This is, perhaps, the result of a general lack of vitality coupled with an uncontrolled influx of sexual energies. The ability of all parties to think clearly is in a state of stasis (or perhaps gestation) indicated by the *ingwaz* in Ljóssálfheimr. This also could mean that certain plans are waiting to be hatched. However, the Aesiric powers also seem to have had a hand in shaping things, as intimated by *ansuz* in Svartálfheimr. The basis of the present situation is rather ambivalent; there seems to be a "velocity toward manifestation."

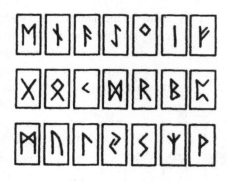

Figure 19.14. Sample layout in the seven realms method.

The present unsettled elements are in archetypal flux, as shown by the presence of *perthro* in the Asgardhr of Verdhandi. This can bode well if higher counsel is heeded in a state of spiritual detachment—do not act further. In the root of things, as shown by the *gebo* in Hel, honor and credit of those in this state will be preserved. Vitality is strongly disciplined and held in protected reserve, indicated by *berkano* in Vanaheimr. The social aspect of *othala* is in great confusion due to its position in Jötunheimr. The present state of crisis shown by *othala's* presence in Jötunheimr is rooted in *naudhiz* in the Urdhr level. Fortunately, rational control *(raidho)* is reinforced in the intellectual realm of Ljóssálfheimr. The presence of *kenaz* in Svartálfheimr may also indicate that craft is being wielded in the creative realm. *Dagaz* in the Midhgardhr of Verdhandi remains ambiguous, as its light may be dimmed by the poor aspect of *raidho* to *dagaz*.

The pairing of *manna* and *wunjo* in the archetypal realms of Skuld seems ideal. This appears to indicate that ultimately there will be an outcome based upon divine principles in a joyous atmosphere. *Elhaz* in Vanaheimr shows a certain upward sweep of vitality, while *uruz* in Jötunheimr suggests that the chaos will be reformed. Cognitive plans will reach their right goals, demonstrated by the presence of *sowilo* in Ljóssálfheimr, and there will be creativity according to law. *Uruz* and *laguz* in Jötunheimr and Svartálfheimr respectively seem to indicate a certain reformation of order out of the chaos and crisis that was rooted in *nauthiz* in the Jötunheimr of Urdhr.

The final outcome is exemplary. *Jera* indicates that right rewards will be gained for beneficial past actions (or non-action). The aspect of the whole of the Skuld realm could not be more hopeful. Ultimately, this disruptive influence will have nothing but a strengthening effect on the social circle—but there may be more rough seas ahead as Verdhandi transits to Skuld.

Alternate Ways of Drawing Lots

In all the methods outlined above the runer is limited to reading each rune only once in every laying of the lots. However, this may not produce the most accurate reading since it is quite possible that a rune could be manifest in more than one stead.

Following are two more ways of generating lots. When using the first method you draw a lot from your bag or box and, depending on which layout pattern you are working with, trace that rune on paper or in the ground in a specially prepared section of loose earth. Put the lot back in the bag or box again and shake it, saying aloud or silently, "Urdhr-Verdhandi-Skuld." Then draw another lot from the box and note it in its proper stead. Continue until you have completed the pattern. Theoretically, you could end up with a reading that contains only one rune!

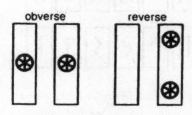

Figure 19.15. The aett staves.

The second method involves the use of an archaic form of Germanic "dice." In order to use this technique, the runer must construct eight staves that are broad and flat enough that they can only land with one faceup when cast upon a flat surface. Two of these staves, the aett-staves, will be marked (for example with a six-spoked wheel) on one side, one will be blank on the reverse, and the other will be marked with two signs on the reverse as shown in figure 19.15. Casting these staves naturally will result in a number 1, 2, or 3. These will give the aett-count of a particular rune.

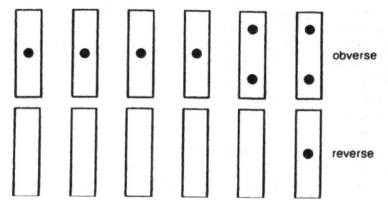

Figure 19.16. The lot staves.

A second set of six staves, the lot staves, is to be prepared with another kind of marking (for example a dot or circle). Four of these have only one mark on one side; one of them has two marks on one side. The reverse of the other five staves are blank. The sixth stave has two marks on one side and one on the reverse. (See figure 19.16.)

Any casting of these lots will result in a number between one and eight. These determine the particular lot or rune within the already determined aett. This system works on the same binary code as the "secret runes" (see chapter 7).

First you cast the aett-staves and get a number from one to three, then the lot staves, to get a number between one and eight. The resulting combination, e.g., 3:6 identifies as particular runestave in the Futhark order—in this case *laguz,* the sixth rune in the third aett.

As each runestave is generated in this manner, note it in its proper stead so you can interpret it according to the kind of reading being done. The same runestave can occur several times in the same reading. Runes that would have been "constrained" to appear in the full "Futhark Layout" may be significantly absent in this type of reading. These methods allow for the element of free play that usually is absent in layout methods.

Yes/No Answers

Probably the most instinctive use of divinatory technique is that of trying to get a "yes" or a "no" answer to a question, e.g., the "he loves me he loves me not" game with the petals of a flower. The runestaves can provide such answers—and something more besides.

In the customary ritual framework, cast the runes upon the cloth with the airt/ Yggdrasill pattern. The only significant pattern for this reading is the outer circle (enclosing the vertical fields of Asgardhr-Hel-Svartálfheimr-Ljóssálfheimr-Midhgardhr). Disregard the lots that fall outside the outer circle. Only those totally within the "circle of advisors" are to be read. If the majority of these are faceup, the answer is "yes"; if the majority are facedown, the answer is "no." The ratio of "yes"-staves to "no"-staves gives you some idea of how "close the call is." An equal number of yeses and nos is, of course, no decision. (But this is the reading—do not try to ask the same question again until the next day.)

This kind of reading also gives you some indications of the "why" of the answer. Reversed lots may tell you the aspects that need to be reversed, if possible, to get an affirmative outcome.

The ritual element in this kind of reading is very important. Because it is a "hit-or-miss" kind of operation, the runer must evoke a strong sense of being "in sync" with the runes before such a casting can be used seriously.

Part Four

RUNE MAGIC

Chapter 20

THE RUNE WORLD

I t is not possible in a book of this scope to present all levels of the runic cosmogony and cosmology. Certain portions of this lore have been used in interpreting and illustrating the properties of the individual runes, and before progressing to the theories of rune magic proper, steps should be taken to explain the cosmos in which these mysteries manifest themselves. A more advanced level of operative runology is presented in the book *Alu: An Advanced Guide to Operative Runology* (Weiser, 2012).

As we saw in chapter 10, the best source for understanding the runic cosmology is found in the Eddas, where we read that before time began there was Ginnungagap, which literally means a "magically charged void." In the present discussion we wish to concentrate on the practical magical aspects of cosmology. The cosmos, or framework of reality, is a beginning point for all magical operations. We have to understand the secrets of the organization of the world if we wish to be able to alter it in any way. Clearly the esoteric cosmology of our ancestors is seen to have been dominated by two opposing forces often called "fire" and "ice." But a close examination shows them to be originally "fire" and "water."

It is also important to realize that: (1) in the first phase of cosmogony there is no personal *Creator*—cosmogony is seen as a natural and organic process; (2) the universe ultimately derives from a *single* source, Ginnungagap, clearly contains two poles within its substance, *two* extremes of fire (expansive energy) and ice (primal matter/antimatter). This polarity is mutually attracted, and from their (re)union the primal essence and archetypal pattern for manifestation are formed. From this framework the multiplicity of being evolves. Beyond this first phase there is indeed a creator figure, or a cosmic reformer: Odin, the All-Father. This god, the first form of consciousness, re-formed the chaotic and disorganized state of existence into a beautiful and rational cosmos. This re-creation makes magic possible for humans to perform.

The Eddas teach us that once existence had been stabilized, the multiverse consisted of nine worlds, contained in and supported by the World-Tree, Yggdrasill. These worlds contain countless abodes and dwellings. In the center is Midhgardhr, with the other worlds arrayed around, above, and below it. In the north in Niflheimr; in the east, Jötunheimr (Etin-world); in the south, Muspellsheimr; in the west, Vanaheimr (Vanir-world). In the middle, above Midhgardhr, is Ljóssálfheimr (light-elf-world) and above that Asgardgr, the enclosure of the Aesir, which houses many dwellings. Below Midh-gardhr is Svartálfheimr ("black-elf-world" or "dwarf-world") and below that Hel, the silent, still, and sleepy realm of the dead. Between and among these worlds the runes and their roadways are to be found—here a great rune lies hidden. In practical work it is essential to remember, to keep in mind, that these worlds exert an effect on Midhgardhr, where our practical work is to find manifestation. By the same token we must realize that we can influence the flow of power from those realms to this one. The beginning of that process is in the realization of their existence and character.

Manifestation of the Rune Row

The manifestation of the runes and their ordering in the Futhark row are bound up with the cosmogonic and cosmologic processes. The runes have no point of origin; they are the substance of the latent energy contained in Ginnungagap. The runes exist simultaneously in an undifferentiated state throughout this void—and thus defy comprehension. At the division between Muspellsheimr and Niflheimr, the runic forces are polarized into shining runes (ON *heidhrúnar)* and dark runes (ON *myrkrúnar.)* These are polarized aspects of the entire corpus of runic power expressed simultaneously. These runic forces attract one another, in order that they might rejoin and create the cosmic seed of manifestation contained in Ymir. The shining runes and dark runes are re-assimilated in a pattern capable of manifestation. The runic forces are at work throughout the cosmogonic processes described above; however, the runes as we know them have not been manifested, because the entire process, up to the sacrifice of Ymir, takes place in an unmanifested state. When Odin, Vili, and Vé sacrifice Ymir (the crystalized seed form of the collective runic pattern), they *arrange* this runic "substance" in accordance with the multiversal pattern. Thus they "create" the nine worlds and Yggdrasill. This primal act brings about cosmic order and manifestation.

At this point the runes are ordered in the Futhark row in their linear form as the primary arrangement at the center of the multiverse. This manifestation unfolds from the "inside out," beginning with the most basic forms of cyclical (:◊:) and vertical (:↑:) force. From that point the other runes manifest themselves in a linear pattern governed by a twelve-fold spherical law. As each succeeding circle is manifested, a pair of runes—esoteric concepts—are isolated within the "space." The laws of sympathy and antipathy determine which runes crystalize in each circle. Also, those same laws govern which of these two concepts will be aligned with which previously manifested rune in the row. The row thus produced is perceived by the intellect in an order governed by the path of the sun, and thereby the runes manifest their numerical values 1 through 24. These numerical values are also part of the innate relative positions of one mystery to the others, and play a determining role in their ordering. A graphic representation shows the full glory of this mystery in figure 20.1 .

These patterns, as well as those that govern the linear alignment of the staves, are fruitful avenues of meditation and will reveal much wisdom and provide great power to the vitki who can unravel their riddles.

Figure 20.1 represents only one of several patterns in which the runes are arranged or divided—each world or "realm of being" has its own particular modality. The aettir are ruled by the pattern of the eightfold "cross" or "star" by which the ancient Northmen divided the heavens (see figure 20.2).

This rudimentary and fragmentary exposition of runic cosmology is only a hint of the secrets and splendors to be discovered by the vitki who perseveres, and penetrates the wisdom of the worlds.

Streams

Much work has been done by German runic magicians concerning the intake and manipulation of streams of runic force. These streams may be classified according to the realms in which they originate: (1) terrestrial streams, which run along the surface of the earth; (2) heavenly streams, which circulate in the atmosphere; and (3) chthonic streams, which

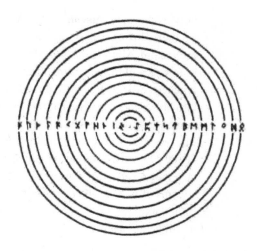

Figure 20.1. Diagram of the futhark pattern of manifestation.

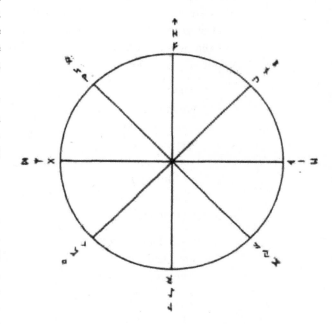

Figure 20.2. The eightfold division of the futhark.

flow in the subterranean sphere. These streams or fields constantly interact upon one another, causing changes and fluctuations in the intensity and form of the force found in each realm. All runes exist in all realms; they are, however, concentrated and intensified in power within the realms most sympathetic to the force they embody. Through the practices of *stadhagaldr* and meditation the vitki is able to draw these cosmic streams into his or her own personal runic sphere, there to be integrated (for increased personal power) or reprojected in order to cause changes in accordance with the will of the vitki. The practical section on *stadhagaldr* explains how to manipulate these streams in more detail. The word "stream" is perhaps a bit misleading. Actually, these runic forces may be *felt* as a variety of sensations within the psyche. Some are indeed similar to flowing streams of power; others are akin to waves, or whirlpools, or utter stillness. Each vitki should explore the "feel" of each rune on its own terms. Once contact has been made, it will be unmistakable.

The Soul and Personal Power Concepts

In chapter 12 we discussed the various ancient Norse soul concepts. Certain soul qualities were given to the primal man and woman (coequally and simultaneously) by the triad of gods. This triad, which is a threefold expression of the god usually known as Odin, was identified above as Odin, Vili, and Vé. In another account, given in the "Völuspá," we read:

> Until the Aesir,
> mighty and loving,
> came from the host
> to the coast;
> on the land they found
> of little might
> Askr and Embla
> yet unfated.

> They had not *önd*,
> they had not *ódhr*,
> neither *lá* nor *laeti*
> nor good *litr;*

> Odin gave *önd*
> Hoenir gave *ódhr*,
> Lódhurr gave *lá*
> and good *litr.*

The last three gifts indicate external qualities (*lá,* appearance; *laeti,* movement; *litr,* health), which are extremely important but not of central interest here. *Önd* is the breath of life, the "spirit" that is the "divine spark" in mankind and that all-pervasive force that penetrates and animates the multiverse. (This is very much akin to the Indian conception of *prana* and is etymologically connected to Sanskrit *atman:* breath, soul.) *Ódhr* is the power of inspiration and ecstasy. The name Ódh-inn is derived from the same root word. This is that pure and irrational numinous power that is the magical faculty of gods and men.

With the entrance of the Nornic force, time and the laws of cause and effect arise (see the P-rune). Furthermore, the infusion of divine structure and consciousness provided by Heimdallr/Odin (see the M-rune) provides another numinous force, which is handed down through the generations. This force is increased or decreased according to human action throughout the life of an individual. These concepts are expressed throughout the rune row. With these qualities the development and concentration of magical power become possible—and even necessary.

Four principal entities arise from this complex interplay of runic forces and are centered in mankind: (1) *hugr,* (2) *hamr,* (3) *hamingja,* and (4) *fylgja.* The *hugr* is the conscious will and intellect. The *hamr* is the personal aspect of the plastic image-forming essence in the cosmos. This is the realm of images, which bridges the worlds and acts as a matrix between the "spiritual" and "physical" worlds. A powerful *hugr* can project and even reform this personal essence in another location in an almost "physical" manner. The Norse sagas abound with accounts of this type. Most readers will be reminded of such phenomena as astral projection, and bilocation. The complex entity that gives this power is known as the *hamingja,* a term that means "shape-changing force," "luck," "power," and on occasion "guardian spirit." *Hamingja* may be transferred from one person to another, from a person to an object, or merely projected into space as indicated above. This force may be increased continuously by ritualized magical action and deeds of honor. The *fylgja* is the storehouse of this action, which is symbolized by a female figure, an animal (specific to the internal nature of the individual), or a crescent shape that hovers before the person. *Fylgja* (fetch) constantly interacts with all levels of the personality imparting the *ørlög* or "fate" of the person in accordance with past action. Both the *hamingja* and *fylgja* may be passed from one generation to the next as a type of "reincarnation." The use of these qualities and entities in magical operations will be elucidated in some of the sections on practical work.

Basic Theories of Rune Magic

The forces used in magic and ritual may be divided roughly into two categories: the dynamistic and animistic. The dynamistic powers are more mechanistic, without a large degree of what we would call consciousness or will, other than their singular (or complex) functions. It is within this category that we may place the runes, and the multiverse generally. However, they do have a degree of "animism" about them, as personal investigation will show. The primal runic forces also are at the root of all being, as the section on cosmogony demonstrated. All the various wights, gods (Aesir and Vanir), elves, dwarves, and giants (thurses and etins) belong in the animistic category. The gods are archetypes, or exemplary models of consciousness, that are perceived as animate primordial images. These forces are ultimately derived from the dynamistic nature of the universe—as is mankind, which they help to form.

These exemplary models are also extremely useful in magic, of course, either as internal consciousness factors or as symbols or vehicles for consciously directed power in invocatory rites. This latter type of rite is infrequent in common runecraft and belongs more to the magical religious expression of Asatru. In the old Nordic multiverse these two categories were closely interwoven. The following is a simplified model for the understanding of the runic processes at work in practical magic.

The rune streams are present in the multiverse, and they have their representative structures in the personal sphere in the *hamingja* of the vitki. This is similar to a macrocosmic-microcosmic model, except there is no definite boundary between the two. The "personal runes" and "world runes" are consciously synthesized in the magical/religious act according to willed or instinctual patterns. This is the essence of the Old Norse concepts *heill* (holy; wholeness) and *heill hugr* (whole mind), a high state of consciousness. The runestaves act as keys to give access to these streams in mankind and in the causal multiversal realms. As *symbols,* the runestaves (with their threefold nature) *are* the forces they "represent." Through willed ritual action the vitki is able to manipulate (through combination, intensification, concentration, direction, etc.) the runic forces in the realms of the nine worlds. By the laws of *perthro* these actions become manifest as the altered rune streams react on and reverberate within the world in accordance with the will of the vitki. The efficiency of the vitki's work is in direct proportion to the intensity and quality of the impression he or she is able to bring to bear on the image worlds that are adjacent to Midhgardhr. The ancients knew that all "things" were filled with runic force—all things "had their runes." Rune wisdom is access to and knowledge of these modalities that penetrate and vivify all the worlds.

Although this book does not contain invocatory magic of a specifically "religious" nature, it is nevertheless important to understand the god-forms that are housed in the rune realms. These gods and goddesses are holy archetypes and consciousness modalities, that preexisted the self-consciousness of mankind but are intensified by human action. These images are culturally distinct exemplary models. They are to varying degrees self-conscious. For example, the rime-giants have practically no consciousness and are almost purely mechanistic, while the god Odin is "structurally" as complex as the most complicated human being. These wights occupy various worlds, each according to their kind. There are, however, no well-defined borders between most of these realms.

For practical purposes and future reference, it would be well to explore the structure of the divine relationships in the worlds of the gods (Aesir and Vanir). The runic god-forms may be understood in a threefold matrix plus a fourth category. To a large degree this divine paradigm is reflected in the social structure of the ancient Germanic (and Indo-European) peoples. The mysteries of the M-rune explain this phenomenon.

The "divine society" is based on a tripartite system. The three levels, or functions, of this system are (1) sovereignty, (2) strength, and (3) production. The first and third functions are dual in structure. The first level contains both the judicial and the magical aspects of "kingship," while the third function encompasses the divine twins and the holy brother and sister. The major gods and goddesses of the Germanic pantheon are arranged according to this pattern:

1. The Judge-King (Tyr) or the Priest-Magician (Odin)

2. The Warrior (Thor, in his oldest aspect)

3. The Providers (Freyja and Freyr, or Alcis)

A short study of these deities will show the complexity that is possible within this paradigm. In Norse theology Odin has aspects in all three levels, true to his shamanistic nature of traversing all worlds. Tyr is considered a god of war because the old ones considered war to be a type of judgment, according to past action and amount of honor/luck (*hamingja*) gathered by that action. Thor is the warrior of the gods. As opposed to Odin and Tyr, he actually fights the battles. But he is also important to the farmers because through his atmospheric power he breaks open the clouds and brings forth the fertilizing rains. Freyja is rather similar to Odin in that she has aspects in all three levels: she is the goddess of fertility and the teacher of the magical arts of *seidhr* to Odin, and half of all warriors slain in battle go to her in the realm of Fólkvangr. (The other half goes to Odin in Valhöll, or Valhalla, "the hall of those slain.")

The fourth realm is that of "deified" dynamistic forces or natural phenomena within the cultic sciences (belonging to the magical function). These would include the sun (Sunna; Sól), the moon (Máni), and fire, which is embodied in the runes *kenaz, naudhiz,* and *dagaz,* and other "elements" and forces.

In ritual work this classificatory system shows the efficiency of these deities in various types of operations. Gods and goddesses that belong to the third level are powerful aids in rites aimed at fertility, art, craft, wealth, and eroticism, while those of the second function rule in operations concerning protection, defense, liberation, and curses. The first level is rather all-encompassing, but the Tyr aspect is most valuable in rites of law and order, justice, and success or victory. The Odin aspect is the most comprehensive and is especially powerful in rites to obtain wisdom, numinous knowledge, and personal power, and to bind or constrict enemies.

Odin has an important lesson to teach all aspiring vitkar. Like Odin, the vitki should search restlessly *all* the worlds, seeking wisdom and power, always willing to sacrifice of self to self, and constantly sharing that wisdom and power with others of like mind. To the Odian no path or door in the multiverse is blocked or closed.

Chapter 21

FOUNDATIONS OF RUNE MAGIC

Through a combination of the runes and the vitki's personal will and ability, all things are possible; but in order to gain this power the vitki must develop the skills basic to all ritual work: concentration, visualization, breath and posture control, and the art of incantation. Many of these skills may be developed haphazardly over the course of practical work. The failures incurred by this method often discourage aspiring vitkar. The best course of action is one in which some time is devoted to exercises designed to develop the basic skills necessary to the successful performance of *rúnagaldr*. It has been noticed by several investigators that the runic power is often slow to develop in people (this may be due to the centuries of widespread neglect) but that when the force manifests itself in the vitki's life, it is all-pervasive in its potency, unshakable in its strength, and overpowering in the stimulation it produces. This may indeed be due to its innate or indigenous nature. A vitki of patience and perseverance will be well rewarded!

Preliminary Exercises

This book is not intended to provide the basics necessary to *all* forms of magic, but the following simple exercises can give some important clues to the nature of the developmental program that each vitki should design for himself or herself. Those who already have considerable experience in the magical arts may dispense with this stage and begin a program of practical experimentation if they desire. It must always be kept in mind that these basic skills should be constantly improved and practiced *daily*, because an increased intensity of will and concentration with more vivid visualizations will greatly expand the success of the magical operations performed by the runer.

1. Consult the runic commentaries and find a rune that is particularly appealing to you. Fashion a meditation card from a piece of white poster board about three inches by five inches in size. Paint the chosen stave on the card in bright red (enamel paint is good for this purpose). Sit in a comfortable position with the card in front of you at eye

level. Begin an even breath rhythm, which should be maintained throughout the exercise. Spend some minutes concentrating on the form of the stave while silently chanting the name three times—pause—then again three times, continuing in this rhythm throughout. Keep all of these elements of concentration on shape, sound, breath, and posture under control for several minutes, then close your eyes and imagine the shape in your *hugauga*—your "mind's eye." Continue practicing this until you can perform it smoothly for ten minutes.

2. Essentially, repeat the process of Exercise I, except sing the name (and basic *galdr* if you wish) out loud while maintaining a breath pattern of ten seconds inhalation—two seconds hold in—ten seconds exhalation (while singing the name or one line of the *galdr*)—and two seconds hold out. At this point begin experimenting with other simple postures, both sitting and standing. Always maintain the posture in a concentrated state, but *do not strain*. Again concentrate on the card for some minutes, and then close your eyes and imagine its form blazing with vivid power. Once you can maintain this complex of action in a concentrated form for ten minutes, you may progress further.

3. Perform this exercise in the I-rune *stadha* with hands overhead. Set up a ten-two-ten-two (or as similar as is comfortable) breathing rhythm while facing north. With your eyes open or closed visualize first the F-rune in blazing red while intoning its name out loud three times. Slowly turn with the sun in a circle, visualizing and vibrating the form and name of each of the runes in turn while maintain the *stadha* and breath rhythm. Once the aspiring vitki is able to perform this exercise in an almost instinctual fashion with few or no breaks in concentration, runework may be confidently undertaken.

Besides a daily program of exercises of this type the vitki should design a course of intellectual and physical development in accordance with his or her will and intentions. The serious study of Norse mythology and religion and the science of runology, as well as the Old Norse language, will greatly improve the vitki's understanding of the processes of runecraft. Because of the syncretic and "pantheistic" view of the multiverse contained in the runic system, a healthy, strong body will reflect itself in more powerful magical abilities. The true rune vitki is an awesome force on all levels of reality!

For anyone interested in a more in-depth initiation into the mysteries of the runes based on an extensive curriculum., see *The Nine Doors of Midgard* (The Rune-Gild, 2016, 5th edition). Taking runework to the next level is found there, and in the book *Alu: An Advanced Guide to Operative Runology* (Weiser, 2012).

At this, the first level of runework, we study and internalize the individual runes as unique and distinct signs which we can combine into formulas. In more advanced work the runes are used within linguistic formulas, often within the languages (Icelandic, Old English) that are suited to specific runic systems, the Younger Futhark and the Old English Futhorc. This is to be expected, just as a Kabbalist works with the Hebrew language at the advanced levels, the runer works with these languages. As outlined in *Alu*, the modern English language can be used (carefully) in conjunction with the Old English runes to effect direct communication with the world at the more advanced levels. But we begin with the *Futhark*—learning the ABCs of the world.

Magical Tools

The foregoing sections have dealt with the "internal tools" of rune magic and their development, but the following pages are concerned with the "external tools" that symbolize internal forces. These are the traditional tools and techniques of *rúnagaldr*, which aid in the manipulation of the rune streams.

Attire

In the practice of runecraft the ceremonial vestments, while important, do not play a central role in the cultic symbolism. The magical attire of the vitki roughly corresponds to the everyday dress of an early medieval Northman, with special symbolic features. The main advantage of liturgical vestments is the magical effect of setting oneself apart from everyday life that the donning and wearing of these garments should have. An ideal set of ritual attire for the rune vitki includes a hooded cloak or frock of a deep blue or black color as the outermost piece. Bright red pants also should be worn; this was a special sign of the vitki in ancient times. Black or natural-color heelless leather shoes may be worn, but many rites, especially those conducted outdoors, should be performed barefoot. A pullover-type tunic of white, blue, or red should be worn under the cloak. This tunic should fit quite loosely and be girdled by a belt made of leather or deerskin. A sheath for the knife may be attached to the belt and a pouch may be hung from it to hold the various other magical instruments. The runes themselves may be represented in two places in the vitki's attire. A white headband may be fashioned, on which the runes are embroidered in bright red, and the wearing of a token on which the futhark row and other magical symbols are engraved is a powerful aid in runic ritual. The runic token should be made of bronze, gold, or silver. It should be designed, created, and consecrated in accordance with the vitki's level of skill and knowledge. An extremely basic design for practical purposes is shown in figure 21.1.

Generally, male and female vitkar dress very much alike; however, the female usually goes bare-legged or wears a long

Figure 21.1. A runic bracteate.

red skirt. Ritual nudity also is practiced, according to the nature and aim of the rite being performed. In this, as in all matters of magic, the vitki should let intuition be the primary guide.

Wand (*gandr*)

The magic wand is known by many names in the technical language of Nordic magic; however, *gandr* is the most generic and expresses the powerful nature of this talismanic object. The *gandr* may be made from any of a variety of woods. The vitki might wish to consult Appendix III for some suggestions in this regard. In all cases the *gandr* should be cut, crafted, and consecrated according to the ceremonial formulas given for the rune tines below. The diameter of the wand should be no smaller than that of the index finger and no larger than the ring made by closing the tips of the index finger and thumb. Its length may be as short as the length of the hand or as long as the distance from the fingertips to the elbow. The *gandr* is blunt or rounded on the hinder end while the forward end may be fairly pointed or moderately rounded. The vitki may carve all twenty-four runes of the Elder Futhark on the wand, arranged in the three rows of aettir—or, in accordance with knowledge, a more unique and perhaps more magically potent formula may be devised for this purpose. An example is shown in figure 21.2 . Notice that the total number of runes is twenty-four, thus magically representing the entire futhark. The formula *ek vitki* is a potent magical statement that declares the power of the vitki and loads the object with his or her force. The numerical value of this part of the formula is 78 or 6 x 13 (see chapter 11 for the section on numerical symbolism). The eight A-runes invoke the power of Odin out of all eight corners of heaven.

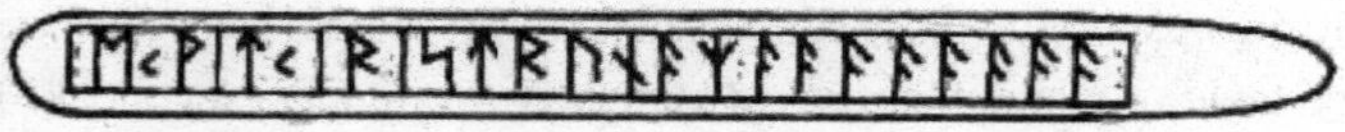

Figure 21.2. A runic wand. The inscription reads: ek vitki rist rúnar aaaaaaaa
(I the Magician carved the runes aaaaaaaa).

Knife (*sax*)

The vitki's knife is often used to carve runes, but it is also employed to cut and prepare wood for talismanic purposes, or in rites of defense and invocation of runic forces. The hilt of the knife should be fashioned from wood or bone, and the blade should be of the "sax" type as illustrated in figure 21.3. Its total length is approximately nine inches with a blade five inches long and a width of about one inch. The name of the vitki, transliterated into runes (see Appendix IV on page 295), may be etched into the hilt. Or a more complex formula may be devised to express the creative, shaping will of the runer. The illustration shows such a formula. It consists of three T-runes, which impart ordering successful force to the instrument, and a series of runes that ideographically express the nature of the knife. (| = the concentrated ego; ⟨ = controlled ability and creativity; ᚼ = the cosmic pattern it is intended to express; ᚠ= an invocation to Odinic force.) The numerical total of these seven runes is 81, which is 9 x 9—the intensified creative force in the multiverse. (See section on numerical symbolism).

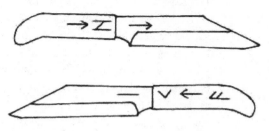

Figure 21.3. A rune knife of the sax type.

Carver

A special carver is often used to etch runes into all types of surfaces. The *ristir* should be extremely pointed and sharp. It is often the most practical tool for the carving of runes. It may again bear the runic form of the vitki's name or a magical formula expressing the purpose of the

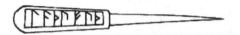

*Figure 21.4. A rune carver (*ristir*).*

ristir. A model for this is shown in figure 21.4. The inscription is *lathu futh:* "I (which means both the vitki *and* the *ristir)* invoke, or load, the futh." The final three-rune formula is the first three staves of the row, and represents the entire futhark. This formula may be called "the womb of the runes." (In Old Norse the word *fudh* actually means vulva and vagina). The numerical analysis is 36, or 4 x 9—the intensified creative force in the multiverse. (See section on numerical symbolism.)

Coloring Tools

The runes were always colored with either red pigments or blood. The magical significance of this is obvious. To the ancient Germanic peoples the verbal constructs "to make red" and "to endow with magical power" were synonymous. German *Zauber* (magic) and Old Norse *taufr* (magic, talisman) are both descended from this concept. In the technical terminology of ancient runecraft the Proto-Germanic word *fahido* and the Old Norse form *fá* meant literally "I color" and "to color," respectively. But these terms came to mean "to fashion runes" in general, describing the entire complex process of carving, coloring, and consecrating the staves.

Pigments used by the old vitkar were red ocher, minium (red lead), and madder. Minium is a latecomer, but ocher was known from neolithic times. Madder is obtained from the root of the plant of the same name *(rubia tincturia).* The Old Norse form of madder is *madhra,* and the magical power of the plant is no doubt increased by the magico-affective association of this world with *madhra*, the Old Norse word for "man" (:ᛗ:). All of these pigments are available in some form at art supply stores. They should be ground with linseed oil, or a gum mixture, in a ritual manner just prior to the beginning of the runic rite. Linseed is, of course, derived from the seed of the flax plant, which is extremely important in runecraft. Its ancient name *lina* often appears in runic talismans for fertility, growth, and well-being. During the grinding process the futhark or the runes to be used in the rite should be intoned, infusing the dye with the potential energy of those runes. All of these pigments are symbolic substitutes for the innate

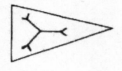

Figure 21.5. A runic coloring tool (reddener) bearing a powerful bind rune.

magical power held by the blood, either human or that of a ritually sacrificed animal. If blood is used no "preloading" is necessary. However, since the blood runes, the sanguine mysteries, are part of the religious expression, many vitkar will not concern themselves with them. All of the rituals in this book certainly may be performed powerfully using these venerable dyes!

A special tool should be made for inlaying the pigments into the carved staves. This can be made from a piece of wood about as thin as a veneer, which is cut in the shape of an isosceles triangle and inscribed with suitable runes. Figure 21.5 shows a *galdrastafr* made up of four K-runes, three in the form ᛦ and the connector in the alternate form ᛤ. Ideographically, this is an intensification of the *kenaz*-force. The numerical symbolism is also quite potent: 4 x 6, or 24 (a magical intensification of *kenaz* in the context of the whole futhark).

Other Magical Tools

Several rites require further instruments, and while the minor ones will be introduced in the pertinent sections, these are a few that bear mention here.

The vitki should possess a drinking horn or cup from which mead is often drunk. The horn may be a natural one, properly prepared, or a horn-shape vessel of precious metal; a cup may be made of wood, earthenware, gold, or silver. In any case, the runes ᛟᛍᚱᚠᚱᛁᛏ should be ritually inscribed on it in the talismanic manner. These runes are transcribed as *ódhrœrir* and mean "the exciter of inspiration." This is the name of the divine mead of inspiration and of the vessel in which it is contained (see the A- and G-runes). The numerical and ideographic symbolism of this formula are powerful. The rune count is 7, and its total is 87, 3 x 29 (see section on numerical symbolism).

A brazier, or fire-pot (ON *glódhker*), also may be needed in some rites. It can be made of metal or earthenware. This fire represents the quickening power of Muspellsheimr. In addition, two pieces of cloth—one black, one white, both preferably of linen—should be on hand. A leather thong, symbolic of the containing, binding force in the multiverse is commonly used.

THE BIG BOOK OF RUNES AND RUNE MAGIC

The equipment of the rune vitki is characterized by its mobility. All major tools needed for the performance of an act of runework should be so well concealed that no one would even notice their presence.

Magical Space

Rune magic may be performed indoors or out, but for atmospheric reasons, as well as for promotion of practical direct contact with the full power of the rune streams, outdoors is preferred. Ideally, the vitki would perform these sacred rites in a holy grove of oak, ash, or yew trees situated high on a hill. However, any secluded place in a wooded area can suffice. The actual work space is conceived of as a sphere, and therefore a circular space should be cleared and ritually set apart in the manner outlined in the "opening ritual" on page 247. Here we are concerned with the symbols to be contained in this magical space. The symbology may be as complex or as simple as the vitki desires; there is no dogma in this matter. Generally, when the work is done within an enclosed space, the symbolism tends to be more complex, and we would expect to find an altar, which may be either circular or rectangular, in either the northern or eastern sector of the space, or even in the center.

At this point a note on Germanic magical orientation should be interjected. From the earliest times the orientation was either to the east (as linguistic evidence shows) or to the north (as archeological evidence demonstrates). The English word "evening" ultimately derives from a Proto-Germanic root *aftan-*, which meant "backward"; hence, it indicates the observer faced eastward at twilight. There exists a large body of lore that speaks for a northward orientation. The Christian missionaries had problems compelling recently "converted" Germanic pagans to pray eastward instead of their heathen custom of facing north. The Icelandic *hof*, or temples, were lined up on a north-south axis, and even in the oldest period the passageways of the grave mounds faced northward.

Figure 21.6. A typical rune magic circle or ring.

It is probable that both these directions were considered powerful and that each was used depending on the type of ritual involved—eastward for matters concerning the earth and northward for matters concerning the "other worlds." Most modern rune vitkar prefer north for the same reason those missionaries hated it.

The altar itself will contain all the objects necessary to the rite. It will also serve as the "workbench" on which the rune tines are carved. In a ritual performed outside, a rock or tree stump serve well, but a portable altar also may be constructed for such cases.

As for the circle that symbolically defines the sacred space, it may be as simple as a circle drawn on the ground with the wand, or it may be complex as a glyph drawn on the floor of a *vé* with chalk or another material. The magic circle should indicate the eight divisions of heaven, which are symbolic representations of the eight otherworlds of Norse cosmology, and the runes should be portrayed in the outer ring, as shown in figure 21.6 on page 243. Other figures or names may be added as the vitki sees fit.

Magical Time

The timing of runic rites also is very important, and while complex, it is not so rigid or complicated as that of traditions more influenced by zodiacal astrology. To fully explain these factors would require an independent study of no small magnitude and would unduly complicate the present work. The most important criteria considered by the rune vitki are (1) season, (2) moon phase, and (3) solar position (time of day). The most auspicious times are dawn, midday, evening, and midnight. For increase of power the waxing moon is desired, but for constriction of force its waning phase is used. The best general time for *any* undertaking is in the nights of the new moon or just after, or the full moon or just before. Again, intuition is the best and most powerful guide in these matters. It should be noted that time and space are considered aspects of one another and both are measured by the *mjötvidhr* (the measuring tree [Yggdrasill]).

Signing and Sending of Runes

The practice of making runic gestures or signs was well known in ancient times. The Norse *godhar* or priests would make the "sign of the hammer" (ON *hamarsmark*) ⊥ or ⃔ over goblets before drinking. The rite of signing persons and objects with holy signs was established well before the coming of Christianity, and in fact they adopted this practice from the Indo-European tribes because they could not eradicate it.

A rune may be traced or drawn in the air in front of the vitki with the palm of the right hand, the right index finger, the right thumb, or the rune wand. Some of the staves may be signed with both hands in a smooth and aesthetic gesture.

Visualization is an important aspect of these *signingar*. The vitki should actually send, or project, the image of the stave from a sphere of brightness in the center of the body, along a shaft of red light to the point where the rune is intended to appear. Once the beam has reached this distance, the vitki traces the form of the stave from the substance of light. The color of the light may be red or some other symbolic hue (e.g., the color ascribed to the rune in Appendix III).

A special rhythm of breath should be observed during this practice. Inhale as the arm is raised, concentrate on the intake of *önd*. On exhalation, send and sign the stave while singing the name and/or *galdr* of the rune, either mentally or out loud.

When the runes are invoked before the vitki, the force may either be reabsorbed into the personal sphere of the runer, infused into an object as an act of loading or "changing," or it may be *sent* to do work elsewhere. This type of ritual work will be more fully treated in its own section below. It is being introduced here as a kind of exercise because it is good practice to use this procedure in daily work and because it is found in the ritual of talismanic loading. This is one of the most powerful techniques available to the vitki, but one that must be practiced and mastered with extremely strong concentration and visualization to be completely effective.

Rituals of Protection

A ritual should be devised by the vitki that serves to banish all forces detrimental to the work at hand and to prevent the return of those powers. These forces may not be "evil," just disadvantageous to the operation. There are three good formulas for such a ritual. The hammer rite (*Hamarssetning*) is the strongest and provides maximal protection and isolation, the *Hagalaz* rite provides the most potent magical atmosphere and potential, and the *Elhaz* rite strikes a balance between these. The formula outlined below gives the hammer rite, but to perform the other two simply substitute the word *hagalaz* or *elhaz* (elk) and sign the corresponding rune in the appropriate places. A rite of this type may be practiced every day and should be used in conjunction with an opening ritual to begin all ceremonial work.

It is most ideal to have a permanently sacred site (ON *vé*) for inner work, one that is always sacrosanct and does not have to be "re-consecrated" every time you do ritual work there.

The Hammer Rite

This example is written in a northward orientation, and appropriate changes of course should be made in the order of *galdrar* in rites of an eastward orientation.

1. With the rune wand in the right hand, face the North Star.

2. Beginning with *fehu* in the north sign and send the runes of the futhark in a ring around you at the level of the solar plexus as far out as the circle on the ground or floor, always "with the sun" in a clockwise direction. The runes should form a complete band ending with *othala* next to *fehu* in the north.

3. Stand in the cross *stadha* and visualize an equilateral cross lying horizontally in the plane of the rune ring and your solar plexus, with that point as the center of the cross. The arms of this cross should end at the points where they intersect the rune band. Imagine a surrounding sphere of shimmering blue light with the red rune band as its

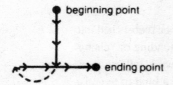

beginning point

ending point

Figure 21.7. Tracing pattern of the hammer sign.

equator. Then visualize the vertical axis coming through your length from the infinite space above and from the infinite space below.

4. Feel and see the force flowing into your center from all six directions as it builds a sphere of glowing red light. The color may be altered depending on the ritual intention (see section on color symbolism).

5. The vitki should touch the hinder part of the wand to the breast at the center of power and thrust it forward, projecting the force from that center to a point on the inside face of the outer sphere. Then the runer should sign the hammer ⊥ from the mass of magical might. The sign should be traced as in figure 21.7. During this process intone:

> *Hamarr í Nordhri helga vé thetta ok hald vördh!*[1]
> (Hammer in the North hallow and hold this holy-stead![2])

Then, turning 90° to the right, send and sign another hammer sign vibrating.

> *Hamarr í Austri helga vé thetta ok hald vördh!*
> (Hammer in the East hallow and hold this holy-stead!)

> *Hamarr í Sudhri helga vé thetta ok hald vördh!*
> (Hammer in the South hallow and hold this holy-stead!)

And in the West:

> *Hamarr í Vestri helga ve thetta ok hald vördh!*
> (Hammer in the West hallow and hold this holy-stead!)

Returning to the north, direct your attention overhead, there send and sign the *hamars-mark* on the "ceiling" of the sphere, saying:

> *Hamarr yfir mér helga vé thetta ok hald vördh!*
> (Hammer over me hallow and hold this holy-stead!)

And then project the hammer sign below to the "floor" of the sphere (*not* the ground or room floor) and intone:

> *Hamarr undir mér helga vé thetta ok hald vördh!*
> (Hammer under me hallow and hold this holy-stead!)

6. Now, strike the cross *stadha* again and sing:

> *Hamarr helga vé thetta ok hald vördh!*
> (Hammer hallow and hold this holy-stead!)

Turning in the center of the *vé*, repeat this once for each of the other four directions and once for the vertical axis. The visual effect should be one of axes connecting all six shining red hammers to your personal center, all engulfed by a field of sparkling deep blue light and surrounded by a band of bright red runes.

7. Finally, center all the forces of the *vé* by folding your arms from the cross *stadha* in toward your center, with your fingertips touching at the solar plexus, and saying:

> *Um mik ok í mér Asgardhr ok Midhgardhr!*
> (Around me and in me Asgardhr and Midgardhr!)

This ritual may be repeated at the end of a working or exercise, and the entire sphere may be drawn into the personal center, or the walls of the globe may be split with the knife, allowing the collected energy to flow to its goal.

The basic form of the rite given here is intended to shield the consciousness of the vitki for magical or meditational work. Modifications in the rite, such as the ones already suggested, may be worked out so that this ritual form may be used as an active magical tool. The runes on the face of the sphere may be drawn from, or projected through to, the outside in order to create magical effects. It is up to the runer to discover the further powers of the hammer rite lying beyond these instructions.

Some people over the years have thought that this rite is based on a cabalistic model, but this, as well as the making of the sign of the hammer over horns of mead, etc., are actually old Germanic forms. A Viking Age runic inscription formula, repeated on several Danish stones, reads: "Thor sanctify these runes (with your hammer)." The power of Thor's hammer, projected in the four quarters and above and below, hallows a place, allowing the space created to be filled with holy power.

The Opening Ritual

In important ritual work the vitki may wish to recite an invocatory *galdr* into which the hammer rite may be incorporated. Such a *galdr* would serve to invoke divine forces or simply act as a general invocation to the runic powers, or both. The knowledgeable vitki will compose his or her own rite and *galdr*, for this would be a great deed of runecraft! Note how the hammer rite is interwoven into this example:

1. Standing in the middle of the *vé*, face north or east, in the *stadha*, and intone:

> *Fare now forth*
> *mighty Fimbultýr[3]*
> *from heavenly homes all eight*
> *Sleipnir be saddled,*
> *hither swiftly to ride:*

Galdrsfadhir,[4] *might to give and gain.*
Holy rune-might flow
from the hoves of Hangatýr's[5] *steed;*
in streams of steadfast strength--
through staves of stalwart standing!

2.   Go to the northern (or eastern) rim of the *vé* and with the wand trace the circle in the direction of the sun, from left to right. During this process sing:

The rune-might is drawn
'round the holy-stead,
unwanted wights wend away!

3.   When the circle is complete return to the center and facing the original direction, perform the rune-ring portion of the hammer rite. When this is complete say:

The worrisome wights
now wend their way
eastward toward etin-home;
hallowed be the hall of Hroptatýr,[6]
with the help of Hrungnir's slayer![7]

4.   Now perform the rest of the hammer rite.

5.   After which, if the ritual calls for a brazier, the fire should be enkindled. If the vitki knows it, and the ritual needs it, this fire may be enkindled by the need-fire friction method; but normally, the runer will light the fire-pot with a previously prepared flame. Also necessary at this juncture are containers of salt and brewer's yeast; a pinch of each should be added to the flame at the point indicated in the *galdr*. Lighting the brazier, sing:

Endless light of life
give thy living gift
fill the night of need;
to the hearth of this hall
bring thy boon so bright
to quicken this salt
and yeast all so cold
together live long and well
in the hearts of Hár's[8] *sib.*

6.   Once the fire-pot is enkindled, the vitki also may add leaves, thin strips of wood from trees, or herbs that correspond to the intention of the rite to be performed (see Appendix III). The body of the magical ritual may now begin in a "loaded" atmosphere.

The Closing Ritual

When a rite has been begun with an opening formula, a closing rite is in order.

1. Face north or east in the *stadha* and intone:

    > *Now is done the holy work*
    > *of word and deed*
    > *helpful to godly children*
    > *hurtful to etin-churls*
    > *hail to (him/her/them) who speaks(s) them*
    > *hail to (him/her/them) who grasp(s) them*
    > *needful to (him/her/them) who know(s) them*
    > *hail to (him/her/them) who heed(s) them.*[9]

2. At this point the hammer rite (without the rune ring) may be performed, although this would be optional.

3. If it is not *totally safe* to allow the brazier to burn itself out, extinguish it by placing a cover over it with the words:

    > *Fire that glows without*
    > *forever be kindled within*
    > *by the might of Odin-Vili-Vé.*

4. If the energy built up by the entire operation is to be internalized, then draw the collected energies into your personal center by standing in the cross position, and while deeply inhaling, draw your arms in so that your fingertips touch your solar plexus. Turn in all four directions and repeat this action, each time visualizing the sphere being drawn into your center. If the energy of the rite has been sent abroad, then you may simply split the sphere with your hand or knife and step out of the circle.

Runic Meditation

The practice of both ceremonially and informally meditating on the runes is a source of vast wisdom—and a direct source of magical power. The vitki should strive to develop a personal link with each rune by communicating with the mystery on a deep level. Once this link has been made—with each individual rune and with the runic cosmology as a whole—a floodgate of runic force is opened, creating a stream of wisdom that always stands open to the vitki. Afterward this stream may be tapped even on an informal basis, in any spare moment that allows for reflection. Often these odd moments provide the vitki with some of the most powerful insights into the runic mysteries.

This meditation is an active, seeking endeavor. One of the most important techniques needed for success is the control of thought—that is, the submersion of thoughts detrimental to the purpose of the meditation and a guiding of the thoughts along the willed rune path. Once the *hugr* (consciousness) has been stilled and thought patterns have been concentrated into a single center—the rune—then the rune wisdom will begin to well up in the consciousness of the vitki. The focal point of runic meditation is threefold: form (which may include color), sound *(galdr),* and root idea (contained in name and key words). The vitki should strive to concentrate, in a relaxed manner, on any one or all elements contained in this threefold complex, quietly leading detrimental thoughts out of the *hugr* and leaving only the runic symbols of form, sound, and name (root idea)—until finally the rune begins to speak directly to the consciousness of the vitki.

Ceremonial runic meditation may be as elaborate or as simple as the vitki desires or is able to perform. Generally, it seems that the wisest path is that which works from simplicity toward complexity. Preparations for meditation include the procurement of a quiet location, mastery of one of the protection-invocation rites, and the creation of a set of meditational cards, as described in the previous section. Later, mastery of the *stadha* of the chosen rune may be necessary. In the first stages of the meditational program the vitki may want to concentrate on one element of the threefold complex only, and include the others according to a self-directed program. A vitki should plan a progressive scheme that is suited to his or her own needs and abilities, always building a richer complex of elements in the inner center of concentration, while including a wider variety of magical techniques in the outer procedure.

The following is a composite outline of various methods of runic meditation from which the vitki may draw in the formation of a meditational program. All procedures may be physically performed, or if more convenient or effective, they may be performed totally within the *hugauga*, or mind's eye.

1. Perform one of the protective-invocatory rites while strongly visualizing the rune ring.

2. Assume a comfortable position, either sitting or standing, or in the *stadha* of the proper rune. You may face north, east, or in the angle indicated by the rune's position in the rune ring.

3. A runic meditation card should be set in such a position—attached to the wall or placed on a simple stand—that it is at eye level during this phase of the procedure.

4. With your eye fixed firmly on the runic form represented on the card, softly sing the rune *galdr* (this may be done inwardly). At the same time, if you wish, you may introduce formulaic *ideas,* such as the rune name, on a secondary level of consciousness. A name is of course included in the *galdr;* however, here we are considering the esoteric *meaning* embodied in the name, which may be included in the "center of con-

centration." In this phrase the vitki should strive toward a strong concentration on the elements of the runic complex that are intended.

5. The vitki should now slowly close his or her eyes, continuing with the *galdr* and contemplation of an esoteric principle (if included). Visualize the form of the rune as it appears on the card and in the mind's eye, and furthermore, attempt to realize the oneness of the form-sound-idea complex. In the beginning you may have to open your eyes to reestablish the stave form, but eventually you may eliminate the fourth phase and proceed directly to a complex inward contemplation once you are confident of your abilities.

6. Maintain this state of inner concentration on the runic complex for at least several seconds, preferably working toward a span of five minutes.

7. After this period of inward concentration the vitki should lapse into inner silence. But remember this is a totally attentive silence! During this void of slumbering thoughts the *word* of the rune will be intoned with a resounding peal. This is a "word" that cannot be expressed by any language, but it is the totality of the runic mystery expressed in a single moment. This is a *holy* experience in which the rune and the *hugr* of the vitki are momentarily unified—or this unity is perceived.

8. The vitki may continue the meditation as long as a link with the runic force is felt. In this meditative state the vitki may be led along a myriad of rune paths, in which secrets concerning the rune itself are revealed or the relationships between certain runes are made clear—the possibilities are infinite.

9. Once the linkage dissipates, or the vitki desires to terminate the meditation, simply repeat a formula such as "Now the work is wrought" and open your eyes. Then ritually break the rune ring according to the hammer rite.

After you feel yourself really becoming a part of the rune world, more informal meditational operations may be undertaken. These will reveal a vast amount of both usable and fascinating wisdom. It has been found that the most useful tools in this endeavor are paper, pen, compass, protractor, and perhaps even a calculator. The procedure is quite simple: Sit at your writing desk or table, surrounded with various runic glyphs and cosmological configurations. Still your mind, turning it toward the rune world. Allow your *hugr* to wander until it lights on a seed concept, then relentlessly follow it, drawing and jotting down your "revelations" as they come to you. These notations can then serve as the basis for further work. It is probably best not to schedule these informal sessions but rather to sit down and delve into the mysteries when the "spirit moves you." Usually, after a short period of time the wisdom of the runes will begin to well up in the *hugr* of the vitki at odd moments. Sometimes the eruption of these forces is so powerful as to cause psychokinetic phenomena in the physical proximity of the vitki!

The regular practice of runic meditation is one of the mainstays in the overall rigging of rune wisdom and one that gives ample rewards for efforts well spent. It may be said that indeed the moments of inspiration gained from these practices are not akin to the discovery of a golden tomb in an exotic desert land but rather to the recovery of a long-lost family heirloom out of the attic (look in the basement too!). What has been lost can be regained if only the will is strong!

Talismanic Magic

In Old Norse there are three principal words for "talisman," "amulet," or "talismanic magic." They are (1) *teinn*, which indicates a piece of wood or twig fashioned into a talismanic object (the word "tine" reflects this); (2) *hlutr*, which may be any object used for talismanic or divinatory purposes (English "lot"); and (3) *taufr*, which means both talisman and magic in general; but in the original sense talismanic magic is particular. All three terms are quite descriptive of various aspects of talismanic runecraft.

The following section on *taufr* will deal with many features of rune magic, such as bind runes and the symbology of number, color, and ideograph, which are of vital importance in *all* areas of *rúnagaldr* but which are introduced here because of the fundamental role they play in the art of *taufr*.

A tine is a living being that has an *ørlög* to live out, one that has been bestowed upon it by the vitki. The runer gives the "object" life and then magically provides it with *ørlög* through the nature of the runic power with which the vitki loads it. The "living nature" of the tine may be so strongly enforced that it will be found to have a "personality." In order to facilitate this high state of autonomous (but vitki-willed) force, the runer may wish to give the tine a name during the loading ritual. This is the mystery behind the many runic talismans (especially weapons) that have been given names.

The technical theories behind tine magic are in perfect accord with the laws of action within the runic cosmology in general. The rune tine acts as a key to unlock the power of particular rune streams. In the loading processes these streams (identical with *hamingja*) are willfully blended in the causal worlds and infused into the object, which has been prepared by the vitki with signs and staves receptive to those forces. There they are intensified or modified and again released, bearing a specific character imparted by the *ørlög* giving *galdrar* and *formálar* of the vitki and the innate power of the symbols depicted on the tine. The talismanic form becomes linked to the essence of the particular rune(s) through a great concentration and energizing of forces directed by the vitki into the tine, using the shape, sound, and color of the runes.

Once the tine has been properly loaded, this power is then "unloaded" according to the form that the vitki impressed upon it. The object is the center of a vortex of force, receiving energy, formulating it in accordance with its *ørlög*, and then re-expressing it in the causal realms, leading to the desired result. This power also may be retained within the personal sphere. The efficiency of this process is dependent on the level of strength in the vitki's *hamingja* and the quality of concentration and visualization the vitki may bring to bear in the loading operation.

Another important aspect of tine magic is that of magical linkage to the "object" of the *taufr*, that is, the person or thing to be affected by the magical force. This may be brought about by attaching a runic formula to the object that represents the person (such as the name transliterated into runes) or by the physical proximity of the tine to the person to be affected. Other techniques of sympathetic magic may also be employed.

There are several distinct types of runic talismans. Usually, they are fashioned from pieces of wood, bone, stone, or metal that readily take their forms. However, paper or parchment also may be used by those less traditionally inclined. The objects on which the runes and signs are carved may be purely magical in function or they may also serve some utilitarian function. The former group is what is usually considered a tine. The latter group may include such objects as belt buckles, pens, automobiles, screwdrivers, guns, and so on, that are thus endowed with *hamingja*. This is valuable for imparting success or protection in the areas where the object is used. This tradition is just as useful and powerful today as it was in ancient Europe, when warriors inscribed their weapons and shields with runes for protection and victory. The imagination of the modern runer should prove to be a fruitful guide in this practice. Another class of talisman is stationary. Any fixed object may be turned into a runic talisman. Trees, large rocks, and houses are good examples. Also, a stationary *taufr* may be a card or stave placed in the vitki's room, or a tine placed near the person to be affected by the magical force. These are used to magically influence a particular place or persons who are regularly in that place. The internally applied talisman is also known and will be discussed below.

The techniques of tine magic may be used in operations of every type. The procedures outlined in these sections should be followed, in one form or another, when fashioning tools to be used in the runic art.

Bind Runes

Tines may be produced that express a single runic force, but one of the most potent techniques of blending several runic forces together for a very specific purpose is that of the bind rune (ON *bandrún*). A bind rune is the combination of individual runic powers into one mighty field of action. This method has the distinct advantage for the modern vitki of using only the ideographic essence of the rune; therefore the contemporary runer does not have to worry about whether his or her inscription is correct or whether it will be effective if written in modern English. In order to properly build and load such a form, the vitki must have a deep understanding of separate runes and how they fit together to form a single powerful expression of force with a single harmonious will. The principles of spiritual and physical aesthetics are important here. This combining aspect is common to all runecraft, but with the bind runes it finds its most obvious expression.

Bind runes have been used by runers from the very beginning. There are two main types of these *bandrúnar:* (1) those used to connect two or more runes together when inscribing words, and (2) those of an apparently purely ideographic type (although this last type may contain a word concealed in its form as a kind of simultaneous anagram). A great amount of "artistic license" is available to the vitki in the construction of bind runes. The alternate forms of the various staves should help in the formation of an aesthetically pleasing shape. When formulating bind runes, the runer should always keep the elements of numerological symbolism and ideological harmony and cooperation in mind. But most importantly the bind rune should be pleasing to the eye.

When used in writing, bind runes may connect two runes or a group of them. This is done to form a magical link between these two runes, to represent two or more words in a coded form, or to reduce the overall count of runes in the inscription. A bind rune is always counted as one rune in the rune count (see section on numerical symbolism). The common grammatical ending -*az* (-*aR*) is often written ⱬ (note the use of an alternate form of the Z-rune to obtain the magico-aesthetic effect). Magically, this links the forces of the A- and Z-runes into a special expression—which is quite powerful! One of the oldest bind runes is ✕ which represents ✕ plus ᚠ.

This stands for the magical formula *gibu auja* (I give good luck) and is often carved on talismanic or ritual weapons. Any runes having adjacent vertical staves are prime candidates for binding, as are words (especially pronouns and verb forms) that are common, for example, ᛖ (*em*: I am); ᛖ (*ek*: I).

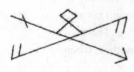

Figure 21.8. Bind rune found on the brooch of Soest, c. 600–650 C.E.

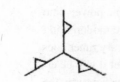

Figure 21.9. Ideographic "three-headed thurs."

The purely ideographic bind runes are the most useful in tine magic, and their multiplicity of levels makes them very effective in refined operations of magic. One of the oldest examples of this is found on the brooch of Soest, circa 600–650 C.E. (see figure 21.8). This is formed from the runes ᛜ, ᛦ, ↑, ✕, and ᚠ twice. The numerical total of these runes is 66, or 6 x 11, with a rune count of 6 (see section on numerical symbolism). This *galdrastafr* is a love talisman carved on a brooch and then given to a woman. The power of the *taufr* draws upon Odinic force ᚠᚠ, with justice and a call for success ↑, out of need ᛦ (note also the sexual symbolism here), for marriage (erotic union) ✕, according to ancestral principles and territory ᛜ The rune count and multiple of 6 emphasizes the erotic nature of the talisman. The runes also may contain an anagram of the old German man's name *Attano* plus the sign ✕ (marriage). The analysis of old inscriptions gives many clues to modern practice.

⊠   THE BIG BOOK OF RUNES AND RUNE MAGIC

Another ideographic example would be the "Three-headed *thurs*" (figure 21.9). Essentially a threefold intensification of the TH-rune, this is used in curses. Further examples of bind runes will be given in the magical formulas.

We will also return to the topic of bind runes in a special section below in which they form their own kind of magic.

Numerical Symbolism

Numerical criteria play an important role in the loading and working of rune tines, and they are often critical in other types of rune magic. In the ancient inscriptions we sometimes find that the vitki has in some way sacrificed linguistic clarity for numerical (or ideographic) potency. This is done by leaving out staves (especially vowels), or by adding or doubling them. We have already discussed the lore of esoteric numerology in the runic tradition in chapter 11. In this section the focus is on the operative aspects of numeric symbolism—that is, how things can be *done* with numeric symbols.

As noted at the beginning of this book, *number* is one of the three keys to each rune. The commentary given under each rune is also pertinent to the symbolism of its number. Indeed much of the interpretation is drawn from numerical criteria. Strong examples of this would be the H-rune (9)—the nine worlds of Yggdrasill; and the J-rune (12)—the twelve months of the solar year. It is necessary only to give the broad outlines of runic numerology here; the true vitki will find the right roads to further power.

The numerical values of inscriptions, tines, and magical formulas place the power of the runes in various "spheres of working" and also draw on the power inherent in that number for their working. Often it is best to aim for a harmonious and broad-based sphere of working to lend maximal overall power to the ideographic and linguistic form of the formula. These formulas also may modify or adjust the overall power of the whole. Since every formula and tine works on various levels simultaneously, a general rule of thumb would be the more levels of meaning you can pack into the least amount of space, and the more cryptic you can make it, the more effective the magic will be. This is important in the shaping as well as the interpretation of talismans.

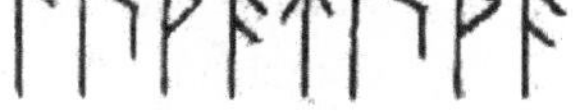

Runic number formulas are analyzed in two ways: (1) the rune count, that is, the number of staves in the formula; and (2) the total of the numerical values of each rune in the formula (as in gematria). These numbers are then broken down into their multiples in order to further analyze their powers. A simple example of this

Figure 21.10. Runic number formula "luwatuwa."

process is shown in figure 21.10: Rune count 8 (multiple: 2 x 4); runic total: 66; (multiple: 6 x 11). This formula is found on ancient talismans, and forms an incantation of great ideographic, phonetic, and numerological power.

Either or both of these systems may be used. The meaning of these numbers is twofold. They indicate the sphere in which the formula is to work and the power by which it works.

There are several "numbers of power" in both of these systems on which the beginning vitki could concentrate. For the rune count, the numbers 1 through 24 are all powerful, and imbue the formula with the force of the rune of that number. Also, the use of any twenty-four runes in an inscription provides a broad base of power and invokes the force of the whole rune row into the formula. To a twenty-four-fold rune count, the number eight and its multiples (and indeed twenty-four and its multiples) may be added to maintain the whole harmony of power while intensifying its force. The multiple of the rune count also modifies the runic potency in subtle and ingenious ways. These are common patterns in ancient inscriptions.

On the second level, that of the numerical total of the runes, there are many possibilities and numbers of power, which direct the runic force in specific directions and give them special magical characteristics. Of course, the sums 1 through 24 indicate the sphere where that particular rune is at work. Prime numbers are especially powerful and express a tremendous amount of will. Whatever the runic total might be, it is through its multiple factors that the root force of the number is revealed. Multiples of three, and especially of nine, are powerful in operations dealing with magical forces working on many levels at once, including the earthly realm. Multiples of ten are especially forceful when the intent is to cause a change in the manifest world of Midgardhr. Twelve and its multiples are also potent in this regard but have a more prolonged and enduring effect. The number thirteen and its multiples are the most universal numbers of power. A vast number of runic inscriptions manifest this numerological pattern. The number is indicative of universal potency and contains the mystery of *eihwaz* as the World-Tree (9) and the three realms (3) in the ontological oneness of Ginnungagap (1). The number by which the "master number" is multiplied further modifies and directs the overall force of the formula according to its runic nature.

All of these principles may be used when constructing rune tines and rituals; however, they need not dominate the form of the operation. Let intuition and natural inclination be your guide. Vitkar may totally dispense with numerical considerations, and their results will in no way diminish. The correct use of runic numerology is an art in itself and one that needs to be supplemented with a large dose of Nordic lore to be completely effective. The study and analysis of inscriptions fashioned by our forebears should be the guiding light in our efforts. It also should be pointed out that the old Germanic attitude toward the concept of number was quite different from that held by their neighbors to the south. To the Pythagorean and Gnostic mystics, number came to be the ἀρχή (rule) of all things, but to the vitkar, number was only one among three equal expressions of the same holy mystery embodied by a rune. While the Gnostics and Pythagoreans tended to look at number as a way of measuring and distinguishing one thing from another, the vitkar saw them as points of connection and interrelation in a cosmos forever in a state of ebb and flow.

The ancient skalds, or poets, counted the number of syllables they used in their lines of poetry in order to make the language more harmonious with the language of the gods. They did this in order to be able to communicate their wishes and messages to the causal realm of the gods in a more efficient and beautiful way. Number and its symbolism is used in a similarly meta-linguistic fashion to convey magical communications more powerfully.

Color Symbolism

The symbology of color in the runic system is somewhat different from that of the Judeo-Christian culture, although the ancient Germanic traditions (among many others) have influenced the Christian color symbology to a certain extent. The source of this color system is to be found in the Eddas and in the saga literature. In the practice of runecraft

Color	Interpretation
Gold	The light of the sun and the spiritual light shining from Asgardhr, the force of *önd* in the universe and a symbol of honor, reputation, and power in all realms.
Red	Magical might and main, protective power, spiritual life and vigor, aggressive force. The principal color of the runes; also a sign of death. Often related to gold. Color emblematic of the warrior class.
Blue	The all-encompassing, all-penetrating, and omnipresent mystical force of the numen, a sign of restless motion, the color of Odin's cloak. In its darkest hues it becomes one with black.
Green	Organic life, the manifested force of fertility in the earth and in the sea, a sign of the earth and nature, passage between worlds.
Yellow	Earthly power, a sign of desire and lust in a will toward manifestation. Related to both green and gold.
White	The total expression of light as the sum of all colors—totality, purity, perfection, nobility, the disk of the sun. Color of the priesthood and kings.
Silver	The disk of the moon, change, transmutation, striving for higher knowledge. A metallic version of white.
Black	New beginning (as night and winter herald the birth of day and summer), all-potential, the root force of all things, knowledge of hidden things, concealment, the container of light. Color indicative of the farmers and craftsmen.

Table 21.1. Color symbology.

this color lore is valuable as material in formulating powerful visualizations and ritual intensification as well as in the construction of more complex talismans. (See table 21.1.)

Appendix III provides speculative color correspondences for each rune, but the best guide is the intuition of the independent vitki. In this manner, as in most others, the perspective of the consciousness alters the perception of the concept, and it is the perception that provides the *best* key for unlocking the concept.

Pictographic Symbolism

Many runestones and rune tines also bear pictographic representations of holy concepts that aid in the formulation and direction of magical power. These are of two kinds: (1) pictographs, graphic representations of naturally occurring objects (see table 21.2 for examples); and (2) ideographs, the holy signs or *galdrastafir* of rune magic (see table 21.3 for examples). These signs and symbols work in conjunction with the runic forces, or they are embodiments of the force expressed by the rest of the formula. They are valuable as talismanic symbols and also as objects of meditation and material for magical visualization.

Symbol	Interpretation
	Serpent or lingworm—enclosure, containment, chthonic force, and the magical unconscious.
	Man and horse—wisdom and magical power of projection, swiftness, command over the worlds and spiritual realms, the Odinic force.
	Ship—passage between life and death, transmutation, fertility, and growth (often appears with ⊕ above it).
	Horn or caldron—sign of Ódhroerir, wisdom and inspiration, invocation of eloquence.
	Hammer—Mjöllnir, the Hammer of Thor, protection, increase, raw power, and will.
	Bird (raven)—swift-moving intelligence and memory.
	Moon—transmutation, ordered change, magical power.

Table 21.2. Pictographs.

Symbol	Interpretation
⊥	Hammer—same as pictograph.
卐	Sun-wheel or hammer—similar to ⊥, but also luck, solar power, the sign of the dynamic solar wheel, transmutation, and magical power under will.
⊕	Solar wheel—spiritual power, law, order, contained religious force, holiness.
✳	Hagall/World-Tree—cosmic pattern of Yggdrasil, the snowflake, protection and magical working by and through the laws of the world.
⊛	*Glückstern* (Star of Luck)—same as Hagall above. Common in Dutch hex signs and a powerful framework for talismans and visual magic.
✳	Heavenly star or cross—the eight corners of heaven, the eight legs of Sleipnir, the World-Tree and the heavens expressed in a single ninefold pattern (center: Midhgardhr, the world of man).
⧓	*Valknútr* (the knot of the fallen or chosen)—the nine worlds embodied in the three realms in eternal unity expressing the evolutionary law of arising-being/ becoming-passing-away to new beginning.
⅄	Trefot—dynamic power from the three realms of being and the threefold evolutionary force. Made from three L-runes (21 + 21 + 21 = 63, or 7 x 9); magical inspiration throughout the cosmos.
♡	"Heart" (actually an ancient representation of female genitalia and buttocks)— sensuality, eroticism, love. In Old Norse books of magic, the sign ⊗ often appears in spells of love magic; a symbol of sexual intercourse.

Table 21.3. Ideographs.

This short analysis should give the aspiring vitki a good basis for practical experiment, while the more curious vitkar will search out books on Norse symbolism and rock carvings for even more of these enchanting signs.

Talismanic Construction

Before attempting to construct a runic talisman the vitki should be well versed in the intellectual content of the rune lore and suitably advanced in the psychic faculties necessary to the successful completion of a talismanic operation. Rune tines should be constructed in accordance with the theories and ideology expressed by the runic system to be of maximal effect.

If the tine is to be constructed of wood, it should be fashioned from a kind of wood that is sympathetic to the aim of the talisman. For this the vitki may consult Appendix III, or better yet, let informed intuition be your guide. The possibilities of using wood are limitless. Metal disks, plates, or rings of copper, bronze, silver, or gold also make excellent runic talismans. Other materials, such as a small and appropriately shaped stone or piece of bone, also are favored. Larger stones are also good for stationary talismans, and in such cases the vitki will find it useful to have a hammer and chisel dedicated to the runic arts with which to construct these runestones. Earthenware is also receptive to rune loading; runes may be etched into the finished product or they may be cut into the soft unfired object, colored properly, and then fired—all in a ritualistic process with powerful potential! Runic talismans also can be formed from parchment colored with pens, inks, and paints dedicated to ritual practice. These parchment talismans may then be carried (in lockets, for example), or they may serve as stationary symbols. The imagination of the vitki is the only limit to the possibilities.

There are certain shapes that are best suited to receive runic forms. The most common are the rectangular solid, the thin wooden stave (1/16 to 1/8 inch thick), the thin disk or rectangular plate, a segment of natural tree branch, or a cylindrical shape of various lengths. Pieces of jewelry of all types are prime candidates for talismanic use. A unique shape that is fairly common for talismans is a thin rhomboid. This is usually cut from wood or bone. Figure 21.11 shows a typical example of this type. By using this design the vitki has four smooth surfaces available for longer inscriptions. This is also an extremely convenient and comfortable shape for tines designed to be carried on the person.

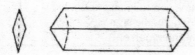

Figure 21.11. A typical talismanic (rhomboid) form.

Necessity will guide the vitki in the construction of utilitarian talismans.

The main requirement in the external formation of these holy objects is that they contain a symbol or symbols describing the purpose and aims of the talisman and a "signature" representing the person, persons, or thing to be affected or altered by the force of the first symbol. This signature may indeed be the name of the person or it may be some other sympathetic link; even physical proximity may serve to form this linkage. Space on the object should be aesthetically allocated and divided according to runestaves, holy signs, and the signature. Any combination of these elements is of course acceptable. Figure 21.12 is an example of a tine for increasing inspiration, magical power, and general success for a person named Erik Thurman.

The vitki should experiment with various surfaces and tools to determine what the best cutting techniques are for each. Time spent in the practice of carving runes will be well invested, because the more skilled the runer becomes in these basic mechanical skills, the more energy and concentration he or she can divert to the work at hand. One

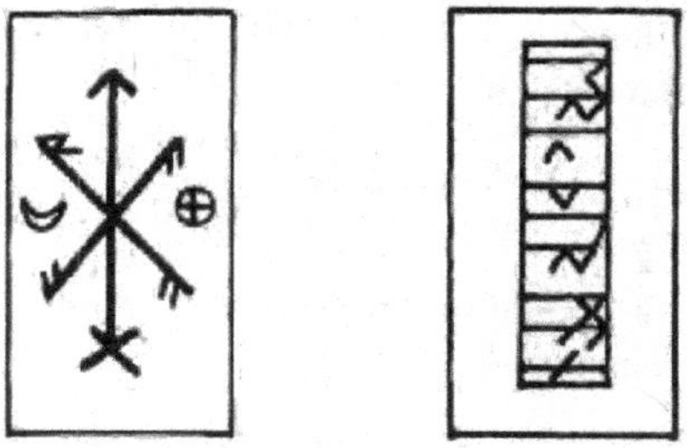

Figure 21.12. Bind rune talisman with signature. A) Obverse. A bind rune formed from ᛏ, ᚨ (twice), ᚠ, ᚱ, and ᚷ, providing success and energy in the realms of inspiration and magic in the natural order of things. B) Reverse. Note that certain runes are bound so that the rune count totals 7, thus linking the name with the power of magical inspiration.

general technique that works well for all types of materials is the precutting of rune bands; that is, cutting two grooves to act as upper and lower limits for the staves.

Cutting Wood for Rune Tines

Once a design has been decided on, the vitki should explore the neighborhood for the right tree from which to cut the tine. After this scouting process is complete, go to the tree in a ritualized attitude, armed with the rune knife, at a time that seems auspicious for the aim of the operation. Generally, the most favorable times are considered to be dawn, noon, and twilight. Find a branch or twig that bends toward a quarter or eighth (of the heavens), because that is sympathetic to the purpose of the tine. The choice of a root at the time of midnight is effective for negative rituals and curses.

The cutting of the tine should be carried out in a ceremonial manner. First, standing to the north or east of the trunk, facing outward, perform the *Hamarssetning* or other suitable rite, envisioning the *whole* tree encompassed within the holy-stead. Then position yourself before the branch, twig, or root that you intend to cut. You may have to climb the tree to do this, of course. Turn your attention to the might and the wight of the tree with the words:

> *Hail to thee, might of (tree name)!*
> *I bid thee give this branch!*
> *Into it send thy speed,*
> *to it bind the might of the bright runes____*
> *(names of the runes to be used on tine)!*

Now proceed to cut the portion of the branch desired, while humming or singing the names and/or *galdrar* of the proper runes during the whole procedure.

Once the future talisman has been removed, the vitki should give thanks to the wight of the tree for its gracious gift.

> *Wight of (tree name), take my thanks*
> *henceforth be thy might in this branch!*
> *Deeply bound to the bright (appropriate rune names)*
> *working my will with speed.*

The branch may then be trimmed and prepared for receiving the stave forms. The tine may be ritually loaded in that place at once, or it may be saved until later and loaded in the runer's usual *vé*.

This ritual process may be adapted easily for the selection and preparation of other materials to be fashioned into holy objects by the runic art.

 The following ritual description provides an example of the complete loading process from which the vitki will be able to devise similar operations for all types of runic talismans. The techniques outlined here are valuable in all kinds of runework.

This *taufr* is built on the runic formula LAUKAZ, which appears very often on ancient bracteate talismans. Literally, the word means "leek" *(allium porrum)*, which is a symbol of growth and well-being. This is also an alternate name for the L-rune. The Proto-Indo European root word from which the Germanic *laukaz* is derived is **leug-* (to bend, turn, wind), a powerful concept and one common to words having to do with magic. This formula promotes healthy growth in the field of things hidden and secret (the root word is also the ancestor of our word "lock").

The numerical analysis of this formula reveals one of its many power sources. Figure 21.13 shows the rune count as 6 (multiple: 2 x 3). The rune total is 52 (multiple: 4 x 13). The number 6 indicates its working in the sphere of will-controlled magical arts (a doubling of the dynamic action of 3). The formula works from a magical (4:ᚨ) intensification of the vertical force of the numen (13:ᛚ) throughout the year of 52 weeks. The ideographic analysis is equally revealing:

1. ᛚ life-law/growth

2. ᚨ transformational numinous force

3. ᚢ unconscious wisdom, health

4. ᚲ conscious knowledge, ability

5. ᚨ transformational numinous force

6. ᛉ protection/"higher" life

The complementary conceptual relationships between the first and last runes, and the third and fourth runes, loaded with the magical "spirit" of the second and fifth runes (which are adjacent to all the others) show the ideological potency and scope of this formula.

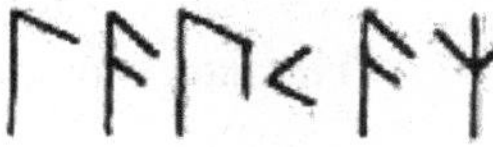

Figure 21.13. The laukaz formula.

For the performance of this rite, the vitki will need a suitable setting for the *vé* with an altar of some type, the *gandr*, the knife or carver, suitably prepared blood or red pigment (and equipment for preparing this onsite), the coloring tool, a black cloth (preferably of linen) large enough to enclose the tine, a leather thong or organic twine long enough to encircle the object nine times, and whatever ritual attire the vitki deems necessary. For optional phases of the rite the vitki also will need a brazier (and kindling) and a cup of water or mead. The talismanic object itself should be fashioned from a piece of willow wood (or its complement, alder wood) having two flat surfaces of suitable size to take the inscriptions. This object should be fully dressed and prepared in its final form and shape except for the magical staves and signs.

Go to the site of the *vé* in silence, preferably at the hour of dawn. Arrange the implements in an orderly fashion on the altar and let the ritual begin.

1. Opening. Facing north, perform the opening rite including the ritual kindling of the brazier if necessary and *Hamarssetning* or other suitable opening formula. This invokes the rune might and calls upon the gods and goddesses as witnesses, while banishing detrimental forces.

2. Preparation of dye (optional). If the blood or pigment has not already been prepared, the vitki may grind it on location. If this is done, sit facing the altar, and grind the pigments with the *galdr:*

> *laukaz laukaz laukaz*
> *[followed by the individual galdrar of all six runes in turn]*
> *Blood of Kvasir*[10]
> *be blessed:*
> *rune-might blooms in the blend!*

3. Name carving. This is to provide the magical link between the power of the formula and the person to benefit from it. Turn the tine so that what is to be on the reverse side is facing up. Using the knife or carver, etch the runes of the person's transliterated name (see Appendix IV on page 295) into the surface, using any formulaic devices that might help integrate the name (and person) with the power of the runic formula. Color the name with the pigments and recite a *galdr* such as:

> *Together the bright runes*
> *are bound and blended*
> *with the might of (name)!*

This does not require a level of intense loading as high as that for the *taufr* formula. (This step is optional if the tine is to be worn on the person at all times.)

4. Preliminary *galdr*. Standing before the altar, *gandr* in hand, invoke the forces of :ᚠᚨᚾᚲᚨᛃ : by thrice intoning the names of each in turn over the tine, and at the same time signing the stave shape over the object with each repetition of the name. This serves to make the material receptive to the streams of these runes.

5. Carving. Sit before the altar in a manner that has been taught to the vitki by personal experimentation. Carve each of the stave forms while singing the simple sound formula of the rune being etched. For continuants (sounds that can be produced as long as the breath lasts) the pure sound is best. In this inscription they are *l, a, u,* and *z.* The *k* sound must be coupled with a vowel and repeatedly intoned (ka-ka-ka . . .). During this process *feel, see,* and *concentrate on* the shining rune might as it willfully flows from the heavens, earth, and subterranean realms via your center, through your arm and carving tool, into the wood in the shape of the stave. The opening ritual engaged these three realms for this purpose. The material on *stadhagaldr* and rune streams is also helpful in mastering this practice. Visualize the shining "substance" in white, red, or electric blue as it is inlaid into the grooves cut by the rune carver or knife. When each has been carefully carved in this manner, the vitki may wish to cut a straight line across the bottom of the staves, connecting their shapes to bind them together in a single form and field of force (in the case of this inscription the K-rune hovers, unconnected).

6. Coloring. Take up the container of paint or blood, and using the knife point or coloring tool, inlay the staves (and connecting bar) with the vivifying substance. This should be done with care and concentration. Throughout this process repeatedly sing the complete runic formula, *lllllaaauuukaaazzz* . . . This imparts basic life force to the tine. At this point the vitki may wish to pause and concentrate on the power of the runes being loaded into the form—*feeling* their presence, as they vibrate with the substance of the wood, in the consciousness of the vitki. Once this is completed, the runer may lightly rub a small amount of linseed oil over the surface of the tine. This serves both an aesthetic and a magical purpose.

7. Enclosure. This is the "dwelling in darkness" before birth and emphasizes the cyclical nature of the runic mysteries. The tine gathers and intensifies its strength during this separation from light. Take up the tine and wrap it in the black cloth, then bind it nine times around with the thong. During this process intone the following *galdr*, or one of your own composition containing similar concepts.

> *Into the den*
> *of darkness deep*

wend thy way
—undoomed yet--
nights all nine
wile away thy spell.
Sleep, gain and grow
in weal and wealth.

Lay the tine down on the middle point of the *vé* and make nine turns (circumambulations) with the sun, while singing the complete word formula: *llllaaaauuukaaazzz. . .* Return the object to the altar.

8.   Birth of the living *taufr*. Unbind the thong and open the cloth while intoning the verse:

Hail thee day!
Hail day's sons
thou art born
—undoomed yet--
bearing my will
wend thy way
toward day's light
with life's law.

Now the vitki should bring his or her mouth close to the tine, and with maximal force of breath intone the holy formula *ffffffaaaaaa . . .*, while feeling and visualizing a great outrush of *hamingja* into the creature. This also infuses the tine with intensified *önd*. In order to awaken the now indwelling wight, take up the *gandr* and gently knock thrice upon the form.

9.   Naming (optional). If the vitki wishes to intensify the animate aspect of the tine, it should be ritually endowed with a name. This name should reflect the purpose of the talisman, and it is usually feminine in form. A good name for this tine might be Groedhing (a) (growth, or the growing one). Pass the tine three times over the fire-pot, intoning a verse indicative of the life-giving force, such as:

Now sparks of fire
with speed spew forth;
lend thy quickness and life.

Then lay the tine on the altar. Dip your fingers into the cup and carefully sprinkle the tine with the water or mead, with the formula:

> *I sprinkle thee with water*
> *and give thee the name (name).*[11]

10. *Formáli*. Now the tine wight must be permanently encoded with its special purpose—its "doom" or *ørlög*. It is newborn but must be provided with "past action," that it may more mightily fulfill its function. This is done by means of a *formáli*, or formal speech of declaration. Stand in the : ᛏ : *stadha* before the tine lying on the altar and proclaim a formula that outlines all the requirements, restrictions, and purposes of the talismanic being. For this tine, the following is appropriate:

> *Thou art wight of my will,*
> *and 'tis thy doom to do as here is deemed:*
> *Thou shalt shield my way, ·*
> *wherever I may wend,*
> *and with Ása*[12]*-might and main,*
> *shower upon me*
> *thy shining law of life*
> *with a love of lust and shaping wisdom,*
> *that I may grow and gain—whole and hale keep me—*
> *as thou art young the whole year through.*
> *In the name of Odin-Vili-Vé*
> *and by the might of Urdhr-Verdhandi-Skuld so*
> *shall it be.*

11. Holding. To bind the might of the rune load to the tine, trace three rings around the wight with the *gandr* while singing:

> *Rune-might hold*
> *the holy runes;*
> *whole may they*
> *work my will.*

Visualize a containing semipermeable sphere of shining force around the tine that allows the desired power to enter and be transformed, intensified, and reprojected but holds the original loading and prevents discharge by contrary forces.

12. Closing. After placing the tine in its intended abode, the vitki may sing a short closing verse:

> *Now the work*
> *has been wrought*
> *with the might*

*of mighty runes
so shall it be.*

Or perform the closing ritual outlined above.

Now the living *hlutr* is to be placed where it is to live its life and perform its function. If the tine is to be worn on the person, it should be next to the skin suspended by a cord, thong, or chain made of sympathetic material.

Talismanic Formulas

The more advanced runers will need no further clues to the successful practice of tine magic, but for those aspiring and talented vitkar who might need more clues, the following ritual and inscription formulas should be of some help. The first three introduce ancient and in some cases rather unique ritual methods that will be of special interest to all vitkar as yet unversed in the hoary and magical literatures of the sagas and Eddas. In the latter section, five talismanic formulas are provided for various magical operations. Some of these are drawn from ancient rune lore, while others are formulas created in the twentieth century. Here again it must be stressed that the most effective rituals will be those designed by talented vitkar based on their own personal relationship to the rune world.

The three special ritual formulas or patterns introduced in the following sections concern three of the most basic drives in magic: (1) love, (2) revenge (curse), and (3) wisdom. The main purpose behind the inclusion of these formulas is to *suggest* paths to greater runic power through a variety of techniques within the general realm of talismanic magic.

Love

Rituals to gain the love of another have been one of the principal subjects of runecraft since ancient times. However, as a previous example has shown, the successful attempts of runic love magic were performed with what we might today call "good intentions." This does not stem from any moralistic accretion in the runic system but rather from the complex nature of sexual energies and relationships. It simply seems that love magic *works* much more effectively, and the variable are kept to a minimum, when the simpler emotion of "true love" is involved.

Figure 22.14. A runic formula for successful love magic.

A runic formula for successful love magic is made up of the staves shown in figure 22.14. The rune count is 6 (multiple: 2 x 3). The runic total is 60 (multiple: 6 x 10). See section on numerical symbolism.

Figure 22.15.
Bind rune of a love-
magic formula.

A tine should be created, perhaps using the bind rune shown in figure 22.15. This bind rune uses the alternate form of the E-rune, ↑.

During the loading process each of the staves must first be carved and loaded separately, then bound together in a single field of force during the coloring phase. On the reverse side of the tine (or next to the *galdrastafir,* if space is a problem) the names of the persons to be brought together should be etched. This of course takes place in step three of the loading ritual. Great care should be taken to bring maximum imaginative and emotional force to bear in the identification of the *three* entities involved—the two lovers and the runic forces of attraction, binding, and love. The loaded tine could be worn by the runer to attract the lover to him/her, or it could be placed in a location near the desired one, such as under his/her bed, under or over a threshold through which the beloved one regularly passes, and so on.

An alternate form of this spell involves etching all the elements of the talismanic formula on a piece of jewelry that is then given to the future lover of the vitki. This of course may be done only in certain special circumstances. The vitki must know the desired one well enough for this to be proper and effective, and it must be known that he or she will wear or be near the object for at least some period of time. This type of rune spell also may necessitate the use of secret runic codes. The future lover might be suspicious of "mystic signs" carved on the jewel. If, for example, a medallion is the object in question, the reverse side might be encoded as shown in figure 22.16. (See section on runic codes in chapter 7 for further information.)

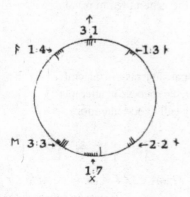

Figure 22.16. Encoded form of a love-
magic formula. The markings at the
top form 3:1, meaning third row,
first rune.

The names could be inscribed using the same code in the side spaces on the rim of the form. In such cases the vitki should perform the loading ritual in the usual fashion, except that when the coded representations are etched, the rune should be strongly visualized and loaded into the numerical symbol. The imagination and talent of the runer are the only limits to the ingenuity this type of talisman may reach. But one must be strong in the basic magical skills and be very familiar with the runic system to make this type of talisman work. One of the most powerful portions of a rite of this kind is the *formáli,* in which a poem of true love and burning lust should be composed and loaded with passionate sexual energy.

Revenge and Defense

This is called "revenge" and "defense" and not merely "curse" because it should be performed only when the vitki has been harmed in some way by the intended victim of the operation or when the victim would have harmed the vitki or his/her loved ones had the dreaded niding pole not been raised to crush the adversary.

The *nidhstöng* or cursing pole (literally "pole of insult or libel") is a long pole on which formulas of insult and curse are carved; then the pole is partially sunk into the ground facing toward the victim's home. The head of the pole is furnished with a horse's head or a representation of the victim in some obscene position. The sagas abound with stories about these niding poles. In order to perform a niding ritual, the vitki will need a stick or pole two feet or more in length, a sculpture of a horse's head or a carved representation of the victim. In ancient times the Ásatúar-skalds often composed niding poems and raised poles against the Christian clerics who were invading the Northland.

The pole acts as a magnet for the deadly forces of Hel, which are drawn up through the pole from the subterranean streams and projected through the horse's head, or other representation, to the victim. The inscription on the pole forms the stream and gives its mission.

The actual performance of a niding-pole ritual is somewhat simpler than other talismanic operations. Find a suitable location to set up the pole (it need not be especially *near* the victim, but it is best if it is within sight of his/her/their dwelling place). Go to the work-stead at midnight and perform a proper opening rite. Spend some time in meditative silence, working up your emotional power against the victim. In this state compose a prosaic or poetic runic formula of niding. An example would be:

> *Three thruses I threw to thee* ᚦᚦᚦ
> *(thurisaz thurisaz thurisaz) and three*
> *ices too* ᛁᛁᛁ *(isa isa isa).*[13]
> *All the wild wights and all the*
> *fierce fetches worried and warted thy*
> *sorry soul — Hel hast thee now*
> *(victim's name)!*

Transliterate the *formáli* into runes (see Appendix IV on page 295) and ritually carve them into the pole. It is *necessary* to color only the staves :ᚦᚦᚦ: and :ᛁᛁᛁ: Set the figurehead on the pole and sink it into the ground, repeating the niding formula. Imagine the forces of Hel—the Goddess of Death—sending forth all her might in streams of blackish (or whatever color the vitki might associate with destruction) "light" toward the doomed victim. Now the vitki should imagine the victim destroyed by the forces of Hel and returned to her dark embrace. The marked soul is smashed by the TH-runes and squashed and restricted by the I-runes. The ritual is concluded by breaking the sphere of working and projecting all residue through the figurehead to the target. Leave the pole standing until the desired result has been accomplished.

In days of yore the niding poles usually were raised against political or religious enemies rather than purely personal ones. The vitki must always ask his or her innermost self whether or not the niding pole is the right (:ᚱ:) solution to the situation.

A curse may also be cast in a talismanic form that is given secretly to the victim or placed somewhere in close proximity to him/her in much the same way the love spell works.

Draught of Wisdom

With the draught of wisdom the vitki loads a rune tine, scrapes the runes into a drink of mead, ale, or beer, and drinks it down—rune might and all! In the sixth stanza of the "Sigrdrífumál" we read a fine example of this practice in the context of an initiatory ritual. The *valkyrja*, Sigrdrífa, says to the hero, Sigurdhr:

> I bring thee beer
> thou warrior of battle[14]
> blended with might
> and mighty renown;
> it is full of songs
> and soothing staves
> good magic[15]
> and mighty runes.

The *valkyrja* then teaches the hero rune lore.

To absorb a dose of rune wisdom the vitki should duly load a rune tine according to ritual form—except do not color the runes with pigment, instead wet them with mead, ale, or beer. Also, do not carve them deeply but rather etch them lightly into the surface of the tine. After the loading is complete, take the rune knife and scrape off the runes into the cup of mead while singing a formula such as

> *I shave the shining runes,*
> *and their shaping-might,*
> *from the wood of wisdom;*
> *into the draught they drop!*

Then mix the contents well with the rune knife, while repeating a formula such as

Rune-might be mixed
with this mead of wisdom,
blended together in a bond of strength.

Now hold the cup or horn aloft with the words:

Ódhrœrir roar into the draught!

Drink the contents of the cup or horn to the dregs. During all this ritual action concentrate on the blending of forces, their vivification in the holy mead of inspiration, and your personal system and its absorption of those forces. This technique may be adopted for a variety of magical or mystical operations, and it is a potent tool in group work and initiatory rites.

ALU: Magical Power and Divine Inspiration

One of the oldest and still most effective runic formulas is ALU, which appears on stones and talismans from as early as 400 C.E. The word literally means "ale." *Alu* originally was a term for magical power and divine inspiration. The term was later transferred to one of the main symbols of this power and inspiration, the intoxicating brew. This power was often used to protect sacred sites from the uninitiated. The formula may be modulated in a variety of ways and may be inscribed a-1-u or u-1-a; the A-rune may fare either direction. The numerical formula also is quite potent. Figure 22.17 shows a rune count of 3 (multiple: 1 x 3 [prime]). The rune total is 27 (multiple: 3 x 9). The force of *alu* seems to be one of almost perpetual motions constantly turning in on itself and intensifying itself. A tine created with this formula will impart general protection, while providing wisdom, inspiration, magical power, and good health within a lawful life.

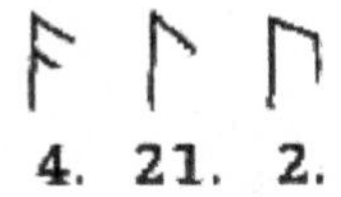

ᚠ ᚱ ᚢ

4. 21. 2.

Figure 22.17.
The alu formula.

The single stave that stood for the yew tree was always a powerful symbol of protection (among other things!). The formula shown in figure 22.18 is a "translation" and magical adaptation of an ancient formula of yew magic. The numerical analysis reveals a rune count of 13 (multiple: 1 x 13 [prime]) and a rune total of 160 (multiple: 10 x 16). The yew force is reemphasized and brought into material manifestation.

ᚠᚷᚨᛁᚾᛊᛏᚨᛚᛗᛁᛁ᛬ᛋ

a g a i n s t a l e͡v i l ᛬ᛋ

Figure 22.18. Adaptation of an ancient formula for yew magic.

Note also the long staves on the A-runes. This distinguishes them for a particular interpretation (3 x 4 = 12), which is intended to say "the blessings of *ansuz* (Odinic force) in all three realms of being throughout the year" (:ᛃ:). If possible, this tine should be fashioned from yew wood. This formula is a good example of how much depth can be plugged into even a modern English version of a runic formula.

The following talismanic *galdrastafir* suggest some of the countless ways in which these bind runes may be used.

For general success in all the affairs of day-to-day life, the runes :ᛏᛋᚦ: may be combined as in figure 22.19—a powerful formula for artists, magicians, and lovers in the realms of action, and also magically powerful as an invocation of force in all nine worlds. Many other levels of potency also may be infused into this *galdrastafir.*

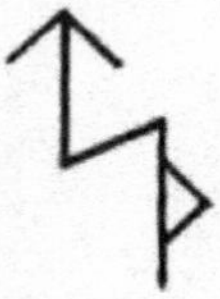

Figure 22.19. A bind rune for success.

For obtaining justice, whether it be from a court of law or from the "court of life," use a combination of the runes :ᛏᚱᛃ: in the form shown in figure 22.20.

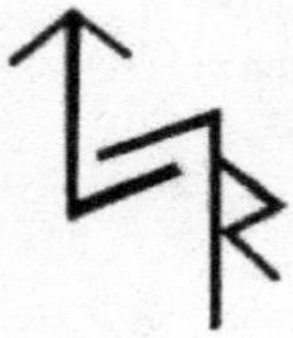

Figure 22.20. A bind rune for justice. The numerical analysis reveals a doubling of the force of the T-rune.

One of the more obvious cosmic and magical concerns of the runic system is that of prosperity and well-being. This is facilitated by a mighty *galdrastafir* made up of two F-runes, four TH-runes, and the NG- and O-runes in the symmetrical configuration shown in figure 22.21. A quick analysis by the runer reveals the manifold sources of power contained in this bind rune.

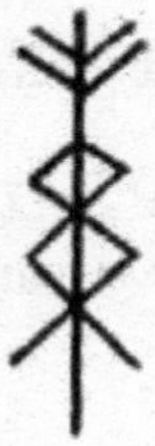

Figure 22.21 A bind rune for prosperity and well-being.

Again it might be well to point out that in the carving and loading of such bind runes *each* intended stave must be either carved individually or reinforced within the collective configuration, and definitely they must be initially charged individually. The order of carving for the talismanic bind rune portrayed above is shown in figure 22.22. After the fifth stage the four

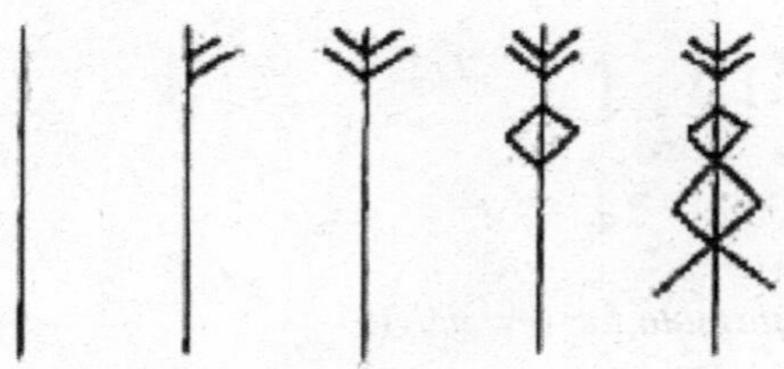

Figure 22.22. Pattern for carving a bind rune.

TH-runes concealed in the figure should be deepened with the proper number of repetitions of the *galdr*.

Death of Rune Tines

In most runic *formálar* not only should the definite purpose of the talismanic being be stated but also the length of time the wight is to live, that is, be vivified with magical force. A convenient formula for this is "until thy work is wrought." Since the wight of the tine is a living being, its death should be attended with proper ritual. This is to insure that the magical force stored up in the form will be redirected back to its source (the vitki), or as a form of sacrifice.

There are two principal methods for effecting this important ritual act. The first emphasizes the *animate* nature of the tine wight and is modeled on funeral rites. There are two types of funeral rituals of reabsorption: cremation and burial. The former is most effective in returning the power to the personal sphere of the vitki through the heavenly streams, while the latter is a powerful way to direct the power through the chthonic streams. The second method, which emphasizes the *dynamistic* nature of the rune might, prescribes a ritual removal of the runes from the tine, using the knife. The scrapings are then burned in the brazier. (This is also a method of banishing the rune magic of another runer.) In all cases this should be done with simple dignity, attended by proper *formálar* of the vitki's own composition. Proper respect should be paid to the wight, the rune might, and the shaper of the tine—the vitki. This "ecology of power" is rather like the ancient Norse lore of rebirth, which postulates that the innate might of the ancestors is continually reformed in the descendants.

Word and Bind Rune Magic

We have met with formulaic words such as *alu* and *laukaz* elsewhere in this book. These formulas are Proto-Germanic words used, written in runes, which convey the essence of the meaning of that word in a magical or operative way. The vitki of today is also free to discover other archaic and powerful words from our ancestral past which can express this same sort of power. The words in Proto-Germanic reflect the original form of many of the words we still use today. In this case, however, they are in their most original and therefore most powerful and essential forms. These are naturally and authentically expressed in the runes of the Elder Futhark and so, with a little work, can be rediscovered and used for magical effects today. This authenticity adds to the magical effectiveness of the work because the forms more perfectly resonate with the original forms from ancient original language.

The topic of bind runes has already been addressed in several sections of this book. I would be remiss, however, if I did not provide more operative information about how to use them in a practical way in their own right. Because we have come to understand, and I hope internalize, the meanings of the runes as unique individual *signs*, "memes" in the current jargon of the day, in order to effect precise and nuanced meanings in our workings we now have to learn how to weld the individual runes together into coherent magical messages which will enter into the causal horizon of events and bring what we desire into our lives.

In ancient times this was done in several ways: with formulaic words (e.g., *alu*) as well as poetic works in which the runic message is incorporated directly into the natural language of the vitki-skald. Poets could cause direct effects with their words *consciously understood in a runic way*. Another way in which this was done, and for which we have direct evidence in the Icelandic magical tradition, is the taking of magically potent words or names, for example names of the god Odin, and turning them into bind runes. The same can be done for words that one finds particularly useful for a specific magical working.

One can find lexicons of Proto-Germanic words in many sources online or in libraries. One that is recent and in English (most of them tend to be in German) is the book *A Handbook of Germanic Etymology* by Vladimir Orell (Brill, 2003). Another source is the etymological appendix in the *American Heritage Dictionary*. By way of example, here are ten Proto-Germanic words, transcribed into runes, which might be used in this manner.

rikjadomaz: ᚱᛁᚲᛃᚨᛞᛟᛗᚨᛉ dominion, wealth
lubo: ᛚᚢᛒᛟ love
frithuz: ᚠᚱᛁᚦᚢᛉ peace
mahtiz: ᛗᚨᚺᛏᛁᛉ power
meduz: ᛗᛖᛞᚢᛉ mead (inspiration)
segaz: ᛊᛖᚷᚨᛉ victory (success)
wurdhawîsaz: ᚹᚢᚱᛞᚺᚨᚹᛁᛊᚨᛉ wise in words
afalan: ᚨᚠᚨᛚᚨᚾ strength
hailaz: ᚺᚨᛁᛚᚨᛉ good luck omen
santhaz: ᛊᚨᚾᚦᚨᛉ truth, justice

The same procedural technique can be used to discover other words of power and simply write them in Elder Futhark runes to create your own magical formulaic words. The key to *accurate* usage is not to try to do grammatical things with the basic words beyond using their simple forms as entered in the lexicons. Technically speaking these are nominate singular forms of the words. If one were to try to make sentences out of them, it would require them to take on different grammatical endings, and so on. The old formulaic words tended to be in this form. The Proto-Germanic language was a highly inflected one with many grammatical changes and endings. Going beyond the basic forms can often lead to confused messages which do not resonate over time and space to effect magical changes.

To create bind runes out of them, one puts them together as a sort of monogram, keeping in mind that repeated runes do not need to be accounted for, and that normal arrangement and orientation of the runes can be altered for aesthetic reasons. To create a *taufr* made in this fashion generally follow the ritual outlined above, and design your formula both in runes and optionally as a bind rune. Write it in red ink on parchment paper, or carve it, and dye it red on a thin flat piece of wood. Once it is completed hide it, or put it in a pouch or small bag to carry on your person, but do not look at it again. Allow the power of the runes to work for you "behind the scenes" from an unconscious level.

Here is an example using the formula *meduz* for inspiration. The runes appear as: ᛗᛖᛞᚢᛦ which can be formed into a bind rune that could appear something like the bind rune shown in figure 22.23. Note, too, that the word can be written as a bind rune in the way shown in figure 22.24 as well:

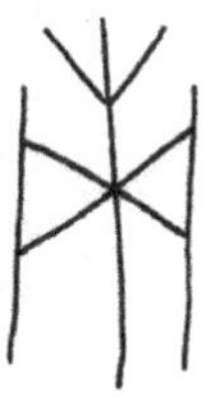

Figure 22.23.
Bind rune for
meduz.

The writing of the sounds in runes opens the sounds to a mode of solidification in the world of events and human experience. The binding of these together into a single form makes their entry into the unconscious and into the causal realm of the world much easier. Make this *taufr* and wear it on your person and let it work and you will be open to the higher realms of the mead of the gods.

Figure 22.24.
Alternate bind
rune for meduz.

Many readers will probably be reminded of the techniques pioneered by the English magician and artist Austin Osman Spare. Evidence that his particular techniques had already been explored by Icelandic magicians many hundreds of years before he lived is shown by the following example.

We find the name of a magical stave in an Icelandic book of magic called *thekkur*. This is a name of Odin with the meaning of "beloved." It would therefore be effective in workings of magic intended to gain a good spouse. The sign is constructed from a bind rune made up of the (younger) runes: ᚦᛁᛦᚴ combined to form the bind rune shown in figure 22.25:

Figure 22.25. Bind rune for
Odin as "beloved."

Figure 22.26. "Thekkur."

This is then stylized in the spirit of fifteenth-century aesthetics to form the final sign called "thekkur" and which appears in the manuscripts as shown in figure 22.26.

This process clearly mirrors that of Spare in many of its particulars. His "rediscovery" of this technique could, I suppose, belong to the category of "atavism" that he was so fond of writing about.

Stadhagaldr

This discipline is heavily indebted to the work of twentieth-century runic magicians of Germany who developed a system they call *Runenyoga*. In the writings of Siegfried Adolf Kummer, Friedrich Bernhard Marby, and Karl Spiesberger there is much concerning *Runen-Asana*, *Runen-mudra*, and so on. Marby called his system *Runengymnastik*. Indeed, they seem a bit too dependent on the kindred Indian discipline. Nevertheless, their practical experiments, invaluable clues, and ritual formulas are the basis for the following work.

Theory and Use

In comparison to what *yoga* became in later centuries, *stadhgaldhr* is an active system of magic that consists of the assumption of runic postures or gestures for operative magical effect, both within the vitki and in his or her environment. Both systems are most probably derived from the same common Indo-European root tradition of magical and symbolic gestures.

Gestures and postures form some part of almost every metaphysical or magical school. They can be seen from the simple folding of hands in prayer to the extremely complex system of *asanas* in the Indian *hatha yoga* school. *Stadhagaldr* is balanced in this respect. The number and intricacy of the postures are varied enough to be expressive of the wide variety of forces present, but none require extensive training or straining of the body. The great advantage of *stadhagaldr* in the runic system is that it allows the actual shape of the stave to be *embodied* in the physical apparatus of the vitki. This can result in the embodiment of the entire runic mystery in the flesh of the vitki, thereby turning the body itself into an awesome magical tool! The overall aims of *stadhagaldr* are:

1) Control of the body through posture *(stadha)*

2) Control of thought through song *(galdr)*

3) Control of breath

4) Control of emotion

5) Becoming aware of the rune realms of the self and of the world(s)

6) Control and direction of the will

Each of these aims should be striven for in turn, until all six have been mastered.

It must be stressed vigorously that the body should not be viewed as something evil or as an enemy to be defeated or whipped into submission but rather as a source for great and holy energy, obtainable through no other medium, if only directed in harmony with the *hugr*. The body is the vitki's personal portion of Midhgardhr, the balanced center of the multiverse containing the potential of all the worlds.

Stadhagaldr is used as a mode of psychological integration and personal transmutation, and it is also employed in *all* other types of magical operations. The vitki may, for example, literally build a numinous, living runic talisman within the body through *stadhagaldr*, so that he or she *becomes a walking rune tine!* The principles of runic combination and blending work with *stadhagaldr* in exactly the same way they function with the tine or sign magic. The *stödhur* are just an alternate mode of expression for the rune might.

Intake of World and Earth Streams

The practice of this magical form is closely connected to the mysteries of the rune streams. The runic postures act as antennas of force by which the vitki may attract, modulate, and reproject rune might for magical purposes.

As the vitki knows, there are three types of rune streams: the heavenly, the terrestrial, and the subterranean or chthonic. The heavenly *and* chthonic streams are world or cosmic streams and are not peculiar to this planet, as are the terrestrial streams that flow just under and above the surface of the earth. The individual self contains counterparts to each of these streams, which act as a matrix through which the rune streams act upon and affect us. These streams are perceived in many different ways: some are vibrations; others are waves, flows, rays, and even contractions. The induction of these forces is the mainstay of *stadhagaldr*.

Power is actually drawn in through the hands and/or feet and head, directly to the central axis of the vitki. There it is absorbed and modulated, then reemitted for specific purposes or assimilated to alter the self of the vitki. Each runic posture receives and/or transmits force in a particular pattern, and from various realms, according to its shape. This power is directly connected to the physical world through the medium of the human nervous system. When performing the various rune *stödhur*, the vitki should visualize and *feel* the flows of force being gathered or projected in a particular pattern through the body, which is in the form of the stave. This will feel as if electric current is passing through your body and will appear as rays of light coursing in angular patterns. Each individual vitki should let personal experience take precedence over anything read in this or any other book. Personal feelings and reactions, rather than "logical" thought processes, are more effective guidelines in the realm of practical magic. This is especially true in *stadhagaldr*.

Table 22.4 on page 278 shows four examples of rune shapes, their patterns of power, and the realms of being they engage, and may give some practical hints for more fruitful development. The arrows indicate the directions in which the force streams.

	Subterranean streams are lifted into the vitki and circulate back to their source.
	Heavenly and subterranean forces flow into the vitki. There they are synthesized and sent out into the terrestrial realm as manifest action.
	A crosscurrent of directed terrestrial force flows through the vertical axis of world streams, resulting in a concentrated intensification of power at the point of confluence.
	Heavenly and subterranean streams are received and assimilated, and all are redirected toward the heavenly realm.

Table 22.4. Some patterns of force streams.

These are based on personal practice and observation and should in no way be taken as dogma. Notice that the diagonals sometimes feel as if they were terrestrial links and sometimes as if they were links to the heavenly or subterranean realms. This is true even with the same rune on different occasions, for the rune world is hardly a static one! A good rune vitki will attempt to experience all of these forces empirically, and with increased skill he or she will then begin to divide and classify the raw forces into their finer runic characteristics. With proper and persistent practice empirical results will arise.

The ancient vitkar knew well the power of the earth streams, for they formed one of their mightiest mysteries. The best work-stead for *stadhagaldr* is a known "power point" where the earth and world streams (the horizontal and vertical) flow together. These are known by all cultures all over the world. The vitki should seek these out for important rites of *stadhagaldr*.

The human being is constantly being bombarded by power flowing from above, below, and all corners of the earth; the task is to control this influx and direct it. We receive the power of brightness from the wide expanse of space, and we induct the constricting force of darkness churning in the center of the earth. It is most important that we realize *both* extremes and consciously seek them out, develop them to their limits, and center them in our consciousness.

Before attempting any practical magical work in this system, the *stödhur* of all the runes to be used in the operation should be mastered through an intense program of meditational exercise with the runic postures in question. The subject of this kind of force in circulation in and around the earth is handled in some more detail in *Rune Might* (Inner Traditions, 2018).

Opening Formula in Stadhagaldr

A work of *stadhagaldr* may begin with the general opening rite given in the section on talismanic magic, or the vitki may use a special *stadhasetning* (posture rite) for engaging the runic forces. This is a powerful rite with which to practice *stadhagaldr,* and therefore these three *stödhur* should perhaps be mastered first. Here, as in the following rites, a stave presented beside a *galdr/formáli* indicates that the vitki should assume the *stadha* of the rune and sing its formulaic *galdr* and/or the *formáli* that loads the ritual actions with more refined intentions (see table 22.5).

ᛁ
Self-knowing, I am a staff
for beams and waves of rune might.

ᚾ
Self-knowing, I shape the might
from the deepest depths
out of the realms of the earth
out of the womb of Hel (or the earth mother).

ᛉ
Self-knowing, I shape the might
from the highest heights
out of the wide world
out of Heimdallr's realm.

Table 22.5. Stödhur for engaging runic forces.

Simple Rites

The performance of any single rune *stadha* may of course be considered a rite. This is especially true if the vitki composes a *formáli* to be recited after the *galdr* is sung. This *formáli* will give specific shape and purpose to the runic force engendered by the operation. The possibilities for potent works of simple beauty are almost limitless. The following rites of combined runic forces are essentially made up of several of these simpler rites blended together to form a more complex magical effect. They describe flows or processes of power aimed toward a specific goal, such as Increase in Magical Power (page 280), Success and Victory (page 281), Increase in Creative Force (page 282), and a Rite of Need on page 283. The advantage of *stadha*-ritual work is that it provides keys to various realms of consciousness, and it inspires the vitki to the greatest power, if properly performed on all levels of being.

Our aim in the rites of *stadhagaldr* is the blending of several runic forces into one single concentrated and directed stream of power with a definite goal or aim. This is to be achieved by combining the forms and sounds of various runes together into a single force field of action. The symbol of the operation may be a series of runes or a bind rune drawn on the floor or ground or on a board lying on the altar or hung at eye level on the wall in front of the vitki. This form should be the focal point of concentration throughout the entire ritual.

These ritual formulas also may be adapted as talismanic or sign magical rites. They are also powerful formulas for the creation of meditative bind-rune sendings.

Increase in Magical Power

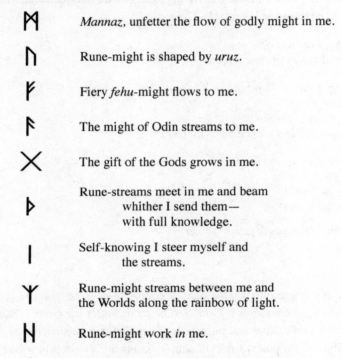

ᛗ   *Mannaz*, unfetter the flow of godly might in me.

ᚢ   Rune-might is shaped by *uruz*.

ᚠ   Fiery *fehu*-might flows to me.

ᚨ   The might of Odin streams to me.

ᚷ   The gift of the Gods grows in me.

ᚦ   Rune-streams meet in me and beam
         whither I send them—
         with full knowledge.

ᛁ   Self-knowing I steer myself and
         the streams.

ᛉ   Rune-might streams between me and
         the Worlds along the rainbow of light.

ᚺ   Rune-might work *in* me.

ᛋ   Rune-might work *through* me.

Success and Victory

ᛏ   Norn-rune fend off the fetters
          of wyrd and turn the need.

ᚠ   Grow and thrive through *fehu*.

ᛋ   Speed overcomes in me!
          Steering might of *sowilo* (the sun)
          lead me from success to success.

ᛏ   *Tyr — Tyr*
          Fruit of the fight — victory!

ᚦ   My deeds make me grow,
          forever in might and main.

ᛗ   *Mannaz*! Word of fullness
          be the fulfiller of my wishes.

ᛚ   Make all the good wax great.

ᛃ   Hail and fullness
          work through the year!

ᚹ   Well-being waxes
          happiness grows in itself.

ᚦ   Our deeds make us grow,
          forever in might and main.

ᛏ   Norn-rune fend off the fetters
          and turn the need!

ᛉ   Warding might of the World, stream to me.
          Warding might of the World, work in me.
          Warding might of the World, work through me.

Increase in Creative Force

ᚠ   Fiery *fehu*-might flows to me.

ᚢ   *Uruz* shapes the rune-might.

ᚦ   Rune-streams meet in me and beam
whither I send them.

ᚨ   The might of my word waxes.

ᚱ   On the right road I wander.

ᚲ   Skill comes to me
through the might of *kenaz*
knowledge and World-wisdom
wax in me through *kenaz*.

ᛋ   The speed of *sowilo* (the sun)
steers me.

ᛏ   Tyr—Tyr
Will of speedy shaping
successfully stream through me.

ᛃ   Hail and fullness—
gifts of the good year!

Rite of Need

ᚾ   Norn-rune fend off the fetters of
       wyrd, turn the need.
       Thou art my need—
       through thee I overcome need.

ᚢ   Wight of the World—wood
       give good speed and help!
       I take up the runes,
       I take up my need!

ᚾ   Need-fire flame in me!

ᛗ   *Mannaz*! Word of fullness
       be the fulfiller of my needs
       and unfetter the flow of rune-
       might.

ᛉ   Rune-might streams between me
       and the worlds
       along the rainbow of light.

ᚾ   Need-fire flame in me!

ᛋ   Steering might of the sun
       lead me forward.

ᚾ   Need-fire flame in me!

(Repeat this until the fire is enkindled in your breast.)

The Ritual Talisman

Whether or not the vitki is performing a talismanic loading ritual, a symbol describing the particular runic operation may be formed to serve as a lasting outward symbol of the holy inner process that takes place in the rite. This is usually a bind rune or rune row, which is incised into or painted on a board or paper. This should be displayed in some place where the vitki will see it regularly and thus constantly reaffirm his or her link to the magical force. It also may be portrayed on a small object the vitki carries.

This technique should be used only in cases where the vitki desires to effect an internal change in his or her own consciousness. For operations that intend to affect the outside environment the vitki should expend all possible energy during the ritual, then make a complete break with the force, thus releasing it to do its work. In the latter case a constant reminder would only hinder the successful fulfillment of the vitki's will.

Sign Magic

The practice of sign magic involves the blending of the techniques of signing and sending with those of *galdr* (incantation). This form of magic is the most difficult because it requires the greatest amount of concentration and visualization to be maximally effective. Once the techniques have been mastered, however, it promises to be the most direct and effective form of *galdr* available to the vitki. The techniques of signing and sending already have been mentioned, and the vitki is by now quite familiar with several aspects of incantation. Here we will deepen this knowledge and direct it in more specific technical channels toward formulating the basis of *signingagaldr* (the magic of signs). The main difference between the signing found in this section and that used in the loading of tines is that here the signs are directed toward and melded with already living systems, be they wights or dynamistic fields of runic force.

The idea behind sign magic is that the vitki actually may cut runes into the living fabric of the multiverse, melding that rune might with a symbolic "target" that has been formulated by the *hugr* of the vitki through concentrated visualization, thus bringing about a change in that target. This is only one of many ways to use the techniques of sign magic. This process may be carried out in the *hugauga* (totally by meditative visualization) or by external ritual work. In both cases the techniques are the same; however, the vitki may wish to begin with the visualization method and work into more difficult ceremonial performance.

The three steps necessary to *signingagaldr* are (1) the formulation of and/or concentration on a target, (2) the formulation and projection of the willed rune might, and (3) the melding of the previous two into a single field of force such that the second influences the first in the desired way.

To formulate a target for the projected magical force, the vitki will need to set off a "target area." This is a framework within which the visualized target is held, so that the rune might may be directed into it. This may be either rectangular or triangular in shape. If a triangle is used, the form ▷ is preferred. In full ritual work a frame may be constructed from wood and suitably painted or otherwise decorated. The frame may contain a symbol form of the target (a picture, for example), but most often the vitki will magically build the form of the target image within the framework using his or her powers of concentration and visualization.

Once the target is firmly established and bound within the frame, the vitki begins to formulate the willed rune might in the center of his or her body. This power is then projected into the target area and signed in the manner described in the section on sending and signing. The *galdr* and/or *formáli* that is sung or spoken should give intention and refined form to the runic power. As the runer signs the rune, it should be as if the force of the sign was actually being infused into the living fabric of the target. The vitki will immediately *see* the change in the target once the melding of forces is complete.

Although the practice of sending and signing is fairly well known by now, the use of *galdr* perhaps needs more development in the context of sign magic. Throughout this book we have seen both the sound-formulaic and poetic forms of *galdrar*. In sign magic both forms may be used, but the vitki should always aim for the more complex poetic form because of the degree of flexibility and exactness that it affords. These "magic songs" are found throughout old Germanic literatures, and indeed for the ancient Teutons (as well as all other Indo-European peoples) the art of poetry grew out of the power of magic.

The *galdr* serves to aid in the invocation/evocation of the rune might and in its formation within the vitki. But it also aids in projection and linkage of that force to the target through its principal quality—vibration.

The following techniques should be followed throughout the practice of sending and signing, for all the elements mentioned in this section must be understood as the multifold expression of a single force—the will of the runer. The breath should be the focal point of concentration throughout the *galdr*. During inhalations the vitki concentrates on the flow of rune might into the personal center.

There it is momentarily held for exact formulation, and then, on exhalation, the portion of the *galdr* that is to be projected is intensely concentrated on. Most *galdrar* of all types require several breaths to perform completely. One line of the incantation may be performed with each breath. In the case of poetic *galdrar* the vitki should "runically" concentrate on each letter-sound of every word in the incantation—*feeling* their force. Do not necessarily *think* about their meaning; if it is well composed, the *galdr* will seem to do its own work. What is important here is the flow of force, its formulation, and its projection in a smooth concentrated pattern that becomes almost unconscious to the accomplished vitki. A unity is built between the rune might, the vitki, and the target in such a way that the special nature of this magical form soon becomes apparent.

The main magical unity on which the runer must consciously concentrate is that of the *sound* (of the incantation) and the *form* (of the stave and the beam of light through which it is projected), all within the common "runic vibration." Meditational exercises will greatly aid in this process. Incantations may be sung either out loud or within the *hugr*. Also, when they are spoken out loud, the *galdrar* may be sonorously and boomingly sung or softly whispered. The former seems more effective when the vitki is performing a rite in solitude or in the company of fellow vitkar, while the latter is often more powerful when non-vitkar are present.

Because this form of galdr comes so close to an unconscious, meditational approach, it is most necessary to *memorize* all aspects of the rite before it is performed. This is generally a good suggestion for all rites, but it is especially necessary here. A successful try at *signingagaldr* is dependent on a curious and magnificent blend of all segments of the runer's psychosomatic complex. The unexpected mystical "fringe benefits" of these operations are often astounding.

Perhaps a further note should be added concerning poetic *galdrar*. These certainly may be composed in English. (See Appendix III for technical suggestions in this matter.) Much thought should go into their composition as to both form and content. The dedicated vitki will undertake the study of Old Norse and/or other old Germanic dialects (e.g., Old English, Gothic, and Old High German), for these languages vibrate with magico-mythic qualities that are hard to conjure up in modern English. But what is most important is that the vitki find a magically potent language and poetic form that speaks with the voice of his or her unconscious realms.

CONCLUSION

When I first encountered the runes in a magical way back in 1974, little to nothing was known of them in esoteric circles in the English-speaking world. Knowledge of the runes has come a long way since then. Much more is known about them, yet they remain as mysterious as ever. This is the nature and character of the runes themselves. They were that way at the dawn of their discovery and first use around two thousand years ago, and they will remain that way forever. That is the proof of their genuine substance.

This book represents a comprehensive introduction to the practical use of runes. Much discussion was dedicated to the history and use of the runes in historical times because the development of deep context for magical lore is essential. Such context is the soil in which the seeds of wisdom can grow and eventually bear fruit. The more context one develops and acquires, the deeper one's work will be. A good resource for continuing your studies in operative runology is my book *Alu: An Advanced Guide to Operant Runology* and perhaps even *The Nine Doors of Midgard*, which provides a detailed curriculum for only the most serious kind of student. Formal entry into the Rune-Gild may be in your future, and if so you may contact the organization at *www.rune-gild.org*. As one advances in runic studies and delves deeper into their meanings, one will discover that they will begin to teach directly, through the agency of the god of the Runes, Odin.

To this conclusion is appended a poem I wrote when I finished the first manuscript for *Futhark*. It was then intended to act as a sort of rune-spell to cast the runes as they really are into the world. Those familiar with the history of the runic revival will know that this, like most magical spells cast by a vitki, worked powerfully, but not always as expected or hoped for. In a way this and all my other books on runes have been an adjustment on that casting.

Galdr for the Runic Revival

Wide stands the door
to the rune-worlds' winds
loud ring their songs' sounds
through the northern night:
the wise wend their way
toward might and main,
again to learn that holy lore.

The sun-born sisters
and brothers bright
call in their night of need:
staves strong and holy
in rune-might standing
enkindle the craft
and cunning ways
to win weal and wisdom.

On a shining plain
runers ply their skill
in a Gard of the Gods
in the northern light—
the runes bloom forth,
roaring their songs,
through a house all whole,
again as aye anon.

Edred Thorsson
Midsummer, 1979

APPENDIX I: RUNIC TABLES

Table 1. The Elder Futhark

No	Shape	Variant Shapes	Phonetic Value(s)	Name	Translation of the Name	Esoteric Interpretation
1	Ꮭ	ᚹ	f	*fehu*	cattle, livestock money (gold)	dynamic power
2	ᚃ	ᚅ ᚃ ᚆ	u	*uruz*	aurochs	primal, formative and fertilizing essence
3	ᚦ	ᚦ ᚦ	th	*thurisaz*	thurs (the strong one)	the breaker of resistance (Thor)
4	ᚨ	ᚨ ᚥ	a	*ansuz*	the Ase, sovereign ancestral god	sovereign ancestral force (Odin)
5	ᚱ	ᚱ ᚱ ᚱ	r	*raidho*	wagon, chariot	vehicle of path of cosmic power
6	ᚲ	ᚳ ᚣ ᚳᚣ	k	*kenaz/ kaunaz*	torch/sore	controlled energy
7	ᚷ		g	*gebo*	gift	exchanged force
8	ᚹ	ᚹ	w	*wunjo*	joy, pleasure	harmony of like forces
9	ᚺ	ᚾ ᚻ	h	*hagalaz*	hail (stone)	seed form and primal union
10	ᚾ	ᚾ ᚿ	n	*naudhiz*	need	need-fire (resistance/ deliverance)
11	ᛁ		i	*isa*	ice	contraction (matter/ antimatter)
12	ᛃ	ᛄ ᛇ ᛃ ✱ ᚱ	j	*jera*	year (good harvest)	orbit (life cycle)
13	ᛇ	ᛢ	i/ei	*i(h)waz*	yew	axis (tree of life/death)
14	ᛈ	ᛗ ᚹ	p	*perthro*	lot cup	evolutionary force
15	ᛦ	ᛪ ✱ ᛉ	-z ~ -R	*elhaz/algiz*	elk/protection	protective and tutelary numen
16	ᛋ	ᛌ ᛋ ᛋ	s	*sowilo*	sun	sun-wheel (crystallized light)
17	ᛏ	ᛏ	t	*tiwaz*	Tyr, the sky god	sovereign order (Tyr)
18	ᛒ	ᛒ ᛒ	b	*berkano*	birch(-goddess)	birch numen (retainer/ releaser)
19	ᛖ	ᚻ	e	*ehwaz/ ehwo*	horse/two horses	twin equine gods (trust)
20	ᛗ		m	*mannaz*	man (human being)	human order from divine ancestry
21	ᛚ	ᛚ	l	*laguz/ laukaz*	water/leek	life energy and organic growth
22	◇	ᚩ ▫ ᛜ	-ng	*ingwaz*	Ing, the earth god	gestation-container (Yngvi)
23	ᛞ	ᛞ	d/dh	*dagaz*	day	twilight/dawn (paradox)
24	ᛟ		o	*othala*	ancestral property	self-contained hereditary power

Table 2. The Anglo-Frisian Futhorc

No.	Shape	Thames Sax	Major Variants	Frisian	Phonetic Values	Old English Name	Translation of Name
1	⻏	⻏	⻏	⻏ ⻏	f	*feoh*	cattle, wealth
2	⋂	⋂	⋀	⋂	u	*ūr*	wild ox
3	⻏	⻏	⻏	⻏	th/dg	*thorn*	thorn
4	⻏	⻏	⻏	⻏	o	*ōs*	a god (or mouth)
5	R	R	R	R ⋔	r	*rād*	(a) ride
6	⻏	⻏	⻏	⻏	c/ch	*cēn*	torch
7	X	X	X	X	g[j/zh]	*gyfu*	gift
8	⻏	⻏	⻏	⻏	w	*wynn*	joy
9	⻏	⻏	⻏⽕⻏	⻏	h	*haegl*	hail
10	⻏	⻏	⻏ ⻏	⻏	n	*nȳd*	need, distress
11	⼁	⼁		⼁ ⻏	i	*īs*	ice
12	⻏	⻏	⻏ ⻏	⻏	y	*gēr*	year
13	⻏	⻏	Z	⼁	eo	*ēoh*	yew
14	⻏	⻏	⻏	⻏	p	*peordh*	dice box
15	⼈	⼈	⼈	⼈	x	*eolhx*	elks/sedge reed
16	⻏	⻏	⻏⻏⻏	⻏	s	*sigel*	sun
17	↑	↑		↑	t	*tīr*	Tiw/sign or glory
18	⻏	⻏	B	⻏	b	*beorc*	birch/poplar
19	M	M		M⻏	e	*eh*	horse
20	⻏	⻏	⻏	⻏⻏	m	*monn*	man (human being)
21	⻏	⻏		⻏⻏	l	*lagu*	sea
22	⻏	⻏	⻏	⻏	ng	*ing*	the god Ing
23	⻏	⻏	⻏	⻏	d	*dæg*	day
24	⻏	⻏	⻏	⻏	e [ay] œ	*ēthel*	ancestral property
25	⻏	⻏			a	*āc*	oak
26	⻏	⻏			ae	*æsc*	ash
27	⻏	⻏	⻏⋀	⻏⻏	y	*ȳr*	gold decoration/bow
28	⻏	⻏	⻏	⻏	ea	*ēar*	earth-grave
29	⻏		⻏	⋀	eo/io	*ior*	serpent
30	⻏		⻏	⻏	q	*cweordh*	fire-twirl
31	⻏		⻏⻏⻏		k	*calc*	chalk/chalice
32	⻏				st	*stān*	stone
33	⻏				g	*gār*	spear

Table 3. The Younger Futhark

No	Shape	Gørlev	Major Variants	Phonetic Value	Old English Nam	Translation of Name	Esoteric Interpretation of Name
1	ᚠ	ᚠ	ᛁ	f	*fé*	cattle, money, gold	dynamic power
2	ᚢ	ᚢ		u/o/ö/v	*úr(r)*	drizzling rain/slag/aurochs	fertilizing essence
3	ᚦ	ᚦ	ᛈ	th/dh	*thurs*	thurs ("giant")	breaker of resistance
4	ᚨ	ᚨ	ᚼ ᛄ	ą	*áss*	(the) god (= Odin)	power of the word, sovereign force
5	ᚱ	R	ᚱ ᚱ	r	*reidh*	a ride, riding/vehicle/thunderclap	spiritual path or journey
6	ᚴ	ᚴ	ᚤ ↓ ⊥	k/g/ng	*kaun*	a sore	internal, magical fire or projection
7	ᚼ	ᚼ	ᛏ ᛏ	h	*hagall*	hail (a special rune name)	ice seed form
8	ᚾ	ᚾ	ᚽ	n	*naudh(r)*	need, bondage, fetters	need-fire, slavery/freedom
9	ᛁ	ᛁ		i/e	*íss*	ice	contraction *prima materia*
10	ᛆ	ᛏ	ᚼ ᛪ	a	*ár*	(good) year, harvest	blooming forth into manifestation
11	ᛋ	ᛋ	ᚺ ᛄ	s	*sól*	sun	sun-wheel/crystallized light
12	ᛏ	ᛏ	ᛀ	t/d/nd	*Týr*	the god Tyr	sovereign heavenly order
13	ᛒ	B	ᛃ ᛒ	b/p/mb	*bjarkan*	birch(-goddess) (a special rune name)	gestation/birth, instrument of the birch numen
14	ᛘ	ᛘ	ᛦ ᛉ ᛁ ᛄ	m	*madhr*	man, human	human order of divine ancestry, power to connect realms
15	ᛚ	ᛚ		l	*lögr*	sea, waterfall (liquid)	life energy and organic growth
16	ᛣ	ᛣ	ᛁ	-R	*ýr*	yew, bow of yew wood	telluric power

Table 4. The Armanen Futhork

No.	Shape	Name	Meaning
1	ᚠ	*fa*	Primal fire, change, reshaping, banishing of distress, sending generative principle, primal spirit
2	ᚢ	*ur*	Eternity, consistency, physicians' rune, luck, telluric magnetism, primal soul
3	ᚦ	*thorn*	Action, will to action, evolutionary power, goal setting, rune of Od-magnetic transference
4	ᚨ	*os*	Breath, spiritual well-being, word, radiating od-magnetic power
5	ᚱ	*rit*	Primal law, rightness, advice, rescue, rhythm
6	ᚲ	*ka*	Generation, power, art, ability, propagation
7	✳	*hagal*	All-enclosure, spiritual leadership, protectiveness, harmony
8	ᚾ	*not*	The unavoidable, "karma." compulsion of fate
9	ᛁ	*is*	Ego, will, activity, personal power banishing, consciousness of spiritual power, control of self and others
10	ᛅ	*ar*	Sun, wisdom, beauty, virtue, fame, well-being, protection from specters, leadership
11	ᛋ	*sig*	Solar power, victory, success, knowledge, realization, power to actualize
12	ᛏ	*tyr*	Power, success, wisdom, generation, awakening, rebirth in the spirit
13	ᛒ	*bar*	Becoming, birth, concealment, song
14	ᛚ	*laf*	Primal law, life, experience of life, love, primal water, water and ocean rune
15	ᛉ	*man*	Man-rune, increase, fullness, health, magic, spirit, god-man, the masculine principle in the cosmos, day-consciousness
16	ᛦ	*yr*	Woman-rune, instinct, greed, passion, matter, delusion, confusion, death, destruction, the negative feminine principle in the cosmos, night consciousness
17	ᛇ	*eh*	Marriage, lasting love, law, justice, hope, duration, rune of troth and of the dual (twin) souls
18	ᚷ	*gibor*	God-rune, god-all, cosmic consciousness, wedding together of powers, the generative and receptive, sacred marriage, give and the gift, fulfillment

THE BIG BOOK OF RUNES AND RUNE MAGIC

APPENDIX II: PRONUNCIATION OF OLD NORSE

The phonetic values provided below are those of reconstructed Old Norse (as it would have been spoken in the Viking Age).

The consonants *b*, *d*, *f*, *l*, *m*, *t*, and *v* are just as in modern English.

a	as in "artistic"	au	as *ou* in "house"
á	as in "father"	ei	as *ay* in "May," *or* as *i* in "mine"
e	as in "men"	ey	pronounced same as *ei*
é	as in *ay* in "bay"	g	always hard as in "go"
i	as in "it"	ng	as in "long"
í	as *ee* in "feet"	h	same as English, except before consonants, then as *wh* in "where"
o	as in "omit"		
ó	as in "ore"	j	always as *y* in "year"
ö	as in "not"	p	as in English, except before *t*, then this *pt* cluster is pronounced *ft*
ø	pronounced same as ö'		
u	as in "put"	r	trilled r
ú	as in "rule"	s	always voiceless as in "sing"
æ	as *ai* in "hair"	th	voiceless *th* as in "thin"
œ	as *u* in "slur"	dh	voiced *th* as in "the"
y	as *u* in German *Hütte* (*i* with rounded lips)	rl	pronounced *dl*
		rn	pronounced *dn*
ý	as *u* in German *Tür* (*ee* with rounded lips)	nn	pronounced *dn* after long vowels and diphthongs

APPENDIX III: RUNIC CORRESPONDENCES

The following table is intended to serve as a guide to further rune understanding as well as stimulation toward further runic investigation by all vitkar. These correspondences are not absolute or dogmatic—as always, the intuition of the vitki is the most reliable guide. Many of these correspondences will be helpful in the construction of rituals, talismans, and so on. Used in conjunction with Appendix I: Runic Tables, this table provides a full range of correspondences, which are partially traditional and partially based on previous research.

No	Shape	Tree	Herb	God/Goddess/Wight	Color	Astrology
1	ᚠ	elder	nettle	Aesir	light red	♈
2	ᚢ	birch	spagnum moss	Vanir	dark green	♉
3	ᚦ	oak	houseleek	Thor	bright red	♂
4	ᚨ	ash	fly agric	Odin	dark blue	☿
5	ᚱ	oak	mugwort	Forseti	bright red	♐
6	ᚲ	pine	cowslip	Freyja, dwarves	light red	♀
7	ᚷ	ash & elm	heartsease	Odin/Freyja	deep blue	♓
8	ᚹ	ash	flax	Freyr, elves	yellow	♌
9	ᚺ	yew/ash	lily of the valley	Ymir	light blue	♒
10	ᚾ	beech	bistort	Nornir, etins	black	♑
11	ᛁ	alder	henbane	rime-thurses	black	☽
12	ᛃ	oak	rosemary	Freyja	light blue	⊕
13	ᛇ	yew	mandrake	Odin/Ullr	dark blue	♏
14	ᛈ	beech	aconite	Nornir	black	♄
15	ᛉ	yew	angelica	valkyrjur	gold	♋
16	ᛊ	juniper	mistletoe	Sól	white/silver	☉
17	ᛏ	oak	sage	Tyr/Máni	bright red	♎
18	ᛒ	birch	lady's mantle	Frigg, Nethus, Hel	dark green	♍
19	ᛖ	oak/ash	ragwort	Freyja/Freyr; Alcis	white	♊
20	ᛗ	holly	madder	Heimdallr/ Odin	deep red	♃
21	ᛚ	willow	leek	Njördhr, Baldr	deep green	☽
22	ᛜ	apple	self-heal	Ing, Freyr	yellow	●
23	ᛞ	spruce	clary	Odin/Ostara	light blue	◑◐
24	ᛟ	hawthorn	goldthread	Odin/ Thor	deep yellow	○

APPENDIX IV: ON THE TRANSLITERATION
OF MODERN ENGLISH INTO RUNES

This topic poses some problems, especially when it comes to putting proper names into runic form. The correspondences reviewed below will provide ample guidelines, but the vitki should let intuition and magical criteria be the final arbiter. In some cases, it may be found best to go with the actual English sound rather than the literal correspondence.

In writing poetry of your own composition in runes, it will be found convenient if you stick to Anglo-Saxon roots. Questions of "correctness" in transliteration are fewer when Germanic words are used.

A	ᚠ	O	ᛟ
B	ᛒ	P	ᛈ
C	ᚲ	Q	ᚲ
D	ᛗ	R	ᚱ (ᛉ in final position)
E	ᛗ	S	ᛋ
F	ᚠ	T	ᛏ
G	ᚷ	U	ᚢ
H	ᚻ	V	ᚢ or ᚹ
I	ᛁ or ᛇ	W	ᚹ
J	ᛁ or ᛃ	X	ᚲᛋ (k + s)
K	ᚲ	Y	ᛃ
L	ᛚ	Z	ᛋ or ᛉ
M	ᛗ	TH	ᚦ / ᛗ (voiceless/voiced)
N	ᚾ	NG	◇

GLOSSARY

Aesir: sg., Áss; genitive pl., Ása (used as a prefix to denote that the god or goddess is "of the Aesir"). ON. Race of gods corresponding to the functions of magic, law, and war.

aett: pl., aettir. ON. Family or genus, used both as a name for the threefold divisions of the futhark and the eight divisions of the heavens. Also means a group or division of *eight*.

airt: Scots dialect word. See *aett*.

Asgardhr: ON. The realm of the Aesir at the apex of the cosmic order.

Atheling: From Old English, a term for noble individuals.

Audhumla: ON. The cosmic bovine who feeds the original creations of Ymir on her milk.

bind rune: Two or more runestaves superimposed on one another, sometimes used to form *galdrastafir*.

Edda: ON. Word of uncertain origin, used as the title of ancient manuscripts dealing with mythology. The *Elder* or *Poetic Edda* is a collection of poems composed between 800 and 1270 C.E.; the *Younger* or *Prose Edda* was written by Snorri Sturluson in 1222 C.E, as a codification of the mythology of Ásatrú for the skalds.

erilaz: pl., *eriloz*. See *Erulian*.

Erulian: Member of the ancient gild of runesmasters who formed an intertribal network of initiates in the Germanic mysteries.

etin: An Anglicized version of the ON term *jötunn*. A giant, or proto-god of the natural universe, known for its strength.

etin-wife: A female etin taken in magical marriage.

fetch: See *fylgja*.

fetch-wife: The fetch in female form. See also *valkyrja*.

formáli: pl., *formálar*. ON. Formulaic speeches used to load action with magical intent.

fylgja: pl., *fylgjur*. ON. A numinous being attached to every individual, which is the repository of all past action and which accordingly affects the person's life; the personal divinity. Visualized as a contrasexual entity, an animal, or an abstract shape.

Futhark: The conventional name for the "alphabet" of the Older and Younger runes based on the sound values of the first six runes of those systems.

Futhorc: The conventional name for the "alphabet" of the Anglo-Saxon runes based on the sound values of the first six runes of that system.

galdr: pl., *galdrar*. ON. Originally "incantation" (the verb *gala* is used also for "to crow"); later meant magic in general but especially verbal magic.

galdrastafr: pl., *galdrastafir*. ON. Literally "stave of incantations." A magic sign of various types, made up of bind runes and/or pictographs and/or ideographs.

Germanic: (1) The proto-language spoken by the Germanic peoples before the various dialects (e.g., English, German, Gothic, Scandinavian) developed; also a collective term for the languages belonging to this group. (2) A collective term for all peoples descended from the Germanic-speaking group (e.g., the English, the Germans, the Scandinavians). Norse or Nordic is a subgroup of Germanic and refers only to the Scandinavian branch of the Germanic heritage.

Gothic: Designation of a now extinct Germanic language and people who spoke it. Last speakers known in the Crimean in the eighteenth century.

hamingja: pl., *hamingjur*. ON. Mobile magical force rather like the *mana* and *manitu* of other traditions. Often defined as "luck," "shape-shifting power," and "guardian spirit."

hamr: ON. The plastic image-forming substance that surrounds each individual, making the physical form. It may be collected and reformed by magical power (*hamingja*) according to will (*hugr*).

Huginn (and Munnin): These are the ravens of Odin. Their names mean "mind" and "memory" respectively.

hugr: ON. A portion of the psychophysical complex corresponding to the conscious mind and the faculty of cognition.

Jötunheimr: ON. The realm of the Jötnar, the giants who are sometimes the enemies, and sometimes the friends of the gods. They belong to the natural order of the universe.

metagenetics: Concept of characteristics of structures, that might at first seem to be "spiritual," inherited along genetic lines. Term first made current by Stephen A. McNallen.

Midhgardhr: ON. The "middle enclosure" of the universe. The material world and the home of humans.

minni: ON. The faculty of "memory"; the images stored in the deep mind from aeons past.

multiverse: A term descriptive of the many states of being (worlds) that constitute the "universe."

Muspellsheimr: ON. The far southern realm of the universe, the point of origin of fiery force.

niding: Developed from ON *nidh* (insult) and *nidhingr* (a vile wretch). Used in the context of cursing by the use of satirical or insulting poetry.

Niflheimr: ON. The far northern realm of the universe, the point of origin of watery force, which becomes ice as it approaches the center.

Norn: pl., Nornir (or English Norns). ON. One of the three complex cosmic beings in female form that embody the mechanical process of cause and effect and serve as a matrix for evolutionary force.

numen: adj., numinous. Living, nonphysical, or magical aspects within the cosmic order, not necessarily meant in the animistic sense; that which partakes of spiritual power.

Odian: A technical term for the "theology" of the Erulian. Distinguished from the Odinist by the fact that the Odian does not worship Odin but seeks to emulate his pattern of self-transformation.

Old English: The language spoken by the Anglo-Saxon tribes in southern Britain from about 450 to 1100 C.E. Also known as Anglo-Saxon.

Old Norse: The language spoken by West Scandinavians (in Norway, Iceland, and parts of Britain) in the Viking Age (ca. 800–1100 C.E.). Also language of the Eddas and of skaldic poetry.

ørlög: ON. Commonly translated "fate," it is really the result of the actions of one's past, even extended into past lifetimes. Literally it means "primeval layers, or laws."

rist: A verb meaning to carve or write the runes.

runecraft: The use of rune skill (esoteric knowledge) for causing changes in the objective environment.

runelore: A general term for esoteric teachings.

rune skill: Intellectual knowledge of runelore.

runestave: The physical shape of a runic character.

runer: A person who seeks the mysteries of the runes and works in a magical way with the runes.

rune wisdom: Ability to apply rune skill to deep-level visions of the world and its workings; runic philosophy.

runework: The use of rune skill for causing changes or development in the subjective universe; self-developmental work.

skald: ON term for a poet who composes highly formal, originally magical verse.

skaldcraft: The magical force of poetry; verbal magic (*galdr*). Also, the "science" of folk etymology in which magical, suprarational associations are made between words based on sounds.

tally lore: Esoteric study of number symbolism.

thurs: From ON *thurs*. A giant characterized by great strength and age, for example, the rime-thurses or frost-giants.

Útgardhr: ON. Literally "outer enclosure." It is the outer realm of the universe, a sort of cosmic wilderness.

valkyrja: pl., *valkyrjur*. ON. "Chooser of the Fallen" (i.e., the slain). Protective *valkyrja*-like numinous qualities that become attached to certain persons who attract them: a linking force between men and gods (especially Odin).

Vanaheimr: ON. "World of the Vanir." The Vanir are the gods and goddesses of production and re-production.

Vanir: sg., Van. ON. The race of gods corresponding to the fertility, prosperity, eroticism functions.

vikti, pl vitkar: ON. Common word for a "magician," literally "one who knows."

World: (1) The entire cosmos or universe. (2) One of the nine levels of being or planes of existence that make up the ordered cosmos.

Wyrd: English word, also spelled "weird" which conceptually corresponds to ON *ørlög*, and phonologically to ON *urdhr*. It literally means "that which has become" and forms the unseen basis for experiential reality.

Yggdrasill: ON. The cosmic tree of nine worlds or planes of the multiverse.

Ymir: The androgynous giant which evolved at the beginning of the natural evolution of the universe. He is sacrificed by Odin in order to construct a rational and beautiful universe from the giant's substance.

ENDNOTES

Part One

CHAPTER 1

1. For the original text, see Frederick Tupper (ed.) *The Riddles of the Exeter Book* (Boston: Ginn, 1910): 14–15. The translation here is my own. See also Paul F. Baum (trans., ed.), *Anglo-Saxon Riddles of the Exeter Book* (Durham, NC: Duke University Press, 1963).

CHAPTER 4

1. Franz Hartmann, "Review: Guido von List. Die Bilderschrift der Ario-Germanen: Ario-Germanische Hieroglyphik." *Neuen Lotusblüten* (1910): 370.

CHAPTER 5

1. Karl Spiesberger, *Runenmagie* (Berlin: R. Schikowski, 1955).
2. Trevor Ravenscroft, *The Spear of Destiny* (York Beach, ME: Samuel Weiser, 1973.)
3. Edred Thorsson, *Futhark: A Handbook of Rune Magic* (York Beach, ME: Samuel Weiser, 1984).

CHAPTER 6

1. Edred Thorsson, *Futhark: A Handbook of Rune Magic* (York Beach, ME: Samuel Weiser, 1984): 121–122.
2. Thorsson, *Futhark: A Handbook of Rune Magic,* 111.
3. For original text see Rudolf Much, *Die Germania des Tacitus,* 3rd ed. (Heidelberg: Carl Winter, 1967): 189. The translation here is my own. Interested readers may also want to pick up the published translation by H. Mattingly: Cornelius Tacitus, *The Agricola and the Germania* (Middlesex, UK: Penguin, 1970.)
4. Julius Caesar, *The Conquest of Gaul* (trans. by S. A. Handford) (Harmondsworth, UK: Penguin, 1951): Book I, 53.

CHAPTER 8

* Originally, perhaps *Hroptr* (the Hidden One [= Odin]). The combination *hr-* was pronounced "kr-" in ON; thus, the alliteration is preserved.

Part Two

CHAPTER 9

1. Edred Thorsson, *Futhark: A Handbook of Rune Magic* (York Beach, ME: Samuel Weiser, 1984): 76.
2. Thorsson, *Futhark: A Handbook of Rune Magic,* chapter 2.
3. For the further cosmological significance of these orderings, see chapter 10 of this volume; see also Edred Thorsson, *Futhark: A Handbook of Rune Magic* (York Beach. ME: Samuel Weiser, 1984): chapter 3.

CHAPTER 11

1. See chapter 9 of this volume; see also Edred Thorsson, *Futhark: A Handbook of Rune Magic* (York Beach. ME: Samuel Weiser, 1984): chapter 2.

Chapter 12

1. See C. G. Jung, "Wotan," in *Collected Works*, vol. 10 (trans. R.F.C. Hull), (Princeton, NJ: Princeton University Press): 179–193.

Chapter 13

1. See Edred Thorsson, *Futhark: A Handbook of Rune Magic* (York Beach, ME: Samuel Weiser, 1984): 79.
2. See Edred Thorsson, *Futhark: A Handbook of Rune Magic* (York Beach, ME: Samuel Weiser, 1984): 79–80, and Georges Dumézil, *Gods of the Ancient Northmen* (ed. by E. Haugen) (Berkeley: University of California Press, 1973): 1–48.

Part Three

Chapter 14

1. Marijane Osborn and Stella Longland, *Rune Games* (London: Routledge and Kegan Paul, 1982).
2. E. Tristan Kurtzahn, *Die Runen als Heilszeichen und Schicksalslose* (Bad Oldesloe: Uranus, 1924).
3. Karl Spiesberger, *Runenmagie* (Berlin: Schikowski, 1955).
4. Roland Dionys Jossé, *Die Tala der Raunen* (Freiburg/Breisgau: Bauer, 1955).
5. Werner Kosbab, *Das Runen-Orakel* (Freiburg/Breisgau: Bauer, 1982).
6. Ralph Blum, *The Book of Runes* (New York: St. Martin's Press, 1982). Blum's rune game opened up the realm of runes for many novices; however, those who go on to become serious students of runology find that the rune game disregards the essentials of the whole futhark system. So despite whatever personal insights Blum was able to provide on individual runes, his whole system must be regarded as artificial.

Chapter 15

1. Edred Thorsson, *Runelore: A Handbook of Esoteric Runology* (York Beach, ME: Samuel Weiser, 1987): 170.
2. Carl G. Jung, *Synchronicity* (Princeton: Princeton University Press, 1973). See also Marie-Louise von Franz, *On Divination and Synchronicity* (Toronto: Inner City Books, 1980).

Chapter 16

1. This was probably *Hroptr* before changed by a Christian copyist.

Chapter 18

1. The term Easter, or *Eostre*, was adopted by the Christians from the already existing name of the Germanic goddess. The Germanic peoples' spring festival celebrated the resurrection of the White Krist.
2. The ancient Germanic peoples counted by nights, not days.

Part Four

1. A literal translation of this phrase would be "Hammer in the North hallow this sacred enclosure and keep watch (over it)!"
2. This version is poetically more effective and therefore better for those wishing to use English in their rites.
3. "The Awesome God" (Odin).
4. "The Father of Incantation (Magic)" (Odin).
5. "The God of the Hanged" (Odin).
6. "The God of Hidden Things" or "The Hidden God" (Odin).
7. Thor is the slayer of the giant Hrungnir.
8. "The High One" (Odin).
9. Freely adapted from the final stanzas of the "Hávamál."
10. Kvasir's blood is the poetic mead of inspiration, used here to invoke the vivifying magical power of that substance in the pigment.
11. Based on the ancient pre-Christian *vatni ausa* formula.
12. The possessive form of Aesir.
13. Sing the names and make the signs.
14. The kenning used in the original is *brynthings apaldr*, literally "apple tree of the court of byrnies."
15. *galdr* in original.

BIBLIOGRAPHY

Arntz, Helmut. *Handbuch der Runenkunde*. Halle/Saale: Niemeyer, 1935, 1944.

Baum, Paul F., trans., ed. *Anglo-Saxon Riddles of the Exeter Book*. Durham, NC: Duke University Press, 1963.

Balzli, Johannes. *Guido von List: Der Wiederentdecker uralter arischer Weischeit*. Vienna: Guido-von-List-Gesellschaft 1917.

Bates, Brian. *The Way of Wyrd*. San Francisco: Harper and Row, 1983.

Blachetta, Walther. *Das Buch der deutschen Sinnzeichen*. Berlin: Lichterfelde: Widukind/Boss, 1941.

Blum, Ralph. *The Book of Runes*. New York: St. Martin's Press, 1982.

Bugge, Sophus. *Norges Indskrifter med de ældre Runer*. Christiana: Brogger, 1905–1913.

Byock, Jesse. Trans. *The Saga of the Volsungs*. Los Angeles: University of California Press, 1990.

Caesar, Julius. *The Conquest of Gaul*. Translated by S. A. Handford. Harmondsworth, UK: Penguin, 1951.

Derolez, René. *Runica Manuscripta*. Brugge: Rijks-Universiteit te Ghent, 1954.

Dickens, Bruce. *Runic and Heroic Poems of the Old Teutonic Peoples*. Cambridge: Cambridge University Press, 1915.

Dumézil, Georges. *Gods of the Ancient Northmen*. Edited by E. Haugen. Berkeley, CA: University of California Press, 1973.

Düwel, Klaus. *Runenkunde. Sammlung Metzler 72*. Stuttgart: J. B. Metzler, 1968, 1983.

Eckhardt, Karl August. *Irdische Unsterblichkeit: Germanischer Glaube an die Wiederverkörperung in der Sippe*. Weimar: Bohlau, 1937.

Eliade, Mircea. *The Myth of the Eternal Return or, Cosmos and History*. Translated by W. R. Trask. Bollingen Series 46. Princeton, NJ: Princeton University Press, 1971.

———. *Shamanism: Archaic Techniques of Ecstasy*. Translated by W. R. Trask. Bollingen Series 76. Princeton, NJ: Princeton University Press, 1971.

Ellis, Hilda R. *The Road to Hel*. Cambridge: Cambridge University Press, 1943.

Ellis Davidson, Hilda R. *Gods and Myths of Northern Europe*. Harmondsworth, UK: Penguin, 1964.

———. "The Germanic World." In: Michael Loewe and Carmen Blacker, eds. *Oracles and Divination*. Boston, MA: Shambhala, 1981.

Elliott, Ralph. *Runes, an Introduction*. Manchester: Manchester University Press, 1989, 2nd ed..

Flowers, Stephen E. *Runes and Magic: Magical Formulaic Elements in the Older Runic Tradition*. Bastrop: Lodestar, [2011].

———. trans., ed. *The Galdrabók: An Icelandic Book of Magic*. Smithville: Rûna-Raven, 2005.

———. *The Rune-Poems*. Bastrop: Lodestar, 2018.

———. *Icelandic Magic*. Rochester: Inner Traditions, 2016.

———. *The Northern Dawn: A History of the Reawakening of the Germanic Spirit. From the Twilight of the Gods to the Sun at Midnight*. North Augusta: Arcana Europa, 2018, vol. I.

Flowers, Stephen E. and James A. Chisholm, eds. trs. *A Source-Book of Seid*. Bastrop: Lodestar, 2015.

Flowers, Stephen E. and Michael Moynihan, eds. trs. *The Secret King: The Myth and Reality of Nazi Occultism*. Los Angeles: Feral House, 2007.

Fox, Denton, and Hermann Pálsson, trans. *Grettir's Saga*. Toronto: University of Toronto Press, 1974.

Franz, Marie-Louise von. *On Divination and Synchronicity: The Psychology of Meaningful Chance*. Toronto: Inner City Books, 1980.

Goodrick-Clarke, Nicholas. *The Occult Roots of Nazism*. Wellingborough, UK: Aquarian, 1985.

Gorsleben, Rudolf John. *Die Hoch-Zeit der Menschheit*. Leipzig: Koehler & Amelang, 1930.

Grimm, Jacob. *Teutonic Mythology*. Translated by S. Stallybrass. 4 vols. New York: Dover, 1966.

Grönbech, Vilhelm. *The Culture of the Teutons*. London: Oxford University Press, 1931.

Hartmann, Franz. "Review: Guido von List. Die Bilderschrift der ArioGermanen: Ario-Germanische Hieroglyphik." *Neue Lotusblüten Jahrgang* 1910, pp. 370–71.

Hauck, Karl. *Goldbrakteaten aus Sievern*. Munich: Fink, 1970.

Heinz, Ulrich Jürgen. *Die Runen*. Freiburg/Breisgau: Bauer, 1987.

Hollander, Lee M. *The Poetic Edda*. Austin,: University of Texas Press, 1962, 2nd ed.

Howard, Michael. *The Runes and Other Magical Alphabets*. York Beach, ME: Samuel Weiser, 1978.

———. *The Magic of the Runes*. Wellingborough, UK: Aquarian Press, 1980.

Hunger, Ulrich. *Die Runenkunde im Dritten Reich*. Berne: Lang, 1984.

Jones, Gwyn, trans. *The Vatndalers' Saga*. Princeton, NJ: Princeton University Press, 1944.

Jossé, Roland Dionys. *Die Tala der Raunen (Runo-astrologische Kabbalistik) Handbuch der Deutung des Wesens und Weges eines Menschen auf Grund der in seinem Namen verborgenen Sckicksalsraunen*. Freiburg: Bauer, 1955.

Jung, C. G. "Wotan" in *Collected Works*, vol. 10. Translated by R. F. C. Hull. Princeton, NJ: Princeton University Press, pp. 179–193.

———. *Synchronicity: An Acausal Connecting Principle*. Princeton: Princeton University Press, 1973.

Kershaw, Nora, ed., trans. *Stories and Ballads of the Far Past*. Cambridge: Cambridge University Press, 1921. (Sörlatháttr, pp. 43–57.)

Kosbab, Werner. *Das Runen-Orakel*. Freiburg: Bauer, 1982.

Krause, Wolfgang. *Was man in Runen ritzte*. Halle/Salle: Niemeyer, 1935.

———. *Die Runeninscriften im älteren Futhark*. 2 vols. Göttingen: Vandehoeck & Ruprecht, 1966.

Kummer, Siegfried Adolf. *Heilige Runenmacht*. Hamburg: Uranus Verlag, 1932.

———. *Runen-Magie*. Dresden: Gartmann, 1933/34.

———. *Rune-Magic*. Bastrop: Lodestar, 2017.

Kurtzahn, E. Tristan. *Die Runen als Heilszeichen und Schicksalslose*. Bad Oldesloe: Uranus, 1924.

Line, David and Julia. *Fortune-Telling by Runes*. Wellingborough, UK: Aquarian Press, 1984.

List, Guido von. *Das Geheimnis der Runen* (= Guido-von-List Bücherei 1) Gross-Lichterfelde: P. Zillmann, 1908.

———. *Die Bilderschrift der Ario-Germanen*. (= Guido-von-List-Bücherei 5) Vienna: Guido-von-List-Gesellschaft, 1910.

———. *Die Religion der Ario-Germanen in ihrer Esoterik und Exoterik*. Berlin-Lichterfelde: Guido-von-List Verlag, 1910.

———. *Die Ursprache der Ario-Germanen und ihre Mysteriensprache*. (= Guido-von-List-Bücherei 6) Vienna: Guido-von-List-Gesellschaft, 1914.

———. *The Secret of the Runes*. Translated by Stephen E. Flowers. Rochester: Destiny, 1988.

———. *The Religion of the Aryo-Germanic Folk*. Translated by Stephen E. Flowers. Bastrop: Lodestar, 2018.

Marby, Friedrich Bernhard. *Marby-Runen-Bücherei*. 4 vols. Stuttgart: Marby-Verlag, 1931–1935.

Marstrander, C.J.S. "Om runene og runenavenes oprindelse." *Nordisk Tidskrift for Sprogvidenskab, 1* (1928), pp. 1–67.

Mayer, R. M. "Runenstudien." *Beiträge zur Geschichte der deutschen Sprache und Literatur, 21* (1896), pp. 162–184.

Mercer, Beryl and Tricia Bramwell. *The Anglo-Saxon Runes*. Amber, UK: Phoenix Runes, 1983.

Moltke, Erik. *Runes and their Origin*. Copenhagen: National Museum of Denmark, 1985.

Much, Rudolf. Die Germania des Tacitus. Heidelberg: Carl Winter, 1967, 2nd ed.

Neckel, Gustav and Hans Kuhn. *Edda. Die Lieder des Codex Regius nebst verwandten Denkmälern.* Heidelberg: Carl Winter, 1962, 3rd ed.

Orell, Vladimir. *A Handbook of Germanic Etymology.* Leiden: Brill, 2003.

Osborn, Marijane and Stella Longland. *Rune Games.* London: Routledge and Kegan Paul, 1982.

Pálsson, Hermann, and Paul Edwards, trans. *Egil's Saga.* Middlesex, UK: Penguin, 1 976.

Page, R. I. *An Introduction to English Runes.* Woodbridge: Boydell, 1999.

Pushong, Carlyle A. *Rune Magic.* London: Regency, 1978.

Saxo Grammaticus. *The History of the Danes,* vol. 1, translated and edited by Peter Fisher and H. R. Ellis Davidson. Suffolk, UK: Boydell & Brewer, 1979.

Schneider, Karl. *Die germanischen Runennamen.* Meisenheim: Anton Hain, 1956.

Shou, Peryt [= Albert C. G. Schultz]. Die "Edda" als Schlüssel des kommenden Weltalters (*Esoterik der Edda* vol 1) Berlin-Pankow: Linser Verlag, [1920].

———. *The Edda as the Key to the Coming Age.* Translated by Stephen E. Flowers. Bastrop: Lodestar, 2017.

Snorri Sturluson. *The Prose Edda.* Translated by A. G. Brodeur. New York: American Scandinavian Foundation, 1929.

———. *Heimskringla.* Translated by Lee M. Hollander. Austin: University of Texas Press, 1962.

Spiesberger, Karl. *Runenmagie.* Berlin: Schikowski, 1955.

———. *Runenexerzietienfür Jedermann.* Freiburg: Bauer, 1976.

Tacitus, Cornelius. *The Agricola and the Germania.* Harmondsworth, UK: Penguin, 1948.

Thorsson, Edred. *Alu: An Advanced Guide to Operative Runology.* San Francisco: Weiser, 2012.

———. *Futhark: A Handbook of Rune Magic.* York Beach: Weiser, 1984.

———. *Green Rúna: The Runemaster's Notebook: Shorter Works of Edred Thorsson.* Volume 1 (1978–1985). Smithville: Rûna-Raven, 1996.

———. *The Mysteries of the Goths.* Smithville: Rûna-Raven, 2007.

———. *The Nine Doors of Midgard.* South Burlington: The Rune-Gild, 2016, 5th ed.

———. *Northern Magic.* St. Paul: Llewellyn, 1992.

———. *Runecaster's Handbook: The Well of Wyrd.* York Beach: Weiser, [1988].

———. *Runelore: A Handbook of Esoteric Runology.* York Beach: Weiser, 1987.

———. *Rune Might.* Rochester: Inner Traditions, 2018.

———. *Rune-Song.* Smithville: Rûna-Raven, 1993.

———. *The Runic Magic of the Armanen.* [unpublished MS, 1975].

Tolkien, Christopher, trans., ed. *The Saga of King Heidrek the Wise*. London: Thomas Nelson & Sons, 1960.

Tupper, Frederick (ed). *The Riddles of the Exeter Book*. Boston: Ginn, 1910.

Turville-Petre, E.O.G. *Myth and Religion of the North*. New York: Holt, Rinehart and Winston, 1964.

Vries, Jan de. *Altgermanishe Religionsgeschichte*. 2 vols. Berlin: de. Gruyter, 1956–1957.

Willis, Tony. *Runic Workbook*. Wellingborough, UK: Aquarian Press, 1986.

Wimmer, L.F.A. *Die Runenschrift*. Berlin: Weidemann, 1887.

TO OUR READERS

Weiser Books, an imprint of Red Wheel/Weiser, publishes books across the entire spectrum of occult, esoteric, speculative, and New Age subjects. Our mission is to publish quality books that will make a difference in people's lives without advocating any one particular path or field of study. We value the integrity, originality, and depth of knowledge of our authors.

Our readers are our most important resource, and we appreciate your input, suggestions, and ideas about what you would like to see published.

Visit our website at *www.redwheelweiser.com* to learn about our upcoming books and free downloads, and be sure to go to *www.redwheelweiser.com/newsletter* to sign up for newsletters and exclusive offers.

You can also contact us at *info@rwwbooks.com* or at

Red Wheel/Weiser, LLC
65 Parker Street, Suite 7
Newburyport, MA 01950